RIGHTS AND SOCIAL JUSTICE IN RESEARCH

Advancing Methodologies for Social Change

Edited by
Kathryn McGarry, Ciara Bradley and Gloria Kirwan

First published in Great Britain in 2024 by

Policy Press, an imprint of
Bristol University Press
University of Bristol
1–9 Old Park Hill
Bristol
BS2 8BB
UK
t: +44 (0)117 374 6645
e: bup-info@bristol.ac.uk

Details of international sales and distribution partners are available at policy.bristoluniversitypress.co.uk

© Bristol University Press 2024

British Library Cataloguing in Publication Data
A catalogue record for this book is available from the British Library

ISBN 978-1-4473-6829-8 hardcover
ISBN 978-1-4473-6830-4 ePub
ISBN 978-1-4473-6831-1 ePdf

The right of Kathryn McGarry, Ciara Bradley and Gloria Kirwan to be identified as editors of this work has been asserted by them in accordance with the Copyright, Designs and Patents Act 1988.

Cover design: Clifford Hayes
Front cover image: Getty/Tim Robberts
Bristol University Press and Policy Press use environmentally responsible print partners.
Printed and bound in Great Britain by CPI Group (UK) Ltd, Croydon, CR0 4YY

FSC
www.fsc.org
MIX
Paper | Supporting
responsible forestry
FSC® C013604

We dedicate this book to all who suffer social injustice in this world and to those who work tirelessly in the name of social justice. We hope this book will help to shine a light on research work which exposes injustice in its many forms and which contributes to tackling social injustices wherever they exist.

Contents

List of figures and tables

Figures

Tables

Notes on contributors

Ciara Bradley is Associate Professor in the Department of Applied Social Studies, Maynooth University, Ireland.

David Donovan is a programme support worker in the Blue Teapot Performing Arts School, Galway, Ireland.

Jamie Gorman is Adjunct Research Fellow at Victoria University, Melbourne, Australia.

Rory Hearne is Associate Professor in the Department of Applied Social Studies, Maynooth University, Ireland.

Lynsey Kavanagh is Co-Director of Pavee Point Traveller and Roma Centre, Dublin, Ireland.

Gloria Kirwan is Senior Lecturer in the Graduate School of Healthcare Management, Royal College of Surgeons in Ireland. She is also Adjunct Associate Professor in the Department of Applied Social Studies, Maynooth University, and Adjunct Assistant Professor in Social Work, School of Social Work and Social Policy, Trinity College Dublin, Ireland.

Kathryn McGarry is Adjunct Assistant Professor in the Department of Applied Social Studies, Maynooth University, Ireland.

Sinead McMahon is Assistant Professor in the Department of Applied Social Studies, Maynooth University, Ireland.

Grainne Meehan is a local development officer with Sláintecare Healthy Communities in South Dublin, Ireland.

Brian Melaugh is Assistant Professor in the Department of Applied Social Studies, Maynooth University, Ireland.

Breda O'Driscoll is Assistant Lecturer in the Department of Applied Social Studies, Maynooth University, Ireland.

Andy O'Hara is Coordinator of UISCE, the Irish National Advocacy Service for People Who Use Drugs.

Johanna O'Shea is Assistant Professor in the Department of Applied Social Studies, Maynooth University, Ireland.

Calvin Swords is Assistant Professor in the Department of Applied Social Studies, Maynooth University, Ireland.

Seamus Taylor is Associate Professor and Head of Department in the Department of Applied Social Studies, Maynooth University, Ireland.

Hilary Tierney is Associate Professor in the Department of Applied Social Studies, Maynooth University, Ireland.

Acknowledgements

The editors wish to acknowledge the support of colleagues from the Department of Applied Social Studies, Maynooth University, and our contributors to this collection for their engagement and dedication to this book project and for sharing their journeys in research for social justice.

We are grateful for the opportunities to work alongside and learn from our partners on the ground for whom challenging injustice is not simply a part of their work but a living praxis.

Bringing this collection together, we are aware of colleagues, partners and friends who are no longer with us but whose legacy of working for social justice provides an ongoing inspiration for our work.

Ultimately, the social justice praxis we aspire to is for the communities we work for, with and alongside, and we are thankful for the opportunities to work together to build relationships, challenge and question, contributing new ways of knowing and imagining new possibilities.

Kathryn, Ciara, Gloria

Foreword

Anastasia Crickley
Emeritus Associate Professor and former Head of Department
of Applied Social Studies, Maynooth University, Ireland and
former Chairperson of the UN Committee on the
Elimination of Racial Discrimination

Researchers at the Centre for Rights, Recognition and Redistribution at Maynooth University, who edited and wrote this book, demonstrate clearly in their contributions their commitment to human rights, social justice and equality. The research lens they apply to this commitment and the articulation of their work in the book's chapters provide readers and users, whether practitioners, colleagues, students or other interested parties, with clear, well thought out and valuable contributions. These have a resonance also beyond the Irish context in the examination and research of parallel concerns globally, and in the associated questions regarding research ethics, outcomes and agenda setting – by whom, for whom and in whose interests.

The short introductions that follow, touching on the book's chapters, attempt to illustrate some of these points. Following the editors' introduction, the philosophy of knowledge construction is robustly interrogated by Kathryn McGarry, while Ciara Bradley and Lynsey Kavanagh continue later with an interrogation of research epistemology and methodology. This is given further clarity in Jamie Gorman's well-argued articulation of the need for research to 'be in' rather than 'reach in' in his very timely work on environmental justice. These concerns are echoed in Rory Hearne's contribution on the co-construction of action research in his own work. Breda O'Driscoll and Gloria Kirwan's thoughtful chapter focuses on children's rights, while Johanna O'Shea's focus on sensitive topics and Gloria Kirwan and Calvin Sword's chapter about research with hard-to-reach groups provide food for thought about the principles and practices which underpin their methodological approaches.

Sinead McMahon, Ciara Bradley and Hilary Tierney outline how their approach to teaching research to community and youth work students is firmly grounded in practitioners' needs for research literacy and capacity to manage research projects, as well as capacity to undertake research. It is, I think, a useful read for anyone involved in teaching research for students for all the social professions, in Ireland and elsewhere.

In a further chapter, Sinead McMahon, based on her research, examines current Irish youth work policy frames, illustrating the impact of policy framing and discursive effect. Grainne Meehan's groundbreaking contribution on research as a deaf woman with deaf and hard-of-hearing women raises questions and challenges regarding deficit frames and ill-informed external perceptions which echo widely, as does Brian Melaugh and Andy O'Hara's chapter on peer-research engagement with drug users. David Donovan continues with an exploration of the rights of disabled people to an intimate life of their own. Seamus Taylor's reflection on his lifetime of UK and Irish practice and research experience provides insights into how rights-focused research can influence policy, with much resonance globally.

Practice and policy remain key for responding to social inequality, but they can, are and should be informed by research. The language and questions raised throughout this book challenge, in both theoretical and research practice terms, the power dynamics and ideological directions often hidden in 'neutral' research work. This has the potential to prompt further discussions on the key areas explored in this volume and to challenge researchers and practitioners to confront the widening inequalities of our time through their work. I encourage readers to reflect on the question I raised at the outset – research by whom, for whom and in whose interests – so that together we can work towards fully realising the just and equal world we aspire to, where rights are realisd.

Researching for social justice: an introduction

Kathryn McGarry, Ciara Bradley and Gloria Kirwan

Introduction

Whom do we conduct research with and for? What kinds of questions do we ask of the social world, and how do we question how knowledge is produced? In what ways do our approaches to research and our manner of carrying out research studies matter? If we, as social science students, academics and practitioners, commit ourselves to social change agendas, then our research endeavour is at the heart of advancing such transformative change. *Rights and Social Justice in Research* is a text which sets out *what* a rights-based approach to research looks like, *why* this framework matters and *how* we can translate a rights-based and social justice agenda into operational research. These questions will be addressed through an examination of numerous case studies based on our contributors' work with and for diverse community groups, including women, young people, migrants, Travellers, sex workers, people who use drugs, people with disabilities, and older people.

This edited collection brings together a range of contributions which explore and illustrate the nature of research for social justice. Taken together, these contributions advance ideas about the transformative potential of social research and demonstrate how a social justice agenda can be operationalised throughout the research process. This collection provides key examples of the tools, processes and outcomes of social justice-relevant research including *where* and *how* social justice frameworks can be utilised in the design and execution of research.

This collection will begin by introducing a frame of social justice in order to unpack how justice is reflected and produced through research and how injustices occur – this will encompass ideas on research on and for rights, research on and for equality, research for social justice and socially just research. Being mindful not to treat these concepts as synonyms, we are also clear on the overarching aims of such an edited collection on research for social justice which ultimately reflects commitments to rights, equality and diversity and social justice.

Why this book and why now?

As a team of social researchers based at the Centre for Rights, Recognition and Redistribution at Maynooth University, the editors of this collection are committed to ideas and principles of social justice in research, teaching and practice. Our commitment through this centre is to promote research that furthers human rights, social justice and equality through research practice as well as through the focus of study and to contribute to the development of the social professions and applied social sciences, as exemplified by the contributions of practitioners and policy advocates to this book.

The social justice agenda is as critical as ever in an increasingly divisive social, economic and political climate. Our teaching, research and practice work is committed to furthering agendas which create conditions for positive social change. This book will be essential reading for those researching and teaching in the area of social justice and will seek to advance rights-based and social justice work with community groups, highlighting key social issues with critical policy and practice implications. While this volume presents examples of social justice-informed research collected within the Irish context, many of the themes and issues to which this approach is applied resonate strongly with issues and challenges found in many societies across the world. Furthermore, this collection holds much potential for extending the learning from and application of theoretical, methodological, policy and practice perspectives to advance social justice goals beyond the context of the publication.

Aims of this collection

This book aims to showcase a social justice approach to research, illustrating how it can be operationalised in methodology and the potential effects such an approach has.

Specifically, the book aims to explore:

1. What does a social justice approach in research mean? How can we define it? Where do we begin? What is our rationale for using a social justice approach?
2. How can a social justice frame be conceptualised? How can we frame research through and for social justice?
3. How can a social justice approach to research be operationalised? How can we design research and develop methodologies that (a) reflect a social justice approach and (b) progress a social justice agenda?
4. What are the potential implications of a social justice approach in research? What does this kind of approach mean for (a) the theory and practice of social research, (b) policy and practice in the social professions and, most importantly, (c) lived lives?

Research for social justice

Creswell (2009) claims that a social justice agenda reflects the philosophical commitment of researchers. Lincoln et al (2011: 102) draw attention to a social justice agenda in research as an ontological position for researchers who 'see the social world as imbued with power struggles that lead to interactions of privilege and oppression'. Indeed, this ontological stance shapes ideas on acquiring and advancing knowledge. In *Fostering Social Justice through Qualitative Inquiry: A Methodological Guide,* Johnson and Parry (2015: 13) usefully describe social justice as 'an epistemology that values emotions, personal relationships, an ethic of care, political praxis, and multivocality to purposefully reveal inequities in all facets of society'. Johnson and Parry bring together methods experts as part of a guidebook on social justice through qualitative research design including ethnography, Participatory Action Research (PAR) and phenomenology.

Taking the critical practice of social justice as this volume's conceptual and epistemological framework, we draw on the work of Nancy Fraser and others to explore the 'how to' of research for social justice. Fraser's theorisations on social justice attend to issues of rights, recognition, redistribution and representation. For Fraser, '[s]ocial justice is the idea that everyone deserves parity in terms of opportunities, political rights and distribution of wealth and privilege to participate as peers in social life and lead fulfilling lives' (McGarry and FitzGerald, 2018: xv, citing Fraser, 2008). To overcome injustice from Fraser's perspective means overcoming institutionalised obstacles which prevent some people from participating on a par with others, 'as full partners in social interaction' (McGarry and FitzGerald, 2018: xv, citing Fraser, 2008). We adopt this frame in our book by using an understanding of social justice that encompasses rights, recognition and redistribution. Thus, we see rights, recognition and participation as contributing to the overall agenda for social justice and not fragmented practices in isolation. In this book, we use the terms social justice research, research for rights and rights-based agendas to reflect this stance.

This book challenges readers to engage with the *what* and the *why* of research for social justice, and it illuminates how the rights-based tools of social justice can be employed and operationalised for research. For readers grappling with what social justice research is, interested in how they might shape their own research, this book aims to provide useful and practical insights.

The wider context of social justice agendas in social policy

Questions of social justice have become as significant as ever in both the study of social policy and in current policy contexts across Ireland, the wider

European landscape and indeed globally. Taking up the mantle of envisioning an agenda for social policy for today, Fiona Williams (2018) theorises that post-2008 austerity politics, the backlash against global migration and the climate change crisis have threatened financial security, social solidarity and environmental sustainability. She draws on Gough's (2017) work *Heat, Greed and Human Need*, which links the threat of climate change, capitalist accumulation and economic growth to the decline in social well-being and equality. These debates are further compounded by the misframing (Fraser, 2008) and the social abjection (Tyler, 2013) some communities experience in their marginalisation through the impact of policy processes and wider discourse. The work of Williams (2018) and others raises critical concerns about our collective responsibilities for today and tomorrow and how agendas for policymaking can adequately address issues of human consumption and redistribution, recognition of intersectionality, the human economy and universal care models and advance rights to social provision.

These fundamental concerns have become an impetus for our work and research as we look at ways not only to promote the funding and operationalisation of such a vision of social policy but to develop and harness methodological tools which can contribute to advancing knowledge in these areas. The research tools themselves are a critical part of a transformative agenda such as that set out by Williams (2018), where well-being, solidarity, voice and equality are at once the embedded values and the desired outcomes of our research endeavour. We turn now to look at how these concerns can be distilled into guiding questions for our work.

Guiding questions for research

The process of knowledge production translates into key questions of social justice which will guide our edited collection:

- What do we need to find out, and why is this important?
- What do we already know, and how has this knowledge come about?
- Whose voices have been heard?
- Where are the silences?
- How do our ways of finding out contribute to particular ways of knowing?
- How can research create inclusionary spaces?
- How can research reflect democratic practices?
- What does the co-production of knowledge really mean?
- In what ways can we call attention to issues of rights, recognition, redistribution and representation in both our questioning of the social world and the practices we employ to find answers?
- How can our research positively challenge normative ideas and practices which have long disenfranchised individuals and communities?

- In what ways can research be used as both a tool and process in *troubling* our taken-for-granted ideas about the social world; in *displacing* such ideas with critical knowledge which calls out exclusion, promotes diversity and equality and builds towards a *reimagining* of positive, inclusive futures?

This book aims to address these questions and offer some tentative answers. The chapters in this volume collectively demonstrate the influence a social justice perspective can exert on the theory and practice of social research.

Overview of the edited collection

This collection is divided into three key sections: Part I, 'Contextualising and theorising research for social justice'; Part II, 'Designing and operationalising methodologies for social justice'; and Part III, 'Exploring case studies in research for social justice'. With reference to practitioner work, policy advocacy work and research activity, the contributions in this edited collection provide a snapshot of the range of rights-based and equality issues that social researchers encounter on a regular basis. Core concepts of social justice, rights-based research and research for transformative social change are explored, described and critically analysed in order to establish the lens used to inform the research presented in this book. Drawing on some of these case studies in social justice allows us to explore core ideas in social science around *ontology* (what is there to know?) and *epistemology* (what counts as appropriate knowledge?) by engaging students, academics and practitioners on issues of relevance to their studies and work and within the contexts in which social policy is produced and has effect. These case studies also allow us to reflect on the *ethical dimensions* of research for social justice as a concept and as a process. We will have the opportunity to delve into *theorising* social justice and *operationalising* it as a framework for research. Furthermore, this edited collection will provide our students and other readers with the opportunity to engage with methodologies for social change. In this way, this edited collection fills a significant gap in the knowledge base on research for social justice in the Irish context. Each of the chapters in our collection ends with a summary of the key lessons arising for social justice research, policy and practice. And this is the key impetus for our collection: to produce a text that foregrounds the practice of social justice in our work in order to bring to life its transformative potential through research.

These ideas are explored throughout the volume as we question and explore the conceptualisation, design and operationalisation of research for social justice, not simply in terms of scrutiny of how our research is produced but in interrogating what critical praxis means for advancing social justice through research. Acknowledging then what we do as researchers and the impacts these 'doings' have, our first contribution in the volume underlines the importance of positionality. McGarry (Chapter 2) draws on the work of Haraway (1988: 587) as 'positioning implies responsibility for our enabling practices'. What kinds of practices does our research enable? How does the knowledge from our research take shape and give shape to lived realities? And how do certain ways of knowing become privileged in research practice?

Operationalising social justice-focused research praxis is explored in the chapter by Bradley and Kavanagh (Chapter 3), who draw on two key examples from their work that actively address themes of stigmatisation, marginalisation and silencing: one a project on the experiences of single women's reproduction in Ireland (Bradley, 2014), and the second a study of the experiences of pregnancy loss with Traveller women in Ireland (Kavanagh, 2018). They argue that 'we may face new contexts and concerns, in different spaces and places, but the same issues still matter in research for social justice: what we research, why, how and with whom'. In their chapter on social justice for community and youth work, McMahon, Bradley and Tierney (Chapter 4) challenge the privileging of established ways of knowing communities and young people and consider the responsibilities of community workers and youth workers to advance and promote knowledge production and access to knowledge. Rather than a separate enterprise, research becomes integral to the values and commitments of community work and youth work, as they argue for a 'social justice praxis that involves the capacity to combine critical awareness, critical analysis and critical action'. As part of this critical awareness, the authors pose the question 'Why have I chosen to pay attention to this research?' This calls us to explicitly acknowledge what we give our attention to in research practice, what gets overlooked, how our paradigms and personal subjectivities shape our research lens and how we might better focus or sharpen our attention to ensure that our research is an integral part of our social justice praxis.

In Part II of our collection, on the design and operationalisation of social justice research, interrogating the assumptions which underpin what we know and how we know is a theme explored in the contribution by McMahon (Chapter 5). In her work drawing on Bacchi's (2009) 'What's the problem represented to be?' framework, McMahon describes the process of problematisation and how we can adapt this to our policy analysis as a tool in our research for social justice praxis. Given the current context of organisational pressure for community and youth work practitioners to prioritise research for funding agendas:

> the promotion of critical policy analysis and the importance of engaging in policy research becomes ever more important ... to return the problematising gaze of policy and policymakers back on to policy itself, producing critical analysis and theorising that has the potential

to inform activism for social justice change and to create knowledge for use in social justice policy.

In her research with deaf and hard-of-hearing women, Meehan (Chapter 6) employs the concept of *flourishing* as a framing device as well as a methodological touchstone. Meehan shows us in this chapter how deaf feminist standpoint theory fulfils both aims by, first, allowing 'exploration of dominant ideologies shaping deaf women's everyday lives', and, secondly, by placing value on 'moving beyond traditional conceptual frameworks to situated knowledge where deaf women from different social locations become "the subjects – the authors – of knowledge"' (Harding, 2004: 4).

The issue of inclusion, which goes beyond tokenistic claims to challenge and transform bounded spaces, is a theme explored in the work of Donovan (Chapter 7) and his case study of arts-based research with people with an intellectual disability. Donovan deftly draws on the notion of 'trespass' as an act of resistance to the exclusion and disempowerment of people with intellectual disabilities and as a means to reclaim these spaces, through the arts, and through the values of social justice. In this contribution, by embracing 'participatory parity' (Lambert and Czerniewicz, 2020: 3), social justice research itself can be seen as an act of trespass.

The primacy of situated knowledges is a theme continued in the chapter by Melaugh and O'Hara (Chapter 8), which presents an important contribution on challenging exclusion. Providing the example of UISCE, the national advocacy service for people who use drugs in Ireland, Melaugh and O'Hara critically argue that for people who use drugs, 'meaningful participation in research not only validates their lived experience as legitimate; the experience of involvement itself affirms their dignity and acts to challenge drug-related stigma and exclusion' (Montañés Sánchez and Oomen, 2009).

In Part III of our collection, resistance and reimagining through anti-extractivist research is explored by Gorman (Chapter 9) in his contribution on researching with a community-based environmental justice group. The environmental extractivism affecting these communities is a mirrored concern in the design of the research of their experience, as Gorman reflexively crafts anti-oppressive research: 'Researchers seeking to understand and support these environmental justice movements must carefully consider our knowledge production practices if we are to avoid replicating the extractivist logic and aggravating the injustice experienced by communities.'

Another approach to 'capturing and amplifying' the 'too often excluded voices' of those from other marginalised communities is explored in the chapter by Kirwan and Swords (Chapter 10), who look at the use of material ethnography in their research with a community group of mental health service users. By selecting objects that represent important experiences for them, the research participants experience the research practice as an opportunity to reveal how 'the objects embody both physical and social meanings in relation to subjective experiences of people in our world' (Broderick et al, 2019). Material ethnography thus provides a useful tool in social justice research that seeks to support participants beyond traditional interviewing techniques to self-report the meaning attached to their experiences.

Researcher positionality is a theme continued in the work of Hearne (Chapter 11), who considers the nature and application of 'engaged research' and PAR methodologies. Drawing on the example of a European-funded PAR project on the structural causes of homelessness (Hearne and Murphy, 2019), this chapter considers the framing of social justice in research through the 'Participatory Action Human Rights and Capability Approach', involving 'the co-construction of new knowledge' of the realities of those experiencing homelessness.

O'Driscoll and Kirwan (Chapter 12) appraise the application of Interpretative Phenomenological Analysis (IPA) as a method through which researchers can access the perspectives and emotional responses of research participants on topics or experiences that are potentially difficult or emotive for the participants to discuss. They consider the application of IPA in O'Driscoll's research, where it was used as a method to elicit the views, feelings and experiences of social workers regarding their efforts – sometimes successful but sometimes not – to support children's participation in decisions that could potentially have lifelong consequences for them.

Another lesson in non-traditional methods to facilitate social justice aims in research is presented in O'Shea's chapter (Chapter 13) on Q-methodology. Presenting a case study on research with probation officers, this contribution describes a process of gathering evidence on 'hard-to-reach' sensitive topics in an organisational context where participation may be viewed as carrying a professional risk. With resonance for social justice frames of research practice, the consideration of such methods demonstrates a reflection on the 'how' of research and the manner in which we can address gaps in knowledge in ways that facilitate participation and minimise harm.

The critical policy analysis approach is further illuminated in Taylor's contribution (Chapter 14), which describes his experiences of using research and practice to advance and promote a social justice agenda in the area of hate crime. Taylor's chapter usefully explores the different traditions of social justice research and the shaping of his own approach to social justice praxis. Recounting his journeying from policymaking to academia provides the opportunity to explore issues of positionality and critical praxis, as well as possibilities for transcending the insider–outsider binary in research. Taylor's 'pracademia' is underpinned by his work in the hate crime domain both as former Director of Equality and Diversity at the Crown Prosecution Service in England and Wales and through his subsequent research on hate crime and associated policy advocacy interventions as an academic, from which he gleans key lessons for readers seeking to influence policymaking processes.

The range of content which makes up this edited collection provides a window into research practices and research issues that are informed and in turn aim to inform the current social landscape in which social injustices and the struggle for recognition and rights are hard fought for many groups within wider society. Research is never neutral, and researchers must be capable of identifying the influences on their work. Across all the chapters, the authors seek to demonstrate how their work is built on a foundation of intention to highlight and seek solutions to social injustices as they exist in many social arenas. Each of the chapters concludes by reflecting on the implications for social justice research and social justice practice and policy in the Irish context and beyond. The shaping of these foundations and the potential they hold for building methodologies for social change are the impetus for sharing this collection with the reader. We turn then together, sharing commitments to reimagining and realising rights within the contexts we engage, to continue our learning journeys in research for social justice.

References

Bacchi, C. (2009) *Analysing Policy: What's the Problem Represented to Be?*, Frenchs Forest, NSW: Pearson Australia.

Bradley, C. (2014) 'Reproducing stigma: Narratives of single women's pregnancy and motherhood in Ireland 1990–2010', PhD thesis, National University of Ireland, Galway, Available from: http://hdl.handle.net/10379/4773

Broderick, G., McNicholas, J., Hegarty, R. and SAOL Project Participants (2019) 'Object poverty', presented at the IASW National Social Work Conference 2019, *Irish Social Worker* (Winter): 19–34.

Creswell, J.W. (2009) *Research Design: Qualitative, Quantitative and Mixed Methods Approaches* (3rd edn), Thousand Oaks, CA: Sage.

Fraser, N. (2008) *Scales of Justice: Reimagining Political Space in a Globalizing World*, Cambridge: Polity Press.

Gough, I. (2017) *Heat, Greed and Human Need: Climate Change, Capitalism and Sustainable Well-being*, Cheltenham: Edward Elgar.

Haraway, D. (1988) 'Situated knowledges: The science question in feminism and the privilege of partial perspective', *Feminist Studies*, 14(3): 575–99.

Harding, S. (2004) 'Rethinking standpoint epistemology: What is "strong objectivity"?', in S. Harding (ed) *The Feminist Standpoint Theory Reader, Intellectual and Political Controversies*, London: Routledge.

Hearne, R. and Murphy, M. (2019) 'Capabilities and human rights in practice; the case study of participatory research on marketisation and homelessness in Dublin', in *Capabilities and Social Policy: Concepts, Measurements and Application*. London: Policy Press.

Johnson, C. and Parry, D. (eds) (2015) *Fostering Social Justice through Qualitative Inquiry: A Methodological Guide*, New York: Routledge.

Kavanagh, L. (2018) ' "Standing alongside" and in solidarity with Traveller women: Minority ethnic women's narratives of racialized obstetric violence', PhD thesis, National University of Ireland Maynooth, Available from: https://mural.maynoothuniversity.ie/11209/

Lambert, S. and Czerniewicz, L. (2020) 'Approaches to open education and social justice research', *Journal of Interactive Media in Education*, 1(1): 1–6,

Lincoln, Y., Lynham, S. and Guba, E. (2011) 'Paradigmatic controversies, contradictions, and emerging confluences, revisited', in N. Denzin (ed) *The SAGE Handbook of Qualitative Research*, Thousand Oaks, CA: Sage Publications, pp 191–215.

McGarry, K. and FitzGerald, S. (2018) 'Introduction: Social justice through an agenda for change', in S. FitzGerald and K. McGarry (eds) *Realising Justice for Sex Workers: An Agenda for Change*, London: Rowman & Littlefield.

Montañés Sánchez, V. and Oomen, J. (2009) 'Use of drugs and advocacy: A research into the participation of drug user organisations in the design of drug policies on a local and European level', Belgium: European Coalition for Just and Effective Drug Policies (ENCOD).

Tyler, I. (2013) *Revolting Subjects: Social Abjection and Resistance in Neo-liberal Britain*, London: Zed Books.

Williams, F. (2018) 'What next for social policy?', University of Oxford Sidney Ball Memorial Lecture, 9 November, Available from: https://podcasts.ox.ac.uk/people/fiona-williams [Accessed 11 May 2023].

PART I

Contextualising and theorising research for social justice

2

Epistemic privilege as a social justice issue: knowing injustice and justice for knowers

Kathryn McGarry

Introduction

> A critique does not consist in saying that things aren't good the way they are. It consists in seeing on what type of assumptions, of familiar notions, of established, unexamined ways of thinking the accepted practices are based. (Foucault, 1994 [1981]: 456)

Foucauldian thinking directs us to interrogate unexamined ways of knowing, how such knowledge of social issues has come to be and what that established knowledge means for regulating behaviours and the shaping of social practices. Considering knowledge as a social justice issue demands a critical analysis of the way knowledge of the social world is produced, how we interact with that knowledge and what these processes mean for lived lives. Considering knowledge through a social justice lens means confronting the relationship between knowledge and power. In this chapter, I will draw on critical theoretical perspectives on the philosophy of the social sciences, which are brought to life in real world research case studies. The chapter will consider how the 'doing' of research and the nature of the knowledge production enterprise and the knower become integral questions of social justice. The vision of social justice described in this chapter is influenced by the work of political theorist Nancy Fraser, who sets out a valuable descriptor of social justice as parity. For Fraser, '[s]ocial justice is the idea that everyone deserves parity in terms of opportunities, political rights and distribution of wealth and privilege to participate as peers in social life and lead fulfilling lives' (McGarry and FitzGerald, 2018: xv, citing Fraser, 2008). Tying Fraserian thinking to issues of knowledge production allows us to consider how our research 'doings' advance or obstruct such parity of participation not only for our research participants but as a ripple effect from our research enterprise.

In the first section, I look at critical theories of knowledge and the relationship between knowledge, discourse and power in order to understand how knowledge can shape realities in ways that call into question social justice. I then introduce two key projects which illuminate some of the issues under discussion and the methodological tools I employed as part of a critical discourse analysis (McGarry and FitzGerald, 2017; McGarry and Ryan, 2020). The remaining part of the chapter explores some of the key themes arising from a critical analysis of knowledge claims and representation in these projects. The aim is to provide readers with a critical discussion of knowledge production and knowledge producers in research; to identify how social injustices occur through epistemic privilege; and to consider how we as thinkers, researchers and practitioners of social justice can contribute to methodologies which challenge injustice, displace traditional inequalities in research, and undertake research and question and empower and ultimately transform ways of knowing.

How is knowledge in research a social justice issue?

> We need the power of modern critical theories of how meanings and bodies get made, not in order to deny meanings and bodies, but in order to build meanings and bodies that have a chance for life. (Haraway, 1988: 580)

Our approach to research says much about our relationship to certain values, concepts and beliefs about the nature of knowledge. It is useful to think of the relationship between these ideas in research through a number of interrelated layers based on core philosophical ideas, namely paradigm, ontology, epistemology and methodology. The philosopher Thomas Kuhn brought the term paradigm into popular usage as the framework or lens through which researchers view the world. According to Guba and Lincoln (1994: 107), 'paradigms are basic belief systems based on ontological, epistemological and methodological assumptions'. Killam (2013) describes terms which define research paradigms – namely axiology, ontology, epistemology and methodology. Axiology refers to the nature of ethics, which in terms of research is concerned with what the researcher deems to be valuable and ethical (Killam, 2013). Ontology refers to the researcher's beliefs about the nature of social reality – is it something out there waiting to be discovered, or are we part of what we observe? According to Killam (2013: 8), '[e]pistemology examines the relationship between knowledge and the researcher during the discovery'. It is concerned with the nature of knowledge, what counts as acceptable knowledge and the relationship between knowledge and knower. Methodology then describes the processes by which researchers go about their discovery – their approach to obtaining knowledge.

An important starting point for our chapter is to draw a connection between knowledge and justice as set out in the challenge posed by Haraway

(1988). As she usefully articulates it, critical knowledge production is required in order to dismantle not only how meanings are made but how meanings are embodied and what the embodiment of knowledge means for lived lives. Embracing this vision through the lens of social justice means asking questions about how the knowledge that is produced shapes lives.

By adapting a Fraserian (2008) approach to our interrogations, the social, economic, cultural and political dimensions of the knowledge-shaping process are our key questions of social justice. The basis of social scientific inquiry is making the social world knowable. The knowledge created through research both produces and shapes epistemological orientations: what becomes known and how we have come to know it. The philosophical journey through the social sciences reveals how the original tenets of positivism were questioned as the one true way of knowing the social world, and an alternative constructivist perspective emerged offering a lens to interpret the subjective nature of knowledge and lived lives. The evolution of such critical inquiry is at the core of our consideration of knowledge as a social justice issue. Ways of knowing the world, how the knowledge of our social world is produced and challenged and the lived effects of such knowledge and ways of knowing are critical issues in a research for social justice agenda.

The fundamental tenets of social science are a starting point for the ideas shared in this chapter, and while a critical interrogation of the foundations of epistemology is beyond the scope of what is possible over these pages, the nature of critical inquiry and what it means for social justice are key dimensions which we will employ in examining knowing, knowledge and the knower.

Critical theories on knowledge

Tracing critical theories of knowledge presents a colossal excavation challenge through the archaeology of social theory. While we can begin at postmodern poststructuralist thinking which signals new avenues of exploration on knowledge and knowing (see Davis, 2004), described in more detail later in the chapter, we stand on the shoulders of neo-Kantian theorists questioning the nature of knowledge and knowledge subjectivity.

This led us to new understandings in terms of both how knowledge is understood by the social actor and how social scientists understand and interpret the actions of those they observe, leading to a method of interpretation and shaping of knowledge, the classic Weberian *verstehen* (Whimster, 2003). Contemporary critical theories of knowledge indeed emerged through a post-Marxist tradition, establishing a new paradigm in the analysis of social change which focused on the significance of ideas and how these ideas come together in the form of ideologies, the shaping and communication of ideologies through practice and the role of key players in perpetuating or disrupting such practices (Ransome, 2010). Gramsci's conceptualisation of intellectual and ideological persuasion around the notion of hegemony became an important conceptual tool in understanding the unifying ideas which relate to practices around knowledge and power: with 'a validity which is "psychological", they "organise" human masses and create the terrain on which men move, acquire consciousness of their position, struggle, etc' (Gramsci, 1971: 376–7). The 'linguistic turn' in social theory further developed conceptualisations of ideological and non-ideological knowledge, with thinkers such as Althusser drawing attention to positive and negative ideologies and the role of the 'intellectual' involved in the development of theoretical skills and activities, an integral part of the structuring process by examining its effects (Ransome, 2010). This pointed the way for poststructuralists to explore how meanings are produced and contested through culture.

Postmodernism, as described by Ramazanoğlu and Holland (2011), refers to three distinct movements: (1) an evolving cultural phase in art and architecture; (2) the poststructuralist writings of Derrida, Foucault, Deleuze and Guattari; and (3) more general sociological theories of late capitalism. Moving beyond the epistemological understandings of modernist theory, which sees knowledge as permanent and accumulating in a linear manner over time, the postmodern thinkers which we draw on for critical analysis of knowledge and discourse (Barthes, Foucault and Derrida in particular – see Payne, 2003; Reynolds and Roffe, 2004) point to the elusive nature of knowledge and its competing discourses. Barthesian ideas provide us with the notion of semiotics, knowledge as a sign–system which produces culturally mediated codes of meaning. Derrida's theories view the nature of knowledge as a sign–system in constant flux, being perpetually deferred to other knowledge claims. For Foucault, knowledge and power are distilled in his conceptualisation of discursive practice and how dominant understandings come to be through the operation of power in society. Yet what of the universalising tendencies of such theoretical lenses? Ramazanoğlu and Holland (2011: 5) argue that 'postmodernism offers feminism both freedom from the grip of modern, humanist thought and the constraints of scientific method, and freedom to open up fresh ways of thinking about gender'. While this chapter looks in more detail at Foucauldian theorising on discourse and its value as both a lens for interrogating knowledge injustice and as a tool in critical methodological practice, the gender blindness of theorising on knowledge and knowledge production has been the mantle taken up by second wave critical feminist thinkers (Gilligan, 1982; Haraway, 1988; Code, 1991): 'Feminism's most compelling epistemological insight lies in the connections it has made between knowledge and power' (Lennon and Whitford, 1994: 1). Indeed, the development of second wave feminist epistemologies as set out by Doucet and Mauthner (2007) was in direct response to issues of masculinity, power and authority in knowledge creation (Code, 1981; Gilligan, 1982). Lorraine Code in 1981 went on to develop ideas on what made feminist epistemology distinct from traditional, 'malestream' epistemology when she posed the question 'is the sex of the knower epistemologically significant?' (cited in Doucet and Mauthner, 2007: 36). Certainly, as Doucet and Mauthner (2007) describe, such movements were in tandem with the rise of critical feminist perspectives of the natural and biobehavioural sciences, where the collection and analysis of data in experimental and clinical biomedical studies had long been exclusively focused on the male subject through the male gaze. As Haraway eloquently argues:

> Histories of science may be powerfully told as histories of technologies. These technologies are ways of life, social orders, practices of visualization. Technologies are skilled practices. How to see? Where to see from? What limits to vision? What to see for? Whom to see with? Who gets to have more than one point of view? Who gets blinded? Who wears blinders? Who interprets the visual field? What other sensory powers do we wish to cultivate besides vision? (Haraway, 1988: 587)

For Haraway, the complex web of the interconnected subject could only ever be partly understood, as the observer, however critical, is similarly multidimensional. Haraway (1988: 589) describes a feminist standpoint which embraces the temporal and imperfect enterprise of knowledge creation as she argues for 'the sciences and politics of interpretation, translation, stuttering, and the partly understood'. She continues by arguing how politics and ethics mediate struggles for what counts as rational knowledge and argues for positionality as a key practice (Haraway, 1988: 587), as '[p]ositioning implies responsibility for our enabling practices'.

   More recent critical feminist theorising moves away from the universalising tendencies of second and third wave feminist concerns to attend to the interconnection of 'gender' with other hierarchies of social identity including race/ethnicity, sexuality, age, social class and position, (dis) ability, culture and nationality (Lazar and Kramarae, 2011). Certainly, the notion of a singular feminist standpoint has been long dismantled by feminist thinkers who emphasise how diverse feminist praxis shapes and creates diverse knowledge processes. These seeds were planted long ago, as Haraway (1988: 590, original emphasis) describes: 'There is no single feminist standpoint because our maps require too many dimensions for that metaphor to ground our visions. But the feminist standpoint theorists' goal of an epistemology and politics of engaged, accountable positioning remains eminently potent. The goal is better accounts of the world, that is, "science."

This strong critical feminist lens provides a valuable launchpad and framework to consider the processes which shape our ways of knowing. We turn now to look at the links between ways of knowing and ways of being and how this helps us reveal social injustice through the crucial connector of power.

Knowledge, discourse and power

> Discourses define what the problem is; they say what is worth knowing and what can be said ... Discourses shape and become institutionalized in social policies and the organizations through which they are carried out. (Clarke and Cochrane, 1998: 35)

Taking a critical feminist approach through engaged, accountable positioning as prompted by Haraway (1988) leads us to consider the connection between knowledge, power and the ways of knowing this makes possible. While Foucault neglected to concern himself with gendered knowledge and power, for him power and knowledge are interrelated, and every human relationship is a site of struggle and negotiation of power: "My problem is to know how men [sic] govern (themselves and others) by means of the production of truth" (Foucault, 1980: 47, in Castel, 1994: 238). As described in Hall's (1997) writings, Foucault is a constructionist concerned with knowledge and meaning through discourse – which is at the heart of constructionist theory of meaning and representation: things and actions take on meaning and become 'objects of knowledge' within discourse. In his seminal work *Archaeology of* Knowledge (1972 [1969]), Foucault describes discourse as systems of thoughts composed of ideas, attitudes, beliefs, practices and courses of action which systematically construct subjects and their worlds. Revealing the power–knowledge nexus, discourses can be understood as media through which knowledge is constructed and power relations are produced and maintained. Hall (1997) describes discourse as a system of representation – the production of knowledge through language.

Understanding the relationship between knowledge and power means exposing the rules and practices producing (historically situated) regulated discourses. Discourse from a Foucauldian perspective relates to power as it operates by rules of exclusion – objects (what can be spoken of), ritual (where and how one may speak), the privileged (who may speak) (in Hall, 1997). Most famously, Foucault explored the history of sexuality (1980) and the history of madness in order to 'problematise' how certain 'truths' about subjects come to be and how such truths lead to ways of knowing and ways of being in relation to such subjects. In this way, then, in any given historically situated context, discourse serves to *rule in* certain ways of talking about knowledge and how it is constructed, and how we conduct ourselves towards, for example, sexuality, and *rules out/restricts* other ways of talking about knowledge and how it is constructed, and how we conduct ourselves towards, for example, sexuality. From such a poststructuralist perspective, subjects such as 'sexuality', 'disability', 'madness' and 'sex work' only exist meaningfully within the discourses about them. We will return to Foucauldian-inspired ideas of problematisation further in the chapter to understand how, as a means to address knowledge as injustice, as critical researchers we can call into question taken-for-granted knowledge and the processes which sustain such injustice.

Inspired by such Foucauldian poststructural analysis (see Bacchi, 1999), we can see how ways of knowing translate into ways of governing behaviour through the production of modes of regulation. While Foucauldian perspectives have provided much currency in poststructuralist analysis, feminist critiques of Foucault have provided valuable shaping to our understandings of the gendered structuring of knowledge and the discursive and wider subjective effects of malestream epistemology (Naples, 2003: Bacchi, 2009). Women's experiences suggest that male power is extra-discursive, that is, it relates to wider realities than those of discourse, and so for some poststructuralist critical feminists Foucault has neglected the way in which 'gendered patterns of power operate so that women's experiences might differ from men's' (Naples, 2003: 113; see also Barrett, 1992).

Taking a pause to recap – how have our learnings about knowledge, power and discourse informing this chapter been influenced by a poststructuralist, Foucauldian-inspired critical feminist perspective? Discourse has materiality as a media through which knowledge is produced and power relations are shaped and sustained. We can reveal how discourse operates through ways of talking about subjects of research, for example how we talk about gender, sexuality, disability, poverty, migration and how this way of talking and knowing such issues at a given point in time leads them to become accepted truths, through rules of formation and institutional practices. Such ways of knowing and the rules imposed for what gets said and how we conduct ourselves in relation to such issues affect behaviours and shape how we act and govern ourselves in relation to such knowledge. Indeed, this is subject to discursive shifts over time as new observed patterns supporting the same political drift/discursive formation (Cousins and Hussain, 1984: 84–5) come to be. Crucially, the evolution of post-Foucauldian critical feminist thinking disrupted the gender blindness of earlier theorising on knowledge, power and discourse and challenged critical theorists to account for the structuring effects of the enterprise of knowledge production.

In the next section, I outline the methodological approach which has shaped the projects I draw on for discussion. The consideration of methodology is not separate from the considerations of knowledge, power and discourse which we have covered so far. Indeed, the methodology is at the heart of that connection. How are our research 'doings' undertaken, and how does this help us to understand the social and political effects of such doings?

Methodology

> [I]f researchers fail to explore how their personal, professional, and structural positions frame social scientific investigations, researchers inevitably reproduce dominant gender, race, and class biases. (Naples, 2003: 3)

We take then as our methodological starting point the notion that knowledge production and the knowledge produced through research is never neutral but infused with questions of social justice. Lynch (1999: 43) observes that 'research is inevitably politically engaged, be it by default, design or by simple recognition'.

Bacchi and Rönnblom (2014: 171) consider it important to initiate a conversation examining theoretical positions 'in terms of the forms of politics they make possible'. Drawing on the work of Mol (1999), they see feminists and other theorists being involved in *ontological politics* or the political shaping of realities. This, they say, prompts new discussions among feminists about the realities shaped by methodologies in Foucauldian-inspired poststructuralist analysis, and they argue that employing uncritical categories in one's analytic framework ignores the politics involved in their production and thus limits feminist change agendas (Bacchi and Rönnblom, 2014). They call for a 'performativity of method' (Law, 2004: 149–50), through reflexivity or more accurately self-problematisation in order to responsibly reflect on the 'realities' one's methods create (Bacchi and Rönnblom, 2014).

What follows in the remainder of this chapter is a teasing out of the key themes related to epistemic politics arising from two research projects (McGarry and FitzGerald, 2017: McGarry and Ryan, 2020), both of which employed critical discourse analysis in whole or in part, one as a distinct methodological approach and the other as part of its analysis in a participatory research project. The first project is a critical discourse analysis study in the context of legislative change on prostitution policy in Ireland, looking specifically at the policy and public debates leading up to the introduction of laws which criminalised sex purchase in Ireland, the Criminal Law (Sexual Offences) Act 2017 (McGarry and FitzGerald, 2017). The second study is a HIV Ireland-commissioned research project which employed Participatory Action Research (PAR) and set out to explore the lived experiences of sex workers following the introduction of these laws in terms of their health, safety and well-being (McGarry and Ryan, 2020).

To undertake this exploration, I draw on key Foucauldian ideas to guide the development of my critical analysis of discourse around knowledge and knowledge producers in these studies. The specific aspects of a Foucauldian-inspired critical discourse analysis are articulated clearly by Stanley Hall (1997):

1. **Statements** about the issue in question – for example 'poverty', or 'drug use', or 'sexuality' and so on, or in the case of this research 'prostitution' or 'sex work' and how such statements give us a particular kind of knowledge about the issue in question.
2. The **rules** which prescribe how we talk about this topic – what gets said – governing what is 'sayable' or 'thinkable' about sex work at a particular historical moment.
3. **'Subjects'** who in some ways personify the discourse – the 'prostitute' or 'sex worker' – with the attributes we would expect these subjects to have, given the way knowledge about the topic was constructed at that particular historical point in time (Hall, 1997).
4. How this knowledge about the topic acquires **authority**, a sense of embodying the '**truth**' about it; constituting the 'truth of the matter', at a historical moment.
5. The **practices** within institutions for dealing with the subjects. In Drawing on Foucault's (1980) work on moral discipline (and medical intervention) for the sexually deviant, I ask whose conduct is being regulated and organised according to which ideas in terms of sex work?
6. Acknowledgement that this is transient – a different discourse or different **episteme** will arise at a later historical moment, supplanting the existing one, opening up a new discursive formation and producing, in its turn, new conceptions of, for example, 'sex work', new discourses with the power and authority, the 'truth', to regulate social practices in new ways.

Moving forward with this critical discursive exercise, I take on board ideas from Ruth Wodak (in Kendall, 2007: 4): '"Critical" means not taking things for granted, opening up complexity, challenging reductionism, dogmatism and dichotomies, being self-reflective in my research, and through these processes, making opaque structures of power relations and ideologies manifest'. In order to establish some operational boundaries for the inquiry and based on the example of the studies selected for this chapter, the specific focus of this critical discursive exercise is on the reproduction of political power and domination through political discourse which establishes a particular way of knowing sex work and 'the discursive conditions and consequences of political *inequality* that results from such domination' (Van Dijk, 1993: 249, emphasis in original).

I turn now to explore how social injustices occur through the example of two relevant projects which employed a critical discourse analysis. This analysis is prefaced by the work of Fraser to draw our attention to the conditions necessary for parity of participation and how a recognition of lack of parity is illuminated through these projects.

How social injustices occur

Understanding how injustices occur is usefully explored through Fraser's (2008) conception of social justice, which is founded on the principle of parity of participation. Such a principle is based on the notion that 'justice requires social arrangements that permit all (adult) members of society to interact with one another as peers' (Fraser, 2008: 27). This necessitates several conditions to be satisfied, as Fraser sees it – first, the 'objective' condition precludes social arrangements which deny some people the means and opportunity to interact with others as peers, thus precluding maldistribution. The second condition is what Fraser terms 'intersubjective' and calls into question the institutionalisation of value systems which depreciate some categories of people, thus denying some people the status of full partners in interaction or misrecognising some groups. Both conditions are thus necessary for participatory parity. While the first condition relates to the distributive elements of justice, the economic structuring of society which positions some people at a material disadvantage to others that is generally associated with class, the second condition relates to the structuring effects of status politics, or, as Fraser describes it, the 'culturally defined hierarchies of status' (Fraser, 2008: 28). As Fraser developed her thinking on her theory of justice, a third element was included relating to the political dimension of justice, which precludes the political constitution of society which leaves a group of people without a voice, or politically misrepresented (Fraser, 2008). Thus maldistribution, misrecognition and misrepresentation become the three major dimensions of injustice in Fraser's thesis which hinder the ability of some groups to participate on par with others in political spaces.

Fraser's theorising on social justice provides important tools for understanding how knowledge and power operate to preclude and silence, and how undemocratic research practices not only prevail but are legitimised and institutionalised. McGarry and FitzGerald's work (2018) uncovered an example of such social injustice in practice by exploring the misrepresentation of sex workers in policy debates on proposed changes to prostitution legislation in Ireland. The analysis of discourse over the course of these debates identified how sex worker 'knowledge' was discredited and delegitimised and how sex workers then became mispresented, through a dominant neo-abolitionist way of knowing sex worker lives. The epistemic privilege awarded to neo-abolitionism in the context of these debates is an important example of how processes of knowledge injustice operate and become institutionalised.

Establishing epistemic privilege in sex work politics

The examples selected for critical review in this chapter stem from a legislative process which set in train the establishment of new criminal laws in the Republic of Ireland governing the purchase of sex, mirroring Nordic-style sex purchase bans elsewhere in Europe. In 2012, the Irish government initiated a consultation process on the future of laws on prostitution in Ireland, and part of this process involved submissions to and public hearings by the Joint Oireachtas Committee on Justice, Law and Equality (hereafter JOC). Research by McGarry and FitzGerald (2018) traced the discursive events around this process by looking at the role of the neo-abolitionist campaign Turn Off the Red Light (TORL)[1] in establishing, in Foucauldian terms, the *rules of formation* of the debates on prostitution – what counts as knowledge, what is worth knowing, who counts as a knower and how the practices around knowledge production or epistemological practices around sex work in Ireland should operate.

As set out in the work of McGarry and FitzGerald (2018), the public hearings held by the JOC provide much evidence of these rules of formation. Drawing on Fraserian theory on political misrepresentation (2009), McGarry and FitzGerald (2018) argue that the evidence from the policy and public debates reveals explicit TORL/neo-abolitionist bounding of political space in discussions on prostitution by establishing *the* truth claims on prostitution (misframing). These tactics were also found to reflect Fraserian ideas on political silencing (misrecognition), as TORL and their discursive influence exclude sex workers from political spaces (meta-political misrepresentation).

TORL delegates provided evidence to the committee which sets out a particular way of knowing prostitution, as a statement by one of its representatives shows:

> The introduction of legislation has great potential to establish a new norm in our society which deems prostitution to be an … unacceptable social phenomenon and sends a strong message to future generations that it is not acceptable for women to be treated as commodities, to be bought and sold for sexual use. (Houses of the Oireachtas, 2012: 6)

The TORL messaging, through a pattern of consistent statements to the JOC and during the process of consultation, established knowledge on prostitution as the 'unacceptable' commodification of women's bodies. The consistency of this framing also set out a powerful message about the bounding of political space, as TORL operate a clear strategy on the terms of the messaging and truth claims on prostitution and how as a collective voice they can establish the authority to represent the issue:

> The important point in terms of where the National Women's Council of Ireland is coming from and discussions among members is that prostitution was viewed within the context of violence against women … it is important that it is seen in the context of violence against women and moving on to supporting a particular model, which is the Swedish model. (Houses of the Oireachtas, 2012: 6)

What is striking is that such messaging seeks to establish the truth of prostitution (knowledge and what is worth knowing) as well as those with authority to speak (knowledge producers), in this case the National Women's Council of Ireland/TORL, and not – surprising though it may seem – sex workers themselves. Their voices, authority, knowledge are conspicuous by their absence. This was revealed in the work undertaken by McGarry and FitzGerald (2017), who looked at the operation of the JOC consultation process and the legitimation provided for the explicit exclusion of sex worker voices. Having received over 800 submissions to its consultation, the JOC held four public hearings between December 2012 and February 2013. During these hearings, 15 organisations were invited to give evidence, 12 of which were TORL members. Of the individuals who presented, five were academics, two were medical professionals and two were media professionals At the end of the public hearings, having not yet heard any evidence from sex workers themselves, the committee agreed to hold one final *in camera* hearing where five individuals were invited to take part (two current sex workers and three with former experience of the sex industry). Notably, the JOC validated their decision to, first, dismiss the evidence provided by current sex workers, and secondly adeptly manage the discursive space to be dominated by neo-abolitionist knowledge, specifically TORL supported "ex-sex worker" accounts:

> The Committee placed a particular value on the evidence provided by those individuals who had exited prostitution and have put some distance between their present life and their experiences in prostitution. They appeared not to have a vested interest in the outcome of the review of the law on prostitution; apart from their concern that others might be exploited through prostitution. (Houses of the Oireachtas, 2013: addendum)

This is an important discursive move in how the JOC justifies the injustice of its silencing of sex workers. McGarry and FitzGerald (2017) found additional evidence of the justification of injustice through pathologising sex workers (discussed in more detail later in the chapter) and their ongoing 'deviant' sexual behaviour as validating the decision of the JOC to devalue their political participation and legitimating the exclusion of sex workers as credible witnesses. The bizarre statement that current sex workers have a 'vested interest' in the outcome of the policy process being used as a justification for discrediting and dismissing them as valid witnesses/worthy knowers indeed shows how the power–knowledge nexus operates to exclude and disenfranchise. In no other policy realm would identification of those with a vested interest in the outcome of the policy process be a credible justification for marginalisation from the policy process, nor would such a manner of political silencing and exclusion be tolerated in rightful democratic processes.

Rules of formation for managing epistemic privilege

To ensure that this abolitionist messaging is awarded the discursive authority in debates, it is important that the rules of formation about the framing, or, in Fraser's words, political misframing, is managed. Misframing in a Fraserian sense is the control of boundaries in political spaces which prevent some who lack the political power from participating on par. Injustice arises when 'partitioning of political space blocks the poor or despised from challenging those who oppress them' (Fraser, 2008: 147). From the analysis of the JOC debates, it is clear that any challenge to the dominant TORL perspective is dismissed and discredited.

Indeed, the rationalisation given by abolitionists for monopolising claims to truth and determining who should be allowed to participate in political space is aptly illustrated in the following statement appearing in *The Irish Times* newspaper by leading TORL campaign group Ruhama:

> '[F]alse consciousness' is a state in which a woman being prostituted denies and disassociates from the psychological reality of her situation in order to survive. Sarah Benson, of Ruhama, says that it is only after these women have left prostitution that their consciousness changes.
>
> Dissociation is a very common experience, a coping mechanism, and our experience of women who have moved on from prostitution, our experience of the survivors' movement, is that the sex trade is harmful for all involved: there are physical and psychological consequences. (Holmquist, 2013)

The clear subjectification effects of this discourse position sex workers who have not yet moved on from prostitution as being incapable of participating in political spaces given the perceived psychological impact on their ability to recognise and speak their truths. Essentially, the strategic use of such discourse by leading abolitionist groups deems current sex workers as incapable of providing credible evidence in a process such as the JOC consultations, and they are thus rendered politically illegitimate. As Bacchi (2009) notes, a key aspect of the knowledge–power relationship is the issue of who is best placed to produce 'knowledges' that will count as 'truth' and how they secure their position of influence. There is much value in the dual idea of discourse suggested by Bacchi, who draws on the work of Ball (1990 in Bacchi, 2009). Drawing on such an idea, we see both the power of discourse used by abolitionists to set the frame and decide who gets to speak, while at the same time we observe the power of abolitionists to deploy particular discourses, thus allowing us to think through both the power that the TORL discourse accrues and the unequal power relations related to the production and reproduction of such discourse.

Establishing epistemic authority

In the tradition of the Habermasian public sphere as exemplified by Fraser's thinking on civic republicanism, where private interests are superseded by the 'common good' (Habermas cited in Fraser, 1990: 58), TORL campaigned upon singular political narratives. Such single narratives inevitably exclude (and particularly exclude those most disenfranchised), devalue political participation by the excluded and preclude 'genuine dialogue between differently located subjects' (Stychin, 2001: 286). The political strategy used by TORL created the 'us' who support the campaign and the 'them' who do not support TORL and by implication support exploitation. As Fraser argues, such a strategy reduces all deliberations to a singular political narrative which masks unequal power relations (Fraser, 1990; McGarry and FitzGerald, 2018). Indeed, the repeated use of this singular political narrative as a strategic discursive practice allowed TORL to become established as *the* authority to speak on the issue of prostitution, representing as it claimed the majority of civil-minded Irish society. The well-worn statement by TORL campaigners conjures the image of the collective across all sectors of Irish society, suggesting a groundswell of support from the majority:

> More than 60 organisations make up the Turn Off the Red Light Campaign representing every aspect of Irish life and it is important that as many as possible are given an opportunity to voice their concerns. We are doctors, nurses, survivors of prostitution, public servants, technicians, human rights campaigners, young farmers and many others. (Immigrant Council of Ireland, 2013)

As a feminist researcher studying and participating in the politics of sex work research, I acknowledge the need to navigate what some deem a 'discomforting space' (Ward and Wylie, 2014). As experienced through my collaborative work, '[w]here evidence-based critiques of neo-abolitionism emerge from informed challengers, abolitionists respond by discrediting "others" who they insist neither understand nor have the authority to speak about the reality of prostitution' (McGarry and FitzGerald, 2018: xix; see also McGarry and FitzGerald, 2017).

I turn now to look at the effects of these discursive practices by drawing on research which centres the voices of sex workers themselves, those deemed 'discreditable' (Goffman,1963) in Irish policy processes, and how their voices challenge such meta-political misrepresentation.

Effects of epistemic privileging practices

Research I undertook with my colleague Paul Ryan (McGarry and Ryan, 2020) sought to uncover the lived experiences of the new laws on sex work in Ireland, introduced following the overwhelming recommendation of the JOC with its clearly articulated leanings towards the TORL. This study was an opportunity to understand lived lives in the context of criminalisation, particularly in terms of health, safety and well-being. What is clear from the research is that the long disenfranchisement of sex workers from the processes which impact their lives compounds the effects of the other oppressions that shape their lives. Iris Marion Young's work (1990) is useful in helping us understand how injustices occur through what she terms the five faces of oppression. According to Young, these oppressions are exploitation, powerlessness, marginalisation, cultural imperialism and violence. Relating this idea to our focus here on knowledge and social justice, we can identify how those in positions of relative power often 'exploit' people for data in research, taking their time and expertise and taking their investment in the research without any attempt to equalise research relationships. Certain groups are mined for data as part of a research project, without realising any ownership on the knowledge that is produced or the outcomes of the project.

Our research (McGarry and Ryan, 2020) attempted to recognise and address such exploitative practices by drawing on a methodological approach which centres the participant as expert in their own lives, while also equalising power in the research process. To this end, we saw a PAR design as being the most valuable approach as both tool and process in a critical and transformative knowledge production enterprise. Given the long tradition of social injustice that has rendered sex workers voiceless and excluded from the production of knowledge on their lives, our research was a commitment to address the injustice of exclusion, misrecognition and misrepresentation and a means to advance an agenda of parity of participation in the research enterprise: to research 'with' and 'alongside', not research 'on' sex workers. As Ledwith (2016: 144) argues, a PAR design provides 'the foundation for co-creating new knowledge as the basis of action for change', and we developed a peer-led approach to research planning, data collection and analysis and reporting as a means to challenge exclusionary research practices controlling knowledge production about sex workers (McGarry and Ryan, 2020; see also Lynch, 1999). The research consisted of a number of focus groups in Dublin, Limerick, Cork and Galway facilitated by peer-researchers and supported by the research team, bringing together sex workers to discuss the key issues arising in terms of sex worker health, well-being and safety in the aftermath of law change.

Some key evidence arising from this study shows how sex workers perceive the law as framing them as 'less than', and the effects of such epistemic manoeuvres is experienced far beyond political spaces, spilling into lived lives: "You're a victim so you need to be taught a lesson. You're victimising yourself by doing all these evil things, and it's like you're an errant child that need to be put back in line" (research participant Kay cited in McGarry and Ryan, 2020: 30).

For Scoular and O'Neill (2008), laws which criminalise aspects of the sex industry perpetuate ideas of sex workers as victims who must 'self-responsibilize' and exit prostitution to be deserving of support. This idea is backed by evidence from Amnesty (2016: 16): '[S]ex workers also frequently face censure, judgement and blame for being seen to transgress social or sexual norms and/or to not conform to gender roles and stereotypes because they are sex workers.' The discursive effects of such 'ways of knowing' sex work and sex workers set a dangerous precedent in terms of the narrative of the inevitability of violence against sex workers, the consequences of which mean that, in line with mounting evidence, sex workers feel they are unable to seek police protection or have access to justice like everyone else. This was exemplified in stark terms by one participant:

> [T]hey allow this group in society to feel so scared, to feel so vulnerable, and marginalised, and thrown away, and ostracised, that this group would do anything, literally anything, to avoid the consequences of having to go to the police, of being found out. So many people live absolutely horrible lives, not because of what they do, but because they don't have any protection when anything happens, unlike any other group in society. (Laura cited in McGarry and Ryan, 2020: 32)

This appears as Young's (1990) second face of oppression, that of marginalisation, what Fraser (2009) describes as a lack of parity of participation, where a group is relegated to the margins, lacking adequate access to the same economic, social and political resources to engage on a par with others. Our participant's remarks can also be seen as a manifestation of Young's (1990) third face of oppression, that is, powerlessness, which occurs through the relative downgrading of the status of some due to their constraints in accessing the social, political and economic resources necessary to engage and be recognised on a par with others. Freire (1998) calls this the most insidious of all oppressions, as powerlessness becomes internalised, leading the powerless to perpetuate such oppressions against themselves and others due to their being indoctrinated that this is the way things are. As Freire describes it, this refers to a culture of silence, where oppressions are not even talked about, injustices are unquestioned and a silence pervades and maintains the power differentials which sustain the oppression.

Challenging epistemic privileging practices

The evidence from these studies shows that, mirroring international evidence, the marginalisation of sex worker voices is part of a long-embedded knowledge–power nexus in sex work politics (Visser et al, 2004; Grenfell et al, 2018; Ryan and Ward, 2018). Young's (1990) fourth face of oppression is cultural imperialism, where the ideas of the most dominant become the normative ideas, leading to an 'othering' and stigmatisation of those holding socially unacceptable ideas or acting in socially deviant ways. Our research demonstrates that sex workers resisted being excluded from conversations about themselves and wanted their voices to be heard:

> I think that is something that would be helpful here, is people recognising that this is their life and their right, and they can stand up and speak out, and obviously it's not made easy, and the people who do need to be heard the most are told to shut up the most. So just having that freedom, of being able to say these things without fear of being persecuted for it. And that falls under freedom of speech, but for goodness' sake, the freedom of speech to what degree. I mean what degree are we actually free to speak our minds and to say what is happening in our world? (Kay cited in McGarry and Ryan, 2020: 32)

Kay's words bring into stark relief the struggle between sex worker resistance and the context which structures their powerlessness. The final face of Young's oppression relates to violence. While the study in question provides evidence of how the most explicit and obvious threats and actual perpetration of physical and sexual violence against sex workers are compounded under new criminal laws (McGarry and Ryan, 2020), we describe processes of structural and symbolic violence impacting the lives of sex workers (Galtung, 1990; Krusi et al, 2014). These processes mean that those in society holding less power and having limited opportunity to acquire power are more likely to be subjected to structural violence. Taking this idea a step further, Scheper-Hughes and Bourgois (2004) describe two processes which are injurious to more vulnerable or marginalised populations – one is everyday violence, where institutionalised and everyday practices such as stigmatisation which render invisible the violence sex workers experience. The other crucial idea is that of symbolic violence (Scheper-Hughes and Bourgois, 2004), where those most marginalised by power differentials and social inequalities accept this as the natural order of things and internalise responsibility for their lower place in the social hierarchy (McGarry and Ryan, 2018). What our study with sex workers shows is that despite the everyday violence which sex workers are subjected to under criminalisation, they are resistant to symbolic violence and wish to disrupt and displace practices and processes which have sustained dominant stigmatised knowledge on sex work and sex workers. One step in supporting this as critical researchers is our commitment to methodologies which advance social justice rather than perpetuate injustice.

Indeed, Sanders et al (2022) highlight the complexities of positionality in sex work research and the more recent contentions in the field between academics and the sex work community, where the 'nothing about us without us' catch call has taken on a new expression to imply that only research undertaken by sex workers themselves is credible and ethical. As researchers committed to social justice, we must acknowledge how our approach to research, the questions we ask of ourselves and others and the collaborations we seek out for knowledge production shape lived realities:

> We sign up to research as an active vehicle for change and as a place to challenge the status quo and to connect evidence to policy and practice for real change. To do this better and more seriously, the democratisation of research (and here specifically sex work studies) should be at the fore of this objective. (Sanders et al, 2022: 7)

Concluding thoughts: lessons for social justice research, policy and practice

A number of key lessons for social justice research, policy and practice arise from the work underpinning this chapter:

- As critical researchers, our task is to support and facilitate such disruption and displacement of the symbolic violence of epistemic privilege which has long oppressed sex workers and other marginalised communities.
- From the perspective of research for social justice, how our practices for acquiring knowledge and the effects those practices have are critical spaces for scrutiny in terms of the manner in which they either perpetuate marginalisation or dismantle taken-for-granted ideas about the natural order of things.
- Our critical praxis must be an acknowledgement of the political resonance of our knowledge creation as our research paradigms and methodologies create different lived realities (Bacchi and Rönnblom, 2014).

- Our research processes have material effect for those lives 'under scrutiny' and the policy and practices which build from research shape and reshape lived lives. How we operationalise our research and the knowledge that is produced matters.
- Guided by Foucauldian ideas on problematisation, research practice for social justice involves critically addressing how we have come to know what we know, and who gets to speak as a legitimate knower.
- Advancing an agenda for change involves engaging in research practices which are transformative not simply in terms of the knowledge that is produced but in terms of critical praxis as a 'politics of doing' (Bacchi and Everline, 2010) for social justice.
- By employing research methods for social justice which are participatory, inclusive and critically address processes which exclude and dispossess already disenfranchised groups, we commit ourselves to building and advancing processes of engagement for knowledge production which deliberately upend hierarchical structures in order to address oppression.

Note

[1] TORL is a coalition comprising feminists, health care professionals, non-governmental organisations from civil and religious society and individuals.

References

Amnesty International (2016) 'Amnesty International policy on state obligations to respect, protect and fulfil the human rights of sex workers', Available from: www.amnesty.org/en/documents/pol30/4062/2016/en/ [Accessed 4 August 2022].

Bacchi, C. (1999) *Women, Policy and Politics: The Construction of Policy Problems*, London: SAGE.

Bacchi, C. (2009) *Analysing Policy: What's the Problem Represented to Be?*, Frenchs Forest, NSW: Pearson Education.

Bacchi, C. and Eveline, J. (eds) (2010) *Mainstreaming Politics: Gendering Practices and Feminist Theory*, Adelaide: University of Adelaide Press.

Bacchi, C. and Rönnblom, M. (2014) 'Feminist discursive institutionalism: A poststructural alternative', *NORA – Nordic Journal of Feminist and Gender Research*, 22(3): 170–86.

Barrett, M. (1992) 'Words and things: Materialism and method in contemporary feminist analysis', in A. Philips (ed) *Destabilizing Theory: Contemporary Feminist Debates*, Cambridge: Polity Press.

Castel, R. (1994) '"Problematization" as a mode of reading history', in J. Goldstein (ed) *Foucault and the Writing of History*, Oxford: Blackwell, pp 237–52.

Clarke, J. and Cochrane, A. (1998) 'The social construction of social problems', in E. Saraga (ed) *Embodying the Social: Constructions of Difference*, London: Routledge, pp 3–42.

Code, L. (1991) *What Can She Know?*, Ithaca, NY: Cornell University Press.

Cousins, M. and Hussain, A. (1984) *Michel Foucault*, Houndmills: MacMillan Education.

Davis, C. (2004) *After Poststructuralism: Reading, Stories and Theory*, London: Routledge.

Doucet, A. and Mauthner, M. (2007) 'Feminist methodologies and epistemologies', in D.L. Peck and C.D. Bryant (eds) *The Handbook of 21st Century Sociology*, Thousand Oaks, CA: Sage, pp 36–42.

Foucault, M. (1972 [1969]) *The Archaeology of Knowledge*, New York: Pantheon Books.

Foucault, M. (1980) *The History of Sexuality, Vol. 1, An Introduction*, New York: Vintage Books.

Foucault, M. (1994 [1981]) 'So is it important to think?', in J.D. Faubion (ed) *Power: Essential Works of Foucault 1954–1984, Vol. 3*, London: Penguin, pp 454–58.

Fraser, N. (1990) 'Rethinking the public sphere: A contribution to the critique of actually existing democracy', *Social Text*, 25–6: 56–80.

Fraser, N. (2008) *Scales of Justice: Reimagining Political Space in a Globalizing World*, Cambridge: Polity Press.

Fraser, N. (2009) 'Social justice in the age of identity politics', in G. Henderson and M. Waterstone (eds) *Geographic Thought: A Praxis Perspective*, New York: Routledge, pp 72–90.

Freire, P. (1998) *Pedagogy of Freedom: Ethics, Democracy and Civic Courage*, Lanham: Rowman & Littlefield.

Galtung, J. (1990) 'Cultural violence', *Journal of Peace Research*, 27(3): 291–305.

Gilligan, C. (1982) *In a Different Voice: Psychological Theory and Women's Development*, Cambridge, MA: Harvard University Press.

Goffman, E. (1963) *Stigma: Notes on the Management of Spoiled Identity*, New York: Simon & Schuster.

Gramsci, A. (1971) *Selection from the Prison Notebooks*, New York: International Publishers.

Grenfell, P., Platt, L. and Stevenson, L. (2018) 'Examining and challenging the everyday power relations affecting sex workers' health', in S. FitzGerald and K. McGarry (eds) *Realising Justice for Sex Workers: An Agenda for Change*, London: Rowman & Littlefield, pp 103–22.

Guba, E.G. and Lincoln, Y.S. (1994) 'Competing paradigms in qualitative research', in N.K. Denzin and Y.S. Lincoln (eds), *Handbook of Qualitative Research*, Sage Publications, pp 105–17.

Hall, S. (1997) 'The work of representation', in S. Hall (ed.) *Representation: Cultural Representations and Signifying Practices*, London: Sage, in association with the Open University, pp 13–74.

Haraway, D. (1988) 'Situated knowledges: The science question in feminism and the privilege of partial perspective', *Feminist Studies*, 14(3): 575–99.

Holmquist, K. (2013) 'Sex trade: Safe or sordid?', *Irish Times*, [online], 4 May, Available from: https://www.irishtimes.com/news/crime-and-law/the-sex-trade-safe-or-sordid-1.1382024

Houses of the Oireachtas (2012) 'Joint Committee on Justice, Defence and Equality debates on the review of legislation on prostitution', 12 December, Available from: https://www.oireachtas.ie/en/debates/debate/joint_committee_on_justice_defence_and_equality/2012-12-12/2/ [Accessed 15 May 2023].

Houses of the Oireachtas (2013) 'Joint Committee on Justice, Defence and Equality report on hearings and submissions on the review of legislation on prostitution', Available from: http://www.oireachtas.ie/parliament/media/committees/justice/1.Part-1-final.pdf [Accessed 15 September 2022].

Immigrant Council of Ireland (2013) 'Prostitution law review resumes 2013 could be the year to end exploitation, abuse and sex trafficking', statement by Immigrant Council of Ireland, 11 January.

Kendall, G. (2007) 'What is critical discourse analysis? Ruth Wodak in conversation with Gavin Kendall' [38 paragraphs]. *Forum Qualitative Sozialforschung / Forum: Qualitative Social Research*, 8(2), Art. 29, http://nbn-resolving.de/urn:nbn:de:0114-fqs0702297.

Killam, L. (2013) *Research Terminology Simplified: Paradigms, Axiology, Ontology, Epistemology and Methodology*, Sudbury, ON: Self-published.

Krüsi, A., Pacey, K., Bird, L., Taylor, C., Chettiar, J., Allan, S. et al (2014) 'Criminalisation of clients: Reproducing vulnerabilities for violence and poor health among street-based sex workers in Canada – a qualitative study', *BMJ Open*, 2014;**4**:e005191. doi: 10.1136/bmjopen-2014-005191

Law, J. (2004) *After Method: Mess in Social Science Research*, New York: Routledge.

Lazar, M. and Kramarae, C. (2011) 'Gender and power in discourse', in T.A. Van Dijk (ed) *Discourse Studies: A Multidisciplinary Introduction*, London: Sage, pp 217–40.

Ledwith, M. (2016) *Community Development in Action: Putting Freire into Practice*, Bristol: Policy Press.

Lennon, K. and Whitford, M. (eds) (1994) *Knowing the Difference: Feminist Perspectives in Epistemology*, London: Routledge.

Lynch, K. (1999) 'Equality studies, the academy and the role of research in emancipatory social change', *The Economic and Social Review*, 30(1): 41–69.

Marion Young, I. (1990) *Justice and the Politics of Difference*, Princeton: Princeton University Press.

McGarry, K. and FitzGerald, S. (2017) 'The politics of injustice: Sex-working women, feminism and criminalizing sex purchase in Ireland', *Criminology & Criminal Justice*, 19(1): 62–79. DOI: 10.1177/1748895817743285.

McGarry, K. and FitzGerald, S. (2018) 'Social justice through an agenda for change', in S. FitzGerald and K. McGarry (eds) *Realising Justice for Sex Workers: An Agenda for Change*, London: Rowman & Littlefield, pp xv–xxxv.

McGarry, K. and Ryan, P. (2020) 'Sex worker lives under the law', Dublin: HIV Ireland.

Mol, A. (1999) 'Ontological politics: A word and some questions', *Sociological Review*, 47(S1): 74–89.

Naples, N.A. (2003) *Feminism and Method: Ethnography, Discourse Analysis, and Activist Research*, New York: Routledge.

Payne, M. (1997) *Reading Knowledge: An Introduction to Foucault, Barthes and Althusser*, Oxford: Wiley.

Ramazanoğlu, C. and Holland, J. (2011) *Feminist Methodology*, London: Sage.

Ransome, P. (2010) *Social Theory for Beginners*, Bristol: Policy Press.

Reynolds, J. and Roffe, J. (eds) (2004) *Understanding Derrida*, London: Bloomsbury.

Ryan, P. and Ward, E. (2018) 'Ireland: The rise of neo-abolitionism and the new politics of prostitution', in S. Jahnsen and H. Wagenaar (eds) *Assessing Prostitution Policies in Europe*, London: Routledge.

Sanders, T., McGarry, K. and Ryan, P. (eds) (2022) *Sex Work, Labour and Relations: New Directions and Reflections*, Cham: Palgrave Macmillan.

Scheper-Hughes, N. and Bourgois, P. (2004) 'Introduction: Making sense of violence', in N. Scheper-Hughes and P. Bourgois (eds) *Violence in War and Peace: An Anthology*, Malden: Blackwell Publishing, pp 1–31.

Scoular, J. and O'Neill, M. (2008) 'Legal incursions into supply/demand: Criminalising and responsibilising the buyers and sellers of sex in the UK', in V. Munro and M. Della Giusta (eds) *Demanding Sex: Critical Reflections on the Regulation of Prostitution*, London: Routledge, pp 13–34.

Stychin, C. (2001) 'Sexual citizenship in the European Union', *Citizenship Studies*, 5(3): 285–301.

Van Dijk, T.A. (1993) 'Principles of critical discourse analysis', *Discourse & Society*, 4(2): 249–83.

Visser, J., Randers-Pehrson, A., Day, S. and Ward, H. (2004) 'Policies towards the sex industry in Europe: New models of control', in S. Day and H. Ward (eds) *Sex Work, Mobility and Health in Europe*, Abingdon, Oxon: Routledge, pp 241–57.

Ward, E. and Wylie, G. (2014) 'Reflexivities of discomfort: Researching the sex trade and sex trafficking in Ireland', *European Journal of Women's Studies* 21(3): 251–63.

Whimster, S. (ed) (2003) *The Essential Max Weber*, London: Routledge.

3

Epistemology, research design and social justice

Ciara Bradley and Lynsey Kavanagh

Introduction

Within the scientific community, values such as honesty, fairness, collegiality and openness have contributed well to the shaping of science as a discipline (Institute of Medicine, 2009: 48). Responsibility in research is an important concept and a growing concern across the social sciences and for bodies and agencies that fund research (Stilgoe et al, 2013; Burget et al, 2016) and extends beyond those that are internal to the scientific community or any particular discipline. Doing good quality work is where 'our responsibilities as researchers begin, not where they end' (Bird, 2014: 171). Researchers also have a responsibility to reflect on how their work and the knowledge they are generating might be used in the broader society (Institute of Medicine, 2009: 48). As members of society, scientists have a responsibility to engage with questions about how science might address societal issues and concerns, and to bring their specialised knowledge and expertise to activities and discussions that promote the education of students and fellow citizens, thereby enhancing and facilitating informed decision-making and democracy (Bird, 2014: 170). Some social science research practice takes on this challenge.

Research is not neutral but shaped by our theory of knowledge, guided by what we believe can be known and how; as such, it is a political act. What we choose to study and how reveals the relationship between epistemology and methodology. Heidegger states that '[e]very inquiry is a seeking … Every seeking gets guided beforehand by what is sought' (Heidegger, 1962: 24). Heidegger argues that one cannot stand outside the pre-understandings of one's experience. Like everyone else, researchers are embedded in the culture and politics of our temporal and spatial experience. An enquiry is framed within the context of a belief about what can be known. Bateson agrees: all researchers hold 'highly abstract principles' (Bateson, 1972: 320) which influence their inherent beliefs about the nature of the world and the way in which it may be investigated and interpreted. These worldviews (Creswell, 2014: 6), paradigms (Lincoln et al, 2011) or comprehensive research methodologies (Neuman, 2000; Creswell, 2014) underpin researchers' assumptions about what constitutes 'knowledge (ontology), how we know it (epistemology), the values that underpin it (axiology), how we write about it (rhetoric), and the processes for studying it (methodology)' (Creswell, 2014: 23). Situated 'inside' rather than external to our philosophical orientations, as Heidegger (1996 [1953]: 56) argues, our worldviews or paradigms guide our investigations, shaping all elements of research (Crotty, 1998; Grix, 2002; Letherby, 2003; Lincoln et al., 2011), including the questions that we ask, the way we choose to ask them and our interpretations of the answers given (Letherby, 2003; Denzin and Lincoln, 2011). Differences in paradigm assumptions cannot be dismissed as mere 'philosophical' differences: they have important consequences for the practical conduct of enquiry, as well as for the interpretation of findings and policy choices (Lincoln and Guba, 1994: 112).

Inevitably, there are power differences between different ways of knowing, and research processes themselves can (re)produce power differences:

> [R]esearch is inevitably politically engaged, be it by default, by design or by simple recognition. No matter how deep the commitment to value neutrality, decisions regarding choice of subject, paradigmatic frameworks and even methodological tools inevitably involve political choices, not only in terms of the discipline, but even in terms of the wider political purposes and goals. (Baker et al, 2004: 169)

Paradigms and hence methodologies matter politically because they create different realities (Bacchi and Rönnblom, 2014). Speaking to this, Mauthner and Doucet cite Lorraine Code (1991) when they argue that researchers must 'know well' and 'know responsibly' (Mauthner and Doucet, 2002: 13). We have 'an obligation and commitment not only to research participants but also to those who read, re-interpret and take seriously the claims that we make' (Doucet and Mauthner, 2002: 3). Social justice research cannot be achieved simply by applying a method but must also start explicitly with the philosophical approach to that method. This chapter takes this as a starting point. We argue for the importance of conscious practice in any kind of research. Researchers should spend time identifying what their ontology and epistemology (worldview) are, what influences it (their training, their personal and professional biography and so on) and how it impacts their research practice.

In addition to this, research for social justice requires an ethical research practice. As Mauthner et al (2002: 6) note, 'principles guide our perceptions of how to conduct ethical research and yet, specific circumstances and contexts inform our decisions'. As a consequence, the tick-box approach to ethics can leave very little room for 'contextualised methods of reasoning'

(Edwards and Mauthner, 2002), and 'the constant neglect of detailed ethical discussions in all stages of research projects renders the enterprise open to being unethical' (Mauthner et al, 2002). Furthermore, these types of processes and committees have developed in particular (Global North) contexts which also influence how they are structured and the meanings they might have in other contexts. Israel (2018) highlights the dangers of 'ethical imperialism' in ways that are, at best, potentially inappropriate and, at worst, at risk of propagating injustice.

It is not always clear how to address these issues, as academic and professional ethics committees as well as research textbooks frequently provide standardised ethical rules such as gaining and maintaining informed consent, privacy/anonymity, avoiding harm, and safely storing data (Neuman, 2000; Silverman, 2007). Notwithstanding the importance of the principles of ethics, the prescribed nature and rigidity of approaches can, in many ways, obscure the messiness and complexity of qualitative research and divert attention away from the core issues of power and voice which are central to research for social justice. Discussions of ethics from anti-colonial (Israel, 2018) and feminist perspectives have tended to separate those that address research practice and those that concern knowledge construction processes, as framed in philosophical or epistemological terms (Doucet and Mauthner, 2002: 1). In this chapter, we see these as integrated issues, and we are both concerned that our epistemological and axiological approaches are congruent with the methodological choices throughout our research.

To explore these points in practice, this chapter reflects on two research projects in the research for social justice paradigm, with and about women. We start by interrogating the ontology and epistemology of these two projects to explore how and why these matter in research that claims to be for social justice and how ontology and epistemology influence everything that follows. We argue that how we conceptualise our research 'participant' matters: it shapes how we engage with them and how they experience the research process. We explore the importance of epistemological, ethical and methodological congruency. We hope this chapter will contribute to the discussion on what we need to consider when taking on social justice research and respond to some of the broad questions raised in Chapter 1: 'How can a social justice approach to research be operationalised?', and 'How can we design research and develop our methodologies that (a) reflect a social justice approach and (b) progress a social justice agenda?'

The research projects

The first example is a study focusing on single women's reproduction in Ireland and in the narrative construction of this experience (Bradley, 2014). Single motherhood has long been stigmatised in Ireland (Viney, 1964;

Darling, 1984; O'Hare et al, 1987; Hyde, 1996, 1997, 1998, 2000; Farren and Dempsey, 1998; Conlon 2006). Until the 1980s, many unmarried pregnant women, especially those from lower social classes and rural backgrounds, were interned in religious institutions, and children were often separated from their mothers (Bradley and Millar, 2021: 2). The last Magdalen institution closed as recently as 1996. Leane and Kiely (1997: 296) describe how single mothers have been 'castigated, punished, stigmatised, ignored, labelled and controlled' by, and within, Irish society.

Despite extensive social change, including improved social security for single mothers, growth in the numbers of single-mother families and improvements in gender equality more broadly, single women with children still experience extreme social and economic inequalities. The Survey on Income and Living Conditions 2018 shows that lone parents in Ireland have the second highest rate of income poverty, persistent poverty and severe deprivation among all EU-15 countries (The Society of St Vincent de Paul, 2019). One-parent families in Ireland experience inequality in health, education and employment and are disproportionately affected by homelessness (CSO, 2019).

Grounded in feminist standpoint epistemology, this study used the Biographic Narrative Interpretive Method (BNIM) (Wengraf, 2012) to interview 12 women who had experienced single motherhood between 1990 and 2010. The interviews were participant-structured open biographic narrative interviews. The study used BNIM to undertake an in-depth analysis of the 'lived life', the 'told story' and the evolving situated subjectivity, emphasising the situatedness by exploring the socio-historical context of the time. The analysis highlighted that single women's experience of pregnancy and motherhood in Ireland is socially located both temporally and structurally. Stigma has shifted in Ireland over the last decades of the twentieth century, yet it remains the key social mechanism that allows inequality to be created and perpetuated at a relational level through social interaction and at a macro level through social construction in media, public discourse and social policy. Social class, ethnicity and time mediate the experience but can also intersect to create a more stigmatised identity (Bradley, 2014; Bradley and Millar, 2021).

The second study explores the experience of pregnancy loss among Irish Traveller women (Kavanagh, 2018), examining the individual, interpersonal and structural factors which mediate this experience over a 30-year period. Travellers are one of the most marginalised groups in Ireland. They experience structural and systematic racism and discrimination, resulting in inequality of access, participation and outcomes in education, employment and health (McGinnity et al, 2018; EU FRA, 2020). For Traveller women, this experience is further compounded by gendered racism and intersectional discrimination, with Traveller women 'facing triple discrimination – as

Travellers, as women, and as Traveller women … Traveller women experience patriarchy in the ways that all women do … they also experience particular forms of abuse as Traveller women, [particularly] when they are brutalized by descriptions in the media' (Fay cited in Reilly, 2005: 1). Similar to other indigenous and minority ethnic women globally, Traveller women experience disproportionate rates of maternal and infant morbidity and mortality (Manning et al, 2015; Manning et al, 2016; Manning et al, 2018).

As highlighted by the All-Ireland Traveller Health Study (AITHS Team, 2010), the infant mortality rate for Irish Travellers is 3.7 times the national rate, and the post-neonatal mortality rate is 4.5 times the EU average. Similar to the overall experience of Travellers in engaging with health services in Ireland, Traveller women experience discrimination and racism (at institutional and individual levels), a lack of trust, a lack of engagement from service providers and a lack of accessible health information and advice (Reid, 2005; Reid and Taylor, 2007; AITHS Team, 2010).

Thirteeen Traveller women were interviewed using the participant-structured BNIM interview (Wengraf, 2012), and the interviews were analysed using the Voice Centred Relational Method (VCRM) (Mauthner and Doucet, 1998). The analysis highlights that the broader structural landscape of discrimination, racism, sexism, marginalisation and inequality is integral to understanding Traveller women's lived experiences, including pregnancy loss (Kavanagh, 2018).

In Irish society, both Travellers and single women have been vilified and their social exclusion normalised and perpetuated at macro and micro levels of society, historically and currently, in a variety of ways. This is further compounded by a historical legacy of voyeurism and exploitation, often under the guise of social scientific 'research' with minority and marginalised groups. Structural social inequalities are significant, and a legacy exists within research in academia (whether intentionally or unintentionally) which has frequently created, perpetuated and enforced sexism, racism and so on. Thus, in research for social justice, the responsibility of the researcher to undertake ethical relational research with these groups cannot be understated, particularly in the context of biographical research that delves into the most intimate and personal aspects of people's lives, making them public for others to also interpret and theorise. At all stages of a research journey involving groups that have this social experience, researchers must start with the question: What do we know, and how do we know it? Whose voices have been heard? Where are the silences? And crucially, how do our ways of finding out contribute to particular ways of knowing?

The following sections discuss how we operationalised a social justice approach to our research by exploring three key areas of the research process: the importance and impact of epistemology on the whole research process; how the ways in which participants are conceptualised connects within epistemology and methodology and how methodological congruency is important in social justice research and how it plays out in our engagements with participants; and the value of reflexivity in data analysis.

Epistemology: feminist standpoint

Both research projects used 'feminist standpoint' as an epistemological starting point to challenge the politics of knowledge production and representation and move to a 'new politics of transparency and accountability' (Dei, 2005: 5) in their research practice. Standpoint theory draws our attention to how knowledge is constructed differently in different social locations by different social groups. 'Standpoint' was a response to the 'brutal history of women's silencing" (Smith, 1974, 1981) by authoritative male discourse. Standpoint seeks to privilege the 'everyday', the unseen, and to 'give voice' to research participants, to bring experiences to the fore, to provide an 'authentic gaze' to research participants' lives (Atkinson and Silverman, 1997: 305). Challenging a positivist scientific neutrality, and acknowledging that knowledge is always situated, standpoint also takes the perspective that oppression can be a source of critical insight, recognising the knowledge of oppressed groups, especially women (Harding, 2004). As Harding eloquently summarises it, 'androcentric, economically advantaged, racist, Eurocentric and heterosexist conceptual frameworks ensure systematic ignorance and error not only about the lives of the oppressed, but also about the lives of their oppressors and thus about how nature and social relations in general worked' (Harding, 2004: 5). Standpoint theory therefore seeks to see 'beneath' dominant discourses and ideologies that have shaped the actualities of women's lives and the conceptual practices of institutions.

Critiques of traditional standpoint include how it gives epistemic privilege to gender oppression over other kinds of oppressions (Bar On, 1993), which can present a 'racially neutral' analysis, ignoring critical differences among women and perpetuating inequality (Hill-Collins, 1997: 375). The approach can also be criticised on the grounds that it presents the oppressed as having 'unique abilities ... to produce knowledge' (Harding, 1991: 57) and for assuming that the 'standpoint' of the oppressed has not been mediated by dominant ideologies (Hawkesworth, 1989, 1999; Flax, 1990; Holmwood, 1995).

To address some of these potential weaknesses, alongside Hill-Collins, Harding (2004: 6) argues for a 'standpoint' perspective where researchers must 'study up': they must be part of critical theory, revealing the ideological strategies used to design and justify intersectional systems of oppression. This 'standpoint' seeks to see 'beneath' dominant discourses and ideologies that have shaped the actualities of women's lives and the conceptual practices of institutions where oppression was 'designed, maintained and made to seem natural and desirable to everyone' (Harding, 2004: 6).

A challenge, then, for researchers using standpoint is how to respect, use and amplify marginalised voices while acknowledging the multiplicity of voice and the collective experience, as well as recognising the impact of the social structure. Hill-Collins (1997) emphasises that the collective experience, particularly that of social structure, such as race, gender and social class, is a primary concern. Hill-Collins (1997) recognises the particularity of individual/everyday experiences (Smith, 1987), but is more fundamentally concerned with the ways social conditions construct such experiences on a collective group level (1997: 375). She argues that intersectionality is crucial to understanding the actual mechanisms of institutional power and how this shapes collective experiences and ways of knowing.

BNIM and VCRM provide a structure within their methodological toolkit to analyse both voice and structure. The VCR method was initially developed by Lyn Brown, Carol Gilligan and colleagues at the Harvard Project on Women's Psychology and Girls' Development as a direct response to the 'uneasiness and growing dissatisfaction with the nature of the coding schemes typically being used at that time to analyse qualitative data' (Gilligan et al, 2003: 157). However, it does not afford an uncritical amplification of voice. Rather, VCRM focuses on the multiplicity of voices embedded in a person's expressed experience (Gilligan et al, 2003; Sorsoli and Tolman, 2008), and as such, the method asks three basic questions: (1) who is speaking and to whom; (2) who is telling what stories about relationships; and (3) in what societal and cultural frameworks (Brown and Gilligan, 1992: 21)? In Lynsey's study, this meant that the analysis started with the Traveller women's narrative and voice; however, following this voice facilitated a deeper analysis of the relationships and the social structure.

The BNIM method of analysis also pays attention to agency and structure. First, the objective biographic data extracted from the narrative interview are analysed on their own terms. Secondly, the way in which the story is told by the teller is analysed. Finally, an analysis of the interview, as a whole and incorporating the first two analyses, is then undertaken. A 'four foci thinking device' based on each of these constituent parts is then devised for analysis of the whole case. This involves constructing a model of phases of the lived life; the told story; the successive subjectivities of the participant over the period concerned; and of the unrolling of the interview itself. BNIM interpretation draws these together to create the final reconstruction of the case contextualised in the social history of the time. The strength of these BNIM interpretation procedures is that it examines both the lived life and the told story from the narrative and contextualises this in a social history perspective facilitating attention to the actor in the narrative, the narrator and the social structure. In Ciara's study, this facilitated analysis of shifting stigma that was temporally and socially located.

Conceptualising research participants: countering labels of 'deviance' and 'vulnerability'

The women we worked with were in diverse ways depicted as both deviant and vulnerable in policy, public discourse and academic literature. In the same breath, both Traveller women and single mothers are vilified and pitied. The concept of 'vulnerability' has become increasingly embedded in and influential across social research, socio-political discourses and policy responses. The uncritical use of this concept has been criticised, highlighting its multiple meanings and practice and research implications (Taylor, 2017; McDonagh, 2019; Meehan, 2019). Taylor (2017) highlights how this discourse exerts a misleading perception that 'vulnerable people' are not rational agents who possess rights, agency and autonomy and is often unproblematically applied to groups without their consent (Taylor, 2017) rather than problematising the social organisation and structure than makes particular social groups vulnerable and affords other groups power. We strove to find ways to stand outside of these social categories and alongside our research participants and were committed to work with them as partners in the process through research. To this end, we carefully considered how potential methods view research participants, how a method might frame the engagement before and during the interview.

This led us to biographic narrative research approached from a feminist participatory perspective. BNIM affords agency and actively tries to create the conditions for full autonomous participation while acknowledging and accounting for the historical, social and political contexts and patterns that have historically oppressed certain groups. Biographical research starts with the individual story for this very reason – the experiences of oppression that silence marginalised groups are otherwise perpetuated (McDonagh, 2000: 244; Clandinin and Rosiek, 2007: 51). Thus, it offers potential for critical transformational research.

Fraser's social justice is concerned with parity of participation, meaning 'social arrangements that permit all to participate as peers in social life' (Fraser in Lovell, 1997: 20). To overcome injustice from Fraser's perspective means overcoming institutionalised obstacles which prevent some people from participating on a par with others, 'as full partners in social interaction' (Fraser in Lovell, 1997: 20). This is important in biographical narrative research: if we are inviting participants to share their stories, we need to create the conditions for these stories to be told and listened to.

The BNIM method invites the participants to 'share their story, all those events and experiences that were important for you personally' and encourages participants to 'start wherever you like and finish wherever/whenever you like' (Wengraf, 2012). Conceiving participants as autonomous actors with agency, the BNIM interview creates the conditions for informed participation which does not end with the start of the interview but is ongoing throughout the interview. In this way, the BNIM interview offers the opportunity to create and hold space for voice of the research participant and to restrain that of the researcher during data collection.

In practice, we strove to create the conditions for 'egalitarian' interviewer–interviewee relationships through our engagement with the research participants. There are several important procedures that were put in place in preparation for, and during, the engagement with research participants to ensure ethical engagement at all stages of the research. Every care was taken to ensure that the participants were able to give informed consent to participate in the research. When recruiting participants, we emphasised that the research participants were invited to participate in the research voluntarily, without coercion. The participants were first contacted by a community-based project with which they were already engaged. When they expressed initial interest, they were provided with a letter of invitation and a consent form. In Lynsey's project, all resources pertaining to the study were developed in partnership with Traveller women to ensure their appropriateness and accessibility for potential participants. In Ciara's project, the letter of invitation provided information about the purposes of the research and the potential uses of the data. The consent form highlighted the purpose of the study; the procedures for data collection, what to expect and so on; the participants' right to withdraw from the study at any time; the procedures undertaken for the protection of participants' confidentiality; and the request for permission to audio-record the interview (Creswell, 1998: 116). They were invited to agree that the community project could share their details with the researchers or to contact the researcher directly themselves.

When we met the participants, we worked to establish a good rapport (Fontana and Frey, 2005) and sought to treat them with respect while creating an environment for an empowering experience. Immediately before each interview, we briefed each woman again about the study including the unconventional approach to the interview. We also reviewed the research information sheet and consent form together to ensure that issues of literacy would not act as a barrier to women's participation. In all cases, consent forms were signed, and verbal consent was recorded at the beginning of each interview. We also discussed their right to stop the interview at any stage or indeed to withdraw from the research at any time without reason. We made it clear that we were grateful for their time and participation.

These actions aimed to address the inherent issue of power imbalance that comes with any research project (McCormack, 2000: 304). Power differentials in research do not simply dissipate just because a feminist approach is used, nor does it ensure anti-racist content or ideology, as power between the researcher and the researched is 'balanced in favour of the researcher, for it is she who eventually walks away' (Mauthner and Doucet, 2006: 30; also discussed in Reinharz, 1992; McDonagh, 2000).

In our experience, the BNIM interviews worked well in both studies. Participants took control of the narrative. Each participant was enabled through the interview design to provide their narrative in their own way, and as a result the narratives were diverse in structure and content. This was important for the research topics, which can be over-researched by outsider researchers. Following the interviews, many participants expressed that they felt listened to and that their story mattered.

In Ciara's study, after the interview was completed and transcribed, the interviews were sent via email and letter to all participants that stated that they wished to receive them for their final consent to use the material. In practice, this had important implications for the research, as three participants withdrew their interviews. This was an important part of the ethics of the project. Nine participants gave their informed consent to continue to participate.

Reflexivity in analysis

A social justice lens demands epistemological accountability in knowledge construction and production and is reflected in the choices through each step of the research design (Doucet and Mauthner, 2002). The analysis of research, according to Mauthner and Doucet (1998, 2002), is where the power and privilege of the researcher is explicitly apparent and where the ethics of the research practice are particularly acute due to the 'invisible nature of the interpretive process''' (Mauthner and Doucet, 2002: 130). They highlight how the image of a neutral researcher simply carrying out a mechanical procedure of data reduction under an elusive veil of objectivity of what essentially remains a 'subjective, interpretative process''' is problematic (Mauthner and Doucet, 1998: 122). The situated, subjective and 'embodied' researcher carrying out the analysis remains invisible and detached from all interpersonal, social and institutional contexts (Mauthner and Doucet, 2003: 414–15). Through the mechanisms provided by BNIM and VCRM, we paid special attention to the analysis of research.

Structured reflexivity for the researcher throughout the process of data analysis is paramount to ensure epistemic accountability. There are a variety of different ways in which this can be put into practice. In this section, we will share two examples. Throughout her research, Lynsey worked in a Traveller human rights organisation. This created the conditions for her to discuss issues as they arose, with Travellers and those working with and along Travellers, specifically in relation to pregnancy, motherhood and loss. In this space, Lynsey actively worked to challenge the concept of the 'settled gaze' (McDonagh, 2000), which historically has led to the exoticisation, objectification and exploitation of Travellers, specifically Traveller women in academic research (Joyce and Farmer, 1985; McDonagh, 2000, 2019). This approach helped support deep analysis at each stage of the research and in particular demanded constant reflection on her epistemology through the analysis. This was particularly important to ensure that assumptions were not left unchallenged, particularly by Traveller women. Again, as McDonagh (2000) reminds us, simply using a feminist approach to research does not guarantee anti-racist content or ideology and garnering feedback from a multiplicity of viewpoints was therefore incredibly valuable to the overall research methodology. The daily conversations meant immersion.

To support her reflexivity during the analysis of the cases, Ciara used the BNIM groups. These are a powerful tool as they challenge the researcher to confront their own biases towards the case and to explore other interpretations. The process in each group begins with the group being introduced piece by piece to the segments of information from the lived life and told story, respectively. Group members are then asked to hypothesise inductively from the bare bones facts of a 'lived life' and the skeleton of the way the story was told – the 'told story'. Through hypothesising inductively bit by bit, the patterns of 'lived-ness' of the lives and the 'told-ness' of the stories emerged. BNIM interpretive groups are about '[c]reating a space in which the individual researcher, and others, dialogically develop their hypothesising, in which each has a different life experience, and defends themselves differently from reality, enables an interpretive group to be less defended and more insightful than any one of its members' (Froggett and Wengraf, 2004: 117).

There are many helpful guides in the literature about the composition of interpretive groups. The first recommendation is that these interpretive groups work better with five to six participants. Froggett and Wengraf (2004: 98) note that 'the involvement of other people of varied class and ethnicity introduces different perspectives and lines of enquiry and greatly aids the [researcher's] understanding of [her] own internal dynamics and habits of reflection'. The second recommendation is that groups should be diverse. Froggett and Wengraf (2004: 118) note that culturally homogenous interpretive groups can be limited in imagination and also in analysis. Volante (2005: 104) emphasises the importance of having someone 'like' the interviewee as a member of the analysis group in addition to some very different people.

The interpretive group sessions require careful preparation. Posters detailing procedures and the list of questions to be posed of each piece of data were affixed to the wall, so that they could be clearly seen by the whole group.

I found that this helped keep the group's focus on issues relevant to the analysis. I followed the procedure of other BNIM researchers in providing refreshments during the sessions (Jones, 2001; Meares, 2007; Corbally, 2009; Wengraf, 2012). The food served a practical purpose in ensuring energy levels were maintained over the three hours and also functioned as a 'thank you' to group members for generously giving up their time to help me with my work. Some of the group members had not met prior to the analysis groups. Consequently, one of my first priorities as a facilitator was to generate a positive, supportive environment in which the participants would feel comfortable sharing ideas.

The interpretive analysis groups were always facilitated dialogically, the dialogue taking place between the participant through their story, with the researcher as interviewer and members of the interpretive analysis groups. The goal of the researcher as facilitator of the interpretive analysis group workshops was to remain open and respectful and avoid judgement or negativity relating to the story. In introducing the session, I stressed that "the important thing is to have as many different ideas as possible'". As Jones (2001) notes, each group member came to the analysis sessions with their own social and cultural biography, 'their own interests and experiences with which to compare and contrast the unfolding dramas and events and the subsequent choices made by the interviewee' (Jones, 2001: 116). They brought more subtle use of their knowledge and experience of popular culture from film, television, novels, art and theatre as well as their knowledge and experience of how single mothers are portrayed within those media. Additionally, the groups drew on the cultural and societal understandings of the world they shared with each other and with the research participant or the 'habitus – our second nature, the mass of conventions, beliefs and attitudes which each member of a society shares with every other member' (Scheff, 1997: 219). The analysis also encouraged a multiplicity of viewpoints evolving from a wide variety of ages, cohort membership and cultural and historical backgrounds among the analysis group members. Harvey et al (2000: 308) argue that as researchers 'we must learn to hear what they can tell us even when this is not what we wish to hear or when their stories do not resemble culturally available plots or match current theories'. The interpretive groups were instrumental in facilitating this process.

Although the process of hosting interpretive panels was labour and resource intensive, it was useful in terms of stimulating thought and generating discussion about the method and the subject of enquiry. It was a powerful means of broadening my interpretation of the data. I did not anticipate the interest, enthusiasm and eagerness of the participants in the research participant's life and in what happens at the end of the story. Corbally (2009) and Jones (2001) also noted this in their respective BNIM research studies.

Mauthner and Doucet also suggest the use of a 'research group' drawing on the insights of others (Mauthner and Doucet, 1998, 2003) in the VCRM method used by Lynsey in this chapter. These groups are somewhat analogous to 'interpretive communities' (Brown et al, 1991: 33), 'conceptual parties', 'critical reference groups' (Miles and Huberman, 1994; Wadsworth, 2001) or BNIM interpretive analysis groups which seek to support the analysis of the cases. Group members read interview transcripts using the four readings prescribed in the VCRM method. The group, ideally, should be as diverse as possible to enhance analysis and support the researcher's understanding of her 'own internal dynamics and habits of reflection' (Froggett and Wengraf, 2004: 98). As Mauthner and Doucet (2003: 418) note, this group provides the necessary space, context and method for operationalising a degree of reflexivity during the analytic stages of research.

According to Moore and Muller (1999, 203) lack of reflexivity means that researchers 'write themselves into their world without stabilising their voice and showing their conditions of production'. They argue that when researchers do not reveal how they produce their knowledge which, in effect, is a 'first person narrative of description … the "voice" of voice discourse erases the text that writes the world of which it speaks'. There are a variety of ways in which reflexivity can be supported using 'critical reference groups'. While Lynsey's study did not have a formal mechanism for feedback, everyday conversations meant that it drew on insights provided by a number of colleagues: both Travellers and non-Travellers who reflect a range of experiences, specifically in relation to pregnancy, motherhood and loss. Using a feminist approach to research does not always guarantee anti-racist content or ideology and therefore garnering feedback from a multiplicity of viewpoints in this regard was incredibly valuable. Researchers can adapt these ideas to find appropriate mechanisms for their context that will challenge their positionality and practice in their research.

Conclusion

This chapter makes the case that research for social justice and socially just research cannot be achieved by simply applying a method but must be built from the ground up, starting with the ontology and epistemology that informs the research. Using examples from two different projects, we illuminate the connections in research practice between ontology, epistemology and methodology and how this impacts social research overall. We argue that there is an imperative for researchers to identify and make explicit in their research the ontology and epistemology that guides their work and how it impacts their research practice.

Within any epistemological frame, how participants are conceptualised becomes reflected in the methodological approach and has a tangible implication for how knowledge is constructed. The women in the examples discussed in this chapter were, in diverse ways, depicted as both deviant and vulnerable in policy, public discourse and academic literature. In the same breath, both Traveller women and single mothers are vilified and pitied. Uncritical use of either conception has real implications for the research outcomes and potentially taints the whole research process. Social justice researchers must be reflexive and conscious in how they conceive of their participants and explicit in how they communicate this.

Reflexivity is as central to analysis and interpretation in research for social justice, as it is for engagement with participants, yet reflexivity in this process is often neglected. We share two examples of how reflexivity might be operationalised in two different contexts and conclude by encouraging researchers to be creative in their development of other approaches that will challenge their positionality and practice in their research context. The social justice lens challenges us as researchers to pay attention to epistemology and congruency across our methodology.

References

All Ireland Traveller Health Study (AITHS Team) (2010) 'All Ireland Traveller Health Study: Our Geels', Dublin: School of Public Health, Physiotherapy and Population Science, University College Dublin.

Atkinson, P. and Silverman, D. (1997) 'Kundera's immortality: the interview of society and the invention of the self', *Qualitative Inquiry*, 3(3): 302–25.

Bacchi, C. and Rönnblom, M. (2014) 'Feminist discursive institutionalism: A poststructural alternative', *Nora – Nordic Journal of Feminist and Gender Research*, 22(3): 170–86.

Baker, J., Lynch, K., Cantillon, S. and Walsh, J. (2004) *Equality: From Theory to Action*, New York: Palgrave Macmillan.

Bar On (1993) 'Marginality and epistemic privilege', in L. Alcoff and E. Potter (eds) *Feminist Epistemologies*, London: Routledge, pp 83–101.

Bateson, G. (1972) *Steps to an Ecology of the Mind*, New York: Ballantine.

Bird, S.J. (2014) 'Socially responsible science is more than "good science"', *Journal of Microbiology and Biology Education*, 15(2): 169–72.

Bradley, C. (2014) 'Reproducing stigma: Narratives of single women's pregnancy and motherhood in Ireland 1990–2010', PhD Thesis. NUI Galway, Available from: http://hdl.handle.net/10379/4773

Bradley, C. and Millar, M. (2021) 'Persistent stigma despite social change: Experiences of stigma among single women who were pregnant or mothers in the Republic of Ireland 1996–2010', *Families, Relationships and Societies*, 10(3): 413–29.

Brown, L., Debold, E., Tappan, M. and Gilligan, C. (1991) 'Reading narratives of conflict and choice for self and moral voices: A relational method', in M. Kurtines and J. Gewirtz (eds) *Handbook of Moral Behavior and Development: Volume 2 – Research*. Hillsdale, NJ: Lawrence Erlbaum, pp 25–62.

Brown, L. and Gilligan, C. (1992) *Meeting at the Crossroads: Women's Psychology and Girls' Development*, Cambridge, MA: Harvard University Press.

Burget, M., Bardone, E. and Pedaste, M. (2016) 'Definitions and conceptual dimensions of responsible research and innovation: A literature review', *Science and Engineering Ethics*, 23: 1–9, DOI 10.1007/s11948-016-9782-1

Central Statistics Office (2019) 'Survey on Income and Living Conditions (SILC) 2018', Available from: https://www.cso.ie/en/methods/socialcon ditions/silc/

Central Statistics Office (2019) 'Survey on Income and Living Conditions (SILC) 2018', Available from: https://www.cso.ie/en/releasesandpublicati ons/ep/p-silc/surveyonincomeandlivingconditionssilc2018/

Central Statistics Office (2022) 'Survey on Income and Living Conditions (SILC) 2022', Available from: https://www.cso.ie/en/methods/socialcon ditions/silc/

Clandinin, D.J. and Rosiek, J. (2007) 'Mapping a landscape of narrative inquiry: Borderland spaces and tensions', in D.J. Clandinin (ed) *Handbook of Narrative Inquiry: Mapping a Methodology*, Thousand Oaks, CA: Sage Publications, pp 35–75.

Code, L. (1991) *What Can She Know? Feminist Theory and the Construction of Knowledge*, Ithaca, NY: Cornell University Press.

Conlon, C. (2006) 'Concealed pregnancy: A case-study approach from an Irish setting', Dublin: The Stationery Office.

Corbally, M. (2009) 'Making sense of the unbelievable: A biographical narrative study of men's stories of female abuse', Unpublished PhD thesis, University of Salford, UK.

Creswell, J. (1998) *Qualitative Inquiry and Research Design: Choosing among Five Traditions*, Thousand Oaks, CA: Sage.

Creswell, J. (2014) *Research Design: Qualitative, Quantitative, and Mixed Methods Approaches*, Vol. 4, Thousand Oaks, CA: SAGE Publications.

Crotty, M. (1998) *The Foundations of Social Research: Meaning and Perspective in the Research Process*, London: Sage.

Darling, V. (1984) 'And baby makes two', Dublin: Federation of Services for Unmarried Parents and Their Children.

Dei, G.J.S. and Johal, G.S. (eds) (2005) *Critical Issues in Anti-Racist Research Methodologies*, New York: Peter Lang.

Denzin, N. and Lincoln, Y. (2011) 'Introduction: The discipline and practice of qualitative research', in N. Denzin and Y. Lincoln (eds) *Handbook of Qualitative Research*, Vol. 4, Thousand Oaks, CA: SAGE Publications, pp 1–20.

Doucet, A. and Mauthner, M. (2002) 'Knowing responsibly: Ethics, feminist epistemologies and methodologies', in M. Mauthner, M. Birch, J. Jessop and T. Miller (eds) *Ethics in Qualitative Research*, London: Sage, pp 123–45.

Edwards, R. and Mauthner, M. (2002) 'Ethics and feminist research: Theory and practice', in M. Mauthner, M. Birch, J. Jessop and T. Miller (eds) *Ethics in Qualitative Research*, SAGE Publications, pp 14–31.

European Fundamental Rights Agency (EU FRA) (2020) 'Travellers in Ireland: Key results from the Roma and Travellers Survey 2019', Vienna: EU FRA.

Farren, G. and Dempsey, A. (1998) 'From condemnation to celebration: The story of Cherish 1972–1997', Dublin: Cherish.

Flax, J. (1990) *Thinking Fragments*, Berkeley: University of California Press.

Fontana, A. and Frey, J. (2005) 'The interview: From neutral stance to political involvement', in N. Denzin and Y. Lincoln (eds) *The Sage Handbook of Qualitative Research* (3rd edn), Thousand Oaks, CA: Sage, pp 695–728.

Froggett, L. and Wengraf, T. (2004) 'Interpreting interviews in the light of research team dynamics', *Critical Psychology*, 10: 94–122.

Gilligan, C., Spencer, R., Weinberg, M. and Bertsch, T. (2003) 'On the listening guide: A voice-centred relational method', in P. Camic, J. Rhodes and L. Yardley (eds) *Qualitative Research in Psychology: Expanding Perspectives in Methodology and Design*. Washington DC: American Psychological Association, pp 157–72.

Grix, J. (2002) 'Introducing students to the generic terminology of social research', *Politics*, 22(3): 75–186.

Harding, S. (1991) *Whose Science? Whose Knowledge? Thinking from Women's Lives*, Ithaca, NY: Cornell University Press.

Harding, S. (ed) (2004) *The Feminist Standpoint Theory Reader: Intellectual and Political Controversies*, London: Routledge.

Harvey, M., Mishler, E.G., Koenen, K. and Harney, P. (2000) 'In the aftermath of sexual abuse: Making and remaking meaning in narratives of trauma and recovery', *Narrative Inquiry*, 10(2): 291–311.

Hawkesworth, M. (1989) 'Knowers, knowing, known: Feminist theory and claims of truth', *Signs: Journal of Women in Culture and Society*, 14(3): 533–57.

Hawkesworth, M. (1999) 'Analyzing backlash: Feminist standpoint theory as analytical tool', *Women's Studies International Forum*, 22(2): 135–55.

Heidegger, M. (1962) *Being and Time*, Oxford: Blackwell.

Heidegger, M. (1996 [1953]) *Being and Time: A translation of Sein und Zeit*, New York: SUNY Press.

Hill-Collins, P. (1997) 'Comment on Hekman's "truth and method: Feminist standpoint theory revisited"; Where's the power?', *Signs*, 22(2): 375–81.

Holmwood, J. (1995) 'Feminism and epistemology: What kind of successor science?', *Sociology*, 29(3): 411–28.

Hyde, A. (1996) 'Unmarried pregnant women's accounts of their contraceptive practices: A qualitative analysis', *Irish Journal of Sociology*, 6: 179–211.

Hyde, A. (1997) 'Gender differences in the responses of parents to their daughter's non-marital pregnancy', in A. Byrne and M. Leonard (eds) *Women and Irish Society: A Sociological Reader*, Belfast: Beyond the Pale, pp 282–95.

Hyde, A. (1998) 'From "mutual pretence awareness" to "open awareness": Single pregnant women's public encounters in an Irish context', *Qualitative Health Research*, 8: 634–43.

Hyde, A. (2000) 'Age and partnership as public symbols: Stigma and non-marital motherhood in an Irish context', *The European Journal of Women's Studies*, 7: 71–89.

Institute of Medicine (2009) *On Being a Scientist: A Guide to Responsible Conduct in Research* (3rd edn), Washington, DC: National Academies Press, Available from: https://doi.org/10.17226/12192

Israel, M. (2018) 'Ethical imperialism? Exporting research ethics to the Global South', in R. Iphofen and M. Tolich (eds) *The SAGE Handbook of Qualitative Research Ethics*, Thousand Oaks: SAGE Publications.

Jones, K. (2001) 'Narratives of identity and the informal care role', Unpublished PhD thesis, De Montfort University, Leicester, UK.

Joyce, N. and Farmar, A. (1985) *Traveller: An Autobiography*, Dublin: Gill Macmillan.

Kavanagh, L. (2018) '"Standing alongside" and in solidarity with Traveller women: Minority ethnic women's narratives of racialized obstetric violence', PhD thesis, National University of Ireland, Maynooth, Available from: https://mural.maynoothuniversity.ie/11209/

Leane, M. and Kiely, E. (1997) 'Single motherhood – reality versus rhetoric', in A, Byrne and M. Leonard (eds) *Women and Irish Society: A Sociological Reader*, Belfast: Beyond the Pale Publications, pp 296–311.

Letherby, G. (2003) *Feminist Research in Theory and Practice*, Buckingham: Open University Press.

Lincoln, Y. and Guba, E. (1994) 'Competing paradigms in qualitative research', in N. Denzin and Y. Lincoln (eds) *Handbook of Qualitative Research*, Thousand Oaks, CA: SAGE Publications, pp 105–17.

Lincoln, Y., Lynham, S. and Guba, E. (2011) 'Paradigmatic controversies: Contradictions and emerging confluences revisited', in N. Denzin and Y. Lincoln (eds) *The SAGE Handbook of Qualitative Research*, vol 4, Thousand Oaks, CA: SAGE Publications, pp 97–128.

Lovell, A. (1997) 'Death at the beginning of life', in D. Fields, J. Hockey and N. Small (eds) *Death, Gender and Ethnicity*, London: Routledge, pp 29–52.

Manning, E., Corcoran, P., Meaney, S. and Greene, R. (2015) 'Severe maternal morbidity in Ireland annual report 2012 and 2013', Cork: National Perinatal Epidemiology Centre.

Manning, E., Corcoran, P., O'Farrell, I., de Foubert, P., Drummond, L., McKernan, J. et al (2016) 'Severe maternal morbidity in Ireland annual report 2014', Cork: National Perinatal Epidemiology Centre.

Manning, E., Leitao, S., Corcoran, P., McKernan, J., de Foubert, P. and Greene, R. (2018) 'Severe maternal morbidity in Ireland annual report 2016', Cork: National Perinatal Epidemiology Centre.

Mauthner, M. and Doucet, A. (1998) 'Reflections on a voice-centred relational method of data analysis: Analysing maternal and domestic voices', in R. Ribbens (ed) Feminist Dilemmas in Qualitative Research: Private Lives and Public Texts, London: SAGE Publications, pp 119–44.

Mauthner, M. and Doucet, A. (2002) 'Knowing responsibly: Linking ethics, research practice and epistemology', in M. Mauthner, M. Birch, J. Jessop and T. Miller (eds) Ethics in Qualitative Research, London: SAGE Publications, pp 123–46.

Mauthner, M. and Doucet, A. (2003) 'Reflexive accounts and accounts of reflexivity in qualitative data analysis', Sociology, 37(3): 413–31.

Mauthner, M., Birch, M., Jessop, J. and Miller, T. (2005) Ethics in Qualitative Research, London: SAGE Publications.

Mauthner, M. and Doucet, A. (2006) 'Feminist methodologies and epistemology', in C. Bryant (ed) Handbook of 21st Century Sociology, Thousand Oaks, CA: SAGE Publications, pp 36–45.

McDonagh, R. (2000) 'Talking back', in A. Byrne and R. Lentin (eds) (Re)searching Women: Feminist Research Methodologies in the Social Sciences in Ireland, Dublin: Institute of Public Administration, pp 237–47.

McDonagh, R. (2019) 'From shame to pride: The politics of disabled Traveller identity', Unpublished PhD thesis, Northumbria University, Available from: https://nrl.northumbria.ac.uk/id/eprint/42036/1/mcdon agh.rosaleen_phd.pdf

McGinnity, F., Grotti, R., Russell, H. and Fahey, É. (ESRI and IHREC) (2018) 'ESRI research series: Attitudes to diversity in Ireland', Dublin: Economic and Social Research Institute.

McCormack, C. (2000) 'From interview transcript to interpretive story: Part 2 – developing and interpretive story', Field Methods, 12: 298–315.

Meares, C. (2007) 'From the Rainbow Nation to the Land of the Long White Cloud: Migration, gender and biography, PhD Thesis, Massey University, Albany.

Meehan, G. (2019) 'Flourishing at the margins: An exploration of deaf and hard-of-hearing women's stories of their intimate lives in Ireland', PhD thesis, National University of Ireland Maynooth, Available from: http://mural.maynoothuniversity.ie/11186/

Miles, M. and Hubberman, A. (1994) Qualitative Data Analysis, Vol. 2, Thousand Oaks, CA: SAGE Publications.

Moore, R. and Muller, J. (1999) 'The discourse of "voice" and the problem of knowledge and identity in the sociology of education', *British Journal of Sociology of Education*, 20: 189–206.

Neuman, L. (2000) *Social Research Methods: Qualitative and Quantitative Approaches*, vol 4, Boston: Allyn and Bacon.

O'Hare, A., Dromey, M., O'Connor, A., Clarke, M. and Kirwan, G. (1987) 'Mothers alone? A study of women who gave birth outside marriage', Dublin: Federation of Services for Unmarried Parents and Their Children.

Reid, B. (2005) 'Re-visioning the provision of maternity care for Traveller women', *Evidence-Based Midwifery*, 3(1): 21–6.

Reid, B. and Taylor, J. (2007) 'A feminist exploration of Traveller women's experiences of maternity care in the Republic of Ireland', *Midwifery*, 23(3): 248–59.

Reilly, N. (2005) 'The struggle for cultural recognition and women's human rights: Lessons from the experience of Irish Traveller women', *Human Rights*, 2(12): 1–3.

Reinharz, S. (1992) *Feminist Methods in Social Research*, New York: Oxford University Press.

Scheff, T. J. (1997) 'Shame in social theory', in M.R. Lansky and A.P. Morrison (eds) *The Widening Scope of Shame*, Analytic Press, pp 205–30.

Silverman, D. (2007) *Interpreting Qualitative Data, Vol. 3*, London: SAGE Publications.

Smith, D. (1974) 'Women's perspective as a radical critique of sociology', *Sociological Inquiry*, 44(1): 7–13.

Smith, D. (1981) *The Experienced World as Problematic: A Feminist Method*, Saskatchewan: University of Saskatchewan.

Smith, D. (1987) *The Everyday World as Problematic: A Feminist Sociology*, Oxford: Alden Press.

Smith, D. (1997) 'Comment on Hekman's truth and method: Feminist standpoint theory revisited', *Signs: Journal of Women in Culture and Society*, 22(2): 392–398.

Sorsoli, L. and Tolman, D.L. (2008) 'Hearing voices: Listening for multiplicity and movement in interview data', in S. N. Hesse-Biber and P. Leavy (eds) (2010) *Handbook of Emergent Methods*, New York: The Guildford Press, pp 495–515.

Stilgoe, J., Owen, R. and Macnaghten, P. (2013) 'Developing a framework for responsible innovation', *Research Policy*, 42: 1568–80.

Taylor, S. (2017) 'The challenges of disablist hate crime', in A. Haynes, J. Schweppe and S. Taylor (eds) *Critical Perspectives on Hate Crime: Contributions from the Island of Ireland*, London: Palgrave Macmillan, chapter 11.

Viney, M. (1964) *No Birthright: A Study of the Irish Unmarried Mother and Her Child*, Dublin: Irish Times.

Volante, M. (2005) 'Biographical landscapes: nurses' and health visitors' narratives of learning and professional practice', Unpublished PhD, University of East London, London.

Wadsworth, Y. (2001) 'What is feminist research?', Bridging the Gap: Feminisms and Participatory Action Research Conference Papers 22–24 June 2001 at Boston College, Available from: https://www.scribd.com/document/51900280/What-is-Feminist-Research [Accessed 13 March 2013].

Wengraf, T. (2012) 'BNIM Short Guide Bound with the BNIM Detailed Manual: Interviewing for life histories, lived periods and situations, and ongoing personal experiencing using the Biographic-Narrative Interpretive Method (BNIM)', London: Wengraf.

4

Using a social justice lens in research engagements for community work and youth work practice

Sinead McMahon, Ciara Bradley and Hilary Tierney

Introduction

Research is where communities, social groups and the issues they face are identified, defined and analysed and is thus of critical value in community work and youth work. In the context of these practices, '[r]esearch-based, theoretically developed and practice informed texts are necessary to the process of creating a discursive field in which the meanings, values and potential of youth work [and community work] as professional activity might be effectively communicated' (Spence, 2007: 4). It is well established in this book and elsewhere that research is not a value-free engagement. Research is a site of knowledge production, and as such it is a form of political action or intervention in the world which has implications for how communities, young people and social issues are problematised and for the solutions policymakers and practitioners seek to apply (Bacchi, 2009).

In this chapter, we discuss some of the ways in which community work and youth work practitioners[1] or others committed to a social justice agenda might engage with research in their work. We are inviting community work and youth work practitioners to bring a social justice lens to all of their engagements with research work as they do in the other aspects of their work. We write this chapter from our experiences as community work and youth work practitioners, researchers and educators, and based on our experiences of working with youth work and community work organisations engaging with research as part of their work for social justice. We present this as a practical chapter for practitioners concerned with social justice and equality, where the actual conduct of research is not their main focus but who still engage with research in a multitude of ways in their everyday practice.

Community and youth work as social justice-oriented practice

Community work is a developmental activity composed of both a task and a process, involving an analysis of social and economic situations and collective action (Crickley and McArdle, 2009) to achieve a more socially just society in which human rights are realised and inequality is addressed. It is a process of working in, with and alongside communities, guided by the principles of equality, participation and community empowerment, with a collective analysis of social issues, aimed at collective action for progressive social change (AIEB, 2016). Similarly, youth work is a developmental practice using informal education methods underpinned by a core set of values and principles including the empowerment of young people, equality, inclusion, social justice and voluntary participation (Devlin and Gunning, 2009). Youth workers engage in anti-oppressive practice and promote equality, diversity and inclusion (Sapin, 2013). Relevant professional endorsement bodies usually refer to the importance of social justice in the training and education of community and youth workers. For example, in Ireland the North/South Education and Training Standards (NSETS) criteria for the endorsement of programmes of study in youth work (NSETS, 2021: 7) recommends that youth work students are facilitated to develop 'an activist identity' and explore models of practice that enable 'greater equality and social justice'. The All-Ireland Endorsement Body (AIEB) sets out standards for community work practice that state 'the pursuit of social justice and sustainable development are core elements of community development' (AIEB, 2016: 15).

Social justice, then, is a core value underpinning the practice of community work and youth work that manifests in models of emancipatory practice informed by a critical analysis of power and inequality and a commitment to social change, equality and the promotion of human rights (Cooper et al, 2015; Ledwith, 2016; Coburn et al, 2017; Beck and Purcell, 2020). For practitioners, these values translate into a commitment to social justice praxis that involves the capacity to combine critical awareness, critical analysis and critical action. Coburn and Gormally (2015), drawing on the work of Freire, who defines 'praxis' as reflection *and* action, point to key characteristics of social justice as a way of working. For example, they suggest that practitioners committed to putting social justice into practice must eschew individual work in favour of collaborative approaches because of the centrality of 'negotiated relationships in emancipatory practice' (Coburn and Gormally, 2015: 75). Ledwith (2016: 141–2), also drawing on Freire, cites the importance of 'a *living critical praxis* for community development to take its stand as a social justice practice', which involves 'critique, reflection and dialogue, lead[ing] to action for change'. Closely related to praxis is the process of 'conscientisation' that pays attention to the structural nature of inequality encountered in everyday life (Ledwith, 2016). This is done by engaging in critical questioning, in dialogue with others, particularly those with lived experiences of discrimination, inequality and oppression, about how power operates even in the everyday. Ledwith (2016) suggests that social justice praxis is not only undertaken with communities but should also be part of the practitioner's own critical reflective practice.

Despite long-established commitments to social justice in youth work and community work practice, these commitments are now under challenge. The policy context shaping youth work and community work has been shifting in ways that now place an emphasis on 'value for money' reforms and its associated economic measurements that seek to calculate such things as unit costs and return on investment (McMahon, 2021). The new policy context means that organisations and practitioners are required to and rewarded for delivering policy-determined outcomes and meeting 'targets', and this has led to increased competition for funding resources (Mayo et al, 2013). Research and in particular evaluation research has increasingly become part of the response to the accountability and 'evidence' drive for more metrics, data and more proof of impact (Mayo et al, 2013; de St Croix, 2018, 2020). Coburn and Gormally (2015) highlight the dominance of neoliberal managerialist imperatives in society generally, as well as in the social professions, which are threatening the social justice dimension of the work and demanding practitioners focus on the technical aspects of practice such as 'what and how we do things' (Coburn and Gormally, 2015: 82). They 'reassert' the underpinning centrality of social justice values for community and youth work practice, and they nudge all of us to follow their lead. With this in mind, our aim in this chapter is to bring social justice to the fore in examining the kinds of praxis (critical analysis, reflection and action) that practitioners might bring to their engagement with research.

Research in community work and youth work practice

Across the community work and youth work literature, there are tensions in the accounts of the relationship between research and practice. Some accounts discuss the dearth of practice-focused and practitioner-led research in the field and point to issues such as a 'lingering anti-intellectualism' that prioritises 'doing' over 'thinking' about practice, a lack of research funding and a lack of research tradition as obstacles. Other accounts point to the dominance of small-scale, applied research and the absence of large-scale and experimental research in the community work and youth work fields (Kouttzi, 2006; Chisholm et al, 2011). Some contributors make a passionate call for more engagement with research in practice in order to advance the work and improve the development of a knowledge base and theoretical perspectives to support practice. Yet others promote the suitability of research approaches, techniques and methods that are aligned with the underpinning values of youth work and community work practice (Barr 2005; Spence et al, 2006; Ledwith, 2016; Cooper, 2018). In more recent literature, the work of de St Croix and Doherty (2018, 2019, 2022), as well as Cooper (2018) and McArdle and Murray (2021) has contributed significantly to challenging technical and number-based evaluation research in favour of evaluation methods and tactics that support transformative and reflective practice.

The politics of research or 'knowledge production' is contentious in the recent literature. One of the most significant debates relates to the issue of 'evidence'. Funders and policymakers are increasingly placing an emphasis on the use of scientific, quantified and independent 'evidence' in many areas of welfare provision and in the social professions. Discussing youth work, Spence and Wood (2011) surface questions about the distribution of power in the evidence approach, suggesting that policymakers and government are directing the research agenda by commissioning external, independent researchers and then imposing the 'evidence' (in some cases produced in very different contexts) on to practice with little role for practitioners. For many in community work and youth work, 'evidence' then conjures negative associations with how research is being put to work to govern and discipline practitioners and communities (Taylor and Taylor, 2013; Duffy, 2017). For example, Oakley (2004), defending the 'researcher's agenda for evidence', argues that it generates more democratic knowledge available to policymakers, service users and the public, yet she fails to mention or address the needs of practitioners in the researcher's quest for evidence. As part of the evidence approach, practitioners' voices have been side-lined, regarded by both policymakers and external researchers as lacking credibility and not counting as 'evidence' (see, for example, House of Commons, 2011). Spence and Wood (2011: 4) argue that this reveals 'a lack of trust in the truth claims of practitioners'. The advocated use of realist evaluation methods and implementation science that produces a narrow focus on programme implementation and that loses sight of broader relational practices and processes not only jars with youth and community work practice values which focus on collective processes and relationship building (Spence and Wood, 2011; Ledwith, 2016; de St Croix and Doherty, 2022) but potentially undermines the integrity of practice as democratic and social justice oriented (Kiely and Meade, 2018). Another significant issue is the treatment of communities and young people in the evidence-based research process. There is a tendency to view communities, young people and community work and youth work as the *site* for enquiry, turning them into 'objects' of the researcher's gaze, which can be extractivist, an issue highlighted and discussed by Jamie Gorman in Chapter 9. This is in stark contrast to Ledwith's (2016: 148) call for community development research to be with and not on people, and that it should be based on a mutual relationship between researchers and the community. For these reasons, in this chapter we eschew narrow references to 'evidence' and reclaim 'research' as a broader activity concerned with knowledge production and infused with politics and ethics.

Community work and youth work are not alone in exploring the tensions surrounding the research–practice relationship, as other social professions share similar concerns, particularly focused on the need to mobilise practitioners to engage with research (see Scanlon, 2000; Fox et al, 2007; Kara, 2017a). Practitioner research constitutes a vitally rich space where practitioners can engage critically with debates from the field, policy and practice (Bradford and Cullen, 2012). Writing about social care practice, Fox et al (2007: 9) note that one of the obstacles to practitioner research is that funders and policymakers give it less status and attention than research carried out by external or academic researchers. However, for social work, Bentley et al (2019: 434) argue passionately that increasing practitioner engagement with research hinges on teaching research to student practitioners (in their case social work) through a social justice lens, saying that 'research is a legitimate form of practice that might be seen as more relevant and influential if we conceptualized and taught research through the lens of social justice, human rights, and diversity'.

The current literature understandably focuses on encouraging more practitioner-based research by providing guidance to practitioners on *how* they might conduct such research (for example, Munford et al, 2003; Bradford and Cullen, 2012; Mayo et al, 2013; Ledwith, 2016; Cooper, 2018). There is also a wide-ranging set of research literature that specifically addresses how to undertake socially just research or research for social justice (see Fassinger and Morrow, 2013; Lyons et al, 2013; Aydarova, 2019; Bailey, 2019; CohenMiller and Boivin, 2021). Despite all of this, the reality is that this ambition remains largely unfulfilled in everyday community work and youth work practice contexts. In our experience, most practitioners in contemporary practice are much more likely to be consumers, participants, gatekeepers or commissioners of research than to be conducting research themselves. There is also a lack of discussion about how a social justice lens might be brought to the arguably more common engagements youth work and community work practitioners have with research in their everyday practice. This chapter attempts to address this gap. We focus on a number of areas of engagement, including consuming and using research to inform practice, participating in and gatekeeping external research, and commissioning and managing research and engaging with funders. We explore the various relationships and roles that practitioners have in these contexts, as well as some key questions that practitioners might ask as they make decisions about if and how they might engage.

Social justice, research and community and youth work

What imperatives does a social justice reflexivity bring to the engagement with research for community workers and youth workers? For Ledwith (2016: 148), research is an important part of pursuing a social justice orientation to community work and youth work because through research practitioners can better integrate theory and practice or 'thinking and doing' to the benefit of values-based practice, a 'unity of praxis', as she puts it. This is an important point because one of the critiques made by policymakers and funders who are increasingly in favour of specific forms of evidence-based practice is that youth work and community work require a stronger evidence/knowledge base. If the field fails to produce research that can build the knowledge base in favour of equality and social justice concerns, it is likely that externally commissioned 'scientific' research processes will be imposed upon practice with potentially limited space for social justice concerns or emancipatory ways of working and with a sole focus on outcomes rather than the process of the work (Spence, 2004, 2007; Spence and Wood, 2011; Cooper, 2012; Ledwith, 2016).

Some contributors draw our attention to the necessity for the underlying values of community work and youth work to be reflected in research that is in, about or for practice (Issitt and Spence, 2005; McArdle and Murray, 2021). In other words, research in practice should uphold the same values base as the practice itself (Spence and Wood, 2011; Ledwith, 2016). Krueger et al posit that practitioners of community work and youth work must engage with research in ways that are consistent with the values of the work and how they are 'experienced, practised and talked about' (Krueger et al, 2005: 370). We argue that practitioners must engage with research in their practice more broadly, in ways that are congruent with their professional values and principles. We must also recognise the imperative that exists for practitioners to contribute to research because of the opportunities it offers to challenge and influence how issues and responses are identified, defined and analysed.

There are synergies with indigenous communities who have been the subjects of 'research' responding over time to develop their own ethical codes, reclaiming research about and for their communities. Their approach challenges Euro-Western perspectives by developing their own ethical codes that assert and prioritise indigenous ways of being, knowing and communicating. One example is the San Code of Research Ethics from South Africa (2017), which highlights the centrality of justice and fairness along with respect, care, honesty and a commitment to collaborative processes in ethical research. Helen Kara situates herself as a student of indigenous research ethics, and her book *Research Ethics in the Real World* (Kara, 2017b) provides a helpful starting point for exploring what Euro-Western researchers can and need to learn from indigenous perspectives. Paris and Winn (2014: 4) describe these approaches as humanising and decolonising forms of research that have at their core a rejection of attempts to create knowledge that pathologises, objectifies or names marginalised communities as deficient. Instead, they say that humanising research is primarily concerned with social justice and involves care, dignity, dialogical consciousness-raising, reciprocity and trust.

Guillemin and Gillam (2004: 263) argue for an 'ethics in practice'. Ethics in practice moves beyond procedural ethics (those subject to institutional approval, 'and which usually prescribe 'do no harm' work instead) and into the realm of the ethical issues that arise in the research process which are not 'usually addressed in research ethics committee applications, nor are they events that are often anticipated when applying for approval' (Guillemin and Gillam, 2004: 263). Sarah Banks, in her work on community-based participatory research, describes the need for a 'virtue-based approach to research ethics, which both complements and challenges dominant principle- and rule-based ethical codes and governance frameworks' (2018: 1). These characteristics are also relevant for community work and youth work practitioners, who often act as advocates and allies for and with communities in all aspects of their work including research engagement. In particular, what community workers and youth workers committed to social justice can bring to their engagement with research is an underlying integrity. Research(er) integrity involves 'practical wisdom' or 'phronesis', which refers to the researcher's capacity to 'deliberate well about ethical issues in research' and includes 'the ability to perceive and appreciate ethically salient features of situations; the exercise of ethical imagination; reflective and deliberative capabilities (to make judgements and act)' (Banks, 2018: 32). For Banks (2018), virtues of courage, respectfulness and trustworthiness are core characteristics practitioners require when facing challenging situations where they need to communicate or advocate the needs and rights of communities to stakeholders who have different agendas in research. This chimes with Sercombe's (2010: 10) idea of an 'ethical commitment to serve' that puts young people and communities first. This type of practitioner integrity, including ethical reasoning and imagination as well as characteristics of courage, respect and trustworthiness, is key to using a social justice lens in community work/youth work research engagements.

Questions to guide social justice thinking in community work and youth work research engagement

As mentioned earlier, there is very little discussion in the youth work or community work literature about the range of engagements that practitioners have with research. Most contributions specifically position the practitioner as a researcher and offer guidance on how to undertake research. Barr (2005) does provide a broad outline of seven types of research that contribute to community development work: explanatory research, policy analysis, market research, practice theory, investigative research, community needs research and practice evaluation. Interestingly, Barr also identifies the potential role of practitioners in each of these seven types of research. In some cases, he suggests practitioners can and do lead the conduct of research, while in others practitioners are involved in commissioning or managing external researchers to conduct the research. In other cases, a participatory approach is taken where practitioners facilitate research among community members as part of their everyday practice or as a tool in a community development process. Additionally, Banks (2018) suggests that practitioners might work in a participatory process with external researchers and/or community members in community-based participatory research. Drawing from this, we can distil four possible kinds of research engagements that practitioners might have in their practice: consuming research done by others and using findings from research to inform their work; invitations to participate in research being conducted by others where the external research agenda is focused on researching the community or issues in the community or practice itself; managing research by bringing in researchers to carry out research in, with or for the community they work with; and finally researching in the community or in practice themselves. As mentioned earlier, since there are many existing guides to support practitioners to conduct their own research, our focus here is on the first two types of engagements since much less has been written on these.

The work of CohenMiller and Boivin (2021) focuses on challenging researchers to engage with what is involved in doing research that is socially just by developing their own critical self-reflection. Their approach uses questions as a central device to support this critical self-reflection. Following their lead, this next section attempts to open up questions for reflection for youth work and community work practitioners about using a social justice lens in their engagements with research in practice. Our own past experiences as practitioners, research educators, researchers and our involvement in research commissioning have informed the following sets of questions.

Consuming research to inform practice

One of the most basic engagements that youth work and community work practitioners have with research is using it to inform their practice. This involves keeping abreast of new knowledge that can support social justice and equality work. Using a social justice lens to inform practice with research involves applying critical thinking to this process. Practitioners need to interrogate the kinds of research they decide to read and engage with. As evidence-based practice is growing in youth work and community work, there are increasing numbers of 'manualised programmes' available to practitioners for immediate use in practice. While these appear to offer an easy and time-efficient way to put research into practice, they do raise questions about the kinds of knowledge assumptions and research methods they are built on, which are usually top-down, positivist approaches using experimental designs and control groups likened to clinical studies. They can study impacts of programme features on individuals and take a psychological, therapeutic intervention approach rather than a social justice, collective empowerment approach. The research may have taken place in a very different geographic, policy or otherwise different context. Using a social justice lens to aid decision-making, practitioners might ask:

- Why have I chosen to pay attention to this research? Can I and should I apply this research in my practice? Are there other research reports that I have ignored that serve social justice and equality better or more fully? What learning can this research bring to my social justice and equality work/practice? How can I use this research in my practice to serve the values of social justice?
- Are there reasons I should not use this research in my practice, particularly if it undermines social justice aims? If this research is damaging to social justice and equality aims, if it further supports power and privilege, what can and should I do about that?
- If this research supports social justice and equality, how can I disseminate and share this research with others – including community members and other practitioners?

Practitioners *who are committed to social justice* need to be *critical* consumers of research that has been conducted and disseminated by others.. At an individual level, practitioners might consider engaging with research as part of their own reflective practice aimed at enhancing their practice skills and approaches or as an aid in tackling a new practice dilemma, and this could be included in regular supervision work. The possibility of bringing research knowledge into a collective setting either with a practitioner network or with young people and communities undoubtedly brings with it the potential for deepening the learning and offers opportunities for social justice praxis through dialogue and discussion. Critically reading and interpreting research reports and publications means paying attention to all aspects of the research, including the people/organisations involved in producing the research; the research agenda and how it was shaped; the underlying assumptions that relate to knowledge production and positionality; research relationships; the research methods used to select participants, gather and analyse information; the representation of research findings; and the dissemination of the research.

People/organisations involved

All research involves a mix of people, organisations and institutional affiliations. Making a list of these (think about researchers/institutions they belong to, funders, commissioners, publishers), practitioners might ask:

- What is the track record of these people/organisations in relation to social justice research? Do the institutions/organisations involved support social justice aims explicitly?
- Have researchers had to make a case/convince organisations/institutions to support the social justice orientation of the research? Have organisation/institutional rules/criteria/norms been an obstacle/hindrance to the production or publication of socially just research in this case?

Research agenda

Most research begins with a set of research problems and aims. It is important to consider this agenda for research as well as any other factors that influenced its shape. From a social justice perspective, being in a position to shape a research agenda, to cast the 'researcher's gaze', is powerful because you shape what/who gets problematised and how (Lyons et al, 2013; Bentley et al, 2019). Research funders in particular, whether institutional, philanthropic or community based, are often an invisible force in the shaping of research agendas. Ask for example:

- Do the research questions reflect an implicit or explicit concern with social justice issues such as inequality, oppression, marginalisation, human rights? Given the topics of the research, are/should/could social justice issues/values have been considered? If not, why might they have been left out? Was this explained or justified or ignored by the researcher?
- What were the initial aims or intentions of the research? Were emancipatory or social change goals part of the agenda? From the initial set of aims, who was to benefit from the research (for example, think about the often-unstated benefits to the researcher like funding, status and career progression)? Is the shape of the research agenda useful to those with less power who might be the focus of the research?
- How were the research questions framed and by whom? Who had the power to shape the research agenda (think about the role of researchers, funders, commissioners, community members and those with lived experience, practitioners)? Was power distributed in shaping the research agenda, was it top-down, shared or bottom-up? Who was left outside the decision-making process that shaped the initial research questions and aims?

- If the research was funded, how was it funded? Was it commissioned, or did the researchers win a research call? What implications did the funding criteria/funders have on the shape and conduct of the research?

Knowledge and positionality

As mentioned earlier, one of the most significant debates in the contemporary literature relates to the issue of 'evidence'. This contested area is essentially about the politics of knowledge production and how knowledge is valued. It represents a power struggle between those who advocate in favour of positivist and science-oriented types of knowledge and others who favour interpretivist, critical, transformative and emancipatory-oriented knowledge. Researchers themselves and the decisions they make are part of this politics (Bentley, 2019). All research and researchers are immersed in this politics of knowledge production, and when critically engaging with research produced by others, practitioners might ask:

- What are the underlying assumptions and worldviews about what is seen as 'truth' or knowledge in this research? What worldviews/types of knowledge/theories are referenced, ignored, celebrated, subjugated, critiqued or heavily relied upon by the research/er? How is the existing body of social justice-oriented research, theory and knowledge treated in this research? What are the political standpoints in this research? What is the status of more marginalised voices (including those of practitioners) in this research?
- How does the researcher position themselves as knowers and producers of knowledge? Do they claim a detachment, objectivity or neutrality; do they talk about the politics of their research and their decisions; do they illustrate an awareness of social justice values; do they deliberately include social justice issues in their own positioning as the researcher; do they address their own subjectivity, lived experiences and positioning (think about class, gender, culture, ethnicity and so on) and relate these to social justice in their research?

Research relationships

Researchers as mentioned earlier have power and privilege to shape knowledge and influence how readers come to understand social problems and their solutions (Bacchi, 2009). For research that involves the gathering of information from others, the researcher is drawn into a relationship of power with participants that often includes the power to select/or not certain participants; shape the questions asked of participants in questionnaires and interviews; code and analyse the words, feelings, ideas and lived experiences of participants; and produce a final account of the research. Guerriero and Correa (2015: 2634) identify differences between scientific research approaches where research participants become 'objects' of researchers' study and critical research approaches, where the view is that knowledge emerges from an 'intersubjective relationship' between the researcher and participants, and participants are not seen as 'objects' to be studied. Though most research ethics boards now require researchers to reflect on these power dynamics, particularly if the research engages with less powerful social groups so as to mitigate risks of harm or direct exploitation or coercion, from the perspective of social justice it might be useful to ask:

- Does the researcher position themselves in relation to the researched? Do they indicate an awareness of their power in the research process? Do they give any account of how they shared power (think about research decisions throughout) with the researched in the research process (thinking about the start of the process and setting the agenda to the end of the process with publication of the research)?
- Who are the researched? If they are members of a marginalised or oppressed group, is this discussed, and in what way are they portrayed? Do the reasons for researching with marginalised groups support social justice aims such as amplifying seldom-heard voices? If it is not discussed, why not, and what does this mean for power dynamics? If the researched are members of a marginalised group, was it appropriate that they be selected to be researched? Could the research problem be more suitably addressed by researching those with more wealth/power/ political influence in society?
- What is the nature of the relationship between the researcher and researched? Are the researched collaborators with the researcher? Are the researched imposed upon or extracted from by the researcher?

Research methods

Researchers face myriad 'choice moments' when designing research and making decisions about how the research will be conducted, including what techniques to use, what questions to ask, how to sample and select participants, what strategies to use to code and analyse data as well as how to produce the final research report (Savin Baden and Howell Major, 2013). Bentley et al (2019: 436) point out that the research process 'has the potential to perpetuate privilege, the status quo, and marginalization of some populations and problems' but they also say that the process 'can sensitively and transparently manage the power issues that emerge and instead empower and give voice to vulnerable populations'. Ledwith (2016) highlights the potential role of some forms of research not just for knowledge production but as a method for achieving social justice through the research methods and processes themselves, though this requires high levels of participation and collaboration between the researcher and researched. When critically reading and interpreting research, it can be useful to ask:

- Are there sufficient details and a rationale given about how the research was conducted and decisions were made? Were social justice values part of the decision-making process? Is there a coherence between the research questions, the research methods used, the rationale given and social justice values?
- Who made the decisions about research design, research methods and research materials used (were research participants involved at any level/ stage)? How has the way this research been carried out met (or not) the values of social justice? How have the methods used contributed to issues of power (sharing, compounding or redistributing)? Were there missed opportunities for advancing social justice aims through the methods and materials used? Did the research techniques, research instruments, questions and materials use culturally appropriate language and images?

Representation and dissemination

In terms of critically consuming research produced by others, some final issues for practitioners to consider are how the research/researcher communicates the outcomes of the research both in terms of representing problems and people and the methods used for reporting and disseminating the research. For Fassinger and Morrow (2013), social justice aims for social change are supported when research participants have a role in deciding on research dissemination. It is important that research participants are not misrepresented or their lived experiences 'colonised' (Lyons et al, 2013). Using a social justice lens might involve asking:

- How are people and issues represented in the final account of the research? What and who is problematised? If the research deals with marginalised groups of people, how are they represented? How are the voices of oppressed or marginalised groups represented, and whom are they represented to (who is the intended audience)? What language and terminology are used?
- Do the reported research findings create harmful outcomes for social justice? Do the research outcomes support, legitimise, 'normalise' inequality, marginalisation, oppression? Do they blame/pathologise individuals but ignore issues of structural inequality? Does the research do harm by creating or perpetuating stereotypes or negative images of those with less power? Do the reported research findings create outcomes to

advance social justice? Do the research outcomes support and promote action for empowerment, emancipation and social change? Is the research used to seek change or hold the powerful to account? Do the research outcomes produce a deeper understanding of the complexity of social justice issues such as diversity and oppression, intersectionality and so on?

- How is the research communicated, reported and disseminated? Who can access the reporting (think about the format it is produced in and cost/accessibility)? Was the reporting disseminated in appropriate formats for participants and practitioners? Where was it published and by what publishers? Was publication shaped by publishing 'norms' and institutional rules about intellectual property that hampered issues of co-ownership? Who 'owns' the research knowledge? How does monetisation through publication impact on social justice aims?

Participating (or not) in external research agendas

Community workers and youth workers are frequently approached in their professional role and asked to support or participate in research projects at the request of external researchers from academic, government or other community organisations. They might be asked to support a project by identifying participants for research projects by sharing a call or targeting people they work with. They might be invited to support or collaborate with external research projects in a variety of ways ranging from having informal conversations about the goals and methodology of the research to sitting on advisory committees that provide more formal consultation on methodology, discussion about the findings in advance of publication or support with dissemination. Practitioners might also be asked to review and provide feedback on external research findings and reports or asked to share research findings with the community they work with. Finally, practitioners may also be invited to become involved directly as research participants themselves. Most often, these requests are for work by the youth worker or community worker that is unfunded and comes in addition to their everyday core work.

In dealing with such requests for participation in external research agendas, practitioners must first consider whether to engage with the research project. Community workers and youth workers have a particular role with the community and young people they work with: they are allies, analysts, equality practitioners with a particular set of values regarding equality, human rights, participation and empowerment and, for community workers, collectivity. From the perspective of community work/youth work, research must seek to promote human rights and solidarity in the process and outcome of the research and contribute to informing the realisation of equality for the group that is the focus of the research. Giving their time in a professional capacity demands reflection on whether the research and their support of it potentially achieves these goals. In effect, they can be asked to take on a gatekeeping role. In these situations, community workers and youth workers might have an opportunity to shape how a community/young people might be engaged in a research project. This could have a very important impact on the quality of the research as well as the further construction of knowledge about the community or about community and youth work practice. In the interests of the community or young people, the better decision might be *not* to support the research. Making this initial assessment of whether to support the research or not is very important and cannot be taken lightly.

Tuck and Yang (2014) reflect on the importance of 'refusing research', particularly where research can be damaging, colonising or exploitative. Following Kosofsky Sedgwick, they question the emphasis that much social science research places on having to *prove* the harms and damage experienced by marginalised communities so that these communities have justification for extra resources. They point to the dangers of research that portends to give voice to oppressed groups but only through the agenda of external researchers. They argue also that social science research is not necessarily deserving of access to some kinds of knowledge held by marginalised communities. For them, it is important that we question the idea that research is always a 'good' or useful thing, as sometimes communities need different kinds of interventions and not research at all.

Using a social justice lens to aid decision-making, practitioners might ask:

- How did the research question(s) emerge? Was there any engagement with the community when conceiving the research question/research focus? What are the aims and objectives of the research? What and who is being problematised? How does this worldview conceptualise research participants? What is the theoretical approach and rationale for this approach? What is the source and requirements of the funding?
- Whose interests are being met in this project? Will the research be of use for the young people/community/interest group we are working with? Has this community/issue already been researched? Have previous experiences of research been damaging and created a research fatigue in the community?
- What is the worldview of the research/er? What is the education/training/experience of the researchers? What is their knowledge and understanding of the issues facing this community?
- How are the voices of oppressed or marginalised groups going to be represented, and whom are they represented to (who is the intended audience)? For what purpose is the community's voice to be used (extractive/beneficial for whom)?
- What is the proposed methodology? Are there any ethical considerations that might emerge? Do the researchers have ethical approval from an

institution? Are there any risks to the group I work with, or otherwise, from the research?

- How does the research align or not with my values as a practitioner? What does my community and youth work analysis bring? What is my potential contribution as a community worker/youth worker? What are the terms of reference for my engagement, and can I negotiate these?
- Is there appropriate funding allocated to support community participation and appropriate systems set up (in funding streams, in partner institutions) to pay expenses for community members to be involved? Is there a recognition for community members' time (if for example they are asked to join a steering group or be a peer researcher)?

Where the support of or engagement of the organisation is requested, the task for the practitioner is to review proposed research projects before they commence to assess the alignment with the mission, values and principles of the organisation and the social justice values of the work. The practitioner might also consider the implications of their involvement and ask:

- Does it align with the mission/strategic priorities of the organisation? Does this research/my involvement (time and other skills) in the research constitute value to my work in X organisation? Could the time spent contributing to this external research be more productively spent (from a social justice perspective) on other forms of work?
- How will this contribution be credited in the research?

Another way in which a practitioner might engage with research is to try to shape the external research funding agenda. This might involve paying attention to debates about research and engaging with these debates by making policy submissions. Community workers and youth workers might not always see this as being part of their work, nor as an area where they are best placed, but as noted at the outset of this chapter, research is a primary site of knowledge production (Bacchi, 2009). Thus there is an imperative for practitioners to engage on behalf of the communities and young people they work with as well as contributing their expert knowledge in equality and social justice practice. Challenging how communities and young people are conceptualised in research and the methodological implications of this is an important part of this work. In addition, how community work and youth work are portrayed and represented, who speaks on behalf of professional practitioners and professional practice is an ongoing challenge for the development of the social professions. According to Banks (2018), 'phronesis' (practical wisdom) and 'courage' are core characteristics practitioners require for engagement. Never more are these important than when engaging with and attempting to shape research funding agendas. Practitioners might ask:

- What are the aims and objectives of the research funding stream? What and who is problematised in the funding call? What are the requirements in the funding stream for engaging with communities? Is the participation of community-based organisations given recognition and recompense/resources?
- Is the time and work of practitioners and community members or young people given appropriate recognition and recompense by the funding stream?
- What outputs are incentivised by the funding call – are these primarily focused on the academic community (for example, journal articles, conferences), or are community-based outputs included in allowable costings (for example, community leaflets, community meetings)?
- What can or should our/other similar organisations do to seek to change or amend funding calls and their policies to better support social justice perspectives?

Conclusion

As we conclude this chapter, we reflect on two key questions: What does this mean for social justice research, and indeed social justice practice and policy as community workers and youth workers, both in the Irish context and beyond? Research is increasingly the space where knowledge is constructed and produced about communities, social groups, the issues they face and practices that might serve as interventions. Research is not a value-free engagement. Like community work and youth work practice, it is an intervention in the social world (Bacchi, 2009). Knowledge production has implications for how communities, young people and social issues are problematised and for the solutions policymakers and practitioners seek to apply (Bacchi, 2009). The evidence-informed agenda is increasingly being imposed on community work and youth work practice, yet often the practitioner voice is silenced. This can be addressed by doing practitioner research, but also by how practitioners engage with research in their everyday practice: how they use, critique or accept research that they use to inform their practice; how they represent community work, youth work as social professions/how they demand community work and youth work are represented in research; how they represent communities and young people; how they support young people or communities to participate. This all takes an enormous amount of work, often work that is unrecognised. In this chapter, we discussed some of the ways in which community work and youth work practitioners or others committed to a social justice agenda might engage with research in their work. Through this chapter, we are inviting community work and youth work practitioners to bring their social justice lens to all of their engagements with research in their everyday practice.

Note

[1] Throughout this chapter, we use the terms 'community and youth work practitioners', and 'youth work and community work practitioners', and at times 'practitioners' for short, recognising the distinct areas of practice but also the overlapping areas of concern with regard to practice, and to research in practice.

References

All Ireland Endorsement Body (AIEB) (2016) 'All Ireland standards for community work', Galway: CWI and AIEB.

Aydarova, E. (2019) 'Flipping the paradigm: Studying up and research for social justice', in K.K. Strunk and L.A. Locke (eds) *Research Methods for Social Justice and Equity in Education*, Cham: Palgrave Macmillan, pp 33–44.

Bacchi, C. (2009) *Analysing Policy: What's the Problem Represented to Be?*, Frenchs Forest, NSW: Pearson Australia.

Bailey, L.E. (2019) 'Thinking critically about "social justice methods": Methods as "contingent foundations"', in K.K. Strunk and L.A. Locke (eds) *Research Methods for Social Justice and Equity in Education*, Cham: Palgrave Macmillan, pp 91–108.

Banks, S. (2018) 'Cultivating researcher integrity: Virtue-based approaches to research ethics', in N. Emmerich (ed) *Virtue Ethics in the Conduct and Governance of Social Science Research*, Advances in Research Ethics and Integrity 3, Bingley: Emerald Publishing Limited, pp 21–44.

Barr, A. (2005) 'The contribution of research to community development', *Community Development Journal*, 40(4): 453–58.

Beck, D. and Purcell, R. (2020) *Community Development for Social Change*, London: Routledge.

Bentley, K.J., Mancini, M., Jacob, A. and McLeod, D.A. (2019) 'Teaching social work research through the lens of social justice, human rights, and diversity', *Journal of Social Work Education*, 55(3): 433–48.

Bradford, S. and Cullen, F. (eds) (2012) *Research and Research Methods for Youth Practitioners*, Abingdon: Routledge.

Chisholm, L., Kovacheva, S., Merico, M., Devlin, M., Jenkins, D. and Karsten, A. (2011) 'The social construction of youth and the triangle between youth research, youth policy and youth work in Europe', in L. Chisholm, S. Kovacheva and M. Merico (eds) *European Youth Studies: Integrating Research, Policy and Practice*, Innsbruck: M.A. EYS Consortium, pp 11–44. Available at https://pjp-eu.coe.int/documents/42128013/47261653/maeys_2012.pdf/38e80a55-bbe2-40fc-b9f7-dd1eb7352a72

Coburn, A. and Gormally, S. (2015) 'Emancipatory praxis: A social-justice approach to equality work', in C. Cooper, S. Gormally and G. Hughes (eds) *Socially Just, Radical Alternatives for Education and Youth Work Practice: Re-imagining Ways of Working with Young People*, Houndmills: Palgrave Macmillan, pp 65–84.

Coburn, A. and Gormally, S. (2017) *Communities for Social Change: Practicing Equality and Social Justice in Youth and Community Work*, New York: Peter Lang.

CohenMiller, A., and Boivin, N. (2021) *Questions in Qualitative Social Justice Research in Multicultural Contexts*, London: Routledge.

Cooper, C., Gormally, S. and Hughes, G. (eds) (2015) *Socially Just, Radical Alternatives for Education and Youth Work Practice: Re-imagining Ways of Working with Young People*, Houndmills: Palgrave.

Cooper, S. (2012) 'Ensuring accountability or improving practice?', in J. Ord (ed) *Critical Issues in Youth Work Management*, Abingdon: Routledge, pp 82–95.

Cooper, S. (2018) *Participatory Evaluation in Youth and Community Work: Theory and Practice*, Abingdon: Routledge.

Crickley, A. and McArdle, O. (2009) 'Community work, community development, reflections: 2009', *Working for Change: The Irish Journal of Community Work*, 1: 17, 14–27.

De St Croix, T. (2018) 'Youth work, performativity and the new youth impact agenda: Getting paid for numbers?', *Journal of Education Policy*, 33(3): 414–38.

De St Croix, T. (2020) 'Re-imagining accountability: Storytelling workshops for evaluation in and beyond youth work', *Pedagogy, Culture & Society*, 30(5): 697–714.

De St Croix, T. and Doherty, L. (2022) '"Capturing the magic": Grassroots perspectives on evaluating open youth work', *Journal of Youth Studies*, 1–17. DOI: 10.1080/13676261.2022.2150540.

Devlin, M. and Gunning, A. (2009) 'The purpose and outcomes of youth work: Report to the interagency group', Dublin: Irish Youth Work Press.

Duffy, D. (2017) *Evaluation and Governing in the 21st Century: Disciplinary Measures, Transformative Possibilities*, London: Palgrave Macmillan.

Fassinger, R. and Morrow, S.L. (2013) 'Toward best practices in quantitative, qualitative, and mixed-method research: A social justice perspective', *Journal for Social Action in Counselling & Psychology*, 5(2): 69–83.

Fox, M., Martin, P. and Green, G. (2007) *Doing Practitioner Research*, London: Sage.

Guerriero, I.C.Z. and Correa, F.P. (2015) 'Ethics, collective health, qualitative health research and social justice', *Ciência & saúde coletiva*, 20(9): 2631–40.

Guillemin, M. and Gillam, L. (2004) 'Ethics, reflexivity, and "ethically important moments" in research', *Qualitative Inquiry*, 10(2): 261–80.

House of Commons (2011) 'Services for young people', London: Stationery Office.

Issitt, M. and Spence, J. (2005) 'Practitioner knowledge and the problem of evidence-based research policy and practice', *Youth and Policy*, 88: 63–82.

Kara, H. (2017a) *Research and Evaluation for Busy Students and Practitioners: A Time-Saving Guide* (2nd edn), Bristol: Policy Press.

Kara, H. (2017b) *Research Ethics in the Real World*, Bristol: Policy Press.

Kiely, E. and Meade, R. (2018) 'Contemporary Irish youth work policy and practice: A governmental analysis', *Child & Youth Services*, 39(1): 1–26.

Koutatzi, M. (ed) (2006) 'The Role of Research in Youth Policy and Youth Work Development in the Broader Euro-Mediterranean', CoE-EU Youth Partnership Seminar Report [online], Available from: https://pjp-eu.coe. int/en/web/youth-partnership/youth-policy-co-operation [Accessed 16 January 2023].

Krueger, M., Evans, E., Korsmo, J., Stanley, J. and Wilder, Q. (2005) 'A youth work inquiry', *Qualitative Inquiry*, 11(3): 369–89. https://doi.org/10.1177/107780040527505

Ledwith, M. (2016) *Community Development in Action: Putting Freire into Practice*, Bristol: Policy Press.

Lyons, H.Z., Bike, D.H., Ojeda, L., Johnson, A., Rosales, R. and Flores, L.Y. (2013) 'Qualitative research as social justice practice with culturally diverse populations', *Journal for Social Action in Counselling & Psychology*, 5(2): 10–25.

Mayo, M., Mendiwelso-Bendek, Z. and Packham, C. (eds) (2013) *Community Research for Community Development*, London: Palgrave Macmillan.

McArdle, O.M. and Murray, U. (2021) 'Fit for measure? Evaluation in community development', *Community Development Journal*, 56(3): 432–48.

McMahon, S. (2021) 'What's the "problem" with Irish youth work?', *Youth and Policy*, 4 August. https://www.youthandpolicy.org/articles/whats-the-problem-irish-youth-work/

Munford, R., Sanders, J. and Andrew, A. (2003) 'Community development: Action research in community settings', *Social Work Education*, 22(1): 93–104.

North/South Education and Training Standards Committee for Youth Work (NSETS) (2021) 'Criteria and procedures for the professional endorsement of higher education programmes of study in youth work', Dublin: NYCI.

Oakley, A. (2004) 'The researcher's agenda for evidence', *Evaluation and Research in Education*, 18(1–2): 12–27.

Paris, D. and Winn, M.T. (2014) *Humanizing Research: Decolonizing Qualitative Inquiry with Youth and Communities*, Los Angeles, CA: Sage.

Sapin, K. (2013) *Essential Skills for Youth Work Practice* (2nd edn), London: SAGE.

Savin-Baden, M. and Howell Major, C. (2013) *Qualitative Research: The Essential Guide to Theory and Practice*, Abingdon: Routledge.

Scanlon, M. (2000) 'Issues in research', in D. Wilkinson (ed) *The Researcher's Toolkit: The Complete Guide to Practitioner Research*, Abingdon: Routledge, pp 2–10.

Sercombe, H. (2010) *Youth Work Ethics*, London: SAGE.

Spence, J. (2004) 'Targeting, accountability and youth work practice', *Practice*, 16(4): 261–72.

Spence, J. and Wood, J. (2011) 'Youth work and research: Editorial', *Youth and Policy*, 107: 1–18.

Spence, J., Devaney, C.A. and Noonan, K. (eds) (2006) *Youth Work: Voices of Practice*, Leicester: National Youth Agency

Taylor, T. and Taylor, M. (2013) 'Threatening youth work: The illusion of outcomes', in Defence of Youth Work [online], Available from: https://indefenceofyouthwork.com/2013/09/15/threatening-youth-work-the-illusion-of-outcomes-part-two-the-critique/ [Accessed 16 January 2023].

TRUST Equitable Research Partnership (2017) 'San code of research ethics from South Africa', Available from: trust-project.eu/wp-content/uploads/2017/03/San-Code-of-RESEARCH-Ethics-Booklet-final.pdf

Tuck, E. and Yang, K.W. (2014) 'R-words: Refusing research', in D. Paris and M.T. Winn (eds) *Humanizing Research: Decolonizing Qualitative Inquiry with Youth and Communities*, Los Angeles, CA: Sage, pp 223–49.

PART II

Designing and operationalising methodologies for social justice

5

Using Poststructural Policy Analysis for social justice

Sinead McMahon

Introduction

While many of the contributions in this book focus on participatory and person-centred approaches to social justice research, this chapter instead points to the potential role for critical discourse analysis using documents as a research focus. In recognition of the vital link between engaging in policy work and achieving progressive social change, this chapter focuses on critical policy analysis as a research method for social justice. The chapter begins with some context, linking policy work and social justice and situating policy work and policy practice as key skills for social justice advocacy. It then moves on to introduce the broad field of critical policy analysis and identifies key differences between traditional and critical policy approaches before settling on a closer look at how poststructural policy analysis is conceptualised. From there, the rest of the chapter focuses on one example of how to apply Carol Bacchi's (2009) 'What's the problem represented to be?' (WPR) analytical framework for poststructural policy analysis in social justice research.

Policy work for social justice

Social policy plays a key role in shaping rights and social justice agendas both for progressive and conservative ends. As such, the policy domain is a key site of contest and struggle. In order for social justice practitioners, advocates and activists to achieve social change, they have to understand and engage with policy work. Social justice advocacy refers to 'activities aimed at influencing public policy (including legislation, provision of resources and services) on behalf of communities experiencing poverty, inequality, discrimination, and social exclusion' (Advocacy Initiative, 2012: 5). Internationally, policy advocacy is regarded as an important function of non-profit organisations seeking to give voice to disadvantaged and marginalised groups (Almog-Bar and Schmid, 2014: Evans and Shields, 2014; Fyall and Maguire, 2015). Policy work, including policy analysis, is a vital element of social justice advocacy and campaigning undertaken by large and small non-governmental organisations (NGOs) across the globe, including for example Oxfam International, Save the Children and Amnesty International. In Ireland, it is estimated that around 40 per cent of NGOs are involved in social justice advocacy of some kind, including lobbying, campaigning, submitting policy proposals and pre-budget submissions and meeting with policymakers (Advocacy Initiative, 2012, 2014).

In the social professions where social justice is a core value, practitioners are expected to have the skills and capacity to engage in policy work in support of progressive social change. For example, the UK Community Development National Occupational Standards specify that practitioners should be able to 'support communities who want to bring about positive social change' and engage in 'participative ways to challenge local and national policy decisions' (Federation for Community Development Learning, 2015: 63). In Australia, the Code of Ethics for Social Workers identifies 'advocacy and policy reform initiatives to achieve equitable access to social, economic, environmental and political resources' and 'promoting policies and practices that achieve a fair allocation of social resources' as part of social workers' ethical commitments to human rights and social justice (Australian Association of Social Workers, 2020: 6).

However, there are significant challenges facing organisations and practitioners who wish to engage with policy advocacy for social justice. Community and voluntary organisations both in Ireland and beyond are increasingly expected solely to provide services and find that policy advocacy is being constrained by funding clauses and charity regulations (Harvey, 2013, 2014; Evans and Shields, 2014; Hemmings, 2017; Anheir and Toepler, 2019). Practitioners also find there is a gap between the potential of their policy practice role and the reality of their everyday work (Saxena and Chandrapal, 2022). Given this backdrop, the promotion of critical policy analysis and the importance of engaging in policy research becomes ever more important as a means to understand the policy context of advocacy work itself as well as to pursue and inform social justice campaigns. Indeed, as the environment for policy advocacy is constrained, some policy advocates, less satisfied with conventional policy work, are engaging with more radical and critical policy analysis methods (Diem et al, 2014).

Critical policy approaches

There are many different approaches to policy research and analysis, and these are often divided into traditional and critical camps (see Diem et al, 2014; Bacchi, 2015; Browne et al, 2018). As a field of study, policy research first emerged in the US in the 1950s. From an early stage in its evolution, policy analysis took on a scientific, rationalist approach in close association with programmes such as the 'War on Poverty' (Fischer et al, 2015). Today, this traditional approach retains a powerful hold on policymaking and remains extremely influential among policy elites. Informed by a positivist orientation to knowledge, it is characterised by an emphasis on gathering 'facts' and developing an 'evidence base' to inform policymaking with the 'best' solutions to social problems (Browne et al, 2018).

Critical policy studies began in the 1970s as a challenge to traditional approaches. The realisation that even when informed with the 'best' science, policy efforts still failed to 'solve' endemic societal problems led to efforts to try to better understand the 'messy' elements of policymaking such as the role of social actors, values, power and knowledge. These early interpretivist, critical approaches developed in part out of dissatisfaction with the technocratic instrumentalism of the scientific approach but also out of concern that the power invested in policy 'experts' might undermine democratic ideals (Fischer et al, 2015). Today, critical policy analysis informed by an 'argumentative turn' pays attention to the mediating role of communication in policymaking. It has influenced mainstream approaches that favour broad (not just expert) democratic involvement in policymaking such as citizen panels, participatory and collaborative planning, and deliberative democracy initiatives (Fischer, 2015). The aim of this type of critical policy approach has been to attempt an improvement in policymaking through a 'political rationalist' approach that focuses on getting consensus between different social actors by taking account of differently held ideologies and values in the policy process (Shaw, 2010). From a social justice perspective, the appeal to broaden policymaking to include the voices of those traditionally silenced, marginalised or oppressed in public and social policy is an important contribution presented by this type of critical policy work.

There has also emerged a 'discursive turn' in critical policy studies (Fairclough, 2013). The emphasis on analysing discourse as part of policy research is a key characteristic of poststructural policy analysis. In their account of the evolution of critical policy studies, Fischer et al suggest that 'the influence of poststructuralism in critical policy studies has been relatively recent, [but] it is now one of the key theoretical orientations in the field' (2015: 10). In this approach to critical policy research, there is a focus on analysing policy discourse to examine, for example: how power operates in policy to produce unequal effects; how policy discourse constructs social 'problems' in certain ways; how policy and policymaking is itself a discourse constitutive of governing; how certain kinds of knowledge and expertise are authorised in policy discourse; how people as policy subjects are produced differently and unequally through categorisations used in policy discourse; how policy discourse produces effects that have material impacts for certain social groups; or how dominant discourses are elevated and counter-discourses are subjugated in policy statements and proposals. From a social justice perspective, the merit of discursive-oriented, poststructural policy approaches is to call into question the 'taken-for-granted' assumptions that pervade policy and policymaking that may 'reinforce the very problems they seek to alleviate' (Allan and Tolbert, 2019: 137). As such, it can act as a critical thinking tool for use alongside reflexive praxis and activism for change (Diem et al, 2014).

Poststructural policy analysis

There are different accounts of the potential of poststructural perspectives in critical policy studies (for example, Howarth and Griggs, 2015; Lövbrand and Stripple, 2015), but the remainder of this chapter will focus specifically on Poststructural Policy Analysis (PPA) as advanced by Australian academics Bacchi and Goodwin (2016) and Bacchi's (2009) associated analytical framework WPR. Bacchi and Goodwin argue that PPA 'provides an important vehicle for questioning how governing takes place', and they advocate PPA as 'a form of critical analysis that allows a refreshing scepticism toward the full range of things commonly associated with policy' (2016: 3). The emphasis on trying to understand how policy works to govern is a key analytical focus for PPA, with implications for how policy is conceptualised and analysed. It also has implications for use in social justice work. The PPA approach and the associated WPR guide for policy analysis have been applied to social justice concerns internationally including research examining policy issues related to the World Health Organization, the World Bank and the International Labour Organization and to issues such as gender inequality, migration and economic policy (see case studies cited in Bacchi and Goodwin, 2016).

Conceptualising and analysing: policy as a technology of governing

PPA is influenced by Foucault and governmentality theory (Bacchi and Goodwin, 2016). Governing refers to 'any more or less calculated and rational activity, undertaken by a multiplicity of authorities and agencies, employing a variety of techniques and forms of knowledge, that seeks to shape conduct' (Dean, 1999: 11). Governing involves the use of technologies of power as well as rationalities or ways of thinking that mobilise power in the form of knowledge (Dean, 1999). There are a vast range of technologies and rationalities that might be used to govern at any particular time and place, but the analysis of policy, given its ascribed role in shaping rules and regulations for conduct, offers a rich source for governmental analysis. As such, governmentality approaches offer 'the most visible questioning of "policy"' (Bacchi and Goodwin, 2016: 8). It appears obvious to conceptualise policy as a technique for governing: after all, many policies are made and promoted by governments, and in a conventional sense policy is understood as a practical way for governments to address social problems. But in poststructural approaches the very idea that modern society and governments take it for granted that policy and policymaking is a 'normal' part of societal problem solving is itself a point of analysis. For example, Bacchi (2016) examines the historical development of policy methods in health, illustrating the normalising of evidence-based approaches underpinned by positivist and critical realist paradigms. In her analysis, many of these dominant health policy models downplay the politics of policy and fail to offer the potential for justice:

> The political focus in these accounts becomes *how we can influence people to behave in desired / 'desirable' ways* instead of how we can produce a just society ... some of these models, specifically those associated with realist evaluation, may actively undermine those justice goals by closing off the space to consider how 'problems' are constituted in policies. (Bacchi, 2016: 8, emphasis in original)

To research policy as a governing technology offers an important field of enquiry for those concerned with understanding how power and governing operate and what this might mean for social justice concerns.

Conceptualising and analysing: policy as discourse

Poststructural perspectives establish discourse as playing a key role in how governing works and in how our conduct, ways of thinking, speaking and acting are shaped. Discourse can be defined in different ways depending on the theoretical orientation. In a poststructural approach, discourse can be understood as something broader than just linguistics and as including 'ways of thinking and speaking about aspects of reality' that help to 'order reality in a particular way' (Cheek, 2012). While many discourses operate in society, they do not all hold the same authority. Some discourses are so dominant they achieve a taken-for-granted truth status that makes them invisible and difficult to question. Dominant discourses help to render 'reality', making it visible and understandable to us in a particular way that makes it almost impossible to think in any other way or to accept there could be alternative knowledge that might provide different realities or truth. Power and knowledge play a supporting role in this (see also McGarry's chapter in this volume). Discourse, as a way of thinking and speaking about reality, is based on certain kinds of knowledge authorised through the exercise of power. Power flows through society, and as social actors take up dominant discourses, these discourses and knowledges are continually reproduced as dominant ways of thinking and speaking (Cheek, 2012). Knowledge supports the exercise of power, while the exercise of power helps to produce knowledge seen to be true or common sense (Alvesson and Skolberg, 2009).

In PPA, there is a considerable focus on analysing policy as discourse (Bacchi and Goodwin, 2016). Analysing policy as discourse involves making a distinction between 'policy as text' and 'policy as discourse' (Ball, 1993, 2015). Policy as text refers to the content – the language and words used in policy. Policy as discourse refers to context – to a much broader analytical framework, including language and the historical and cultural context of policy as well as the knowledges that inform policy and its meaning. Policy is not just a set of words on paper or in a speech; it also reflects and produces broader social practices of power/knowledge. Analysing policy as discourse provides the opportunity to examine the governing techniques and rationalities that are constituted in policy as well as the operation of power/knowledge. For example, 'value for money' is an economic knowledge accepted to be common sense, and politicians today often reference the appeal for 'value for money' to justify difficult budget decisions. From a policy as discourse perspective, what is interesting here is questioning how 'value for money' ideas became common sense, what kinds of knowledge and expertise informed this 'truth', how did these ideas gain 'truth status', and how economic knowledges like this shape the thinking and conduct of policymakers and social justice workers. In researching policy as discourse, we might also be interested in the role that policy plays in shaping, carrying, promoting and producing 'value for money' as a common-sense knowledge. In addition, we might look at the elevation of economic experts and economic theories in the production of policy alongside paying attention to the absence of alternative discourse such as an ethics of care. Further, we might also analyse the productive effects of policy as discourse. Policy does not just reflect reality, or dominant discourses, but also plays a role in reproducing or constituting reality, and so has effects (Bacchi and Goodwin, 2016). Here, for example, we might ask how 'value for money' policy discourse has material or lived effects for the funding of social justice organisations and if economic calculation can account for the contributions that social justice work make to the health of democracy.

Conceptualising and analysing: policy as problematisation

Problematisation is an important analytical device for exploring and understanding governing (Dean, 1999; Miller and Rose, 2008). Whenever an issue is called into question or is *problematised*, it is made to take on a problematic character, and once problematic the issue is open to intervention and solution. Through problematisation, any part of life can be 'transformed into a zone that is considered to need governing' (Miller and Rose,

2008: 14). For Bacchi (2009), governing is based on problematisations which act as 'framing mechanisms' for deciding on what is and is not to be governed: 'Problematizations thus become part of how we are governed. That is, governing takes place *through* the ways in which "problems" are constituted in policies. Put in other words, we are governed through *problematizations*, rather than through policies, signaling the importance of critically interrogating problem representations' (Bacchi, 2016: 9). Recognising and analysing problematisations is of key importance in governmental analysis because they help to locate when 'actors and agents of all sorts must pose the question of how to govern' (Dean, 1999: 27). In PPA, there is a clear deviation from the conventional understanding that policy is a means of providing solutions to existing social problems. As Bacchi explains: 'The premise behind a policy-as-discourse approach is that it is inappropriate to see governments as responding to "problems" that exist "out there" in the community. Rather "problems" are "created" or "given shape" in the very policy proposals that are offered as "responses"' (Bacchi, 2000: 48).

Instead of a focus on problems, there is a focus on analysing policies as types of problematisation (Bacchi, 2000). This means that policies, located as they are in certain times and places, can be understood as problematising an issue as a particular kind of 'problem'. Since every policy proposal for change and every policy 'solution' has, implied within it, a 'problem' to be addressed, policy discourse can be analysed for the work it does to problematise, to constitute and construct 'problems' of a particular kind, and PPA aims to reveal the problematising work of policy and the role it plays in governing conduct (Bacchi and Goodwin, 2016). The centrality of problematisation to PPA is illustrated in the title given to Bacchi's (2009) associated analytical framework 'What's the problem represented to be?' (discussed in detail in the next section) that can be used to guide PPA.

Conceptualising and analysing: policy research as political

Wetherell (2001) points to a tension between the ontological positioning of poststructural discourse analysts and their capacity to occupy an activist or politically engaged position. While acknowledging that poststructural analysts, given their commitment to radically questioning what constitutes truth, often face the charge of relativism that can lead to 'political quietism', since 'if there are no truths, then why bother with any critique at all?', she makes clear that 'relativists also have commitments to social movements' (Wetherell, 2001: 394). She suggests that for poststructural analysts a 'politically engaged stance of some kind is probably the most common position' (Wetherell, 2001: 384). Bacchi and Goodwin (2016: 24) similarly address a concern about 'the usefulness of post-structural analysis', making reference to the challenge that taking a poststructural stance means rejecting any kind of 'right' course of action and that the outcomes of PPA research do not produce 'precise recommendations'. Can this sit comfortably with social justice approaches underwritten by an activism and a desire to shape progressive social change? Their answer to the question 'Is it possible to claim to support an egalitarian politics while refusing to advocate specific reforms?' is that the two are indeed compatible and 'necessary to each other' (Bacchi and Goodwin, 2016: 25). There are many examples of the use of PPA and WPR to address social justice issues: Bacchi (2010), for example, examines gender inequality by analysing Irish and Dutch gender mainstreaming policies; Blestas (2007, 2012) analyses poverty as a governmentality; Brodin and Peterson (2019) analyse gender and race issues in equal opportunities policy in Sweden; Dawson et al (2020) examine indigenous groups and disadvantage in policy representations in Australia; Helakorpi et al (2018) critically analyse Traveller and Roma equality in education policy in Scandinavia; and Horsell (2020) examines disability issues in social welfare in Australia. But it is vital to note that in PPA 'social justice', 'human rights' and other forms of egalitarian politics do not escape critical analysis or problematisation (see for example Cruikshank's [1999] critique of empowerment or Meriluoto's [2019] more recent analysis of empowerment and participatory policy decision-making involving service users). All discourses, all reforms and proposals for change (including those of the researcher themselves), whether conservative or progressive, seek to govern conduct in particular ways, and from a poststructural perspective all must be opened up to problematisation in order that there is governing 'with a minimum of domination' (Foucault, 1987: 129, cited in Bacchi and Goodwin, 2016: 24). For these reasons, Bacchi and Goodwin (2016) argue that undertaking PPA research is political work.

There are a number of points to consider in relation to PPA policy research as political work. As a form of research, it involves knowledge production. Knowledge as mentioned earlier is intermeshed with power, so that all knowledge production is political. Rönnblom's (2012: 122) discussion of poststructural research points out that 'methodology matters' since researchers shape reality by the methodological choices they make. How researchers engage with the world, the kinds of research they do, the decisions about what is studied and how, has effects. From a poststructural perspective, research contributes to constructing reality, and it is therefore far from neutral – it is political. Making the decision to engage with PPA policy research is a political one (Bacchi, 2012). The WPR tool (discussed in the next section) used to undertake PPA is a tool for analysing policy as discourse, and Bacchi and Goodwin (2016) argue its main aim is 'making politics visible'. As dominant discourses operate to represent and construct reality and as they become accepted truth and 'common sense', they also help to obscure the existence of alternative discourses and that 'things could be otherwise' (Bacchi, 2009). Analysing policy as discourse involves paying attention to the production of common-sense problems and solutions in policy, paying attention to what is obscured from view, silences and the alternative discourses not present in policy. Undertaking PPA and analysing policy as discourse using WPR helps to reveal, call out and expose hidden problem representations and as such is 'part of a political process of challenge' (Bacchi, 2000: 49). The outcomes and effects of PPA policy research may also be political. WPR as a tool for critical questioning opens up space for analysing how we are governed through problems constructed in policy discourse, and this questioning is a 'strategy for intervention', an act for change (Bacchi, 2009). Though, as mentioned earlier, there is no list of recommendations that emanates from PPA research, the WPR process does offer potential 'opportunities for disruption' (Bacchi, 2009: 44). The work of critically analysing policy as discourse helps to: problematise policy as problematisation; disrupt dominant discourses and certainties about 'problems' that circulate in rationalist policy and policymaking; highlight contradictions and tensions in policy and point to potential harmful effects of policy. For Bacchi and Goodwin (2016: 8), PPA and WPR analysis 'is counter discursive': it is a resistance activity in itself.

Applying PPA: WPR as an analytical tool in social justice research

WPR is an analytical framework that Carol Bacchi (1999, 2009) developed to support poststructural critique. It is one of a small number of poststructural frameworks specifically dedicated to 'the realm of policy' (Bacchi and Goodwin, 2016: 17). The WPR framework consists of a set of seven question prompts to guide PPA. The question prompts are to act more like a 'conceptual checklist' than a strict set of instructions or a 'step by step process' (Goodwin, 2011: 171). There is a great deal of flexibility in using WPR, and Bacchi (2009) recommends using it in a way that best fits the research aims and scope. In some cases, it may be useful to only address one or two prompts, while in other cases application of all seven questions in the framework might be appropriate. Bacchi (2009) also recommends watching out for problem representations that 'nest' within each other, so that more than one cycle of applying the question prompts might be required. The following is a summary of the question prompts adapted from Bacchi (2009) and Bacchi and Goodwin (2016). Some examples of application from previous doctoral work that analysed 'value for money' policy discourse and its effects for Irish social justice organisations who promote equality, social justice and democratic principles in their work with marginalised young people are also provided (McMahon, 2019, 2021).

Question 1: What's the 'problem' represented to be in the selected policy?

The starting point in WPR is to look at the selected policy in an overall sense, treating the policy as problematisation and searching for implied 'problems'. The aim is to identify and clarify how these implied 'problems' are represented in policy discourse. By working backwards from the stated policy recommendations or 'solutions', problem representations become easier to identify. Once the dominant problem representations are identified, they then become the focus of the rest of the WPR analysis.

In the 'value for money' research, the main policy text analysed was a government-produced economic evaluation of funding programmes used to support work with young people via a number of voluntary youth work organisations. The evaluation report concluded with frustration that a reliable 'value for money' assessment could not be carried out because of a range of 'problems' associated with the autonomy of the voluntary organisations and the youth work professionals carrying out the work. Twelve recommendations for reform were provided in the evaluation report as 'solutions' that would help to create top-down 'governance chains' ensuring much stricter regulation of voluntary organisations receiving state funding for youth work. Working backwards, the research found that the dominant problem in the 'value for money' policy discourse represented youth work agencies and workers as having too much discretion in the work and too little desire or capacity to produce reliable quantitative data about the economic value or impact of their work with young people. The WPR analysis pointed to a number of problem representations that were nested or layered together within the 'value for money' policy discourse including representations of youth work organisations as ungovernable, as risky, as underperforming and as lacking evidence of their impact.

Question 2: What assumptions underpin this representation of the 'problem'?

To address the second WPR question prompt, the researcher needs to analyse policy discourse looking for the assumptions or knowledges that underpin the conceptual logic that the problem representation rests on or rather the 'unexamined ways of thinking' that make it possible to see the 'problem' in this way. Paying attention to policy language as well as the production of binaries and categories that are used to produce the 'problem' in a particular way is important here.

For example, the doctoral research examined the assumptions and knowledge underpinning the logic of representing social justice organisations as problems of value for money and underperformance. The WPR analysis illustrated how by using an economic evaluation device like a value for money assessment, government policy produced an economically framed problematisation of youth social justice organisations as various types of economic performers and service providers. The main assumptions embedded in these problem representations were that the 'success' of youth social justice organisations and workers should be motivated and measured solely by economic thinking and knowledge.

Question 3: How has this representation of the 'problem' come about?

The concern of this WPR question is to trace the history of how the problem representation has come about. By searching historically through earlier connected policy, it may become possible to illustrate the contested nature of the problem representation over time, thereby disrupting the certainty it appears to have in current policy. This involves finding and analysing a potentially large volume of interacting policy texts.

In the doctoral research project, it was necessary to understand how youth social justice organisations suddenly became a target for 'value for money' reforms. This meant tracing back through hundreds of contemporary and historical government policy texts. The WPR analysis found various interacting policy threads that seemed to influence the production of youth social justice organisations as problematic in terms of governance, risk and underperformance, including broader policy reforms of children's services with a heightened focus on risk and evidence as well as public outrage as a number of financial 'scandals' in the voluntary sector were exposed. However, the main policy development influencing the production of youth social justice organisations as problems of 'value for money' was found to be an austerity-inspired public sector reform programme that was committed to risk management and improving performance in all areas of state spending.

Question 4: What is left unproblematic in this problem representation? What are the silences? Can the 'problem' be conceptualised differently?

This question supports the analyst to think broadly about the limits of problem representations by identifying not just what has been said but more importantly what has not been said or left out in policy discourse. To undertake this analysis, it is useful to draw on resources generated in questions 2 and 3 and also draw from a significant range of secondary literature (current, historical and international) so as to identify silences through comparison. The analyst is also encouraged by this prompt to find alternatives, to re-problematise and discuss other ways it might be possible to represent the 'problem' other than the one produced in the current policy.

In the 'value for money' research, it became clear that the dominant economic thinking and assumptions pervading the policy discourse failed to take account of very important social justice perspectives. For example, some of the key values of the work such as the voluntary participation of young people, the open inclusion of all young people and the idea of empowering young people to take part in decision-making about the design of youth work programmes were ignored or silenced in the economic evaluation. Instead, this values-based approach was produced in the policy discourse as problematic because it meant too much uncertainty (increasing risks) and could not be measured against any standardised set of outcomes. The WPR analysis also revealed that an alternative problem representation that was completely ignored by the policymakers was the 'problem' of how to ensure quality in youth social justice organisations that had undergone a 30 per cent cut in funding over the three years prior to the 'value for money' assessment.

Question 5: What effects are produced by this representation of the 'problem'?

This question seeks to bring attention to the potential implications of the problem representation that is outlined in the selected policy. This aspect of analysis goes beyond identifying and analysing the problem representations to illustrate the uneven effects of policy discourse and the potential harms and disadvantages that are created by the way in which 'problems' are represented in policy. There are three types of interacting effects ranging from symbolic to material that should be considered, including discursive effects, subjectification effects and lived effects. Discursive effects refer to the limits that are set by certain problem representations on how we think about 'problems'. Subjectification effects refer to the ways people are called to imagine themselves as a result of policy discourse and problem representation. The issue of how people are categorised so that they can be governed in different ways and how some groups may be blamed or made responsible for 'problems' is of interest here. Lived effects are the impacts of problem representations on people's lives, for example financial, emotional or physical.

In the doctoral research, it was found that by producing youth social justice organisations as problems of governance, risk and underperformance, the 'value for money' policy discourse had harmful effects. Discursively, the policy discourse created significant suspicion about the value of the work of youth social justice organisations as well as their accountability to the public taxpayer. 'Value for money' catchphrases and calculations such as 'unit costs', 'social return on investment' and 'outcomes measurement' got taken up in the discourse of organisations and workers while silencing older values commitments to 'start where young people are at'. The 'value for money' policy discourse also had subjectification effects, creating new categories for youth social justice organisations as 'good' and 'weak' performers that clearly pitted them against each other, thereby eliciting new desires to prove performance through competitive comparison and ranking. There were lived effects too, in that the 'value for money' policy discourse opened up reform solutions that meant radical changes to funding arrangements. Recommendations included that youth social justice organisations would have to conduct work with young people according to pre-established outcomes and produce quantified, database-friendly reports as well as agree to new inspection regimes including unannounced visits to youth projects. All of these effects interlinked to create new disciplinary modes and methods for governing youth social justice work that are likely to delimit the potential for open, creative and democratic modes of work with young people.

Question 6: How and where has this representation of the 'problem' been produced, disseminated and defended? How can it be disrupted or replaced?

This question focuses first on analysing how problem representations have achieved their possibility, authorisation and legitimacy. This involves identifying practices that helped to support and promote dominant ideas about the 'problem'. State and national as well as international non-state actors may play a role here, a range of expertise may play a role including policy entrepreneurs and policy actors, policy travel across different jurisdictions may play a role as well as certain knowledges like science, economics and psychology, for example. Secondly, the analyst is prompted to consider how dominant problem representations in policy might be contested and resisted. Resistance analysis might include finding contradictions and tensions in policy discourse that might be exploited, drawing on the multiple discourses at play that reveal alternative ways of thinking about the 'problem' that have been ignored in policy discourse and using other dominant discourses to re-problematise the 'problem'.

In the 'value for money' research, by analysing the main policy text and the hundreds of interacting policy texts (linked to question 3), various authorising actors and agencies could be identified. For example, it became obvious that similar 'value for money' reforms had taken place in England, and there were many overlapping research references, authors, research agencies and approaches to economic and outcomes measurement shared between two policy jurisdictions. Many of the research agencies quoted and used could be linked together as part of a global evidence industry with ties to strategic American philanthropy and with expertise in 'scientific' evaluation methods. In drawing on alternative dominant discourses, the research pointed to some contradictions in government youth policy that promoted the United Nations Convention on the Rights of the Child (UNCRC). In accordance with the UNCRC, the Irish government commits to promoting children's participation in the services they are part of. The discourse of children's rights was largely absent from the economic 'value for money' discourse and could be used to illustrate competing ways of understanding the work of youth social justice organisations.

Question 7: Self-problematisation – apply this list of questions to your own problem representations

The work here is slightly different from the other prompts. Here it is the researcher's own problematisation that is to be problematised. This requires reflexivity and an analysis of the potential governing effects of the research work, thinking about questions 1 to 6 as they might apply to what is being said or proposed by the researcher.

Applying PPA: stages in the research process

This final section describes one possible way of operationalising the WPR research process. The focus here is on researching policy documents as a sole method, but WPR can also be used in research combining policy analysis and interviews (Bacchi and Goodwin, 2016). Despite the neat presentation and sequencing of WPR as a set of seven prompts, the experience of putting WPR into practice is not at all linear. Thinking about the movements of a spinning top, WPR application works more like a spiral research process that involves an entry point, moving backwards, forwards and around as well as moving inwards and outwards (McMahon, 2019). The following considers some key points in data gathering, data analysis and write up in a WPR research process.

Determining an entry point for WPR involves selecting one or more policy texts to begin with. Written policy texts are an obvious starting point for WPR and can include 'organisational files and records, legislation, judicial decisions, bills, speeches, interview transcripts, media statements, budgets, program contracts, research reports and statistical data' (Bacchi and Goodwin, 2016: 18). It is important that the selected text(s) have a clear rationale for selection: they may be chosen because they stand out as unusual examples of 'a moment of crisis' in governing or because they have the appearance of being quite mundane (Goodwin, 2011). From here, moving forwards, backwards and around the first text chosen, it is necessary to identify and find a set of related documents. Working backwards involves searching for historical documents that enable a genealogical tracing of how the policy text chosen came into being. Researchers can then work outwards from the chosen text to search for contemporary interacting policy documents. They must also work around the chosen policy text to find as much related secondary literature as possible. In practical terms, though WPR focuses on analysing one or two main policy texts, the researcher can end up with many hundreds of related texts to find, read and analyse in order to resource the WPR analytical process. Decisions must be made to 'map the territory' of a WPR process, meaning that, depending on the scope of the research, some things may be included and others left out, and though this is 'an interpretive act' (Goodwin, 2011), it is important to catalogue, describe and provide a rationale for the search and selection process. Deciding on date ranges, geographical spread and whether to focus solely on government policy texts or to include the policy work of non-state actors will help to put boundaries on the research.

After gathering the chosen documents, the process of data analysis begins with moving inwards, involving detailed reading and becoming very familiar with the texts. Bacchi (2009) does not refer to any process of coding in WPR, but it can be useful in the early stages of analysis to use some forms of inductive (open-ended) coding alongside deductive (theory-driven) coding (Allan and Tolbert, 2019). Though WPR is not a linguistic analytic device, attention to language used and counting the frequency of terms used are useful to aid analysis (Bacchi, 2011). A focus on language used to problematise or solve – for example 'problems', 'propose', 'solve', 'should', 'could', 'would' – is useful, as is paying attention to any recommendations made. Once familiar with the texts, you can begin to move outwards to really engage with WPR analysis itself. Developing a WPR template is useful here so that as each document is read and analysed, important points can be identified and recorded. The template might include sections for problems/solutions, knowledges, genealogical links, silences, implications/effects, expertise/policy actors, contradictions and alternatives. This can be a paper exercise or some type of computer-aided approach. Decisions will need to be made about how many rounds of WPR will be applied in the research process, taking account of the research scope and the time resources available as well as consideration of how 'nested' some problem representations are within each other. The first round of WPR means applying the WPR prompts to the chosen policy text (entry point) to look for the *dominant* problem representations. Once these are identified, a second round of WPR analysis can be applied to each individual problem representation and so on. This process of WPR analysis will also be influenced by the focus of the research. For example, if the study is looking at gender inequality, then the WPR analysis will be guided at a conceptual level by this, so that the WPR prompts act as a lens to examine the problem representation of gender and gender inequality.

Poststructural perspectives reject the idea of 'objective' truth-finding in research, and so there are no traditional research 'findings' sections presented in the research write up. The WPR framework can be used as a structuring device for representing the study's outcomes, but it is not necessary to use it in this way. There are no 'rules' for representing a WPR analysis, and the researcher will need to shape the write up in a way that best conveys the research story based on the social justice orientation of the analytical work undertaken. For a PPA study, there will be a focus on describing the policy texts that were analysed, focusing on policy as discourse and policy as problematisation, and it is common to use extracts from policy texts to illuminate the analysis for the reader. It is also helpful to draw upon a wide range of policy literature, as well as literature associated with governmentality perspectives and the research topic in order to provide depth in the analysis. There is no commitment to produce any kind of final, fixed or 'true' version of discourse in PPA, and the researcher will need to reflect on their own positioning in the research and their own problem representations within the write up.

Conclusion

It is likely this chapter stands in contrast to many of the surrounding chapters that focus on interpretivist research methods where people, such as those from oppressed, marginalised or minority groups and communities, might be engaged in interviews, narratives and participatory methods, so that their lived experiences and voices might be brought to bear on efforts to achieve social justice. Undertaking a PPA has implications for the conduct of social justice research because it requires a shift from focusing on researching people and their views on policy as well as their experiences of policy and policy enactment to a focus on researching discourse and the 'vita activa' of texts and documents (Prior, 2016). For poststructuralist policy analysts, this shift is deliberate: it aims to problematise 'the work that policy does' (Bacchi, 2009), illustrating an interest in the constituting power of policy and standing in contrast to those who might view policy as neutral or even as 'boring' piles of paper. In PPA, the researcher is emboldened to return the problematising gaze of policy and policymakers back on to policy itself so as to disrupt the taken-for-granted assumptions that policy is about solving social problems and that it can be a progressive vehicle for the achievement of social justice aims. PPA instead enables the social justice researcher to engage in a deeper critical analysis of the role of policy in constructing social problems in particular ways and potentially undermining social justice principles and values. Ultimately, this type of research approach offers a means of theorising that can help to inform activism for social justice change and to create knowledge for use in social justice policy and campaign work. Undertaking PPA also has implications for doing social justice research that enriches the analytic connections between policy and practice. This was illustrated by the 'value for money' research example outlined earlier in the chapter showing how contemporary policy works to (re)form the practices of social justice practitioners and organisations on the ground. The example also illustrated the potential that a PPA has for revealing 'policy travel' (Bacchi,

2009) or the international connections between policy developments in one jurisdiction and another as the imposition of 'value for money' policies on social justice organisations could be traced beyond Ireland, and the kinds of economic knowledges required in these policies had also travelled globally.

As this chapter closes, it is hoped that readers who are interested in social justice research will have been inspired to consider the importance and the potential of policy research generally and of poststructural policy analysis in particular. Bacchi (2009: 44) clearly signals the normative commitments of PPA and its potential for social justice research and action when she states that 'some problem representations benefit the members of some groups at the expense of others' and that PPA 'takes the side of those who are harmed'.

Further resources

Bacchi and Goodwin (2016) *Poststructural Policy Analysis: A Guide to Practice* provides many examples of the application of WPR to policy areas in health, migration and gender equality. The book also contains an appendix devoted to doing interviews using a poststructural approach.

Bacchi's (2009) book *Analysing Policy: What's the Problem Represented to Be?* is a key resource for anyone starting out with WPR as it provides detailed advice and guidance on its potential use.

Bacchi's website https://carolbacchi.com provides access to many different resources including videos of WPR workshops that provide an overview of WPR and how to use it.

References

Advocacy Initiative (2014) 'Breaking through: The future of social justice advocacy', Dublin: Advocacy Initiative.

Advocacy Initiative and CM Advice (2012) 'Mapping of social justice advocacy in Ireland', Dublin: Advocacy Initiative.

Allan, E.J. and Tolbert, A.R. (2019) 'Advancing social justice with policy discourse analysis', in K. Strunk and L. Locke (eds) *Research Methods for Social Justice and Equity in Education*, Cham: Palgrave Macmillan, pp 137–49.

Almog-Bar, M. and Schmid, H. (2014) 'Advocacy activities of nonprofit human service organizations: A critical review', *Nonprofit and Voluntary Sector Quarterly*, 43(1): 11–35.

Alvesson, M. and Skoldberg, K. (2009) *Reflexive Methodology: New Vistas for Qualitative Research* (2nd edn), London: Sage.

Anheier, H.K. and Toepler, S. (2019) 'Policy neglect: The true challenge to the nonprofit sector', *Nonprofit Policy Forum*, 10(4): 20190041. https://doi.org/10.1515/npf-2019-0041

Australian Association of Social Workers (2020) 'Code of ethics for social workers', Melbourne: AASW.

Bacchi, C. (1999) *Women, Policy and Politics*, Thousand Oaks, CA: Sage.

Bacchi, C. (2000) 'Policy as discourse: What does it mean? Where does it get us?', *Discourse: Studies in the Cultural Politics of Education*, 21(1): 45–57.

Bacchi, C. (2009) *Analysing Policy: What's the Problem Represented to Be?*, Frenchs Forest, NSW: Pearson Australia.

Bacchi, C. (2010) 'Poststructuralism, discourse and problematization: Implications for gender mainstreaming', *Kvinder, Køn & Forskning*, 4: 62–72.

Bacchi, C. (2011) 'WPR workshop' [video online], Available from: https://www.adelaide.edu.au/graduate-research/career-development/online-training/resources-tools/the-wpr-approach#wpr-workshop [Accessed 12 February 2022].

Bacchi, C. (2012) 'Strategic interventions and ontological politics: Research as political practice', in A. Bletsas and C. Beasley (eds) *Engaging with Carol Bacchi: Strategic Interventions and Exchanges*, Adelaide: University of Adelaide Press, pp 141–56.

Bacchi, C. (2015) 'The turn to problematization: Political implications of contrasting interpretive and post-structural adaptations', *Open Journal of Political Science*, 5(1): 1–12.

Bacchi, C. (2016) 'Problematizations in health policy: Questioning how "problems" are constituted in policies', *Sage Open*, 6(2): 1–16.

Bacchi, C. and Goodwin, S. (2016) *Post-structural Policy Analysis: A Guide to Practice*, New York: Palgrave Pivot.

Ball, S.J. (1993) 'What is policy? Texts, trajectories and toolboxes', *Discourse: Studies in the Cultural Politics of Education*, 13(2): 10–17.

Ball, S.J. (2015) 'What is policy? 21 years later: Rreflections on the possibilities of policy research', *Discourse: Studies in the Cultural Politics of Education*, 36(3): 306–13.

Bletsas, A. (2007) 'Contesting representations of poverty: Ethics and evaluation', *Policy & Society*, 16(3): 65–83.

Blestas, A. (2012) 'Spaces between: Elaborating the theoretical underpinnings of the "WPR" approach and its significance for contemporary scholarship', in A. Bletsas and C. Beasley (eds) *Engaging with Carol Bacchi: Strategic Interventions and Exchanges*, Adelaide: University of Adelaide Press, pp 37–53.

Brodin, H. and Peterson, E. (2019) 'Equal opportunities? Gendering and racialising the politics of entrepreneurship in Swedish eldercare', *NORA – Nordic Journal of Feminist and Gender Research*, 28(2): 99–112.

Browne, J., Coffey, B., Cook, K., Meiklejohn, S. and Palermo, C. (2018) 'A guide to policy analysis as a research method', *Health Promotion International*, 34(5): 1032–1044.

Cheek, J. (2012) 'Foucauldian discourse analysis', in L.M. Given (ed) *The Sage Encyclopaedia of Qualitative Methods*, Thousand Oaks, CA: Sage Publications.

Cruikshank, B. (1999) *The Will to Empower: Democratic Citizens and Other Subjects*, Ithaca, NY: Cornell University Press.

Dawson, J., Augoustinos, M., Sjoberg, D., Canuto, K., Glover, K. and Rumbold, A. (2020) 'Closing the gap: Examining how the problem of Aboriginal and Torres Strait Islander disadvantage is represented in policy', *Australian Journal of Social Issues*, 56(4): 522–38.

Dean, M. (1999) *Governmentality: Power and Rule in Modern Society*, London: Sage.

Diem, S., Young, M.D., Welton, A.D., Mansfield, K.C. and Lee, P.L. (2014) 'The intellectual landscape of critical policy analysis', *International Journal of Qualitative Studies in Education*, 27(9): 1068–90.

Evans, B. and Shields, J. (2014) 'Nonprofit engagement with provincial policy officials: The case of NGO policy voice in Canadian immigrant settlement services', *Policy and Society*, 33: 117–27.

Fairclough, N. (2013) 'Critical discourse analysis and critical policy studies', *Critical Policy Studies*, 7(2): 177–97.

Federation for Community Development Learning (2015) 'Community development national occupational standards', Availabe from: https://clds tandardscouncil.org.uk/wp-content/uploads/CDNOStandards2015.pdf

Fischer, F. (2015) 'In pursuit of usable knowledge: Critical policy analysis and the argumentative turn', in F. Fischer, D. Torgerson, A. Durnová and M. Orsini (eds) *Handbook of Critical Policy Studies*, Cheltenham: Edward Elgar, pp 47–66.

Fischer, F., Torgerson, D., Durnová, A. and Orsini, M. (2015) 'Introduction to critical policy studies', in F. Fischer, D. Torgerson, A. Durnová and M. Orsini (eds) *Handbook of Critical Policy Studies*, Cheltenham: Edward Elgar, pp 1–24.

Fyall, R. and McGuire, M. (2015) 'Advocating for policy change in nonprofit coalitions', *Nonprofit and Voluntary Sector Quarterly*, 44(6): 1274–91.

Goodwin, S. (2011) 'Analysing policy as discourse: Methodological advances in policy', in P. Freebody, L. Markauskaite and J. Irwin (eds) *Methodological Choice and Design*, Dordrecht: Springer, pp 167–80.

Harvey, B. (2013) 'Funding dissent: Research into the impact on advocacy of state funding of voluntary and community organisations', Dublin: Advocacy Initiative.

Harvey, B. (2014) 'Are we paying for that?', Dublin: Advocacy Initiative.

Helakorpi, J., Lappalainen, S. and Mietola, R. (2018) 'Equality in the making? Roma and Traveller minority policies and basic education in three Nordic countries', *Scandinavian Journal of Educational Research*, 64(1): 52–69.

Hemmings, M. (2017) 'The constraints on voluntary sector voice in a period of continued austerity', *Voluntary Sector Review*, 8(1): 41–66.

Horsell, C. (2020) 'Problematising disability: A critical policy analysis of the Australian national disability insurance scheme', *Australian Social Work*, 76(1): 47–59.

Howarth, D. and Griggs, S. (2015) 'Poststructuralist discourse theory and critical policy studies: Interests, identities and policy change', in F. Fischer, D. Torgerson, A. Durnová and M. Orsini (eds) *Handbook of Critical Policy Studies*, Cheltenham: Edward Elgar, pp 111–27.

Lövbrand, E. and Stripple, J. (2015) 'Foucault and critical policy studies', in F. Fischer, D. Torgerson, A. Durnová and M. Orsini (eds) *Handbook of Critical Policy Studies*, Cheltenham: Edward Elgar, pp 92–108.

McMahon, S. (2019) 'Governing youth work through problems: A WPR analysis of the "Value for money and policy review of youth programmes"', PhD thesis, National University of Ireland, Maynooth.

McMahon, S. (2021) 'What's the problem with Irish youth work?', *Youth & Policy Journal*, https://www.youthandpolicy.org/articles/whats-the-prob lem-irish-youth-work/

Meriluoto, T. (2019) 'The will to not be empowered (according to your rules)': Resistance in Finnish participatory social policy', *Critical Social Policy*, 39(1): 87–107.

Miller, P. and Rose, N. (2008) *Governing the Present: Administering Economic, Social and Personal Life*, Cambridge: Polity Press.

Prior, L. (2016) 'Using documents in social research', in D. Silverman (ed) *Qualitative Research*, London: Sage, pp 171–86.

Rönnblom, M. (2012) 'Post-structural comparative politics: Acknowledging the political effects of research', in A. Bletsas and C. Beasley (eds) *Engaging with Carol Bacchi: Strategic Interventions and Exchanges*, Adelaide: University of Adelaide Press, pp 121–40.

Saxena, A. and Chandrapal, S. (2022) 'Social work and policy practice: Understanding the role of social workers', *British Journal of Social Work*, 52(3): 1632–42.

Shaw, S.E. (2010) 'Reaching the parts that other theories and methods can't reach: How and why a policy-as-discourse approach can inform health-related policy', *Health*, 14(2): 196–212.

Wetherell, M. (2001) 'Debates in discourse research', in M. Wetherell, S. Taylor and S.J. Yates (eds) *Discourse Theory and Practice: A Reader*, Milton Keynes: Open University, pp 380–400.

6

Research with deaf and hard-of-hearing women: reimagining social justice as flourishing

Grainne Meehan

Introduction

In this chapter, I explore social justice research carried out with deaf and hard-of-hearing women in Ireland. I aim to contribute to understandings of how methodologies for social justice research with deaf and disabled people can be designed and operationalised in order to develop an agenda for change both within the Irish context and beyond. In particular, I delve into the opportunities that are presented for reimagining radical possibilities through research and for achieving social justice by problematising and displacing common concepts used in social policy discourse in relation to disability and deafness. I also set out some ways by which research can be designed to illustrate how equality, participation and inclusion by design can take place within research – ethics in practice. This is not to say 'one size fits all' – there is no prescribed approach to take in research with deaf people/signing communities, and as Young and Temple (2014: 58) write, the 'fundamental issue of heterogeneity has a range of implications for ethical research practice'.

This chapter draws on my doctoral research exploring sexuality and sexual health with deaf and hard-of-hearing women. Deaf women's narratives and knowledge have been neglected on a national and international scale, and thus we possess limited understandings of deaf women's lives in Ireland and elsewhere (Ladd, 2003; Coogan and O'Leary, 2018). I was inspired by bell hooks (1989) urging us to look to perspectives 'from the margins' and to reimagine 'from the margins, from spaces of resistance' (1989: 20). The issue of who should be doing research within different communities is a contested issue (Young and Temple, 2014) and one that I will touch on again in this chapter. It is an issue that any researcher carrying out social justice research with marginalised groups must be reflexive in relation to. My experiences as a deaf woman formed a strong starting point for the research framework used, and my values as a community worker – collectivity, community empowerment, human rights, equality, anti-discrimination, social justice and sustainable development and participation (CWI, 2016) – informed how I engaged with, designed and operationalised my research. It is important to mention that I did not grow up using Irish Sign Language (ISL). I attended mainstream school settings and used English as my first language. In my 20s, I began to mix with deaf groups and the Deaf Community and also began to learn ISL. Thus I did not grow up as a 'native' sign language user. Therefore, my positionality in relation to my research and the research participants is very much shaped by this lens, and my biography was discussed with research participants.

The politics of doing

It is also pertinent to reflect on the methodology used and acknowledge that first and foremost my research was grounded in the constructivist view that deaf knowledge of the world, understanding the deaf lens (the deaf way of seeing the world) and deaf ways of thinking and knowing (for example, not viewing oneself through a disability lens but a cultural and linguistic one) is formed through seeking deaf accounts of deaf lives (Holcomb, 2010). This standpoint emerged from groundbreaking work considering the language and culture of deaf people that challenged hearing ways of seeing deaf people (see Padden, 1980; Padden and Humphries, 2005; Wolsey et al, 2017): 'Deaf epistemology is focused on visual access, visual learning and visual language' (Wolsey et al, 2017: 574). It inspires academics to challenge audism when producing knowledge (deClerck, 2010). On the other hand, it was also crucial to bear in mind that deafness is made up of multiple, intersecting, embodied identities (Hauser et al, 2010) that lead to diverse ways of being deaf and encountering other deaf bodies. Not all deaf people will use or want to use visual language and visual learning, and that must be navigated during research with deaf people. Embedding deaf epistemologies into research with deaf people is imperative but must be carried out in line with taking a nonessentialist and non-positivist, deaf-inclusive approach that understands that not all deaf participants in a research project may regard themselves as fully culturally deaf (Young and Temple, 2014). This is a useful stance to work from as it allows for a focus on the diverse lives of deaf people, pays attention to subjectivity, reimagines what it is to be deaf and articulates resistance to hearing and traditional scientific ways of viewing the deaf experience.

Blending deaf and feminist standpoint epistemology

In my research with deaf women, I sought to foreground and value the voices of deaf women in relation to marginalised and overlooked experiences of deafness and sexuality. Exploring the intersection between sexuality, gender and deafness was strengthened by rooting the research in deaf epistemologies (Kusters et al, 2017) and feminist standpoint epistemology (Harding, 2004 [1993]). Deaf feminist standpoint theory is important for two critical reasons. First, it allows for exploration of dominant ideologies shaping deaf women's everyday lives and, secondly, places value on moving beyond traditional conceptual frameworks to situated knowledge where deaf women from different social locations become 'the subjects – the authors – of knowledge' (Harding, 2004 [1993]): 4). It considers experiences of oppression and structural inequalities of power and explores deaf issues from multiple perspectives in order to produce a 'more realistic form of knowledge' (Fawcett, 2000: 4). Using deaf feminist standpoint theory means also considering how gender, sexuality and deafness work together from multiple perspectives. This understanding built from situated narratives can be used as a resource to challenge and transform unjust dominant, hegemonic normative discourses. Given the limited body of research from deaf feminist perspectives, using this approach presents new directions for knowledge production and contributes to the advancement of deaf feminist methodology.

Disrupting ways of knowing

Troubling common concepts linked with any topic of study is a core part of forming the conceptual framework of a research project. It is this integral step that propels us into embracing, reimagining and advancing new ways of knowing. My research on sexuality with deaf and hard-of-hearing women explored the deliberate use of positive language and frameworks in order to challenge normative ways of perceiving and locating deaf women and disability that are uncritically grounded in notions of 'deficit', audism[1] and ableism[2] (Humphries cited in Bauman, 2004: 240; Campbell, 2009; Joharchi and Clark, 2014). I did so to ensure I broadened the horizons of the research to allow for possibilities of seeking out alternatives, new ways of knowing and disrupting our ways of knowing in relation to deaf women and sexuality (Kennedy, 1999). Deaf scholars have begun to shift their conceptual language and lens towards the value and positive attributes of being deaf. Examples of this are concepts of 'deaf value' (Freidner, 2015) and 'deaf gain' (Bauman and Murray, 2009). I aligned myself with this turn in the scholarship and contend that doing so led to uncovering a research narrative that told a story of deaf women flourishing because of, not despite, being deaf – a critical point for how knowledge about being deaf and deaf women's lives was disrupted and troubled (Meehan, 2019). In this chapter, I set out the concepts problematised and suggest that other researchers may also find value in drawing on this conceptual framework.

I interrogated tensions linked with the concept of vulnerability. Using Carol Bacchi's (2009) 'What is the problem represented to be?' (WPR) approach, I scrutinised policies and strategies framing sexual health and well-being in Ireland. Designed for policy analysis, Bacchi's framework revealed that the concept of vulnerability is central to how deaf women are positioned and recognised at discursive and policy level. With this understanding at the forefront of my conceptual framework, I worked with participants in my research to explore deaf women's own embodied knowledge and subjective experiences, which exposed the importance of troubling the concept of vulnerability as it is applied and used in relation to deaf women.

Troubling and disrupting ways of knowing is critical as both an act of social justice and a social justice issue. The act of reframing or shifting traditional narratives that are embedded into policy and social, political and economic structures can allow for steps towards transformative social change around social justice issues. It is also important as a social justice issue because it is a process by which the task of social justice is carried out. In the next section, I set out how engaging with this process has potential to achieve social justice in relation to sexuality and deaf and hard-of-hearing women.

Troubling vulnerability

Traditionally, discursive practices surrounding deaf and disabled people along with law and policy draw on the influential concept of 'vulnerability' to make a case for the rights and entitlements of disabled people across policy sectors. Brown (2012) proposes that the concept used in policy, practice and academia initially appears favourable and frames groups or individuals encompassed by the term as victims of structural factors (Brown et al, 2020). However, as Taylor (2017) highlights, further interrogation of the concept reveals that its common use exerts a powerful perception that 'vulnerable people' are not rational agents who possess rights, agency and autonomy. The concern then is that it promotes a false perception that vulnerability is an innate characteristic of a person, meaning they require protection or, as Brown suggests (2020), manifests in varying policies of paternalistic intervention, control and discipline (Taylor, 2017). Other theorists concerned with vulnerability such as Hollomotz (2012) and Munro and Scoular (2012) agree that the protective discourse embedded in vulnerability language can further create situations of individual dependency, protection and intervention that perpetuate exclusion and marginalisation by failing to acknowledge and devise collective solutions to overarching systemic inequalities. Importantly, disabled people have challenged and resisted notions of vulnerability as bound up with disability, maintaining that this overlooks society's role in constructing vulnerable situations for disabled people (Oliver and Sapey, 2006). Alternative framings of vulnerability contend that it is a state of being that unites all human beings (Lynch, 2010) and that 'universal vulnerability' is a more appropriate understanding of the concept (Butler, 2004b; Fineman, 2008). Additionally, it can be harnessed to advocate for greater access to social protections and services (Brown, 2015; McLaughlin, 2017).

I begin from the standpoint that it is crucial to challenge connotations of vulnerability in relation to disability and sexuality and suggest that not to do so will shape and restrict how we see bodies and possibilities for bodies. In addition, it is important to consider that vulnerability is a label that many individuals and communities may resist and reject (Brown, 2015). They might disrupt and displace problem representations and reimagine new ways of knowing. Key to my research was how participants' narratives presented an opportunity to disrupt and reimagine through challenging the common perception that deaf people 'survive' or do well 'in spite of' being deaf, as opposed to because of being deaf. I explored the concept of vulnerability formally with some research participants, as well as informally with deaf friends, and received firm responses that the descriptor was not relatable, and the term was viewed in a negative light with another more appropriate term needed if one was needed at all.

Displacing and reimagining the vulnerability discourse

Troubling the concept of vulnerability with research participants in this way opened up real opportunities for disrupting, displacing and reimagining new ways of knowing. Displacing vulnerability and understanding that deaf women are not 'always and inevitably vulnerable' (Brown, 2015: 67) allowed for this discourse to be replaced with another – that of flourishing: 'Positive frameworks for human flourishing provides the language and insights for engaging new questions about how best to develop communities of belonging, connectedness and compassion' (Cherkowski and Walker, 2013: 200). By centring flourishing as a core concept through which to understand deaf women's experiences, I asked what conditions contribute to psycho-emotional well-being in relation to sexual subjectivity and how this can be nourished to ensure flourishing for all deaf women. In terms of asking new questions, this meant moving away from understanding the barriers and instead asking what is working, what is doing good and how can we do more of this. To understand this, I engaged with deaf women participating in the research to ask what opportunities deaf women have, what their feelings are about these and how such opportunities can be enhanced and supported. The following quotes highlight the stories of two deaf women who were limited in their exposure to deaf role models when young. As they grew up, they met deaf people and then realised the possibilities they also had access to. These stories thus illustrate the need to continue to support opportunities for deaf people to engage in the Deaf Community.

'I remember my mother saying "oh well, you'll probably never meet anyone who wants you, you'll have to accept that". She wasn't very positive about me ever thinking about that. So I grew up with no expectations. But I remember being shocked when I came into the Deaf Community and saw [incredulously] "people can get married, deaf people can get married and have relationships!"' (Kerry, mid 40s)

'When I was small I always think I was the only deaf in the world … Funny when I was child mother said "you're not able to look after child because you're deaf." I was like [expresses totally baffled but accepted] "okay". So my mother look after my daughter for two/three years. Until I meet deaf – saw a lot of deaf mothers. [Expresses thinking to myself] "you and you and you and you and you" – but my mother said deaf can't look after children. But no, but no, but, but, but. I was like [expresses thinking in confusion] so after saw loads said "Mam you're wrong."' (Vivian, late 30s)

There have been many contributions to understandings of flourishing from the philosophical and positive psychology literature considering how individuals might achieve well-being, happiness and flourishing (Keyes, 2002; Seligman, 2011; Gaffney, 2016), and human development ideas (Nussbaum, 2000) that explore how we as a society can live 'the good life'. As a concept, flourishing has been primarily used to measure human feelings and functioning to ascertain if people are feeling good and functioning effectively (Hone et al, 2014). We can first look to Aristotle's eudaimonia work, which promoted an understanding of flourishing as living well and as the achievement of one's potential as a human being as an end in itself (Younkins, 2008). This standpoint considers flourishing as something that is done in and achieved through partnership with others (Annett, 2016). Positive psychology espouses similar ideas, exploring factors that support people and communities to thrive and prioritises flourishing as something to be valued in its own right in order to achieve overall life satisfaction (Huppert and So, 2013).

However, although useful starting points, these perspectives tend to burrow in on how individuals can achieve well-being, which fails to take account of the structural change that is a non-negotiable requirement for flourishing. To build in this dimension to understandings of flourishing, it is useful to draw on Nussbaum, who draws on these ideas in her capabilities approach to argue for the need to consider the wider structural factors affecting individual well-being. She asks to what degree can a person be (beings) and do (doings) what they want to (2000). Nussbaum contends that the achievement of social justice involves creating and nourishing conditions that afford individuals opportunities to develop their capabilities and in turn to engage with others to their fullest potential and flourish. This is operationalised by specifying ten basic capabilities that should be available to people so that a flourishing life is possible: (1) life; (2) bodily health; (3) bodily integrity; (4) senses, imagination and thought; (5) emotions; (6) practical reason; (7) affiliation; (8) other species; (9) play; and (10) control over one's environment (2003).

Importantly for enhancing opportunities of 'displacing' and 'reimagining' in research exploring disability, Nussbaum has extended the capabilities approach to include disabled people and has argued that traditionally disabled people have not been considered as primary subjects of justice but instead objects of compassion (Kulick and Rydström, 2015). She insists that disabled people are equally entitled to define their own understandings of what is 'the good life' and to develop and flourish in their capabilities to achieve this.

Using the concept of flourishing in social justice research will spark many possibilities for asking questions that we might not otherwise ask and assist us with contributing to a discursive shift and building up a more accurate, deeper picture not just of the causes and determinants of flourishing, but as VanderWeele (2017) asserts, unrealised strategies to nourish flourishing. The following examples illustrate how being in deaf spaces with other deaf people contributed to both research participants feeling confident, assured and safe in their deaf identity and with deaf people growing up. In contrast, the first participant in the following excerpt did not know or mix with LGBT+ people and thus accepting her identity as a lesbian woman was difficult. The second participant met a hearing man but did not feel safe or at home in the hearing world. These stories thus highlight a potential strategy for how flourishing as a deaf person can be fostered.

Liv (mid 40s):	Oh I already accept deaf when young growing up (expresses that was never an issue). I always accept, always accept that.
Grainne:	Yes, but lesbian that was more difficult?
Liv:	Yes difficult. Very, very difficult. I found it difficult because I'm worried how society view me.
Shauna (early 70s):	David was hearing. I didn't want to marry him.
Grainne:	You only wanted to marry a deaf man?
Shauna:	Yeah at that time I was only happy in the Deaf Community and didn't want to live in a hearing community.

Addressing the misrecognition of deaf women

Through troubling the concept of vulnerability and by centring flourishing in my research, I sought to ensure that deaf women could address the misrecognition (Fraser et al, 2004) of deaf women – in other words, challenge the dominant discourse in relation to deaf women. As referred to earlier in the chapter, deaf women are often problematised in terms of individualised 'deficits', for example lack of knowledge about sexual health (Heiman et al, 2015; Wakeland et al, 2017); concerns related to deaf women's sexuality; how deaf and disabled people are 'vulnerable'; barriers' deaf women experience to services and information (Block et al, 2012); or the 'risks' for deaf women relating to sexual assault/intimate partner violence.[3] Acknowledgement or even consideration of the positive aspects of deaf and disabled sexuality is meagre in contemporary research (Block et al, 2012). In contrast, as Block et al (2012: 164) sets out through their framework, there are four dominant approaches to disability/sexuality research that:

1. perceive disabled people's sexuality as an individual problem to be solved;
2. explicitly or implicitly are concerned with treatment objectives;
3. focus on how individuals stack up on a scale of sexual functioning; and
4. view disabled sex in terms of physiological, social and relational norms derived from research with nondisabled people.

Disabled feminists have long resisted the exclusion generated by such approaches to disability/sexuality research that position disabled/deaf women's intimate lives on the periphery of research analysis exploring gender and sexuality (Finger, 1992; Morris, 1996). They argue that sexuality has been dominated by normative, ableist discourses. As a result, disabled people have been 'positioned largely as asexual [and] assumed to lack the capabilities and capacity to embody sexuality, sensuality, expression and desire' (Liddiard, 2018: 1). Reviewing literature at the intersection of gender, sexuality and deafness demonstrates that such research also employs a similar victimisation/deficit/risk/vulnerability framework which serves to reinforce Joharchi and Clark's (2014: 1536) contention that 'our understanding of sexuality in Deaf individuals is almost non-existent' and 'available information focuses on myths, misunderstandings and problems related to sexual health and behaviour'. These myths have been documented as contributing to the continued marginalisation of disabled people within the sexual politics arena (Morris, 1996; Shakespeare et al, 1996) and reinforcing barriers.

In contrast to these dominant approaches, my research unfolded a story of how deaf women seek to thrive and flourish in their intimate lives through nurturing their relational connections. I found that there are many ways by which deaf women resist and navigate sexual and intimate normalcy to claim their intimate agency and construct positive sexual subjectivities. The three stories that follow show how in different ways each participant navigates personal and professional relationships to allow their authentic deaf embodiment to flourish:

> '[Y]eah well, one of the reasons why we split up is, he just didn't know me, the real me, my culture, my identity.' (Aileen, late 20s)

> 'Foo, but the other day I found myself talking to him and I was like "foo" and he was like "what?", I was like emm, its Deaf English … It was nice though to have, to actually share my deaf language with him you know, and it's important to me because I naturally say "foo" all the time and it's good to know what it means.' (Addison, early 20s)

> 'I have noticed … a lot of GPs will look at all Deaf and consider them vulnerable and they need to change that attitude. They will shorten the language they are using to the point that it is patronising … It's like they look at me and make an automatic assumption that I am deaf so I don't know or understand what they are saying … I am quick to let them know that I do know what they are talking about.' (April, mid 30s)

I began my research with a different standpoint, one which was grounded in the largely negative focus on the intimate lives of deaf women. My expectations were centred on the themes of lack of control, disempowerment and discrimination which were to the forefront of the research available to me. I realised that these assumptions positioned deaf women in an oppressive, victim-centred narrative that did not reflect the lived lives shared with me.

In contrast, strong themes of 'intimate agency' and 'relational autonomy' (LeFeuvre and Roseneil, 2014) emerged from the research findings and challenged what I anticipated would be the dominant themes – those of oppression, marginalisation and exclusion. This is what led me to the 'flourishing framework' and to a story that was quite hopeful. It was not completely rosy of course and was still a story of the many audist/ableist contours of deaf women's intimate citizenship and illustrated that there are complex relationships between language, community, gender, sexuality and deafness as well as other intersectional social divisions and systems of inequality. However, my research uncovered that deaf women's narratives resist the vulnerability discourse regarding deafness and sexuality and spoke truth to power to disrupt the knowledge/power dynamic, a dynamic that has developed problematisations from a starting point of audism/ableism. Thus, I argue it is important to shift our language, problem representations and challenge and displace taken-for-granted ideas in relation to disability and sexuality which perpetuate limited ways of knowing and knowledge production. To advance flourishing as opposed to vulnerability is to advance a new political language, new meanings and new ways of knowing and enquiring into intimate lives, with discursive and subjective effects. Additionally, there is potential for pragmatic steps to be taken and collaborations to be fostered by which the conditions for flourishing can be operationalised, for example by designing service provision with diversity in mind from the beginning such as building an accessible website that includes text to voice, ISL interpreting being provided, clear visuals and so on for service users who engage with services in diverse ways. This leads me to highlighting how I embedded the conditions for meaningful participation in my research within my research design and how this process itself is a social justice issue.

Deaf research framework

Research design is crucial to research with deaf people as deaf people have consistently reported negative encounters with researchers and research processes (Singleton et al, 2014). Inaccessible research methods and research unavailable in 'accessible contexts and language' are two prominent issues. Such practices are aligned with an unethical approach to doing research 'on' rather than 'with' deaf women. Harris et al (2009: 104) comment that there are 'uniquely difficult challenges for the ethical conduct of research because of issues of power that surround the cultural and linguistic legacy in the Deaf Community'. Their terms of reference and principles for what ethical research with sign language communities looks like contribute to the deaf research framework embedded in my research.

The first step is to consider cultural competency,[4] whereby the researcher must deeply reflect on understanding themselves in relation to the community. They must seek to build trust, examine their own biases and be reflexive. The researcher must have 'trusted or verifiable cultural competence to engage in research alongside, with and for deaf people' (Young and Temple, 2014: 64), and this enhances the research validity. This is also related to building rapport, an essential research skill. Singleton et al (2015) state that building rapport shows personal respect for participants. Before I commenced research, I spent over two years building my relationships in the Deaf Community both formally through sitting on the board of two deaf organisations and informally through community activism, for example membership of Deaf Community Together for Yes, a deaf Repeal the 8th campaign group,[5] deaf friendships, attending cultural events and mingling at such events. All this was an important commitment to building cultural competence. However, this was not all to further my own research. I wanted to mix with other deaf people and build friendships, friendships which are still maintained.

This also means that research boundaries can be blurred. To resolve this I had to rigidly preserve confidentiality. While some research participants divulged that they had taken part in the research, I never indicated if someone was a participant. For example, at a group dinner a participant discussed our interview. Cautious not to inadvertently reveal anything raised in the interview, I just listened and did not engage in conversation about the interview. Additionally, during interviews participants divulged information about other deaf people I know. It was important to manage this, which Young and Temple term (2014: 71) 'keeping information confidential from myself'. This required a process of 'forgetting' information shared.

O'Brien (2017: 67), a deaf academic, has developed four preliminary principles for deaf research[6] which provided a strong guide to build my deaf research framework around:

1. The primacy of sign languages
   To value and demonstrate respect for sign language as a central part of deaf life. Putting this into practice in my own research meant offering interviews in ISL, discussing informed consent through ISL, offering to employ an ISL interpreter for interviews and video recording interviews to ensure all communication during an interview was captured.
2. Self-determination
   Self-determination is understood as deaf research being designed, led and disseminated by deaf people. Research produced needs to be 'valued by deaf communities and give back tangible benefits to deaf people, with direct impact on policies or practices that have negative effects on their lives' (O'Brien, 2017: 68).
3. Identity preservation
   Holding a positive attitude towards deaf identity is crucial, along with actively seeking to promote and develop a deaf academic identity. This principle specifically refers to deaf academics.
4. Community development
   'All research conducted under a deaf research framework should contribute in some way to the development of deaf communities' (O'Brien, 2017: 69). There are many ways in which this can happen and will be tied into the research itself.

Ethically reflexive research practice

This book is concerned with how society can be a more just place for people to live and flourish in. It is inherently politically motivated and argues that research must assist this. Research that explores issues of exclusion, discrimination, marginalisation and so on must be carried out with a goal of 'social transformation' (Harris et al, 2009: 108). In addition, it means that it is critical research is carried out in an ethical way. For example, in my research I challenged dominant, normative discourse around vulnerability and argued that we must think and do differently in relation to audist/ableist voices that are embedded in discourse and policy. All research concerned with social justice is required to do the same.

Carrying out deaf-related research requires consideration of research practice. First, 'failure to understand population-specific issues means that research practices might well be unethical in their application in specific contexts; and secondly, lack of awareness of the culturally mediated nature of fundamental ethical principles including informed consent, anonymity and confidentiality' (Young and Temple, 2014: 57). This means that components of ethical research, such as gaining informed consent, are not simple 'box-ticking exercises' but must be culturally mediated. In addition, Young and Temple (2014) advise that ignoring accessibility can result in making invisible the realities of some deaf people and perpetuate inequalities, for example that of deaf people with a learning disability.

Research participants had varying levels of literacy.[7] I used the following strategies, among others, to ensure parity of participation and develop a process that would not serve to exclude 'certain kinds of d/Deaf people':

- providing information on my research project through an ISL vlog and clear English written material;
- meeting some participants face-to-face before interviews and securing initial consent through ISL;
- posting an ISL vlog in deaf Facebook groups.

I understood that one-off interviews would be most successful, and a 'pure' version of narrative enquiry would not work in this research context. Co-producing knowledge is formally regarded as requiring multiple engagements with participants to work through their data. However, I agree with Young and Temple, who contend that universal ethical principles should be culturally mediated (2014: 60). Twenty-nine deaf women with varying literacy requirements took part in my research. To return to 29 deaf women repeatedly with a stack of paper would have been challenging. Furthermore, in my view, it would be disempowering for many of the participants to be required to work closely with me on the (re)presentation of their stories in the written form given literacy issues. It would not have been ethical, I believe, to ask this. I did work with participants around issues of anonymity, confidentiality and negotiating the data to be used but did not ask for further contributions. This might have been possible if I worked with a smaller group and had access to a research assistant/ISL interpreter. Even so, that would have excluded some deaf women and further marginalised voices that are so rarely heard. Additionally, some participants would not have participated with an interpreter. There is a small body of interpreters available in Ireland, and it is likely that participants would know them and feel uncomfortable sharing private topics through an interpreter that they may also use in other contexts.

Additional ethical nuances attached to my research relate to the ethics of researching intimate lives. Shakespeare (1997) has pointed out that researching and presenting disabled people's sexual lives must be approached with care, as such research can potentially be used in voyeuristic ways. Liddiard (2013: 3) found tension in her research between accessing the data and 'enabling disabled people to speak about their sexual lives and subjecting their lived experience to a lack of privacy experienced throughout public and private life; thus serving to objectify their sexual selves and desires'. I referred to the philosophical and pragmatic aspects of challenging vulnerability earlier in this chapter. I also challenge the idea of inherent participant 'vulnerability' regarding 'sensitive' research. As discussed, 'vulnerability' is a contested concept (Brown, 2015), and I found it problematic to apply it to participants. This is not to say that there is not a requirement to be accountable and follow the tenets of 'do no harm' and minimise potential risk. However, I believe all participants in research are vulnerable, and my participants were not vulnerable because they were deaf. At all stages, my research was committed to minimising risks because this is good, ethical practice.

Thus, I sought to build a supportive environment through careful, sensitive questioning that minimised the risk of being unnecessarily intrusive. I reminded participants that they did not have to answer any questions, and I remained alert to the need to move on from any topics of discomfort or distress. An additional risk to be aware of is confidentiality – in two cases, I chose to exclude stories to maintain confidentiality and anonymity.

Ethics in practice

Prior to interviews, participants were sent information sheets about the research questions and their rights. This was followed by a face-to-face conversation before an interview. Once participants indicated consent, I turned on the camera to record an interview. Three options were provided to document informed consent: signing a consent form, giving consent through ISL and a video recording or giving a verbal recording. I gave the issue of attaining informed consent careful consideration. Young and Temple (2014) referring to Pollard (1998) advise that informed consent may not be familiar to some participants (2014). While researchers warn against placing participants in a 'victim' or 'vulnerable' role by automatically assuming a lack of knowledge, it is still good practice to give time to drawing out the concept of informed consent with research participants. I adopted the following practices to ensure ongoing informed consent:

• checking before, during and after interview for consent;
• providing accessible written and signed information and using suitable, accessible terms and translating everything into ISL;
• ensuring the purpose of the research was fully explained to participants, what would happen with the data, where and how it would be stored and what would happen with the research;
• reminding participants that they could leave the research at any stage including after the interview;
• sharing transcripts with participants and noting that we could work together to review and alter where required.

The importance of identifying the act of translation/interpretation is prominent in literature exploring research with Deaf Communities. The research is published in English. This raises 'hierarchies of language power' (Young and Temple, 2004) – translation in this context is not a simple one of translation from one language to another but, in a way, 'collusion with the historically oppressive significance of English in deaf people's lives' (Ackerman and Young, 2001: 186). English has long been promoted as a 'better way' for Deaf people to communicate, with sign language ignored as a legitimate language. This has deep resonance for Deaf people and consideration must be given to how to challenge this disempowering language hierarchy.

I sought to represent each interview as closely as possible – including humour, gestures, laughter, pauses, silences and facial expressions. My approach was also to try to follow ISL grammar as best as I could and to include deaf words such as Foo. This followed interpretive and constructive epistemologies where attention is paid to how something is said in recognition that it is important how a point is constructed (Young and Temple, 2014). However, my representation was imperfect and raised dilemmas of how to navigate complex issues such as producing expressions in written English. West (2013: 5) notes that 'the recording and re-presentation (by a hearing person) of stories told by, for and about, deaf people – whose history is arguably largely one of discrimination and marginalisation – is a methodological, epistemological and political minefield. It places issues of power, representation, cultural translation and conceptual equivalence firmly in the spotlight.'

I am a deaf person, but the issues of power and representation remain pertinent. I negotiated narrative presentation with participants. For example, I emailed transcripts, some of which followed an ISL grammatical structure. One participant asked me to rewrite the interview following English grammatical structure. Stone and West (2012) note that one must be mindful of presentation of sign language narratives and think of the readership, losing something in the translation, as well as readers thinking this is simply poor English. The researcher must think carefully about their aim when representing interviews. My aim is to strengthen the representation of the diversity of language use along with the depth of expression and embodied communication within interviews.

Conclusion

What do my findings mean for social justice research?

'Promoting a just society involves promoting policies and practices that challenge injustice, poverty, inequality, discrimination and social exclusion and valuing diversity of identities and approaches' (Community Work Ireland, 2016: 15). As noted earlier in the chapter, troubling and disrupting ways of knowing is critical as both an act of social justice and a social justice issue. To build policies and practices that challenge all forms of injustice, it is important to carefully consider the conceptual framework and methodology to ensure injustice is not perpetuated through the research design, which will likely translate into the findings.

In this chapter, I present a positive methodological and theoretical scaffold that centred deaf women's voices and subjectivities and which allowed for exploration of social structures as a 'politics of doing' (Bacchi, 2009). The flourishing framework allowed for rethinking and reimagining; for gaining insight into how to promote what is going well and how we can create sustainable conditions within which to facilitate positive social change. The 'politics of flourishing' is the process that works in tandem with the 'politics of doing', whereby the conditions for flourishing can be created and nourished in line with the principles of equality, inclusion, participation and empowerment. It allows us to identify 'where to from here' – how injustice can be rectified and, as Fraser (2007) writes, how parity of participation can be achieved.

The research framework set out within this chapter offers social justice research points of reflection in relation to how social justice research with deaf people can be designed and operationalised, an approach applicable both in the Irish context and beyond. Embedding strong principles of equity and accessibility into the research process and working from a starting point of valuing diverse and deaf ways of seeing and knowing the world will support building a rich, insightful analysis that challenges audism.

What do my findings mean for social justice practice and policy, both in the Irish context and beyond?

My findings contribute both to international accounts of deaf women's lives and deaf ways of seeing the world. My research offers another way of thinking about and understanding disability, deafness and sexuality through dismantling the vulnerability framework and suggesting the flourishing framework as a way to ask new questions, garner new perspectives and understand deaf sexuality. Within work that is involved with both the process and task of achieving social justice, we must interrogate deeply held assumptions in order to disrupt and then shift how we see the world and the process of achieving change. Looking to and drawing from global research grounded in different contexts concerned with challenging the dominant discourse can have transformative implications for local social justice work.

Notes

[1] Audism frames the systemic nature of oppression and negative attitudes and experiences encountered at different levels (individual, institutional, metaphysical) to understand how discrimination against deaf people is perpetuated (Bauman, 2008).

[2] Ableism has been defined (Campbell, 2009: 5) as 'a network of beliefs, processes and practices that produces a particular kind of self and body (the corporeal standard) that is projected as the perfect, species-typical and therefore essential and fully human. Disability is then cast as a diminished state of being human.'

[3] See Obinna et al, 2005; Anderson et al, 2011; Anderson and Pezzarossi, 2012; Williams and Porter, 2014; Elliot and Pick, 2015; Ballan et al, 2017; Opshal and Pick, 2017; Wakeland et al, 2017.

[4] Cultural competency is understood as

> a systematic, responsive mode of inquiry that is actively cognizant, understanding, and appreciative of the cultural context in which the research takes place; it frames and articulates the epistemology of the research endeavour, employs culturally and contextually appropriate methodology, and uses community-generated, interpretive means to arrive at the results and further use of the findings. (SenGupta et al, 2004, cited in Harris et al, 2009: 112)

[5] The Repeal the 8th Campaign advocated for an amendment to the Constitution of Ireland which would permit legislation for abortion.

[6] This framework emerged from his research on Kaupapa Māori research principles and a workshop of deaf academics.

[7] It is important to understand the particular learning and visual needs of deaf people and to include this in written research material, for example the information and consent form. There is limited information in relation to literacy levels of deaf people in Ireland (Mathews and O' Donnell, 2018). Internationally, there is greater availability. Irish researchers Mathews and O'Donnell recently carried out a study exploring literacy among deaf mainstream students in Ireland (2018). They cite findings from 'Holt's (1993) landmark study ... which found the median reading age of 17-year-old school leavers was 9.5 years. Similar results were found in a 1990 study carried out in Ireland which reported average reading ages for 16-year-old DHH pupils at 9.2 years of age (James, O'Neill and Smyth, 1991) and again in the US nearly a decade later (Traxler, 2000).

References

Ackerman, J. and Young, A.M. (2001) 'Reflections on validity and epistemology in a study of working relations between deaf and hearing professionals', *Qualitative Health Research*, 11(2): 179–89.

Annett, A. (2016) 'Human flourishing, the common good, and Catholic social teaching', in J. Helliwell, R. Layard and J. Sachs (eds) 'World Happiness Report 2016', Update, vol 1, New York: Sustainable Development Solutions Network, chapter 2, pp 39–57.

Bacchi, C. (2009) *Analysing Policy: What's the Problem Represented to Be?*, Frenchs Forest, NSW: Pearson Australia.

Bauman, H-D.L. (2004) 'Audism: Exploring the metaphysics of oppression', *Journal of Deaf Studies and Education*, 9: 239–46.

Bauman, H.-D.L. and Murray, J.J. (2009) 'Reframing: From hearing loss to deaf gain', *Deaf Studies Digital Journal*, 1: 1–10.

Bauman, H-D.L. and Murray, J.J. (eds) (2014) *Deaf Gain, Raising the Stakes for Human Diversity*, Minneapolis: University of Minnesota Press.

Block, P., Shuttleworth, R., Pratt, J., Block, H. and Rammler, L. (2012) 'Disability, sexuality and intimacy', in N. Pollard and D. Sakellariou (eds) *Politics of Occupation-Centred Practice: Reflections on Occupational Engagement across Cultures*, Chichester, West Sussex: Wiley-Blackwell, chapter 12, pp 162–74.

Brown, K. (2012) 'Re-moralising "vulnerability"', *People, Place and Policy Online*, 6(1): 41–53.

Brown, K. (2015) *Vulnerability and Young People: Care and Social Control in Policy and Practice*, Bristol: Policy Press.

Brown, K., Ellis, K. and Smith, K. (2020) 'Vulnerability as lived experience: Marginalised women and girls in the UK', in M. Kuronen, E. Virokannas and U. Salovaara (eds) *Women, Vulnerabilities and Welfare Service Systems*, London: Routledge, pp 13–25.

Butler, J. (2004) *Precarious Life: The Powers of Mourning and Violence*, London: Verso.

Campbell, F.K. (2009) *Contours of Ableism: Territories, Objects, Disability and Desire*, London: Palgrave Macmillan.

Cherkowski, S. and Walker, K. (2013) 'Schools as sites of human flourishing: Musings on efforts to foster sustainable learning communities', *Journal of Educational Administration and Foundations*, 23(2): 139–54.

Clandinin, J.D. (2006) 'Narrative inquiry: A methodology for studying lived experience', *Research Studies in Music Education*, 27(1): 44–54.

Community Work Ireland (CWI) (2016) 'All Ireland standards for community work', [online], Available from: https://www.cwi.ie/wp-content/uploads/2016/03/All-Ireland-Standards-for-Community-Work.pdf [Accessed 16 March 2017 and 23 April 2023].

Coogan, A. and O' Leary, J. (2018) 'Deaf women of Ireland (1922–1994)', in L. Leeson (ed) *CDS/SLSCS Monograph No. 4*, [online], Available from: http://www.tara.tcd.ie/bitstream/handle/2262/86028/PDF%20D EAF%20WOMEN%20OF%20IRELAND.pdf?sequence=1&isAllowed= y [Accessed 3 January 2019].

De Clerck, G.A.M. (2010) 'Deaf epistemologies as a critique and alternative to the practice of science: An anthropological perspective', *American Annals of the Deaf*, 154(5): 435–46.

Fawcett, B. (2000) *Feminist Perspectives on Disability*, New York: Pearson Education.

Fineman, M. (2008) 'The vulnerable subject: Anchoring equality in the human condition', *Yale Journal of Law and Feminism*, 20(1): 1–23.

Finger, A. (1992) 'Forbidden fruit: Why shouldn't disabled people have sex or become parents?', *New Internationalist*, 233, [online], Available from: http:// newint.org/features/1992/07/05/fruit/ [Accessed 31 January 2016].

Fraser, N. (2007) 'Feminist politics in the age of recognition: A two dimensional approach to gender justice', *Studies in Social Justice*, 1(1): 23–35.

Fraser, N., Dahl, H.M., Stoltz, P. and Willig, R. (2004) 'Recognition, redistribution and representation in capitalist global society: An interview with Nancy Fraser', *Acta Sociologica*, 47(4): 374–82.

Friedner, M. (2015) *Valuing Deaf Worlds in India*, New Brunswick: Rutgers University Press.

Gaffney, M. (2016) *Flourishing: How to Achieve a Deeper Sense of Well-being, Meaning and Purpose – Even When Facing Adversity*, Dublin: Penguin.

Heiman, E., Haynes, S. and McKee, M. (2015) 'Sexual health behaviours of Deaf American Sign Language (ASL) users', *Disability Health Journal*, 8(4): 579–85.

Harding, S. (2004 [1993]) 'Rethinking standpoint epistemology: What is "strong objectivity"?', in S. Harding (ed) *The Feminist Standpoint Theory Reader, Intellectual and Political Controversies*, London: Routledge, chapter 8, pp 127–40.

Harris, R.L., Holmes, H.M. and Mertens, D.M. (2009) 'Research ethics in sign language communities', *Sign Language Studies*, 9(2): 104–31.

Hauser, P.C., O'Hearn, A., McKee, M., Steider, A. and Thaw, D. (2010) 'Deaf epistemology: Deafhood and deafness', *American Annals of the Deaf*, 154(5): 493–6.

Holcomb, T.K. (2010) 'Deaf epistemology: The deaf way of knowing', *American Annals of the Deaf*, 154(5): 471–96.

Hollomotz, A. (2012) 'Disability, oppression and violence: Towards a sociological explanation', *Sociology*, 47(3): 477–93.

Hone, L., Jarden, A., Schofield, G. and Duncan, S. (2014) 'Measuring flourishing: The impact of operational definitions on the prevalence of high levels of wellbeing', *International Journal of Wellbeing*, 4(1): 62–90.

Hooks, B. (1989) 'Choosing the margin as a space of radical openness', *Framework: The Journal of Cinema and Media*, 36: 15–23.

Huppert, F.A. and So, T.T.C. (2013) 'Flourishing across Europe: Application of a new conceptual framework for defining well-being', *Social Indicators Research*, 110(3): 837–61.

Joharchi, H.A. and Clark, M.D. (2014) 'A glimpse at American deaf women's sexuality', *Psychology*, 5(13): 1536–49.

Kennedy, P. (1999) 'Women and social policy', in G. Kiely, A. O'Donnell, P. Kennedy and S. Quin (eds) *Irish Social Policy in Context*, Dublin: University College Dublin Press, chapter 13, pp 231–53.

Keyes, C.L. (2002) 'The mental health continuum: From languishing to flourishing in life', *Journal of Health and Social Behaviour*, 43(2): 207–22.

Kulick, D. and Rydström, J. (2015) *Loneliness and Its Opposite. Sex, Disability and the Ethics of Engagement*, Durham, NC: Duke University Press.

Kusters, A., De Meulder, M. and O'Brien, D. (eds) (2017) *Innovations in Deaf Studies: The Role of Deaf Scholars*, New York: Oxford University Press.

Ladd, P. (2003) *Understanding Deaf Culture: In Search of Deafhood*, Clevedon: Multilingual Matters.

Le Feuvre, N. and Roseneil, S. (2014) 'Entanglements of economic and intimate citizenship: Individualization and gender (in)equality in a changing Europe', *Social Politics: International Studies in Gender, State and Society*, 21(4): 529–61.

Liddiard, K. (2018) *The Intimate Lives of Disabled People*, Oxon: Routledge.

Liddiard, K. (2013) 'Reflections on the process of researching disabled people's sexual lives', *Social Research Online*, 18(3): 10.

Lynch, K. (2010) *Affective Inequalities: Challenging (re) distributive, recognition and representational models of social justice*. Unpublished paper presented at: ISA XVII World Congress of Sociology Conference. Sweden, July 11–17.

Maynooth University (2019) 'Maynooth University research ethics policy', [online], Available from: https://www.maynoothuniversity.ie/sites/defa ult/files/assets/document/Maynooth%20University%20Research%20Eth ics%20Policy%20June%202016_0.pdf [Accessed 1 May 2016].

Meehan, G. P. (2019) *Flourishing at the margins: An exploration of deaf and hard-of-hearing women's stories of their intimate lives in Ireland*. PhD thesis, National University of Ireland Maynooth.

McLaughlin, K. (2017) 'Disabling the subject: From radical vulnerability to vulnerable radicals', *Annual Review of Critical Psychology*, 13: 1–15.

Morris, J. (ed) (1996) *Encounters with Strangers: Feminism and Disability*, London: Women's Press.

Munro, V. and Scoular, J. (2012) 'Abusing vulnerability? Contemporary law and policy responses to sex work in the UK', *Feminist Legal Studies*, 20(3): 189– 206.

Nussbaum, M. (2000) *Women and Human Development: The Capabilities Approach*, Cambridge: Cambridge University Press.

O'Brien, D. (2017) 'Deaf-led deaf studies: Using Kaupapa Māori principles to guide the development of deaf research practices', in A. Kusters, M. De Meulder and D. O'Brien (eds) *Innovations in Deaf Studies: The Role of Deaf Scholars*, New York: Oxford University Press, chapter 2, pp 57–76.

Oliver, M. and Sapey, B. (2006) *Social Work with Disabled People* (3rd edn), Houndmills: Palgrave Macmillan.

Padden, C. (1980) 'The Deaf Community and the culture of deaf people', in C. Baker and R. Pattison (eds) *Sign Language and the Deaf Community*, Silver Spring: National Association of the Deaf, chapter 3, [e-book], Available from: https://archive.org/details/signlanguagedeaf00stok/page/n3 [Accessed 18 March 2017].

Padden, C. and Humphries, T. (2005) *Inside Deaf Culture*, Cambridge, MA: Harvard University Press.

Pollard R.Q. (1998) 'Psychopathology', in M. Marschark and D. Clark (eds) *Psychological Perspectives on Deafness*, Mahwah: Lawrence Erlbaum, chapter 8.

Seligman, M. (2011) *Flourish: A Visionary New Understanding of Happiness and Well-being*, New York: Free Press.

Shakespeare, T. (1997) 'Researching Disabled Sexuality', in C. Barnes and G. Mercer (eds) *Doing Disability Research*, Leeds: The Disability Press, chapter 11.

Shakespeare, T., Gillespie-Sells, K. and Davies, D. (1996) *The Sexual Politics of Disability Untold Desires*, London: Cassell.

Singleton, J.L., Martin, A. and Morgan, G. (2014) 'Ethics, deaf-friendly research, and good practice when studying sign languages', in E. Orfanidou, B. Woll and G. Morgan (eds) *Research Methods in Sign Language Studies: A Practical Guide*, Oxford: John Wiley & Sons, chapter 1, pp 8–18.

Singleton, J.L., Martin, A. and Morgan, G. (2015) 'Ethics, deaf-friendly research, and good practice when studying sign languages', in E. Orfanidou, B. Woll and G. Morgan (eds) *Research Methods in Sign Language Studies: A Practical Guide*, Oxford: John Wiley & Sons, chapter 1.

Stone, C. and West, D. (2012) 'Translation, representation and the Deaf "voice"', *Qualitative Research*, 12(6): 645–65.

Taylor, S. (2017) 'The challenges of disablist hate crime', in A. Haynes, J. Schweppe and S. Taylor (eds) *Critical Perspectives on Hate Crime: Contributions from the Island of Ireland*. London: Palgrave MacMillan, chapter 11, pp 209–32.

VanderWeele, T.J. (2017) 'On the promotion of human flourishing', *PNAS*, 114(31): 8148–56.

Wakeland, E., Austen, S. and Rose, J. (2017) 'What is the prevalence of abuse in the deaf/hard of hearing population?', *The Journal of Forensic Psychiatry and Psychology*, 29(3): 434–54.

West, D. (2013) 'What's in a sign? Narrative inquiry and deaf storytellers', in S. Trahar (ed) *Contextualising Narrative Inquiry, Developing Methodological Approaches for Local Contexts*, Oxon: Routledge, chapter 1, pp 1–18.

Wolsey, J.L.A., Dunn, K.M., Gentzke, S.W., Joharchi, H.A. and Clark, M.D. (2017) 'Deaf/hearing research partnerships', *American Annals of the Deaf*, 161(5): 571–82.

Young, A. and Temple, B. (2014) *Approaches to Social Research: The Case of Deaf Studies*, Oxford: Oxford University Press.

Younkins, E. (2008) 'Toward the development of a paradigm of human flourishing in a free society', *The Journal of Ayn Rand Studies*, 9(2): 253–304.

7

Sanctuary: trespassing the enclosure of rights

David Donovan

Introduction

Research for social justice emphasises that equality is a process, a never finished project, a negotiation balancing the individual and the community; it is deeply concerned with issues of empowerment, power, the allocation of resources and social transformation (Griffiths, 1998). Here, 'the researcher's pre-eminent commitment should ... be ... to the fundamental principles of social justice, equality and participatory democracy' (Troyna and Carrington, 1989, in Griffiths, 1998: 3). This chapter seeks to locate the play and film *Sanctuary* as an example of such a commitment.

The title of this chapter refers to how the rights of people with an intellectual disability to an intimate life of their own choosing were fenced off, enclosed, by others such that to actively exercise their right to an intimate life would potentially have seen them criminalised under the provisions of the Criminal Law (Sexual Offences) Act 1993. As a result, 'people with cognitive disability are not respected as sexual decision-makers on an equal basis as others' (Arstein-Kerslake, 2015: 1459).

Sanctuary by Galway-based Blue Teapot Theatre (BT) Company involves acts of resistance, and trespass, into the enclosure of the right of people with an intellectual disability to an intimate life, a right immured under Section 5 of the Criminal Law (Sexual Offences) Act 1993 (Arstein-Kerslake, 2015). BT used the rehearsal process as a period of research, gathering stories from the lived experience of the actors, all of whom are people with an intellectual disability. These stories were then fashioned into performances that highlighted both the desire for and the denial of their right to an intimate life of their choosing. And while it might not be seen as research in academic enclosures, it serves to illustrate how the arts can and do play a significant role in exposing situations of social injustice.

Trespass

Trespass refers to a 'voluntary wrongful act against the person or property of another, esp. unlawful entry to a person's land or property' (Concise Oxford Dictionary, 1995: 1488). Laws of trespass are ways of enforcing enclosure, the separation of place in such a way as to ensure that others remain excluded. Enclosure acts as a border, a line drawn around a territory, a means of 'unifying the identity of believers and dividing them from the non-believers' (Nail, 2016, in Hayes, 2020: 99). Borders keep out the 'Other', the different, the troubling. Borders, sold as a means of ensuring safety, may in fact lead to fragmentation (Hudson, 2006).

As a state, Ireland, along with other countries, has a long history of enclosure, of immurement, of separating out the troubling 'Other' (Clapton, 2009; Ferriter, 2012; Hornstein, 2017; Conroy, 2018; Kelly, 2022; McDonagh, 2021; Scull, 2022). Peppering the country, asylums, prisons, mother and baby homes, laundries and other institutions housed those the state deemed to be 'beyond the pale'. Enclosure and separation, enforced through legislation and policy, ensured, as far as possible, that everyone stayed in their place. Enclosure seeped into the public's consciousness in other ways too. The media, research and the arts played their part, performing and reinforcing acts of enclosure (Ledwith, 2005; McConkey et al, 2010; Collin, 2020; Gray, 2022).

Trespass may sometimes be used as an act of resistance, an act of reclamation, an act of re-insertion, whereby those excluded re-enter enclosed spaces. Acts of deliberate trespass have a long association with struggles for social justice: for example, the sit-in, the die-in and mass trespass on land have all been used to highlight situations of injustice (McKay, 1988, 1996, 2011; Blunt and Wills, 2000; News from Nowhere, 2003; Hayes, 2020, 2022). Social justice research is an act of trespass, endeavouring 'to promote human development and the common good through addressing challenges related to both individual and distributive justice' (Crethar et al, 2008, in Ponterroto et al, 2013: 44). The arts have often been embraced as acts of trespass into public conversation and consciousness, highlighting situations of injustice (Zinn, 2003; Macphee and Reuland, 2007; KCAT, 2009; McConkey et al, 2010; Gray, 2022).

In shining a light on the 1993 Act and its implications for people with an intellectual disability, BT also drew attention to Ireland's non-ratification of the 2006 United Nations Convention on the Rights of Persons with Disabilities (UNCRPD). This situation, a massive enclosure of the rights for the whole community of people with disabilities, sanctioned the continuance of injustice and inequality.

The author must at the outset state the non-neutrality of their position. They have a long association with BT as prop-maker, board member, tutor and latterly programme support worker in the BT Performing Arts School. Their involvement with the *Sanctuary* project was solely as audience member for repeated viewings of both stage and film versions. The questions asked by *Sanctuary* as both process and product continue to trespass into their mind and influence their practice.

Blue Teapot Theatre Company

BT was founded in 1996 as a project for people with intellectual disability to participate in the arts. Over time, BT developed to include a full-time acting ensemble, a performing arts school, a youth drama project and a community outreach programme (Blue Teapot Theatre Company, nd). Since its inception, BT has participated in St Patrick's Day parades, performed as part of the opening ceremony for the 2003 Special Olympics, staged bespoke shows in various indoor and outdoor settings and played a central role in the establishment of the pan-European Crossing the Line Festival (Galway 2020, 2021).

Through a series of conversations over a number of years, Petal Pilley, appointed BT Artistic Director in 2006, gradually became aware of the barriers the ensemble performers faced in their desire to form relationships: '[B]eing around in their lives and suddenly realising they are adults … they have the same urges, the same wants, the same needs that we do, but in order for them to fulfil that there are a lot more barriers in the way' (Pilley in *Sanctuary* Electronic Press Kit [EPK], 2015). In 2012 Pilley commissioned the playwright Christian O'Reilly to develop a play exploring this issue (Galway International Arts Festival, 2013).

The writing of *Sanctuary* involved time spent getting to know the actors and their world (Ojrzińska, 2017; O'Reilly, 2020). Conversations focused on "their feelings about relationships and the challenges they faced in having relationships" (O'Reilly, 2020: 241). The story had to come from the actors so they felt "invested in the work … they were going to create together" (Collin, 2020: 222). These dialogues were vital in ensuring the accuracy of the story to be told. Critically, listening to and hearing their voices trespassed on the enclosure of sexuality and relationships in the lives of people with intellectual disabilities.

Equally important was the fact that BT actors would perform in both the play and the film. This undermined the practice of ' "cripping" up or "cripdrag", industry terms describing the practice of an able-bodied actor playing a character with a … disability' (Creedon, 2020: 64). Actors with an intellectual disability playing characters with an intellectual disability 'expose the exploitation of disability and deny its metaphorical use' (Creedon, 2020: 65), meaning the audience can no longer hide behind this illusion and claim it did not know.

In commissioning this play, BT drew on two traditions prominent in the struggle for social justice: arts-based research (ABR) and art as resistance (AAR) (Boal, 1998; McNiff, 1998; Goldbard, 2006; Clover and Stalker, 2007; Cleveland, 2008; Naidus, 2009; Ganguly, 2010; Cohen and Varea, 2011a, 2011b; Mykitiuk et al, 2015).

Arts-based research

ABR has its roots in diverse fields, including art therapy, narrative methods, social justice movements, critical theory (McNiff, 1998; Leavy, 2010; Coemans et al, 2015) and 'epistemologies of the south' (Santos, 2014). ABR involves a 'coming together of storytelling and social change' (Viscardis et al, 2018: 1292) in 'a process of disciplined inquiry' (McNiff, 1998: 21). As a methodology, ABR acknowledges that people communicate and story their worlds through a variety of means (Eaves, 2014; Chamberlain et al, 2018). ABR has proven useful in 'accessing subjugated voices' (Coleman, 2019: 19), thus surfacing often forgotten and overlooked stories, thereby building the well-being and creativity of the participants (Mykitiuk et al, 2015).

ABR as social justice research acknowledges 'that we have a choice, to be open to the fact that for societies to evolve an old order must change' (Malik, 2019: 263). Injustice experienced in this 'old order' is a visceral experience (McIntosh, 2012), inscribed on the body and etched into the soul. ABR facilitates the braiding of personal stories regarding this 'old order' into collective stories, offering ways to trespass on hegemonic enclosures (Leavy, 2010; McNiff, 2012; Horsford et al, 2014; Viscardis et al, 2019; Kuri, 2020). A similar process underlies community work/community development (Westoby and Dowling, 2013; Ledwith, 2016) and social justice activism (Doetsch-Kidder, 2012).

For McIntosh (2012: 52), in the contemporary world 'our illness is a loss of soul and we must find the courage to call it back'. It was this loss of soul that drove policies and practices of immurement and separation of people with intellectual disabilities. How then to research such experiences if, as has been argued, the body has been, if not written out of research, then underprivileged, while 'detachment, objectivity, and rationality have been valued and masculinised as part of a gender politics of research to the detriment of engagement, subjectivity, passion and desire, which has been feminised' (Anderson and Smith, 2001, in de Craene, 2017: 455)? It is as if we begin at the 'neck and go upwards' (Neill nd, in Miller, 1966), ignoring the body and the emotions.

An arts-based methodology with a focus on 'embodied experience, lends itself to exploration of sensory and psychological experience' (Boydell, 2021: 1) and not only opens new methods of research but also new routes of dissemination, for example poetry readings, art installations and dramatic presentations (Pickering and Kara, 2017). Having previously researched art as a way of building community (Donovan, 2011) and used narrative enquiry to research community workers' ways of being in and seeing the world (Donovan, 2019), and reflecting on many years of experience as an arts worker in community and socially engaged arts, I would concur with Boydell's (2021) statement.

Art as resistance

Kearns (2007a: 140) states that 'within the disabled activist cohort, disabled artists have always been at the forefront'. Many of these artists have an affinity with the Disability Arts movement. This movement involving disabled 'activists, artists and creatives' campaigned against the marginalisation of disabled people and championed their social, civil, political and cultural rights (Rocco, 2019). It challenged the prevailing assumptions and depictions of people with disability (Kuppers, 2003, 2011; Cameron, 2007, 2009, 2016; Gold, 2021) as 'pitiable and pathetic; an object of violence; sinister and evil; atmosphere or curio; super cripple; object of ridicule; own worst enemy; broken; sexually abnormal; incapable of participating fully in community life; normal' (Barnes, 1992, in Collin, 2020: 218–19). The arts become both a means of consciousness-raising, shifting the 'medical discourse of impairment to a social discourse of disabling barriers', engendering 'collective celebration and pride' (Swain and Cameron, 1999: 77), and critique of the system in which 'differences get organised on a hierarchical scale of decreasing social and symbolic worth' (Braidotti, 2016, in Viscardis et al, 2019: 1289). In a process linking the personal to the collective, Disability Arts takes the 'power of storytelling, space-making, truth-saying, time-shaping' in order to 'make the frames of everyday experiences, private experiences, and public knowledges visible' (Kuppers, 2003: 9).

This process contests 'hegemonic forms of truth and harmful assumptions ... acknowledging the impossibility of claiming to know' any 'group fully' (Kuri, 2020: 208). For example, the songs composed by people with intellectual disability in institutional settings 'clearly show that people with learning difficulties were speaking up for themselves, demonstrating resistance and resilience long before the terms "advocacy" and "self-advocacy" came into common usage' (Ledger and Shufflebotham, 2006: 68). The Disability Arts movement did not take hold in Ireland in the same way it did elsewhere (Daunt, 2007; Kearns, 2007a; Lynch, 2007). Daunt (2007: 37) says of his experience of running the Disability Cabaret that "it can be uncomfortable to speak about such issues" [(collective celebration and pride)] "in the cosy model that is the Irish disability movement". 'The cosy model' mirrored the prevailing Social Partnership, an arrangement in which trade unions, employers, farmers and the State were the dominant forces with the community and voluntary sector having much reduced role, a melange of overlapping enclosures (Kearns, 2007a; Toolan, 2007). Thus 'the term "disabled people" came to include parents and carers while the idea of stakeholders threw service providers into the mix' (Daunt, 2007: 38).

Behind this 'Irish solution to an Irish problem' lies 'the non-disabled world's fear to lose power and privilege if disabled people were to run their own lives, their own art' (Kuppers, 2007: 16). Political linkage and access to budgets can work to mute if not silence artists seeking to trespass this particular enclosure (Daunt, 2007; Kearns, 2007a; Lynch, 2007). Hadley et al (2021: 1502) assert that while this larger group may 'travel through life with disabled people' and 'come to know the barriers they deal with by proxy ... they can forget that their experience is at one remove from the actual experience of disability'. Arts and Disability Ireland (ADI), 'the national development and resource agency dealing with arts and disability issues', also adheres to this model, stating that 'the "disability community" is understood to include a broad coalition of people with disabilities, their families, friends, advocates, and representatives' (Arts and Disability Ireland, 2017: 9). ADI, while acknowledging the 'broad coalition' in the Irish context, has as its ambition the creation of 'an Irish arts and cultural environment that is at its core inclusive and responsive' (ADI, 2017: 23).

On the ground, though, some artists and arts organisations continued, and continue, in their endeavours to change 'hierarchical' orderings of difference (KCAT, 2009; Kearns, 2009).

In research with people with intellectual disabilities, arts-based methods have been used to 'co-create with and share ... voices ... to illuminate inequities' (Schnellert et al, 2023: 4). Co-creation is a process which 'invites people into an intimate engagement of their stories and creativity, hospitality towards one another's ideas and perspectives, and giving attention and care to building a shared analysis of ways forward' (Westoby and Dowling, 2013: 59).

Sex lives and relationships

Relationships are central to who we were, who we are and who we will become: 'Relationships of all kinds help define who we are ... Without relationships with others we cannot know what we are like, or what kind of person we would like to be' (Firth and Ripley, 1990, in Bayley, 1997: 19). However, the life histories of people with intellectual disabilities are often ones of fragmentation, dislocation and separation (Bayley, 1997; Johnson and Traustadóttir, 2005; Clapton, 2009; Hamilton and Atkinson, 2009; Johnson et al, 2010; McConkey et al, 2010; Oliver and Barnes, 2012; McConkey, 2015, 2021; O'Byrne and Muldoon, 2015; Merrells et al, 2019). Loneliness remains a significant experience in their lives (Callus, 2017), contributing to 'known mental and physical health inequalities that further exacerbate social exclusion' (Wilson et al, 2017: 847).

People with intellectual disabilities consistently express a desire to have more control over relationship choices in general (Bane et al, 2012; Inclusion Ireland, 2021) and sexual relationships in particular (Healy et al, 2009; Bane et al, 2012; Azzopardi-Lane and Callus, 2015; Wilson et al, 2017, 2019; Correa et al, 2022; de Wit et al, 2022). Wilson et al note how

> sexuality in the lives of people with intellectual disability is mediated by ideas about capacity and competence, assumptions of desirability and overshadowed by a discourse of risk and vulnerability … underpinning this discourse is a 'paternalistic regime' whereby the sexual lives of people with intellectual disabilities are strongly surveilled, often by parents or other care givers. (Wilson et al, 2019: 989)

Consequently, in order to have a sexual relationship, people with an intellectual disability 'are expected to demonstrate achievement of autonomy and self-determination in aspects of living that are rarely obtained by people with an Intellectual Disability (ID), such as financial independence or home ownership' (Healy et al, 2009: 906). The existence of Section 5 of the 1993 Act 'led to concerns among service providers about supporting people with intellectual disabilities to develop relationships or express their sexuality' (Johnson et al, 2009: 4). While service providers had a range of sexuality and relationship programmes in place, the possible legal implications for both provider and people with intellectual disabilities if they chose to fully express their desires led to practices of over protection (Kelly et al, 2009; Feely, 2016; Whittle and Butler, 2018; Onstot, 2019; Santinele Martino and Perreault-Laird, 2019). Notwithstanding the legal arguments being made on proposals for how to amend the 1993 Act (Arnstein-Kerslake, 2015; Arnstein-Kerslake and Flynn, 2016), the situation on the ground remained unchanged for people with an intellectual disability.

Writing *Sanctuary*

The research process for *Sanctuary* unfolded over a period of years. Pilley (2022) noted how listening to and engaging in conversations with BT actors together with observing several spontaneous enactments of marriage ceremonies by the actors during break times alerted her to a profound yearning on the part of the actors for relationship and connection with a significant other of their own choosing. The actors were aware of such relationships through being part of their own families, as fans of TV soaps, movies and other media. But they watched from the outside separated from such attachments by multiple visible and invisible fences, for example religion, house rules, lack of privacy.

One particular conversation stands out for her. Here, she "explained how it was for me" (Pilley, 2022). She could act on her desires should she so wish. The conversation shifted to whether the actors thought this situation was fair, with Pilley being free to act compared to the multiple constraints placed on their freedom to act. This conversation exposed "a lot of pain and discomfort in the room" (Pilley, 2022).

It was the discovery of the "legal piece" (Pilley, 2022) that provided the final motivation to commission a writer to make a piece of theatre to expose this unjust and painful situation (Pilley, 2022). O'Reilly was given the commission (Pilley, 2022), as he seemed to be someone who would be sensitive to 'difference, spontaneity and the fun of individual creativity' (Griffiths, 1998: 147).

The writing process began with actors and writer participating in workshops together as a way of getting to know each other. These workshops used the Meisner technique as a way of 'co-creating a spontaneous, unpredictable, affective engagement in the moment' (Esper and DiMarco, 2008, in Strandberg-Long, 2019: 96). This approach facilitated "honest observation and interaction", leading to "connection and communication" between actors and playwright (Pilley, 2022). Through this process, conversations were initiated drawing on the experiences of the actors and feeding into the development of the script (Pilley, 2022). O'Reilly's presence in the workshops involved 'listening, learning, supporting, witnessing' (Watkins, 2019: 184), an 'outsider witness … [creating] a setting where people can tell their preferred stories to a group of outsiders who then amplify and accredit the stories they witness' (Combs and Freedman, 2012: 1049). The script evolved with O'Reilly writing and then presenting the script for workshopping with the actors, a practice of "collectively articulating" (Pilley, 2022) the stories that were being revealed by the actors, stories that ranged from the light to the profoundly dark. In working this way, O'Reilly as accompanist worked from 'a faith in what can arise from common efforts, rather than solely through his or her own expertise and efforts' (Watkins, 2019: 186). This allowed for the pathos and humour of the stories to be present in the characters as they were developed in the room.

Tronto (1993, in Buser et al, 2020: 1042) defines care as 'everything that we do to maintain, continue and repair our world so that we can live in it as well as possible. That world includes our bodies, ourselves, and our environment, all of which we seek to interweave in a complex, life-sustaining web.' Pilley was conscious throughout the process of her role as director to both tell a story while at the same time being mindful of a sense of "ownership and belonging", such that the actors had "a real place in there", a place of "great safety" (Pilley, 2022). Caring in the sense proposed by Tronto was central to this. The actors were being asked to "open personal" stories around a "hard-core topic" that contained both "light and dark" (Pilley, 2022). Stories would be translated into a script to be performed before an audience. This caring and trust was something that had been built between Pilley and the actors over the years since Pilley's appointment as Artistic Director in 2006 (Galway International Arts Festival, 2013).

Sanctuary (play)

O'Reilly had already been exposed to enclosure regarding the arts and disability. He had developed a film script based on his experiences of working with the disability activist Martin Naughton, who in the early 1990s had been instrumental in setting up Ireland's first Centre for Independent Living. This script posed a significant 'challenge' to 'the rehab culture that prevailed in Ireland at the time' (O'Reilly, 2020: 237), a culture where despite public rhetoric around rights-based approaches, 'services specific to disabled people … exist at a discretionary level' (Toolan, 2007: 121), thus giving service providers enormous 'control … over disabled peoples' lives' (Toolan, 2007: 122).

O'Reilly was "taken off my own project" (O'Reilly, 2020: 239), and a different film, *Inside I'm Dancing*, was produced. As a result, he felt he "had failed the community that had entrusted me to tell its story" (O'Reilly, 2020: 239). For Kearns (2007b: 129), the film 'does not truly portray what it is like to be a disabled person in Ireland today'. Casey (2014: 9) argued 'a narrative that marked an important moment in the Disability Rights movement was abrogated in favour of a sentimentalised melodrama by the filmmakers'. Critically, 'cripping up' casting 'relieved [the audience] of doing anything about Irish society's problematic relationship with disabled people' (Kearns, 2007b: 126). No wonder O'Reilly was both "fascinated and daunted" by this commission (*Sanctuary* EPK, 2015).

For O'Reilly, the success of the play was down to the:

> clarity of the agreement between the director the actors and I about … the story we wanted to tell … full participation of actors with ID in the creative process, both as collaborators in the play itself and performers in the production … actors with ID playing characters with ID. This had a tremendous impact on the audience, who were seeing something they had never seen before, performed by actors who occupied a world they knew nothing about. (O'Reilly, 2020: 243)

The play centred on a subject "most of us know very little about" (Pilley in Crawley, 2013). Research involved a 'deep hanging out' of 'localised long term vernacular field research' (Wogan, 2004, in Walmsley, 2018: 277).

Here, through a facilitated series of 'conversation-in-context … a mutual and critical process of building shared understanding' (Westoby and Dowling, 2013: 21) around personal relationships, the actors were able 'to reveal that which would remain unseen' (Hernández-Hernández and Fendler, 2013, in Eaves, 2014: 149). For example, people with intellectual disabilities often repurpose 'social fields' like day centres 'into sexual fields as a means of responding to lack of access to and exclusion from mainstream sexual fields' (Santinele Martino, 2021: 1). BT actors' voices shaped the story being told, serving to speak to and critique understandings of sexuality and relationships in the lives of people with intellectual disabilities. These conversations, while taking place in the rehearsal room and building on the knowledge present, also paid attention to the fact that that space was 'connected to the larger community outside the physical boundaries of [the] workshop' (Capra 2007 in Diamond, 2007: 18), for example ongoing conversations concerning the 1993 Act.

This process sought to 'uncover and challenge the power relations embedded' (Strega and Brown, 2015: 8) in the process of writing a story about the intimate lives of 'Others' while at the same time working to 'uncover and challenge hegemonic assumptions about the nature of the world' (Strega and Brown, 2015: 8). And while 'theatre … is a collaborative medium, but rarely a democracy' (Lambert, 2009: 138), the diversity of ideas, suggestions, thoughts and actions trialled in workshops and discussed in conversations were, through this practice involving 'an ontology of "being with" rather than simply "listening to"' (Macpherson et al, 2016: 373), moulded into a script, a script that accurately reflected the lives of the actors. This process meets the criteria outlined by Pickering and Kara (2017) and Brannelly and Barnes (2022) for an ethical representation of and engagement with the actors and their input into the writing. It also illustrates what Schmidt (2017: 452) labels the 'spectrum of collaboration', which acknowledges 'the care and integrity required in inter-abled artistic relationships' (Gold, 2021: 222). A further point of investment was having the actors choose the name for the character they would perform in the production.

The story reveals how Larry and Sophie (both adults with intellectual disabilities) use the cover of a group outing to the cinema to spend time together in a hotel room that Tom (a care-worker) has booked and Larry has paid for. Meanwhile, back in the cinema the others noticing the absence of their friends go in search of them. Finally, everyone ends up in the hotel room, where Sophie (who also has epilepsy) has had a seizure from mixing alcohol and her medication. The story ends with the friends calling an ambulance to take Sophie to hospital while the rest wait for the minibus to take them home.

The critical reception was extremely positive: 'Blue Teapot have set the bar … for professional theatre productions with roles for and about people with intellectual disabilities' (Shannon, 2012, in O'Reilly, 2020: 242); 'The most important stage kiss in Irish theatrical history' (Daunt, 2013, in O'Reilly, 2020: 243); 'Blue Teapot Theatre Company ... cracks open a political quandary about the sexuality of people with special needs and asks intriguing questions of the theatre' (Crawley, 2013). In doing so, BT foregrounds in a very public way the abilities, experiences and voice of a much marginalised community (Crawley, 2013). This objective nestles at the heart of any social justice research.

Sanctuary (film)

Under the direction of Len Collin, O'Reilly's script was developed into a film (Collin, 2020). The supporting cast played a bigger role than they had in the original stage version, rendering them more visible. Collin and O'Reilly wanted to ensure that the film script avoided fantasy, 'a device that ... allowed audiences off the hook as they were given quick and simple solutions' (Collin, 2020: 226). In so doing, they followed the advice of Barnes (1992, in Collin, 2020: 226): 'Living with a disability means being confronted with environmental and social barriers daily; any portrayal of disabled people, in whatever context, that does not reflect this experience is both grossly inaccurate and a major cause of their continued existence.' *Sanctuary* as a film held the potential to highlight the barriers people with intellectual disabilities faced in developing intimate relationships. The film deliberately trespassed the stereotyped depictions of disabled people, allowing the audience to 'vicariously experience the lives of others' (Nguyen, 2018), thus developing an emotional connection to the enclosures they live under. Illustrating the potential reach of this project film, Schlozman (2021: 2) notes it is 'discussed in the ivory towers of academia ... the bedlam of social media ... highbrow journals and on the stalls of a public restroom'.

Great care was taken to ensure that the settings and situations portrayed in the film accurately reflected the actors' lives. Throughout the film, as with the play, the various characters make references to how many aspects of their lives are not under their control. In doing so, they subtly questioned 'the right of people with IDs to sexual autonomy ... their infantalization ... their right to privacy and the question of independent living' (Ojrzyńska, 2017: 235).

The filming process too trespassed into the already existing taken-for-granted ways of doing things of the cast, crew, families and service providers. For families, service providers and cast, it meant adjusting to longer days than they would normally be used to. For the crew, it meant being constantly aware of following 'the principles laid out by Barnes' (Collin, 2020: 232) and taking their lead from the actors.

Film acting involves receiving, processing and responding to information arriving (often simultaneously) from multiple sources, for example continuity, make-up, lighting and so on. In observing how the actors adapted to the world of film making, Collin questions the definition of intellectual disability as 'a significantly reduced ability to understand new or complex information, to learn new skills' (Department of Health, 2001, in Collin, 2020: 231).

Such questioning is vital, particularly as 'in the professional literature on people with intellectual disabilities, little reference is made to their positive qualities' (McConkey et al, 2010: 7). While McConkey et al made that observation over ten years ago, in a conversation this author had with one of the writers, they said they had no reason to believe the situation had changed (Dunne, 2015). The professional literature is read by psychologists, social workers, medical practitioners, occupational therapists, policy advisors and makers, people with immense power of enclosure over the lives of people with intellectual disabilities. They are therefore conditioned to 'pay attention to the shadow side of those we support, so much so it distorts our images of their full humanity' (McConkey et al, 2010: 7). In placing the stories and bodies of people with intellectual disabilities centre stage, *Sanctuary* reminds us that 'the arts of learning disabled people are the strongest tools to enable society to put an end to its own difficulty in learning' (Masefield, 2006: 77). If only society could be made to pay attention.

Closing act

Sanctuary serves as an illustration of how ABR, aligned with AAR, makes it possible to 'creatively … do things differently that will have a huge impact without necessarily thinking inside the box' (Schnellert et al, 2023; 9–10). As both play and film, *Sanctuary* trespassed into the ongoing enclosure of the intimate lives of people with intellectual disabilities. Barucha (2011, in Rusi-Pyykönen, 2021: 300) asks 'when the play ends what remains/when the play ends what begins'. In choosing to present this story, in the very public arenas of theatre and cinema, BT played a not insignificant part in not just broadening public awareness of the unjust nature of the 1993 Act but ultimately in the conversations that led to its repeal. This illustrates the potential of the arts as a method of social justice research 'to bring people together, to build community to develop empathy, and share a common humanity' (Freebody and Finneran, 2021: 5).

BT followed approaches common in both ABR and AAR. Both of these approaches can be used as methods in social justice research in seeking to critique and re-story social injustice (McNiff, 1998, 2012; Kearns, 2007a, 2009; Eaves, 2014). This process of re-storying enmeshes the personal into the collective, braiding 'how people live their lives and work for social change' (Doetsch-Kidder, 2012: 160). ABR and AAR are acts of trespass, acts of remembering, processes of breaking down walls and fences that serve to silence voices and experiences of injustice, and work to re-vision different and inclusive futures.

The conversational research, central to the writing process, foregrounded the lived experience of BT actors, all of whom are people with an intellectual disability (Collin, 2020; O'Reilly, 2020). This process acknowledged the authority of people to speak about their experience of the world. It allowed O'Reilly to listen to, and hear, little-told tales and for those to be fashioned into a script. This process is not without difficulties, as some of the richness of the original stories may get lost in the act of translation (Pickering and Kara, 2017) when, for example, a composite story is composed. From the start of the process, there was a commitment that this was the BT actors' story that was being told, it was their world that was being represented and they would be playing the various characters (Collin, 2020; O'Reilly, 2020). Through ongoing dialogue, the actors, playwright and director ensured an ethical, and accurate, representation of their world.

Sanctuary considered as social justice research illustrates how the arts have the potential to trespass the enclosure of rights and thereby disrupt the power of taken-for-granted ways of seeing the world. It shows how people 'tell stories in many ways' (Brannelly and Barnes, 2022: 145) and how 'patient listening' (Brannelly and Barnes, 2022: 146) and hospitality on the part of the researcher is essential for those stories to be heard and for the seeking of 'just outcomes' for those telling their stories (Brannelly and Barnes, 2022: 19).

What *Sanctuary* highlighted was how policies and practices need to be examined from multiple perspectives in order to become aware of any unintended consequences that follow from their enactment. Policymakers and enactors need to acknowledge and listen to the voices of those most affected. *Sanctuary* serves as a marker pointing towards the possibilities that might be realised if policies were enacted with Tronto's (1993) definition of care noted earlier as their starting point.

Section 5 of the Criminal Law (Sexual Offences) Act 1993 was changed on 27 March 2017. Despite this, the rights of people with intellectual disabilities to pursue sexual intimacy remain largely unfulfilled. Tellingly, the National Disability Inclusion Strategy 2017–21 contains nothing 'that seeks to address the specific area of personal or intimate relationships for people with disabilities' (Magee et al, 2018: 66). Further, Inclusion Ireland's 2021 UNCRPD shadow report indicated that while progress had been made, there was still significant distance to travel with regard to personal choices and relationships (Inclusion Ireland, 2021).

While the public appears to be becoming more supportive around certain rights of people with disabilities in general (sexual fulfilment, having children, attending mainstream education), they are less so towards people with intellectual disabilities (McConkey, 2019). Cultural, social and legal barriers remain, complicating the wishes of people with intellectual disabilities 'to consider (let alone experience) sexuality as a humanly intrinsic part of life and a right' (Wilson et al, 2017: 989). That this situation exists despite the state signing, in 2006, and ratifying, in 2018, the UNCRPD (Irish Human Rights and Equality Commission, nd), says something about how people with intellectual disabilities are respected and valued. Enclosure continues. Undeterred, BT actors 'continue to imagine a world that has a place for them despite the difficult "given reality"' (Westoby and Dowling, 2013: 137).

References

Arnstein-Kerslake, A. (2015) 'Understanding sex: The right to legal capacity to consent to sex', *Disability and Society*, 30(10): 1459–73.

Arnstein-Kerslake, A. and Flynn, E. (2016) 'Legislating consent: Creating an empowering definition of consent to sex that is inclusive of people with cognitive disabilities', *Social & Legal Studies*, 25(2): 225–48.

Arts and Disability Ireland (2017) 'Leading change in arts and culture: Strategic plan 2017–2021', Dublin: Arts and Disability Ireland.

Azzopardi-Lane, C. and Callus, A.M. (2015) 'Constructing sexual identities: People with intellectual disabilities talking about sexuality', *British Journal of Learning Disabilities*, 43(1): 32–7.

Bane, G., Deely, M., Donohoe, B., Dooher, M., Flaherty, J., Garcia Iriarte, E. et al (2012) 'Relationships of people with learning disabilities in Ireland', *British Journal of Learning Disabilities*, 40(2): 109–22.

Bayley, M. (1997) 'Empowering and relationships', in G. Roberts, G. Grant, P. Ramcharan and J. Borland (eds) *Empowerment in Everyday Life*, London: Jessica Kingsley Publishers, pp 15–34.

Blue Teapot Theatre Company (nd) 'Training', [online], Available from: https://blueteapot.ie/programmes/ [Accessed 16 August 2022].

Blunt, A. and Wills, J. (2000) *Dissident Geographies*, Harlow, Essex: Prentice Hall.

Boal, A. (1998) *Legislative Theatre*, Abingdon, Oxon: Routledge.

Boydell, K. (2021) 'Introduction', in K. Boydell (ed) *Applying Body Mapping in Research*, Abingdon, Oxon: Routledge, pp 1–5.

Brannelly, T. and Barnes, M. (2022) *Researching with Care*, Bristol: Policy Press.

Buser, M., Payne, T., Edizel, Ö. and Dudley, L. (2020) 'Blue space as caring space: Water and the cultivation of care in social and environmental practice', *Social & Cultural Geography*, 21(8): 1039–59.

Callus, A.-M. (2017) 'Being friends means helping each other, making coffee for each other: Reciprocity in the friendships of people with intellectual disability', *Disability and Society*, 32(1): 1–16.

Cameron, C. (2016) 'Disability arts: The building of critical community politics and identity', in R.R. Meade, M. Shaw and S. Banks (eds) *Politics, Power and Community Development*, Bristol: Policy Press, pp 199–216.

Cameron, C. (2007) 'Whose problem? Disability narratives and available identities', *Community Development Journal*, 42(4): 501–51.

Cameron, C. (2009) 'Tragic but brave or just crips with chips? Songs and their lyrics in the Disability Arts Movement in Britain', *Popular Music*, 28(3): 381–96.

Capra, F. (2007) 'Foreword', in D. Diamond (ed) *Theatre for Living: The Art and Science of Community-Based Dialogue*, Oxford: Trafford Publishing, pp 14–18.

Casey, J. (2014) 'Disability, deficiency and excess: A critical re-examination of the construction, production and representations of physical disability in contemporary European film', Unpublished PhD thesis, National University of Ireland, Galway, Available from: https://www.academia.edu/download/53982669/PhD_James_Casey.pdf [Accessed 24 June 2022].

Chamberlain, K., McGuigan, K., Anstiss, D. and Marshall, K. (2018) 'A change of view: Arts-based research and psychology', *Qualitative Research in Psychology*, 15(2–3): 131–9.

Clapton, J. (2009) *A Transformatory Ethic of Inclusion*, Rotterdam: Sense Publications.

Cleveland, W. (2008) *Art and Upheaval*, Oakland, CA: New Village Press.

Clover, D. and Stalker, J. (eds) (2007) *The Arts and Social Justice: Re-crafting Adult Education and Community Cultural Leadership*, Leicester: NIACE.

Coemans, S., Wang, Q., Leysen, J. and Hannes, K. (2015) 'The use of arts-based methods in community-based research with vulnerable populations: Protocol for a scoping review', *International Journal of Educational Research*, 71: 33–9.

Cohen, C.C., Varea, R.G. and Walker, P. (2011a) *Acting Together: Volume 1; Resistance and Reconciliation in Regions of Violence*, Oakland, CA: New Village Press.

Cohen, C.C., Varea, R.G., and Walker, P. (2011b) *Acting Together: Volume 2; Building Just and Inclusive Communities*, Oakland, CA: New Village Press.

Coleman, C. (2019) 'Dancing through the fourth wall: Process drama as an enactment of critical pedagogy', Unpublished PhD thesis, University of Auckland, Available from: https://researchspace.auckland.ac.nz/handle/2292/49823 [Accessed 15 October 2022].

Collin, L. (2020) 'Shooting actors who have intellectual disabilities: A reflexive analysis on the making of the feature film Sanctuary', in K. Ojrzyńska and M. Wieczorek (eds) *Disability and Dissensus: Strategies of Disability Representation and Inclusion in Contemporary Culture*, Leiden: Brill, pp 217–35, Available from: https://brill.com/view/book/9789004424678/BP000019.xml [Accessed 10 April 2022].

Combs, G. and Freedman, J. (2012) 'Narrative, poststructuralism, and social justice: Current practices in narrative therapy', *The Counseling Psychologist*, 40(7): 1033–60.

Conroy, P. (2018) *Disability in Ireland*, Dublin: Orpen Press.

Correa, D.A., Castro, A. and Barrada, J.R. (2022) 'Attitudes towards sexuality of adults with intellectual disabilities: A systematic review', *Sexuality and Disability*, 40: 261–97.

Crawley, P. (2013) 'Special-needs actors centre stage: "For once they have the power in the room"', *The Irish Times*, Wednesday, 17 July, Available from: https://www.irishtimes.com/culture/stage/special-needs-actors-centre-stage-for-once-they-have-the-power-in-the-room-1.1465457 [Accessed 24 August 2022].

Creedon, E. (2020) 'Disability, identity, and early twentieth-century Irish drama', *Irish University Review*, 50(1): 55–66, Available from: https://www.euppublishing.com/doi/abs/10.3366/iur.2020.0434 [Accessed 09 September 2022].

Daunt, S. (2007) 'The power of dance', in K. O'Reilly (ed) *Face On: Disability Arts in Ireland and Beyond*, Dublin: Arts and Disability Ireland, pp 34–9.

De Craene, V. (2017) 'Fucking geographers! Or the epistemological consequences of neglecting the lusty researcher's body', *Gender, Place and Culture*, 24(3): 449–64.

De Wit, W., van Oorsouw, W.M. and Embregts, P.J. (2022) 'Attitudes towards sexuality and related caregiver support of people with intellectual disabilities: A systematic review on the perspectives of people with intellectual disabilities', *Journal of Applied Research in Intellectual Disabilities*, 35(1): 75–87.

Doetsch-Kidder, S. (2012) *Social Change and Intersectional Activism*, New York: Palgrave Macmillan.

Donovan, D. (2011) 'A submarine in the King's river: KCAT and inclusive arts practice', Unpublished MASS dissertation, National University of Ireland, Maynooth.

Donovan, D. (2019) 'Practice bold as love: "Professing" community work', Unpublished DSocSc thesis, Maynooth University.

Dunne, J. (2015) Personal communication.

Eaves, S. (2014) 'From art for arts sake to art as means of knowing: A rationale for advancing arts-based methods in research, practice and pedagogy', *Electronic Journal of Business Research Methods*, 12(2): 154–67, Available from: https://academic-publishing.org/index.php/ejbrm/article/view/1324 [Accessed 21 August 2022].

Feely, M. (2016) 'Sexual surveillance and control in a community-based intellectual disability service', *Sexualities*, 19(5–7): 725–50.

Ferriter, D. (2012) *Occasions of Sin*, London: Profile Books.

Freebody, K. and Finneran, M. (2021) *Critical Themes in Drama: Social, Cultural and Political Analysis*, Abingdon, Oxon: Routledge.

Galway 2020 (2021) 'Blue Teapot: Crossing the Line', [online], Available from: https://galway2020.ie/en/event/blue-teapot-crossing-the-line/ [Accessed 16 August 2022].

Galway International Arts Festival (2013) 'Theatre; Blue Teapot Sanctuary', [video online], Available from: https://www.youtube.com/watch?v=ScnG_oSuD3U [Accessed 19 June 2022].

Ganguly, S. (2010) *Jana Sanskriti: Forum Theatre and Democracy in India*, Abingdon, Oxon: Routledge.

Gold, B. (2021) 'Neurodivergency and interdependent creation: Breaking into Canadian disability arts', *Studies in Social Justice*, 15(2): 209–29.

Goldbard, A. (2006) *New Creative Community: The Art of Cultural Development*, Oakland, CA: New Village Press.

Government of Ireland *Criminal Law (Sexual Offences) Act 1993 S,5*, Dublin: Dublin Stationary Office.

Gray, J. (2022) 'Relational and aesthetic accountability: Considerations of a research-based playwright', *Qualitative Inquiry*, 29(2): 314–22, Available from: https://journals.sagepub.com/doi/abs/10.1177/10778004221098203 [Accessed 3 September 2022].

Griffiths, M. (1998) *Educational Research for Social Justice: Getting Off the Fence*, Buckingham, UK: Open University Press.

Hadley, B., Batch, M. and Whelan, M. (2021) 'The entitled ally: Authorship, consultation, and the "right" to stage autistic people's stories', *Disability & Society*, 36(9): 1489–509.

Hamilton, C. and Atkinson, D. (2009) 'A story to tell: Learning from the life stories of older people with intellectual disabilities in Ireland', *British Journal of Learning Disabilities*, 34(4): 316–22.

Hayes, N. (2020) *The Book of Trespass*, London: Bloomsbury Circus.

Hayes, N. (2022) *The Trespasser's Companion*, London: Bloomsbury Publishing.

Healy, E., McGuire, B.E., Evans, D.S. and Carley, S.N. (2009) 'Sexuality and personal relationships for people with an intellectual disability: Part I; Service-user perspectives', *Journal of Intellectual Disability Research*, 53(11): 905–12.

Hornstein, G.A. (2017) *Agnes's Jacket*, Monmouth, UK: PCCS Books.

Horsford, R., Rumbold, J., Varney, H., Morris, D., Dungan, L. and Lith, T.V. (2014) 'Creating community: An arts-based enquiry', *Journal of Applied Arts & Health*, 5(1): 65–81.

Hudson. B. (2006) 'Punishing monsters, judging aliens: Justice at the borders of community', *The Australian and New Zealand Journal of Criminology*, 36(2): 232–47.

Inclusion Ireland (2021) 'Respect our rights!', [online], Available from: https://inclusionireland.ie/wp-content/uploads/2021/12/Respect-Our-Rights-Report-November-2021.pdf [Accessed 18 August 2022].

Irish Human Rights and Equality Commission (nd) 'The Convention on the Rights of People with Disabilities', [online], Available from: https://www.ihrec.ie/crpd/ [Accessed 17 September 2022].

Johnson, K. and Traustadóttir, R. (2005) 'Introduction: In and out of institutions', in K, Johnson and R. Traustadóttir (eds) *Deinstitutionalisation and People with Intellectual Disabilities: In and Out of Institutions*, London: Jessica Kingsley Publishers, pp 13–29.

Johnson, K., Walmsley, J. and Wolfe, M. (2009) *People with Intellectual Disabilities: Towards a Good Life?*, Bristol: Policy Press.

KCAT (ed) (2009) *Art and Inclusion: The Story of KCAT*, Callan, County Kilkenny: KCAT.

Kearns, P. (2007a) 'Emancipatory art processes', in K. O'Reilly (ed) *Face On: Disability Arts in Ireland and Beyond*, Dublin: Arts and Disability Ireland, pp 138–46.

Kearns, P. (2007b) 'Inside I'm Dancing', in K. O'Reilly (ed) *Face On: Disability Arts in Ireland and Beyond*, Dublin: Arts and Disability Ireland, pp 124–9.

Kearns, P. (2009) 'Being a subversive 'Activist Crip' on a fixed contract', *The Ahead Journal*, [online], Available from: https://www.ahead.ie/jour nal/Being-a-subversive-Artivist-Crip-on-a-fixed-contract [Accessed 26 August 2022].

Kelly, B. (2022) *In Search of Madness*, Dublin: Gill Books.

Kelly, G., Crowley, H. and Hamilton, C. (2009) 'Rights, sexuality and relationships in Ireland: "It'd be nice to be kind of trusted"', *British Journal of Learning Disabilities*, 37(4): 308–15.

Kuppers, P. (2003) *Disability and Contemporary Performance: Bodies on Edge*, Abingdon, Oxon: Routledge.

Kuppers, P. (2007) 'Introduction', in K. O'Reilly (ed) *Face On: Disability Arts in Ireland and Beyond*, Dublin: Arts and Disability Ireland, pp 12–17.

Kuppers, P. (2011) *Disability Culture and Community Performance*, London: Palgrave Macmillan.

Kuri, E.L. (2020) 'Ethics in arts-based research: Drawing on the strengths of creative arts therapists', *Canadian Journal of Counselling & Psychotherapy/ Revue Canadienne de Counseling et de Psychothérapie*, 54(3): 197–219.

Lambert, M. (2009) 'Theatre in the round: Exploring an inclusive model', in Kilkenny Collective for Arts Talent (ed) *Art and Inclusion: The Story of KCAT*, Callan, County Kilkenny: Kilkenny Collective for Arts Talent.

Leavy, P. (2010) 'Poetic bodies: Female body image, sexual identity and arts-based research', *LEARNing Landscapes*, 4(1): 175–87.

Ledger, S. and Shufflebotham, L. (2006) 'Songs of resistance', in D. Mitchell, R. Traustadóttir, R. Chapman, L. Townson, N. Ingham and S. Ledger (eds) *Exploring Experiences of Advocacy by People with Learning Disabilities: Testimonies of Resistance*, London: Jessica Kingsley Publishers, pp 68–90.

Ledwith, M. (2005) *Community Development: A Critical Approach*, Bristol: Policy Press.

Ledwith, M. (2016) *Community Development in Action*, Bristol: Policy Press.

Lynch, Y. (2007) 'Betwixt the devil and the deep green sea', in K. O'Reilly (ed) *Face On: Disability Arts in Ireland and Beyond*, Dublin: Arts and Disability Ireland, pp 40–7.

Macphee, J. and Reuland, E. (eds) (2007) *Realizing the Impossible*, Edinburgh: AK Press.

Macpherson, H., Fox, A., Street, S., Cull, J., Jenner, T., Lake, D. et al (2016) 'Listening space: Lessons from artists with and without learning disabilities', *Environment and Planning D: Society and Space*, 34(2): 371–89.

Magee, C., Murphy, T., Turley, M., Feely, M., García Iriarte, E. and McConkey, R. (2018) '19 stories of social inclusion: Ireland: stories of belonging, contributing and connecting', Dublin: National Disability Authority.

Malik, N. (2019) *We Need New Stories*, London: Weidenfeld and Nicolson.

Masefield, P. (2006) *Strength: Broadsides from Disability on the Arts*, London: Trentham Books.

McConkey, R. (2015) 'Measuring public discomfort at meeting people with disabilities', *Research in Developmental Disabilities*, 45–6: 220–8.

McConkey, R. (2019) 'Public perceptions of the rights of persons with disabilities: National surveys in the Republic of Ireland', *Alter: European Journal of Disability Research*, 14: 128–39.

McConkey, R. (2021) 'A national survey of the social and emotional differences reported by adults with disability in Ireland compared to the general population', *Disabilities*, 1(2): 89–97.

McConkey, R., Dunne, J. and Blitz, N. (2010) *Shared Lives: Building Relationships and Community with People Who Have Intellectual Disabilities*, Rotterdam: Sense Publications.

McDonagh, R. (2021) *Unsettled*, Dublin: Skein Press.

McIntosh, A. (2012) 'The challenge of radical human ecology to the academy', in L. Williams, R. Roberts and A. McIntosh (eds) *Radical Human Ecology*, Farnham, Surrey: Ashgate, pp 31–56.

McKay, G. (1996) *Senseless Acts of Beauty*, London: Verso.

McKay, G. (1998) *DIY Culture: Party and Protest in Nineties Britain*, London: Verso.

McKay, G. (2011) *Radical Gardening*, London: Francis Lincoln.

McNiff, S. (1998) *Arts-Based Research*, London: Jessica Kingsley Publishers.

McNiff, S. (2012) 'Opportunities and challenges in art-based research', *Journal of Applied Arts and Health*, 3(1): 5–12.

Merrells, J., Buchanan, A. and Waters, R. (2019) '"We feel left out": Experiences of social inclusion from the perspective of young adults with intellectual disability', *Journal of Intellectual & Developmental Disability*, 44(1): 13–22.

Mykitiuk, R., Chaplick, A. and Rice, C. (2015) 'Beyond normative ethics: Ethics of arts-based disability research', *Ethics, Medicine and Public Health*, 1(3): 373–82.

Naidus, B. (2009) *Arts for Change*, Oakland, CA: New Village Press.

News from Nowhere (eds) (2003) *We Are Everywhere*, London: Verso.

Nguyen, M. (2018) 'May: The creative and rigorous use of art in health care research', *Forum Qualitative Sozialforschung/Forum: Qualitative Social Research*, 19(2), [online], Available from: https://www.qualitative-research.net/index.php/fqs/article/download/2844/4225?inline=1 [Accessed 15 October 2020].

O'Byrne, C. and Muldoon, O. (2015) 'Stigma, self-perception and social comparisons in young people with an intellectual disability', *Irish Educational Studies*, 36(3): 307–22.

Ojrzynska, K. (2017) Populating the Irish stage (dis)abled bodies: Sanctuary by Christian O'Reilly and Blue Teapot Theatre Company, in A. Etiene and T. Dubost (eds) *Perspectives on Contemporary Irish Theatre: Populating the Stage*, London: Palgrave Macmillan, pp 231–47.

Oliver, M. and Barnes, C. (2012) *The New Politics of Disablement*, Houndmills: Palgrave Macmillan.

Onstot, A. (2019) 'Capacity to consent: Policies and practices that limit sexual consent for people with intellectual/developmental disabilities', *Sexuality and Disability*, 37: 633–44.

O'Reilly, C. (2020) 'Christian O'Reilly talks about his writing on disability for the stage and screen', in K. Ojrzyńska and M. Wieczorek (eds) *Disability and Dissensus: Strategies of Disability Representation and Inclusion in Contemporary Culture*, Leiden: Brill, pp 236–44.

Pickering, L. and Kara, H. (2017) 'Presenting and representing others: Towards an ethics of engagement', *International Journal of Social Research Methodology*, 20(3): 299–309.

Pilley, P. (2022) Personal communication.

Ponterotto, J.G., Mathew, J.T. and Raughley, B. (2013) 'The value of mixed methods designs to social justice research in counseling and psychology', *Journal for Social Action in Counseling & Psychology*, 5(2): 42–68.

Rocco, L. (2019) Reflections on the Disability Arts Movement'. *Unlimited*, [online], 21 May, Available from: https://weareunlimited.org.uk/an-interview-with-tony-heaton-david-hevey-jo-verrent-members-of-the-disability-arts-movement/ [Accessed 12 May 2023].

Rusi-Pyykönen, M. (2021) 'Object companionship: An artistic research method and object-led praxis in participatory theater', *Research in Arts and Education*, 4: 283–302.

Sanctuary Electronic Press Kit (2015) [video online] Directed by Len Collin. United Kingdom: Noncents Films, Available from: http://blueteapot.ie/our_performances/sanctuary-film/ [Accessed 27 June 2022].

Santinele Martino, A. (2021) '"I don't want to get in trouble': A study of how adults with intellectual disabilities convert and navigate intellectual disability sexual fields', *Culture, Health & Sexuality*, 24(9): 1230–42.

Santinele Martino, A. and Perreault-Laird, J. (2019) "'I don't' know if I can talk about that": An exploratory study on the experiences of care workers regarding the sexuality of people with intellectual disabilities', *Disability Studies Quarterly*, 39(3). Available at: http://dsq-sds.org/article/view/6383 [Accessed 7 Sepember 2023].

Santos, B. (2014) *Epistemologies of the South*, Abingdon, Oxon: Routledge.

Schlozman, S. (2021) *Film*, Bingley: Emerald Publishing.

Schmidt, Y. (2017) 'Towards a new directional turn? Directors with cognitive disabilities', *Research in Drama Education: The Journal of Applied Theatre and Performance*, 22(3): 446–59.

Schnellert, L., Tidey, L., Co-creators, R.R.R. and Hole, R. (2023) "'You have the right to love and be loved": Participatory theatre for disability justice with self-advocates', *Qualitative Research*, 23(2): 467–85.

Scull, A. (2022) *Desperate Remedies*, London: Penguin Random House.

Strandberg-Long, P. (2019) 'The reaction in counter-action: How Meisner technique and active analysis complement each other', *Stanislavski Studies*, 7(1): 95–108.

Strega, S. and Brown, L. (2015) 'Introduction: From resistance to resurgence', in S. Strega and L. Brown (eds) *Research as Resistance* (2nd edn), Toronto: Canadian Scholars Press, pp 3–16.

Summerhill (1966) [film] Directed by David Miller, Canada. National Film Board of Canada, Available from: https://www.nfb.ca/film/summerhill [Accessed 14 January 2023].

Swain, J. and Cameron, C. (1999) 'Unless otherwise stated: Discourses of labelling and identity in coming out', in M. Corker and S. French (eds) *Disability Discourse*, Buckingham: Open University Press, pp 68–78.

Thompson, D. (ed) (1995) *Concise Oxford Dictionary* (9th edn), Oxford: Clarendon Press.

Toolan, D. (2007) 'Ten years after "A strategy for equality"', in K, O'Reilly (ed) *Face On: Disability Arts in Ireland and Beyond*, Dublin: Arts and Disability Ireland, pp 117–23.

Viscardis, K., Rice, C., Pileggi, V., Underhill, A., Chandler, E., Changfoot, N. et al (2019) 'Difference within and without: Health care providers' engagement with disability arts', *Qualitative Health Research*, 29(9): 1287–98.

Walmsley, B. (2018) 'Deep hanging out in the arts: An anthropological approach to capturing cultural value', *International Journal of Cultural Policy*, 24(2): 272–91.

Watkins, M. (2019) *Mutual Accompaniment and the Creation of the Commons*, New Haven: Yale University Press.

Westoby, P. and Dowling, G. (2013) *Theory and Practice of Dialogical Community Development*, Abingdon, Oxon: Routledge.

Whittle, C. and Butler, C. (2018) 'Sexuality in the lives of people with intellectual disabilities: A meta-ethnographic synthesis of qualitative studies', *Research in Developmental Disabilities*, 75: 68–81.

Wilson, N.J., Jaques, H., Johnson, A. and Brotherton, M.L. (2017) 'From social exclusion to supported inclusion: Adults with intellectual disability discuss their lived experiences of a structured social group', *Journal of Applied Research in Intellectual Disabilities*, 30(5): 847–58.

Wilson, N.J., Frawley, P., Schaafsma, D., O'Shea, A., Kahonde, C.K., Thompson, V. et al (2019) 'Issues of sexuality and relationships', in J.L. Mastson (ed) *Handbook of Intellectual Disabilities: Integrating Theory, Research, and Practice*, Springer, pp 989–1010.

Zinn, H. (2003) *Artists in Times of War*, New York: Seven Stories Press.

8

Using peer engagement to support the participation of people who use drugs in research

Brian Melaugh and Andy O'Hara

Introduction

The purpose of this chapter is to outline the theory and application of employing peer engagement with people who use drugs (PWUD) to inform research and policy development. The chapter will outline the research practice of the drug advocacy organisation Union of Improved Services Communication and Education (UISCE) for PWUD and highlight how the approach of UISCE reflects social justice methodologies. First, the chapter will open with a description of UISCE. This will be followed by a discussion of drug use in Ireland and the opportunities and challenges drug policy presents for engagement with PWUD. Thirdly, we will provide a description of peer-led research conducted by UISCE to inform the development of Ireland's first drug consumption room and the development of the National Drugs Strategy. The fourth section will review what works to support the engagement of PWUD in research and the relationship of this engagement to social justice. Finally, the chapter will conclude with a review of the overall learning with regard to peer engagement and social justice research.

Before proceeding with the chapter, it is important to address two areas: our approach to social justice research and the issue of language and terminology when addressing drug use. Turning to social justice, we accept the definition of the United Nations: 'Social justice may be broadly understood as the fair and compassionate distribution of the fruits of economic growth' (UN, 2006). We also accept that four principles need to be achieved for social justice to be effective: human rights, access, participation and equity (Soken-Huberty, 2022). These principles are reflected in UISCE approach to research, and in the chapter we highlight how and why PWUD should participate in research. With regard to human rights, it is necessary to link social justice with human rights as a framework that acts as a 'mechanism against exclusion' (Hibbert, 2017). Again, this reflects the mission of UISCE, namely to 'contribute to improving the quality of life of people who use drugs through a human-rights based approach' (UISCE, 2022).

Addressing the theme of language, the chapter accepts the position adopted by the International Network of People who Use Drugs (INPUD) about the need to avoid terms such as 'drug user' or 'problem drug user'. As these terms reduce the complexity of an individual's experience to the act of drug use, they have the potential to denigrate the individual (INPUD, 2011). INPUD recommends the use of the term 'people who use drugs' and the specific term PWID for 'people who inject drugs' (INPUD, 2011), terminology which we will use in this chapter.

Union of Improved Services Communication and Education

UISCE was established in the 1990s, with a remit to provide an independent representative voice for PWUD and to promote their human rights. In meeting this remit, UISCE is aware of the importance of conducting research that informs the development of service delivery and wider reform of drug policy. As a representative organisation, UISCE is aware that for research to fully reflect the voice of PWUD it needs to be conducted in partnership with PWUD. This commitment to peer engagement is reflected in UISCE's earliest research, exemplified in this extract from 'Methadone: What's the story?' (UISCE, 2003):

> A unique aspect of the methodology was the fact that the focus groups and questionnaires were co-facilitated and designed by drug service users. This is in marked contrast to the external evaluation commissioned by the Eastern Health Board … From UISCE's point of view, the omission of service users from the research process could be seen as indicative of an invalidation of their views. Methadone patients are rarely seen as a consumer group whose expectations and experiences need to be taken into account when designing and operating treatment programmes. (UISCE, 2003: 10)

It is refreshing to note that UISCE's perspective on the inclusion of PWUD in research and policy is accepted as essential by the EU Drugs Strategy 2021–25 (Council of the European Union, 2020) and Ireland's National Drug Strategy 'Reducing harm, supporting recovery. A health-led response to drug and alcohol use in Ireland 2017–25[1] (Department of Health, 2017). This focus on participation makes sense, as evidence suggests that the inclusion of PWUD supports service development and coherent drug policy (Hunt, 2002; Kerr et al, 2006; Lianping et al, 2012; UISCE, 2022). On this point, INPUD (2008a) states:

People who use drugs themselves are often best able to identify what works in their community – a community that others know little about. Their voices need to be heard to ensure the shaping of effective responses to blood borne pathogen epidemics and other drug-related harms. Research has provided evidence of the benefits of greater involvement of people who use drugs. In particular, people who use drugs are able to expand the reach and effectiveness of prevention and harm reduction services by making contact with people at greatest risk. (INPUD, 2008a: 39)

For PWUD, meaningful participation in research not only validates their lived experience as legitimate; the experience of involvement itself affirms their dignity and acts to challenge drug-related stigma and exclusion (Montañés Sánchez and Oomen, 2009).

The Irish and wider drug policy context

Whereas the commitment to support participation in the EU and Irish policy is notable, the existence of organisational and legal barriers that limit participation must also be acknowledged (Lianping et al, 2012; Wilkinson, 2021). Organisational barriers include a reluctance to share power or to fully involve PWUD as equal partners in decisions about research (Wilkinson, 2021), while the fact that certain drugs are 'criminalised' means people who use these 'illicit' drugs are often reluctant to engage because of concerns about disclosure. As PWUD are constructed as 'criminals' and drug use as 'morally wrong', these labels create a perfect climate for the stigmatisation and marginalisation of PWUD (Grosso and Gruppo, 2008; Wilkinson, 2021).

This prevailing legal and moral context means that PWUD take steps to hide their drug use, often using drugs on the 'street' or in hidden locations and eschewing contact with health services. As a consequence, PWUD can be defined as 'hidden' populations:

Criminalisation and stigmatisation of drug use have led to a situation where problematic drug use is to some extent hidden … Some individuals are not interested in reporting their abuse to authorities because they are worried about negative consequences, and others with problematic drug use have no contact whatsoever with the social or health care system. (Dahlberg and Anderberg, 2013: 149)

The literature also suggests that PWUD take active steps to hide their drug use, often linked to concerns about engaging with law enforcement or parental concerns about contact with social services (Corr, 2002; TUSLA, 2019). As a consequence, PWUD are described as 'hard–to–reach' populations:

> Hard to reach is a term used to describe those sub-groups of the population that are difficult to reach or involve in research or public health … Hard-to-reach populations may also actively try to conceal their group identity due to fear of confrontation with legal authorities (e.g. drug users) or simply because of social pressure they feel from other members of the broader community. (Shaghaghi et al, 2011: 87)

Because of their experience of social marginalisation and drug use practice, PWUD are defined as 'vulnerable drug-using populations' (EMCDDA, 2017).[2] As a population, they experience the most serious health problems, including significant levels of morbidity because of overdose (INPUD, 2011; Duffin et al, 2020; O'Carroll et al, 2021). The number of PWUD who reflect the criteria of high-risk drug use in Ireland is not inconsequential, with the number of high-risk opioid users estimated at 18,988 (EMCDDA, 2019). Research suggests that around 13,000 of this cohort are in contact with services for the purpose of opioid substitution treatment (such as methadone) and/or needle exchange provision (EMCDDA, 2019; Merchants Quay Ireland, 2020; Kelleher et al, 2021) Therefore, about 6,000 PWUD can be considered as a hidden/hard-to-reach population.

The paradox for researchers is that the views of the group with the highest need are often absent from research findings and recommendations. Since its creation, UISCE has taken active steps to ensure the voice of hard-to-reach PWUD is included in research and representation. This commitment is again affirmed in the organisation's current strategic plan 'Peer partnership for change 2022 to 2025' (UISCE, 2022: 8): 'UISCE continues to focus on the group of people who have the least opportunity to have their voice heard, actively seeking out people who are currently using on the street, many of whom are experiencing homelessness.'

UISCE approach to research: peer-led consultations with PWUD

This commitment to engaging with hard-to-reach PWUD is reflected in UISCE's early research, for example 'Methadone: What's the story?' (UISCE, 2003), which pioneered the use of peer-led street outreach to engage with PWUD. While acknowledging the importance of this early research, the purpose of this section is to explore UISCE's recent research to illustrate what works to engage with PWUD and how this engagement reflects social justice research. This approach reflects UISCE's view that to be effective, research for social justice must reflect principles such as participation and human rights. In practice, this means working to ensure PWUD participate in the planning, implementation and dissemination of research. It places demands on UISCE to manage the challenges of making contact with 'hidden populations' to ensure their voice is part of health and policy decisions that affect their lives. Again, this commitment to meaningful participation is in keeping with declarations that promote the human rights of PWUD, namely the 'Vancouver Declaration' (IAUD, 2006) and '"Nothing About Us Without Us": A manifesto by people who use illegal drugs' (INPUD, 2008b). On this point, the manifesto states: 'Today we demand to have a say and we need to: be treated as equals and respected for our expertise and professionalism in addressing drug use … and other health, social and human rights issues that affect our lives. We need to be involved in research that affects us' (INPUD, 2008b). The research/consultation process is divided into four phases: planning, implementation, data analysis and dissemination. While the stages may need to be tailored to meet the particular context of the research, all research conducted by UISCE starts with the Advisory Committee. This committee, responsible for the planning and management of the research, is normally composed of UISCE staff, academics and policymakers, and central to its composition is the involvement of PWUD as peers. The Advisory Committee ensures that the research is based on the needs of PWUD and is responsible for research design, planning, evaluation and strategies for dissemination. As the committee is responsible for the overall governance of the research, it is essential that PWUD are empowered to play an active role in the committee. This demands training, support, flexibility and policies and procedures that respect PWUD as equal peers in the research process. Without these elements, peer engagement is tokenistic and cannot be viewed as meaningful participation (Kools, 2013; Marshall et al, 2015). The implementation stage is based on peer-led research approaches, with peers acting as 'gatekeepers' to engage with PWUD. The research is primarily conducted in open/street locations, and peer knowledge of locations PWUD access is central for the research to happen. Peers receive training on, for example, informed consent, personal safety and engaging with law enforcement. The analysis stage is focused on making sense of the data (for example, thematic analysis), and peers are actively involved in how the final findings of the research will be documented. The final stage is dissemination, which for UISCE includes dissemination to PWUD, for example through the UISCE publication *Brass Munkie*. UISCE is also committed to ensuring that peers and PWUD play a central role in meetings with policymakers to explore, for example, how the research can contribute to policy change/service planning (UISCE, 2022).

The research initiatives we will cover in this chapter are the 'Public consultation to inform the development of a new Safer Injecting Facility' (UISCE, 2017) and 'UISCE submission for 2017 National Drugs Strategy

(UISCE, 2016a) to inform the development of 'Reducing harm, supporting recovery. A health-led response to drug and alcohol use in Ireland 2017–2025' (Department of Health, 2017).

Before describing these research projects, it is important to touch on the theme of research ethics. As these research projects are defined as consultations, with the aim of discovering what people know about service delivery and/or wider organisational need, there is not a requirement (in Ireland) to apply for research ethics approval (HSE, 2018;[3] TUSLA, 2020). However UISCE complies with ethical frameworks that guide engagement with PWUD, for example 'Nothing About Us Without Us consulting with people who use drugs: Do's and don'ts' (INPUD, 2008a). The INPUD framework requests that researchers respect confidentiality when meeting with PWUD in low threshold settings or in settings where PWUD congregate. It also requests that the voice of both current and former PWUD is included in the research. These frameworks offer international benchmarks that respect and protect the dignity of PWUD who engage in research/consultation.

Public consultation to inform the development of a new Safer Injecting Facility

In 2016, UISCE was invited by the Health Service Executive to become part of a working group planning the development of Ireland's first Safer Injecting Facility (SIF). Supervised injecting facilities, also referred to as 'Medically Supervised Injecting Centres', are 'medically supervised spaces where people can inject drugs in a clean and hygienic setting off the street' (Ana Liffey Drug Project, 2015). SIFs are effective in addressing the needs of high-risk drug-using populations and also reduce the risks associated with public injecting (EMCDDA, 2018). A key milestone in the development of the SIF was the passing of the Misuse of Drugs (Supervised Injecting Facilities) Act 2017, which provided for the establishment of a pilot supervised injecting facility in Dublin. In order to ensure the proposed facility reflected the opinions and concerns of PWUD, especially PWID, UISCE carried out a consultation with the community. To manage the process, UISCE established an Advisory Group of PWUD and other stakeholders to oversee the design and management of the consultation, for example developing the survey to guide the interview. The survey was conducted through peer-led outreach, and 93 PWUD were interviewed.

The findings provide interesting information on prevalence and drug-using patterns: for example, heroin was the main drug of choice, with 90 per cent of respondents sharing that they were currently injecting heroin. With regard to environments for consuming drugs, 86 per cent of the sample confirmed they had injected in public, with 75 per cent sharing they considered this practice unsafe. However, as 76 per cent of respondents defined themselves as homeless, the options for finding safe spaces to consume drugs were limited (UISCE, 2017). It is important to note that in a UISCE consultation with PWUD in 2016, the research highlighted that the opening of an SIF 'would reduce the harm to people who use drugs and the general population' (UISCE, 2016a).

Central to the consultation was finding out the views of respondents on service location, opening hours and the internal layout of the facility:

> While some people affirmed that they would travel "anywhere" or "everywhere" the majority said they would like it to be near the city centre or even close to a clinic. Regarding opening hours, the majority of respondents agreed it should be a service available 24/7 with a few exceptions. Finally, regarding the ideal set-up of the facility, it was agreed that some basic equipment, such as mirrors, tables and chairs, were essential. In the recovery space ... there will need to be coffee and tea facilities as well as a smoking area. (Millar, 2018: 10)

Because of planning objections and a judicial review, a final decision on the opening of the SIF has yet to be made (McCann and Duffin, 2022). Despite this reality, the consultation to inform the development of Ireland's first SIF is evidence of UISCE's commitment to social justice by ensuring the voice of PWUD is central in the planning and design of the SIF.

Public consultation to inform the development of National Drugs Strategy 2017 to 2025

The process of developing a drug strategy to replace the National Drugs Strategy (interim) 2009–16 (Dublin: Department of Community, Rural and Gaeltacht Affairs, 2009) started in 2015, with the establishment of the National Drugs Strategy Steering Committee. The purpose of the committee was 'to provide guidance and advice in the development of the new strategy and advise the Minister on the new policy' (RPA Consulting, 2017). UISCE was appointed to the National Steering Committee in 2016. This decision to appoint UISCE to the National Steering Committee is important both at a strategic and symbolic level. The appointment of UISCE followed consultations with government and acceptance of the UISCE position that the voice of PWUD should inform the emerging drugs strategy. Strategically, a goal for UISCE was to develop a holistic model of representation through membership of policy fora at local and national levels. While representation at the local level was developed, UISCE was not represented on any national policy forums. Membership of the National Steering Committee addressed this strategic goal. Symbolically, political support transmits a message to PWUD that their perspectives are valuable and their participation in decisions on the development of drug policy is essential (Kools, 2013; Wilkinson, 2021).

A core task for the National Steering Committee was to oversee a public consultation to inform the development of the new strategy. A key concern for UISCE was to ensure that the voice of more marginalised PWUD was included in this consultation, which meant engaging with people on the street and outdoor locations. Conducting a consultation in outdoor environments requires a concise, clear and accessible research instrument that allows researchers to manage different variables. These include weather and the needs of PWUD, for example the need to access drugs and leave a space because of law enforcement. A review of the questionnaire to guide the consultation highlighted some concerns about its length (long and repetitive), use of negative language to describe drug use (misuse of drugs) and because of the language used it was not widely accessible for PWUD (RPA Consulting, 2017). UISCE requested permission to 'redraft' the questionnaire to ensure it met the requirements for engaging with PWUD. The request was granted, and in practice 'UISCE spent the first 10 days of the consultation working with this community to rewrite the questions while maintaining the core message and ensuring relevance to the level of exposure to the strategy' (UISCE, 2016b: 14). The approach to the consultation was influenced by participatory research approaches with PWUD, for example the 'Participatory Research in Ottawa Understanding Drugs' (PROUD) study in Canada (Lazarus et al, 2014). The PROUD study is grounded in community based participatory research and adopts a peer-led approach to conduct research with PWUD. The study provides practical information on how to recruit, train and manage the power dynamics of working with PWUD as peer researchers. To support its work, UISCE has several 'peer-led volunteers' who conduct street outreach and lead out on research initiatives.[4] UISCE established an Advisory Committee composed of peer volunteers, academics and staff to oversee the consultation. The knowledge and expertise of peers were central in the redrafting of the questionnaire and conducting the street-led outreach. The peers also played a central role in the dissemination of the findings, for example by meeting with policy representatives and ensuring the findings of the consultation were shared with the wider community of PWUD.

Informed consent is central to research and indeed for any form of meaningful participation (Souleymanov et al, 2016). Using a collaborative process to make the language of the questionnaire more accessible, with regard to what it means to take part in the consultation and ensuring the form reflected a 'plain English' style, is evidence of research informed by a social justice approach, namely ensuring language is clear and simple enough to allow all to participate.

Through peer-led outreach, UISCE engaged with 51 people who completed the questionnaire (88 per cent identified as male and 11 per cent identified as female). As part of its commitment to ensuring information is shared with the community, the final submission 'Your voice: 2017 National Drugs Strategy' was shared widely among PWUD. In December 2016, a full copy of the submission was included in a special edition of the UISCE magazine *Brass Munkie* (UISCE, 2016b).[5] The article is available online, and over 1,000 copies were distributed to individuals and services through outreach (Melaugh and Rodrigues, 2017). A rationale for the wide dissemination of the submission was linked to answers evoked by the question 'Did you know Ireland has a National Drug Strategy for the years 2009–2016?' (UISCE, 2016a). Most respondents were not aware of the existence of the strategy (68 per cent). This level of awareness is a concern – a national drug strategy has real implications for PWUD, as Hunt et al (2010: 333) state 'the structure of the drug scene affects what users' groups can do and how they function'. The *Brass Munkie* is also evidence of a social justice approach in that it highlights how a marginalised community can fully participate in the creation of knowledge that reflects their lived experience.

Hunt (2002) maintains that the development of drug policy is a two-way process, involving an exchange of knowledge between professionals and PWUD. This exchange allows for drug policy to remain current and responsive: 'Professionals undoubtedly have important expertise, but much valuable knowledge for understanding how services can best be organised and delivered – what might work in a given locality and identifying emerging needs – is possessed by drug users, not professionals' (Hunt, 2002: 16). As this professional knowledge of drugs is partial, the experience of PWUD is essential for the development of robust drug policy. As this chapter highlights, engaging PWUD in research to inform service and policy delivery is not without its challenges, specifically how to engage with hard-to-reach/hidden populations. However, the review of consultations conducted by UISCE does present evidence on what works to support the meaningful participation of PWUD in research. Three themes emerge: first, using community development approaches to empower PWUD to fully participate in the design, governance and wider dissemination of research; secondly, the use of peer-led outreach approaches to collect data; and finally, social research informed by social justice principles of participation, taking steps to support access and employing a rights-based approach.

People who use drugs are part of the solution: engaging with people who use drugs

The manifesto by people who use illegal drugs, 'Nothing About Us Without Us' (INPUD, 2008b), states that PWUD 'are part of the solution and not part of the problem'. With regard to the problem, the manifesto does not sugar-coat the issue: We are among the most vilified and demonized groups in society. Simply because we use illegal drugs, people and governments often deny us our rights and dignity. The solution is to adopt community development approaches to involve PWUD in all decisions that affect their lives towards the end goal of promoting their dignity and human rights. UISCE reflects the manifesto's perspective and is committed to working 'for and with PWUD through a community development approach' (UISCE, 2022). As a concept, community development is defined as: 'A developmental activity comprised of both a task and a process. The task is social change to achieve equality, social justice and human rights, and the process is the application of principles of participation, empowerment and collective decision making in a structured and co-ordinated way' (Community Work Ireland, 2016: 5).

This thinking is reflected in Lianping et al's (2012) definition of peer engagement with PWUD as a 'community-based' and a 'bottom-up' approach. Drawing on community development, the task for UISCE is to develop an organisational culture where PWUD feel they are part of all decisions around research and are empowered to take up their role as peers in the research process. The way to achieve this aim is through appropriate training for PWUD (research approaches and team building, for example) and the establishment of peer-led advisory groups that oversee the governance of research (Melaugh and Rodrigues, 2017). With regard to building cultures that support the meaningful participation of PWUD, Hunt (2002) makes a distinction between 'involvement' and 'empowerment'. While involvement is valid and is the preferred approach for service review, it has a tendency to construct the PWUD as 'client/s' with limited roles in decision-making, while empowerment is wider, with the goal of including PWUD as equal partners in research, valuing their lived experience and ensuring they have equal power in the governance and dissemination of research. Empowerment is closely associated with social justice approaches to research, as both focus on how marginalised groups can identify and change the issues that impact on their lives (Crickley and McArdle, 2009). Specifically, social justice-focused methodologies, for example participatory and collective action, are named as central in reducing barriers that prevent PWUD from engaging in research (Lianping et al, 2012; Kools, 2013; Wilkinson, 2021), a perspective captured in the following excerpt from the '"Nothing About Us Without Us": Manifesto for people who use illegal drugs:' (INPUD, 2008b: 1): 'Through collective action, we will challenge existing oppressive drugs laws, policies and programs, and work with governments and international agencies to formulate evidence based policies and programs that respect our human rights and dignity and protect and promote our health.'

Peer-led approaches to engage with people who use drugs

Regarding the consultations to collect the views of PWUD on policy and service development, a challenge was making contact with hard-to-reach PWUD. A review of the literature highlights that peer-led outreach and street-based recruitment approaches are named as effective in accessing hard-to-reach and at-risk PWUD (Abrams, 2010; Lianping et al, 2012). The value is that peers use their lived experience of drug use to access members of their community for the purpose of research. Referring to the practice of peer-led approaches, Grosso and Gruppo (2008) distinguish between the roles of the 'initiative group' who want access to PWUD and the 'peer operator' who support access to happen. As stated earlier in the chapter, a strategic objective of UISCE (initiative group) 'is to engage with the PWUD who have the least opportunity to have their voice heard by actively seeking out people who are using drugs on the street' (UISCE, 2022). Drug use in this population, particularly PWID, typically takes place in hidden locations such as alleyways, and a knowledge of these locations is necessary for access. As people who are currently using drugs have knowledge of these locations and are likely to be trusted by the drug-using community, it makes sense to use their expertise as peer operators (Wilkinson, 2021). It should be stated that peer-led outreach is part of the daily work of UISCE, and the learning from the consultations is that this daily contact is essential to support research. When the peer is known to the community, access is easier, and indeed there is the opportunity to use the sampling technique of 'snowballing', as respondents are more comfortable providing details of individuals who may participate in the research (Shaghaghi et al, 2011). The research methods employed by UISCE to collect data include semi-structured interviews and participant observation. In many ways, street outreach reflects 'purposive sampling' approaches, as the research is guided by the 'researcher's judgement and interest' (Robson, 2002). The strength of using purposive and snowball sampling is that it allows peers to use their judgement. As peers have valuable knowledge of the local drug scene, they can get access to concealed populations. They can also make the decision not to engage with PWUD, for example if access is considered unsafe for peers and/or participants. The challenge of using more flexible research designs includes the logistical demands of street outreach, which can be time-consuming. While the sampling strategy of snowballing is useful for identifying members of hidden populations (Robson, 2002), its weakness is the challenge of generalisability, the extent to which the data can be applied to the wider population (Shaghaghi et al, 2011).

A significant challenge in the consultations was how to fully include the experience of peers in the process of data analysis. Consultations typically need to be completed in a short time, and because of the pressure to complete the final report the engagement of peers in the analysis was limited. This decision was taken by the research steering committees, and while not perfect, this excerpt from Melaugh and Rodrigues (2017) on the experience of conducting a consultation to inform the National Drugs Strategy offers some justification for the decision:

> When planning the consultation we wanted to include the peers in the process of analysing the data from the questionnaires. However, the goal was to ensure that the voices of PWUD on the streets of Dublin were included in the consultation. As the consultation period was short (six weeks) we took the pragmatic decision for a staff member to collate, analyse and write a submission. Before the submission was finalised it was shared with the peers who conducted the consultation. (Melaugh and Rodrigues, 2017: 13)

Peer engagement and social justice – the main learning

It is important to note that there are gaps in the research on how PWUD can be engaged as peers in research initiatives to inform drug policy and service development (Lianping et al, 2012; Greer et al, 2016). This lack of engagement is an issue for research and practice. As stated earlier in the chapter, both Irish and European National Drugs Strategies are committed to the active participation of PWUD in drug policy, and if this voice is absent then the drug policy cannot be viewed as robust. Irish and international research (UISCE, 2003; Marshall et al, 2015) highlights obstacles (for example, exclusionary policies/criminalisation) that prevent PWUD from engaging as peers in research. Because it reflects the principles of human rights, access and participation, social justice research creates a research culture that supports the meaningful engagement of PWUD as peers. While this approach cannot remove all the obstacles faced by PWUD, it affirms that knowledge, expertise and access to research participants that comes from lived experience is central to research and policy development.

To evaluate the learning gained from employing social justice research with PWUD, the chapter will use the 'Lundy model' of participation (Lundy, 2007). While the model was developed to support child participation in the area of children's rights, the elements of space, voice, audience and influence are applicable to the work of UISCE.

With regard to the element of 'space', this chapter highlights that the meaningful participation of PWUD in research is linked to the development of inclusive peer-led spaces, such as research steering committees. This demands the sharing of power and from a social justice perspective developing a culture that supports access, participation and respect for the dignity and experience of PWUD. The element of 'voice' is typified in the use of peer-led street outreach to engage with 'hard-to-reach' PWUD to ensure their voice is part of research informing national drugs strategy and service (SIF) development. A social justice perspective highlights that barriers such as criminalisation and stigma act as obstacles to participation, while 'audience/influence' highlights that the views of PWUD must be acted upon. As drug policy is a contested space, if peer-led research dissents from current drug policy, for example legalisation/regulation of drugs, this knowledge should be acknowledged and respected. As social justice research is concerned with human rights, the purpose of research with PUWD is about change: 'Through collective action, we will fight to change existing local, national, regional and international drug laws and formulate an evidence-based drug policy that respects people's human rights and dignity instead of one fuelled on moralism, stereotypes and lies' (Vancouver Declaration, 2006).

Finally, to summarise the findings of the chapter for social justice research, practice and policy, the chapter highlights that UISCE's use of social justice research supported the meaningful participation of PWUD as peers. Because of the research, the voice of PWUD informed the development of the Irish National Drugs Strategy and the development of Ireland's first proposed SIFs. As there are gaps in evidence about how to engage PWUD as peers in the development of research (Lianping et al, 2012; Greer et al, 2016), the findings extend the research and outline ways to engage with PWUD as peers in research, policy and service development in an Irish and wider context.

In conclusion, the purpose of the chapter was to outline the theory and application of using peer-led approaches to engage with PWUD. The chapter presents research examples from the drug advocacy organisation UISCE to highlight that peer approaches are effective in engaging with PWUD and specifically with 'high-risk and vulnerable' PWUD. Finally, social justice research, because of its adherence to the principles of participation, access, equity and human rights, is named as an approach that supports meaningful engagement with PWUD.

Notes

[1] The EU Drugs Strategy 2021–2025: Priority 7 and the National Drug Strategy; Reducing harm, supporting recovery 2017–2025; Priority 4.2.44 highlight the importance of engagement of PWUD.

[2] The European Monitoring Centre for Drugs and Drug Addiction (EMCDDA, 2017) define vulnerable drug-using populations as people who experience homelessness and mental health problems, for example. The population may also engage in 'high-risk drug use', the regular use of opioids, stimulants, cannabis and new synthetic substances and may use these substances in a potentially harmful way (including injecting/slamming). Slamming is a term used to describe the injection of drugs during sex.

[3] Further information on research ethics and consultations is available from the Health Service Executive: https://hseresearch.ie/what-is-research-2/

4 Further information on peer-led volunteers is available from UISCE: https://myuisce.org/volunteer-with-uisce/
5 Please follow this link to access the article on the consultation: https://myuisce.org/wp-content/uploads/2020/01/Brass-Munkie-Issue-30-Winter-2016.pdf

References

Abrams, L. (2010) 'Sampling "hard to reach" populations in qualitative research: The case of incarcerated youth', *Qualitative Social Work*, 9(4): 536–50.

Ana Liffey Drug Project (2015) 'Position paper on the provision of medically supervised safter centres in Dublin', Dublin: Ana Liffey Drug Project.

Community Work Ireland (2016) 'All Ireland standards for community work', Galway: CWI.

Corr, C. (2002) 'Engaging the hard to reach: An evaluation of an outreach service', Dublin: Merchants Quay Ireland.

Council of the European Union (2020) 'EU drugs strategy 2021–2025', Brussels: Council of the European Union.

Crickley, A. and McArdle, O. (2009) 'Community work, community development: Reflections 2009', *Working for Change: The Irish Journal of Community Work*, 1(1): 14–27.

Dahlberg, M. and M. Anderberg (2013) 'The hidden population: Some methodological issues about estimation of problematic drug use', *Nordic Studies on Alcohol and Drugs*, 30(3): 149–66.

Dublin: Department of Community, Rural and Gaeltacht Affairs (2009) 'National drugs strategy (interim) 2009–2016', Dublin: Department of Community, Rural and Gaeltacht Affairs.

Department of Health (2017) 'Reducing harm, supporting recovery. A health-led response to drug and alcohol use in Ireland 2017–2025', Dublin: Department of Health.

Duffin, T., Keane, M. and Millar, S.R. (2020) 'Street tablet use in Ireland: A Trendspotter study on use, markets, and harms', Dublin: Ana Liffey Drug Project. Available at https://www.aldp.ie/content/uploads/2020/04/Trend spotter-Report_Street-Tablets-Ireland_FINAL-21.04.20.pdf [Accessed 18 January 2023].

EMCDDA (2017) 'High-risk drug use and new psychoactive substances', Luxembourg: European Monitoring Centre for Drugs and Drug Addiction.

EMCDDA (2018) 'Perspectives on drugs: Drug consumption rooms; An overview of provision and evidence', Lisbon: European Monitoring Centre for Drugs and Drug Addiction.

EMCDDA (2019) 'Ireland, country drug report 2019', Lisbon: EMCDDA.

Greer, A.M., Luchenski, S.A., Amlani, A.A., Lacroix, K., Burmeister, C. and Buxton, J.A. (2016) 'Peer engagement in harm reduction strategies and services: A critical case study and evaluation framework from British Columbia, Canada', *BMC Public Health*, 16: 452–460.

Grosso, L. and Gruppo, A. (2008) 'Empowerment: Models of good practice; Heroin use and peer support; What lessons have been learnt?', in G. Bröring and E. Schatz (eds) 'Empowerment and self: Organisations of drug users; Experiences and lessons learnt', Amsterdam: Foundation Regenboog AMOC Correlation Network.

Hibbert, N. (2017) 'Human rights and social justice', *Laws*, 6(2): 1–16.

Hunt, N. (2002) 'Involvement and empowerment Why bother?', Drug Link (January/February).

Hunt, N., Albert, E. and Sánchez, V. (2010) 'User involvement and user organising', in T. Rhodes and D. Hedrich (eds) *Harm Reduction: Evidence, Impacts and Challenges*, Luxembourg: EMCDDA, pp 333–54.

IAUD (2006) 'Vancouver Declaration: Why the world needs an international network of activists who use drugs', Vancouver Canada: The International Activists Who Use Drugs.

INPUD (2008a) 'Nothing about us without us: Greater, meaningful involvement of people who use illegal drugs; A public health, ethical, and human rights imperative', International edn, Toronto: Canadian HIV/AIDS Legal Network, International HIV/AIDS Alliance, Open Society Institute.

INPUD (2008b) 'Nothing about us without us: A manifesto by people who use illegal drugs', Toronto: Canadian HIV/AIDS Legal Network, International HIV/AIDS Alliance, Open Society Institute.

INPUD (2011) 'Statement and position paper on language, identity, inclusivity and discrimination', London: INPUD.

Kelleher, C., Carew, A. and Lyons, S. (2021) 'National drug treatment reporting system 2014–2020 drug treatment data', Dublin: Health Research Board.

Kerr, T., Small, W., Peeace, W., Douglas, D., Pierre, A. and Wood, E. (2006) 'Harm reduction by a "user-run" organization: A case study of the Vancouver Area Network of Drug Users (VANDU)', *International Journal of Drug Policy*, 17(2): 61–9.

Kools, J.P. (2013) 'Drugs participation greater meaningful involvement of people who use drugs in 7 key principles and 13 examples of good practice', Amstedam: Correlation Network product.

Lazarus, L., Shaw, A., LeBlanc, S., Martin, A., Marshall, Z., Weersink, A. et al (2014) 'Establishing a community-based participatory research partnership among people who use drugs in Ottawa: The PROUD cohort study', *Harm Reduction Journal*, 11(26).

Lianping, T., Tzemis, D. and Buxton, J. (2012) 'Engaging people who use drugs in policy and program development: A review of the literature', *Substance Abuse Treatment, Prevention, and Policy*, 7.

Lundy, L. (2007) '"Voice" is not enough: Conceptualising Article 12 of the United Nations Convention on the Rights of the Child', *British Educational Research Journal*, 33(6): 927–42.

McCann, E. and Duffin, T. (2022) 'Working paper empathy, evidence, & experience learning from overseas to respond to street-based drug injecting in Dublin city centre'. Available at https://www.aldp.ie/content/uplo ads/2022/01/Dublin-SIF-Working-Paper-Jan-22-McCann-Duffin.pdf [Accessed 18 January 2023].

Marshall, Z., Dechman, M.K., Minichiello, A., Alcock, L. and Harris, G.E. (2015) 'Peering into the literature: A systematic review of the roles of people who inject drugs in harm reduction initiatives', *Drug Alcohol Dependence*, 151: 1–14.

Melaugh, B. and Rodrigues, H. (2017) '"The voice of the street": Using peer led outreach with people who use drugs to inform the development of Ireland's National Drug Strategy', *Social Work & Social Sciences Review*, 19(3): 7–16.

Merchants Quay Ireland (2020) 'Annual review 2020', Dublin: Merchants Quay Ireland.

Millar, S. (2018) 'Public consultation for a new safe injecting facility in Dublin', *Drugnet Ireland*, 65: 9–10.

Montañés Sánchez, V. and Oomen, J. (2009) 'Use of drugs and advocacy: A research into the participation of drug user organisations in the design of drug policies on a local and European level', Belgium: European Coalition for Just and Effective Drug Policies (ENCOD).

O'Carroll, A., Duffin, T. and Collins, J. (2021) 'Harm reduction in the time of COVID-19: Case study of homelessness and drug use in Dublin, Ireland', *The International Journal of Drug Policy*, 87: 102966.

Robson, C. (2002) *Real World Research*, Oxford: Blackwell Publishing.

RPA Consulting (2017) 'Report on public consultation undertaken to inform the new National Drugs Strategy', Dublin: Department of Health.

Shaghaghi, A., Bhopal, R.S. and Sheikh, A. (2011) 'Approaches to recruiting "hard-to-reach" populations into research: A review of the literature', *Health Promotion Perspectives*, 1(2): 86–94.

Soken-Huberty, E. (2022) 'Social Justice 101: Meaning, Principles, Facts and Examples' Austria: Human Rights Careers. Available from Social Justice 101: Meaning, Principles, Facts and Examples', Available at https:// www.humanrightscareers.com/issues/social-justice-101-meaning-princip les-facts-and-examples/ [Accessed 2 September 2023].

Souleymanov, R., Kuzmanović, D., Marshall, Z., Scheim, A.I., Mikiki, M., Worthington, C. et al (2016) 'The ethics of community-based research with people who use drugs: Results of a scoping review', *BMC Medical Ethics*, 17 25). Available at zttps://bmcmedethics.biomedcentral.com/articles/ 10.1186/s12910-016-0108-2 [Accessed 18 January 2023].

TUSLA (2019) 'Hidden harm practice guide', Dublin: TUSLA.

TUSLA (2020) 'Determining when ethical approval is required: Guidance for Tusla Child and Family Agency staff', Dublin: TUSLA.

UISCE (2003) 'Methadone: What's the story?', Dublin Union for Improved Services, Communication, and Education.

UISCE (2016a) 'UISCE: Submission for National Drugs Strategy', Dublin Union for Improved Services and Education.

UISCE (2016b) 'Your voice: 2017 National Drug Strategy', Brass Munkie, Dublin Union for Improved Services Communication and Education, 30 – Winter.

UISCE (2017) 'Public consultation to inform the development of a new safer injecting facility', Dublin: UISCE.

UISCE (2022) 'Peer partnership for change: UISCE's strategy to build inclusion & participation of people who use drugs 2022–2025', Dublin: UISCE.

UN (2006) 'Social justice in an open world: The role of the United Nations', International Forum for Social Development, ST/ESA/305, New York: United Nations.

Wilkinson, R. (2021) 'Rapid evidence review of peer-based harm reduction interventions for people who inject drugs', Available at https://data.sout hampton.gov.uk/images/peer-based-hr-evidence-review-injected-drugs_ tcm71-440420.pdf [Accessed 18 January 2023].

PART III

Exploring case studies in research for social justice

9

Beyond research extractivism in environmental justice research

Jamie Gorman

Introduction

What does a social scientist have in common with an oil rig operator? The answer is that both can be miners engaged in the extraction of a precious resource. Fossil fuel companies engage in extractivist practices that create 'sacrifice zones' (Lerner, 2010), where communities and environments are devalued, degraded and often displaced so that commodities can be mined (Raftopoulos, 2017). Similarly, researchers can mirror the practice of commodity extractivism by extracting resources like knowledge, wisdom and stories in the form of data from communities. In this chapter,[1] I theorise the issue of research extractivism, which I define as research which extracts data from the social world in ways that obscure the researcher's subjectivity, deny inter-subjectivity in the research relationship and condemn the researched 'other' to objectification for presentation to external audiences. Following the seminal publication of Linda Tuhiwai Smith's *Decolonizing Methodologies* (2021 [1999]), responses to colonial and extractivist research practices have been advanced by indigenous researchers challenging neo-colonial research practices (Gaudry, 2011; Kouritzin and Nakagawa, 2018; Held, 2020; Thambinathan and Kinsella, 2021; Hui, 2023). The issue of research extractivism is also increasingly being debated by environmental justice and social movement researchers (Milan, 2014; Luchies, 2015; Temper et al, 2019; Owens, 2020; Cieslick et al, 2021; Colectivo Mariposas, 2022; Solera, 2022). In this chapter, I explore this literature and reflect on my own efforts to develop an anti-extractivist standpoint for research design and operationalisation. In doing so, I aim to contribute to collective scholarly efforts to overcome what Ndhlovu (2021: 196) calls 'methodological stasis': 'a situation where we have remained tied to methodologies that sustain the very same epistemological hegemonies we are seeking to unsettle' as emancipatory and justice-focused researchers.

My consideration and attempts to address the issue of research extractivism are motivated by my positionality and professional interests. As a white-Irish person with working-class origins, my work lies at the intersection of the social professions of community and youth work with environmental social movements and policymaking. I am particularly interested in how young people and communities navigate power and knowledge asymmetries to have voice and impact in environmental governance. Strongly influenced by Freirean pedagogy and Freire's (1996) critique of the teacher/student binary, I am concerned with how this hierarchical dualism may be replicated in the researcher/participant relationship. This consideration inspired the case study design of my PhD research with the anti-fracking movement in Ireland. In this research, I noted the potential for researchers to mirror the logic of the fracking process by seeking to extract a valuable resource (data) from the community and refine them for profit and external consumption.

Extractivism is a mode of capitalist accumulation based on the removal of minerals, fossil fuels and agri-crops from the earth, which is often degraded and despoiled at the point of extraction (López et al, 2015; Raftopoulos, 2017). Within the logic of accumulation, such areas are deemed necessary to sacrifice in order to realise the economic value of their resources on the global trading markets. In the process of this accumulation, extractivism contributes to and distributes environmental degradation and human rights abuses across multiple scales. Often it is poor, marginalised and racialised communities, those on the periphery – without power/voice – who become sacrifice zones (Lerner, 2011; United Nations, 2019). With little access to political power, these communities must mobilise to overcome power asymmetries and procedural injustices in order to achieve recognition and redistributive justice. As a result, extractivism catalyses an 'environmentalism of the poor' (Martinez-Alier, 2001), and globally there are thousands of grassroots community campaigns contesting the destruction of their local environment and the associated threats to health, livelihoods and other human rights (EJ Atlas, nd).

Research practice has the potential to mirror this extractivist violence. Researchers are often involved in data collection in a local setting and the interpretation and presentation of that data on the global market of academic knowledge (Paasi, 2005). An important aspect of this commoditisation is the enclosure of knowledge, with research often placed behind a paywall, which 'upholds intellectual monopolies and prevents publicly subsidized research from entering the public domain' (O'Donovan, 2014: i24). For emancipatory, rights-focused researchers, and particularly those working with environmental justice movements, it is important to consider how we can avoid replicating the extractivist logic in our research practice. As this chapter will demonstrate, an anti-extractivist stance foregrounds a concern for justice in the process of undertaking research. It seeks recognition for diverse identities and voices, honouring alternative knowledges. It calls for a redistribution of power in the research relationship that challenges hierarchies. Finally, it emphasises enhanced involvement of participants in the research process.

In writing this chapter, I draw on my experience of PhD research with the community-based movement Love Leitrim, which formed in opposition to the proposed extraction of shale gas by hydraulic fracturing, or fracking (Gorman, 2022). I undertook a case study of Love Leitrim which explored the participatory barriers and procedural injustices they faced as a local environmental campaign attempting to influence national political change for environmental justice. The research was rooted in sustained dialogue, exchange and collaboration-in-action with Love Leitrim over the course of a year and a half. Data were collected through semi-structured interviews, participant observation, documentary and audio-visual analysis. This was then analysed thematically in order to identify the strategies and practices which enabled campaigners to overcome participatory barriers and procedural injustices and prevent fracking.

Understanding research extractivism

Data miners: exploring extractivist epistemology

How might we prefigure a post-extractivist world through the research process? We must begin, I suggest, by considering the nature of research today, and in particular the place of the researcher in the modern 'knowledge economy'. Brinkmann and Kvale (2018) offer two contrasting metaphors of the miner and the traveller for what researchers are doing when conducting interviews. In the miner metaphor, 'knowledge is waiting in the subject's interior to be uncovered, uncontaminated by the miner'. The researcher 'digs nuggets of knowledge out of a subject's pure experiences', 'strips the surface of conscious experience' and using 'a variety of data-mining procedures … extracts the objective facts or the essential meanings' from the data. This meaning is then reported objectively as fact by the impartial miner. This paradigm remains the dominant model of modern social science today. The second researcher metaphor offered by Brinkmann and Kvale (2018: 20) is that of the traveller, who 'wanders through the landscape and enters into conversations with the people he or she encounters'. The traveller 'walks along with' people, listening to 'their own stories of their lived world' and unfolding the 'potentialities of meanings in the original stories' through interpretive narratives. In this process, the traveller opens themselves to questioning and change. The metaphor of the traveller has its origins in ethnography but has come to increasing prominence as scholarship began to shed light on the social construction of knowledge even in the 'hard' sciences.

Since the 1960s, scholarship in the field of science and technology studies has revealed the social nature of knowledge production, demonstrating that scientific knowledge is constructed through social structures and practices (Janasoff, 2007; Sismondo, 2009; Martin et al, 2012). This mutual interplay of science and society means that, far from being ahistorical, knowledge 'is a temporarily stable outcome of heterogeneous activities of scientists and engineers and their entanglement in wider social and political relations' (Rohracher, 2015). Knowledge – and therefore truth – is situated and embodied rather than universal. This understanding of the nature of science reveals the violence of the realist position, which attempts to impose a single, totalising truth through the obfuscation of the socio-cultural practices involved in knowledge production. This is what Haraway (1988) calls the *god-trick*, 'a doctrine of objectivity which promises transcendence'. Yet, she argues, such attempts to portray objectivity in knowledge production are 'power moves, not moves towards truth'. Knowledge is 'produced by and productive of power' (Strega, 2005: 226), and this symbiotic relationship led to Foucault's theorisation of 'power/knowledge' as a unified concept. Power/knowledge allows us to 'expose historical contingency and instability in purported scientific and social truths, to intervene in their contested and political operation' (Luchies, 2015: 2).

Yet, the doctrine of objectivity remains hegemonic in Western society and politics, demanding the production of empirical knowledge in the service of evidence-based policymaking. This social scientific endeavour relies on highly trained researchers capable of employing complex methodologies to undertake systematic studies of social phenomena. This approach to knowledge generation came to the fore in 18th-century Europe as the empirical positivist epistemological approach. The scientific method of developing theory through experimentation, observation and data analysis influenced the development of the social sciences in the 19th century (Comte's positivism) and 20th century (Popper, 2002 [1959]). While purist positivists may be thin on the ground today, dominant popular conceptions of science – despite qualitative critiques (Denzin and Lincoln, 2017) – continue to echo the functionalist view (Merton, 1973) that research's social function is to provide certified truth which progressively reveals the structure of the material world through the adherence to the norms and standards of the scientific method. This common understanding of how knowledge is produced and evaluated leads to an emphasis on rational and objective knowledge production even in the applied fields of policy formation and the social professions. This has significant implications for participatory researchers in the emancipatory tradition because it enmeshes us within a realist paradigm of intellectual enquiry which imagines our role is to uncover universal abstract truths. This erases the workings of power in the power/knowledge binary.

This modernist perspective on the nature of intellectual activity and of knowledge has shaped our understanding of ourselves as much as it shapes our understanding of the world around us. Modern scientific enquiry engages in symbolic and epistemic violence (de Sousa Santos, 2018) to establish a 'positional superiority of Western knowledge' (Smith, 2021: 62) rooted in the Cartesian fallacy that organises the world according to hierarchical dualities such as mind/body, humans/nature, colonial metropole/periphery and the subjects/objects of research. These binaries are separated by what de Sousa Santos (2018: 6) describes as 'abyssal lines', which in the case of colonisation enforce 'false universalisms that are based on the social experience of metropolitan societies and aimed at reproducing and justifying the normative dualism metropolis/colony'.

Writing from within the metropole, Bruno Latour (1993) demonstrates that while modernity seeks a strict delineation of hierarchical boundaries, we have never in fact been 'modern': human activity has always involved hybrids of binary categories and continues to do so today. Latour (2007) points out that the social world is characterised by major uncertainty around the nature of identity, agency, social actors, groups, actions, objects, facts and indeed what exactly qualifies as empirical social research. Such critiques have been furthered by feminist and qualitative scholars (Pascale, 2011), yet positivist intellectual enquiry continues to rest on these dualistic assumptions, assuming that ideas are manufactured through rational processes which can control for socio-cultural bias to produce abstract truths for the knowledge economy. Just as with the manufacture of goods, the raw materials for knowledge creation must be mined, extracted and refined by skilled workers before they are opened up to global markets. As a result, the miner metaphor remains dominant in shaping our understanding of the nature of social scientific enquiry today.

Dynamics of research extractivism

In the research process, as carried out by data miners, knowledge is extracted from situated, embodied local contexts and reconstituted as universalist empirical data and presented as truth in reified forms to elite audiences. Boulet (2018: 104) highlights how in Western intellectual culture there is a strong assumption of 'the centrality of the speaking, writing or thinking author/subject – or more generally of the individual person – in the entirety of the living and changing context and the complexity of the interconnections they report on'. The effect of this privileging of the 'I' is to centre the eye of the one who writes. This point is increasingly well understood within the social sciences thanks in particular to feminist and indigenous scholars, and qualitative researchers are expected to reflect on their positionality. Yet the reflexive consideration of positionality, necessary though it is, does not guarantee that the research will present a full picture of the living context in all of its complexity and interconnectedness. It is not, in itself, a guard against extractivist research practices of the modern knowledge economy. We must fully understand the extractivist dynamic and think critically and creatively about how to move beyond it.

Boulet (2018: 106) points out that notions of objectivity 'lead to the paradox of both denying subjectivity in the researcher, inter-subjectivity in the research relationship and condemning the "researched other" to objectification (or a form of "enclosed subjectivity")'. Boulet's reflections on this triple movement helpfully illuminate the dynamic of research extractivism, which can be understood as a research practice which extracts data from the social world in ways that deny the subjectivity in the researcher, inter-subjectivity in the research relationship and condemn the researched other to objectification. While quantitative and positivist research may be more likely to enact an extractivist dynamic, qualitative researchers may also do so. Although the research produced in this frame may in some ways produce useful knowledge, I advance the normative perspective that for researchers concerned with social justice it is important to be concerned with both the means and ends of research. Gaudry (2011), writing from an indigenous perspective in the United States, emphasises that extractivist research is common practice in contemporary academia, where 'research and publishing expectations drive researchers to take deeply meaningful information often from a marginal or "underresearched" community and present it to ... a highly educated academic audience or government bureaucracy' (Gaudry, 2011: 113). This sheds further light on the dynamics of research extractivism: it involves researchers removing knowledge from its immediate context and presenting it to highly specialised outsiders. In this process, both the research design and outputs are externally orientated – 'communities rarely participate in the development of research questions or are entitled to determine the validity of the research process' (Gaudry, 2011: 114). Similarly, the means of dissemination is most often through academic conferences and peer-reviewed journal articles, where the 'jargon-laden prose ... density and self-referential nature of [journal] articles ... make them incomprehensible to anyone without a graduate-level degree' (Gaudry, 2011: 116). While peer-review can be an important tool for scrutiny of research results to counter unscrupulous researchers, it maintains a hierarchical relationship between researchers and those who participate in research when results are *only* published in such forums without other more democratic forms of dissemination. Yet dissemination by peer review alone is often expected within the university system as a prerequisite – although not a guarantee – for jobs, permanent contracts and promotions for the individual researcher.

The issue of research extractivism has been most thoroughly examined and critiqued by decolonial scholars in indigenous contexts (eg Gaudry, 2011; Kouritzin and Nakagawa, 2018; Held, 2020; Smith, 2021) as well as in social movement scholarship (Milan, 2014; Luchies, 2015). Table 9.1 offers a summary of the key ethical principles this literature offers. Taken together, they present a strong critique of the claims of objectivity and neutrality of traditional Western research, calling attention to its replication of regimes of truth that sustain hetro-patriarchal, White supremacist capitalist worldviews

Table 9.1: Emerging principles of non-extractivist research in the decolonial and social movement literatures

Author(s)	Gaudry (2011)	Milan (2014)	Luchies (2015)	Kouritzin and Nakagawa (2018)	Held (2020)
Research Literature	Decolonial	Social movements	Social movements	Decolonial	Decolonial
Ethical principles	• Employ indigenous worldviews. • Orientate knowledge creation towards indigenous peoples and their communities. • See responsibility directed almost exclusively towards the community and participants. • Promote community-based action and a liberatory praxis.	• The question of relevance. • The question of risk. • The question of power. • The question of accountability.	• Movement-relevance. • Anti-oppression. • Prefiguration.	• Intent in undertaking the research. • Integrity in the process. • Focus on process. • Social hostage. • Post-humanist outlook.	• Respect. • Relevance. • Reciprocity. • Responsibility. • Relationality.

in the academy, policymaking and civil society. This challenges those of us working in institutional contexts such as universities to interrogate and extend our ethical frameworks and procedures.

Designing anti-extractivist research

How can we move beyond research extractivism as justice-focused scholars working with environmental movements? I believe that we must begin by humbly listening to those communities and groups who are themselves engaged in liberatory praxis to resist extractivism and be guided by their needs and interests. In the remainder of the chapter, I present the results of my listening to the emerging literature on anti-extractivism. Intertwined with an exposition of the themes, I reflect on my own experience of PhD research with communities resisting fossil fuel extraction in Ireland and attempts at anti-extractivist praxis. Through this process of 'listening' and reflection, I explore the issues and implications of an anti-extractivist standpoint for research design and operationalisation.

Reflect on our position and intentions

Given the power/knowledge dynamics of the research process, it is imperative for researchers to reflect on their positionality and intentions when negotiating access in fieldwork and developing the research design. As researchers, we must understand and consider our deeply held attitudes, opinions and concerns about the phenomenon we are investigating. We must also develop a reflexive discussion of our positionality, making clear questions of identity, status and role and continuously consider how these are affecting research design and implementation. However, it is important that positionality statements do not become merely 'self-centred biographies or disclaimers that often distance or distract researchers from participating in struggles for social justice' (Luchies, 2015: 9). Rather, positionality statements should position us for active, respectful engagement in the field (Held, 2020).

Beyond making conscious our personal stance and positionality, it is important to be clear about our intentions in conducting research. Kouritzin and Nakagawa remind us that:

> any researcher who is officially entitled to do research can, with the consent of the ethics review board, enter into humans' hearts and minds, using them as research data without being asked important questions: 'is this person fit to enter into people's hearts?', 'Is this researcher interested in the research participants' well-being and happiness?' and 'For who's sake is the researcher doing research?' (Kouritzin and Nakagawa, 2018: 7)

Table 9.2: Luchies' (2015) guiding questions for anti-oppressive research

---

- Who owns the research project?
- Whose interest does it serve?
- Who will benefit from it?
- Who has designated its questions and framed its scope?
- Who will carry it out?
- Who will write it up?

Indeed, they suggest that the 'most important question of all' is 'whose approval is most important to the researcher?' If approval from the studied group or individual is not more important to the researcher than approval from the institution and other academics, then questions arise about the true emancipatory nature of the research. Similarly, Luchies (2015: 8) offers several guiding questions (Table 9.2) to foreground an ethic of anti-oppression in social movement research and support researchers to 'engage in contextual and contingent negotiations towards reciprocal research relationships'. In answering these questions, he suggests, researchers should foreground a commitment to activists involved in contesting relations of oppression and a commitment to furthering intersectional resistance.

In reflecting on my own place within the dynamics of modern research practice, I recognise that it would potentially be very easy for me to build a successful academic career as a data miner. I am a White man who is middle class by virtue of the education I have received. Yet two factors have caused me to question the dynamics of research extractivism. First, my upbringing in a working-class community gave me a lived experience of inequality and made me alive to questions of voice and power. Then in my early 20s I trained as a community development and youth work practitioner, where I was challenged to develop a deeper analysis of power and oppression. As a researcher with roots in practice, I am drawn to the emancipatory tradition of research which is concerned with articulating and amplifying the voices of marginalised and disadvantaged groups. In my PhD research, my central concern was to hear and amplify the voices of those impacted by fracking and facing participatory injustices in their attempts to prevent drilling in their communities. I was conscious that the fracking Licensing Options had been awarded without community consultation and that significant power imbalances existed between Leitrim campaigners, the companies and the state, which made it difficult for the voices of frontline anti-fracking communities to be heard.

Interrogating my own PhD research with Kouritzin and Nakagawa (2018) and Luchies' (2015) questions, I find that while I embodied the spirit of anti-oppressive research, I could do more to support the co-creation of the research question and design. My motivation in doing the research was to support the community in their campaign, and so it was and continues to be the community's approval which matters most to me. Yet I continued to have ownership over the research question construction and research design, and ultimately I carried out and wrote up the project independently, albeit with regular consultation with the community. Greater levels of co-creation were not sought by community activists, who were extremely busy and under pressure as they ran a campaign alongside their day-to-day lives. Yet I recognise that if I had been a more confident researcher at the outset of my PhD, I would have developed my research question and scope through a more deliberately participatory process. All the same, the questions and scope evolved somewhat organically through my engaged approach to fieldwork, living for a year in the community impacted by fracking. This expanded my perspective on the phenomenon of Love Leitrim's anti-fracking mobilisation and allowed me to better understand it in the context of campaigners' lives and rural social, political and economic life more broadly. I allowed this engagement to challenge my initial conceptualisation of the case, which had focused too heavily on the role of environmental NGOs without understanding the variety of actors which local campaigners engaged with in their efforts to stop fracking.

Interrogate the limitations of institutional ethical frameworks

Communities resisting environmental injustices like extractivism often face disproportionate risks due to their political opposition to the status quo and powerful economic interests. When researching movements, we must be aware that recording and reporting on activist activities could be of use to government and commercial interests. This issue was raised with me by someone who refused to participate in my PhD research and was an important point of reflection. As Flacks (2005: 7) notes, researchers with such social movements 'ought to be sensitive to the possible ways your work could be used to perpetuate established social arrangements and repress opposition'. This elevated risk calls scholars to deep reflection on the ethics of research design and fieldwork with communities and movements. This must begin with a critical consideration of our ethical frameworks and how we might deepen them beyond what is required by institutional ethical review boards. Indeed, we must consider critiques of these ethical standards coming from the decolonial and social movement literature.

Writing from a Canadian indigenous perspective, Kouritzin and Nakagawa (2018) note that institutional research ethics is concerned with protecting autonomy, welfare and justice in the research relationship.

However, they suggest that in practice these principles inculcate an ethical culture primarily concerned with a 'one dimensional ethic' (Kouritzin and Nakagawa, 2018: 4) of risk management and mitigation. The standard research ethics concerns have nothing to say about the ethical dilemma raised with me that the knowledge I gathered might be used to undermine community resistance. While it is indirect, such an act would be a form of harm to participants. Furthermore, Kouritzin and Nakagawa (2018) note that when data is seen as private property, ethical concern centres on contractual written consent, privacy and the ownership and storage of data. Yet, with indigenous social structure based on deep relationality (discussed further later in the chapter), which facilitates oral decision-making, consensus and accountability, 'the request for a permanent record of consent from the research participants violates community ethics' (Kouritzin and Nakagawa, 2018: 8). Written consent, they suggest, exchanges personal accountability for a contract. By examining Western research practices such as obtaining written consent, they contest that research ethics are a 'regime of truth' (Foucault, 2020 [1975]), which, when applied to indigenous community research, maintains the power of Western knowledge, cognitive structures and ideology through 'an increasingly specialised and esoteric discursive practice, managing the relationship between the researcher and the research by means of surveillance and control' (Kouritzin and Nakagawa, 2018: 2).

Kouritzin and Nakagawa suggest that research ethics, as a regime of truth, transmit the norms and values of Western society to indigenous communities. They argue that this consolidates hierarchies of power and 'solidifies pre-determined Western "truth"' (Kouritzin and Nakagawa, 2018: 3). Just as resource extractivism destroys the local environment, hegemonic and totalising research ethics regimes are 'ethical imperialism', which can destroy local cultural, linguistic practices that are ecosystems of indigenous knowledge. I was not navigating the same power/knowledge dynamics in my work with Irish environmental activists. My research ethical review process was undoubtedly rigorous and encouraged me to reflect on how I protected participants from harm. Yet it is also true that the culture of ethics which I was working in was based around the management of risks and contractual consent. This did not require me to consider ethics in a more non-extractive frame which centres the relationality of local knowledge and considers the ethics of its removal from local contexts. Held (2020) emphasises that for indigenous communities, epistemology is relational: knowledge is transactional and embedded in a context rather than being something objective and easily disembedded from context. Reflecting on ethics from this perspective encourages us as researchers to consider our relational accountability to the community, to which I now turn.

Develop deep relational accountability

Across the ethical principles set out in Table 9.1, the importance of sustained engagement over time emerges as a crucial research design element. This enables the development of a deep relational accountability and mutuality which is central to anti-extractivist research. Milan (2014) writes as a European social movement scholar and highlights how 'bridging the significant gulf between researchers and activist groups requires a serious effort to build research relationships based on clarity, reciprocal respect and trust'. Indeed, this is most strongly emphasised by indigenous scholars writing from a worldview which understands that 'humans are not alone. They are connected and made by way of relationships with a wide range of beings, and it is thus of prime importance to maintain and strengthen these relationships' (Graham, 1999). Gaudry (2011: 118) proposes a model of 'insurgent research' with indigenous communities which binds researchers into the community through 'webs of close personal relationship and even kinship [which] make them accountable to the community'. Kouritzin and Nakagawa (2018: 10) take this further, suggesting the concept of a 'social hostage' which is 'a physical manifestation of the researcher's social and cultural capital that has been established over a lifetime'. Researchers should make themselves accountable to research participants throughout the course of their career and lifetime, always acting to protect them from harm and enable their well-being. While I am no longer living in the community where I carried out my research, I continue to consider the 'social hostage' principle as a guide to my actions as a researcher.

Relational accountability was core to my own research with anti-fracking communities. My research design emphasised a dialogical (rooted in conversations and active engagement) and diachronic (committed over time to people and places) process. The most significant research decision which shaped my PhD research was the decision to move to the community affected by fracking and to participate in the day-to-day activities of the campaign against drilling. This decision fundamentally changed the nature of the research by enabling a richness and depth of engagement with campaigners and insight into the social, cultural and economic milieu which shaped local resistance to fracking. In a very real sense, I travelled the journey of the last year of the campaign alongside the community.

Some Western methodologists might criticise such an approach as 'going native' (Bryman, 2012: 445). Indeed, Held (2020: 3) stresses that relationality 'is a concept not easily translated into Western approaches to research'. Yet recognising relationality is crucial to developing an anti-extractivist research ethic. Epistemologically, relationality challenges the god-trick of objectivity and recognises that the relationship between the knower and the known is interrelated. From this perspective, it becomes clear that knowledge production is historically situated, culturally specific and constituted through an interplay of discursive and material practices (Foucault, 2002 [1969]; Haraway, 1991, 2016). Methodologically, relationality requires us to consider how we support the emergence of knowledge which is situated and locally relevant, while making ourselves as researchers directly accountable to participants in the process.

Reciprocal relationality is central to the ethics of social movement research advocated by Milan (2014) and Luchies (2015). Milan (2014: 457) notes the importance of 'creating connections, situating oneself in the activists' environments and relating to their value systems'. She offers a detailed discussion of the ethical challenges involved in establishing oneself as a trusted interlocutor with activist groups, including managing relevance, risk, power and accountability. Luchies (2015) calls for researchers to develop a triple ethic of movement relevance, anti-oppressive practice and prefiguration. Movement relevance calls on researchers to study questions of concern to movements and to make their research available to inform and support movement praxis. Anti-oppressive practice involves examining issues of power in the research process through an intersectional lens to prevent and contest relations of oppression. Finally, prefiguration requires researchers to contribute concrete alternatives to oppressive power hierarchies and regimes of truth through their research practice and dissemination. These principles, Luchies suggests, enable 'a reorientation of knowledge production from the extractive imperatives of enlightenment truth-making to supporting and feeding struggles for collective liberation' (Luchies, 2015: 12). This supports an 'insurrectionary power/knowledge' that liberates local and subjugated knowledges from the powerful Western liberal regime of truth. This validation of local knowledge is also emphasised by Gaudry's (2011) insurgent research, and he calls on researchers to employ indigenous worldviews in their theorising. Similarly, Kouritzin and Nakagawa (2018) emphasise a post-human perspective that challenges the assumptions of humanity's dominance over the planetary ecosystem in line with indigenous worldviews.

Being present over time in my research with the anti-fracking campaign meant that I was accountable to the community and campaigners in a variety of ways. This included intermittent reporting to campaign meetings and discussing my emergent findings with campaigners. It also involved the informal accountability of being a member of the community and having countless everyday conversations on the street and in shops. Being present in and with the community over time was an ethical commitment to be accountable to those I was working with to explore the social world. In this process, I sought to understand local knowledge in its situated context and to present it within the bounded system of a case study. My aim in this was to produce a case study which can aid other communities in their liberatory praxis for environmental justice. Epistemologically, this produced abductive knowledge (Brinkmann, 2014), producing an account of the social world from the perspective of the community which might support the phronesis (practical, reflexive wisdom) of readers. As a PhD researcher, I had the freedom to live in the community for an extended period. Researchers whose commitments do not allow such immersive engagement might nonetheless consider how to build meaningful relationships and hold themselves accountable to research participants beyond what is required by institutional ethical review boards.

Balance introspective reflexivity with relational accountability

Seeking to build a deep, relational and reciprocal accountability brings into focus the need for ongoing critical reflexivity around the questions of relevance, risk, power and accountability inherent in engaged research (Milan, 2014). It requires ongoing self-awareness, 'which aids in making visible the practice and construction of knowledge within research in order to produce more accurate analyses of our research' (Pillow, 2003: 173). But more than just providing an audit trail of our decision-making, and improving the accuracy of our research, reflexivity is a key tool for addressing power/knowledge asymmetries. Milan (2014: 449) stresses that 'reflexivity is an iterative and permanent process, and a dialogical one, transforming the researcher into the object of his [sic] own scrutiny, and potentially able to situate the researcher in horizontal relationship with the researched'.

Reflexivity can serve to address power and knowledge hierarchies because it requires us as researchers to critically reflect on the power and privilege which may be associated with our social identities and roles. How might we be perceived and understood by others within the cultural context of our work? How might the social and cultural assumptions we are making shape our sense of self and constrain our ability to understand issues in the field? In answering these questions, reflexivity supports researchers to act with ethical integrity in the research process. But interestingly, the decolonial literature reviewed, with its emphasis on relationality, does not have a great deal to say about reflexivity as an introspective activity of the individual researcher. Rather than stressing reflexivity as a task, these scholars emphasise the importance of integrity in the process (Kouritzin and Nakagawa, 2018) to develop reciprocal and trusting relationships (Held, 2020) in which the researcher is accountable to the community (Gaudry, 2011). Implicit in this is the effective negotiation of power/knowledge asymmetries through a relational ethic of accountability. However, reflexivity continues to be important for researchers in societies with embedded inequalities and prejudices who wish to navigate their way out of the extractivist paradigm, as Gerlach (2018) demonstrates.

In my research with the anti-fracking movement, there were a number of dynamics to consider and manage. Being from the capital city, I was an outsider to the rural community where I undertook fieldwork. It was important for me to adopt a listening and learning stance in relation to rural life. But I was an insider within the movement: I was active in the campaign for several years before my research, and at the time of my fieldwork I was a board member of a national environmental NGO. This interesting insider/ outsider dynamic was important to reflect on. I sought to use my voice on the NGO board to support the grassroots campaign, and so I found myself in a bridging role between NGO and grassroots environmentalism. I was aware that my association with the NGO, which had campaigning resources at its disposal, could place me in particular power relations with local campaigners, or indeed lead to prejudice from campaigners who disagreed with the NGO's strategy. On top of this very specific dynamic, there were of course considerations related to my gender, ethnicity and level of education to remain aware of.

I developed a researcher positionality statement to clarify the personal values, experiences and positions which informed my approach to the field. Throughout the fieldwork process, I kept a journal to reflect on my own subjectivity as a researcher in relation to the field (participants/context) and research issue. Through my research journal, I reflected on conversations I had, considering how my ideas and biases shaped the encounter. I also took several steps to address power and knowledge dynamics in the research process, including sharing my emerging analysis and draft findings chapters with participants. In the final stages of the research, I presented my tentative analysis for consideration and critique by campaigners at a findings workshop. In checking for validity, my key question was 'does this ring true to you?'

In this process, I also sought to address the ethical concern that research may be used against activists to perpetuate established social arrangements and repress opposition (Flacks, 2005). Participants were afforded the opportunity to provide their consent to the publication of the research findings in the public domain and were able to appraise the benefits and risks involved in publication. This enhanced ethical concern mitigated a potential risk of harm to participants and the wider movement. From a social justice perspective, it was also an important step in equalising power in the research dynamic.

Make relevant and reciprocal contributions

When conducting anti-extractivist research, it is essential to ensure that our research and our participation in people's lives are of direct and immediate benefit to those who are participating in our research. Relevance and reciprocity are a strong ethical concern among the decolonial and movement scholars reviewed in this chapter. Indeed, the issue of relevance must be considered from the outset of research design and begins with the researcher reflecting on their intentions in the research. Held (2020) suggests that relevant research is based on a community-identified research need, generating knowledge relevant to the community and supporting them to advance their goals. Similarly, Gaudry's (2011: 133) insurgent research is distinguished by its orientation towards action that achieves self-determination and empowerment for indigenous communities. He calls for a 'sense of responsibility towards community liberation and challenging the colonial system'. From a social movement research perspective, Luchies (2015) stresses an ethic of relevance which emphasizes academics' responsibility to find [the] places in which to meaningfully contribute to movement-building. This implies mutual struggle and respect, including mutual struggle to overturn the imperatives of power/knowledge that are hostile to such relationships. For both Gaudry (2011) and Luchies (2015), an important element of this liberatory praxis is articulating, developing and realising meaningful alternatives to existing oppressive social structures. This is something that Gaudry (2011: 133) suggests may be easier for indigenous researchers 'because there is in many cases a living memory of another way of being' among elders in the community. For those of us not working in indigenous contexts, the memories of other ways of being may have faded further, perhaps requiring consciousness raising and popular education.

Regardless of the context we find ourselves in as researchers of environmental justice struggles, it is important to ask what we bring to the community or the campaign. What value do we add above and beyond what is already happening? We may say that we hope that our research reaches decision-makers and impacts future policymaking. While this may be a benevolent aim, it remains within the extractivist paradigm, where data is removed and presented to an expert audience. It does not contribute to the community's own liberatory praxis or support those impacted by an issue to advocate for themselves. We might also suggest that as a researcher we are a cataloguer and storyteller of movement knowledge, which is indeed a worthy aim, but if this alone is our aim then we may remain detached and disengaged from the community's campaign and fail to engage with the calls of the decolonial and social movement scholars to participate, theorise and transform alongside the communities we work.

In our reflections on positionality, we can begin to unpack and understand our standpoints and locations within the broader social context of a campaign and make note of what we may be uniquely placed to do. For example, I recognised my position as board member of an environmental NGO and sought to articulate grassroots perspectives in that space. Indeed, for the campaign, engaging with researchers and students was an important strategy to enable them to disseminate their message to a wider audience.

Additionally, I recognised that I could add value through my community development and youth work practice. This included participating in relevant working groups, co-facilitating an anti-fracking youth arts summer camp and writing a number of news articles about the campaign in the media and on movement platforms.

Plan for democratic dissemination

A final element to consider in designing and carrying out anti-extractivist research is the dissemination of our research results. How and where are we publishing our results in ways that are accessible to the community and to other communities and groups who could benefit from the knowledge? Here we can recall Gaudry's (2011) critique of the jargon-laden and self-referential nature of academic journals. It is also important to consider issues of ownership and control of knowledge in a time when much academic knowledge is produced to sit behind a paywall. This is an issue which has been critiqued by scholars of the commons (Harvey, 2011) and by those who are contributing to a 'knowledge-commons' of freely available information through projects such as open access repositories and databases (O'Donovan, 2014). In this regard, democratic dissemination forms an important element of Luchies's (2015) ethic of prefiguration. The formats and modes of dissemination which support access to the research for a wider variety of people may vary depending on the research area and the community with whom you wish to communicate. Social movement research might be disseminated through pamphlets that can be shared through zine libraries. Communities where oral culture is more prominent might appreciate the research dissemination being conducted in workshop format. My research has informed my education and training activities for activists and community workers (Nolan and Gorman, 2023). I further sought to disseminate research findings in ways that are relevant and useful for both frontline environmental justice activists and community development workers (Gorman, 2022; 2023).

Conclusion

My aim in writing the chapter is to work towards a time when oil rig operators and social scientists are governed by very different operating paradigms. As researchers concerned with social justice, guarding against extractivist research practices is an important task that can contribute to the strengthening of a social justice orientation in our work. This requires us to problematise the dominant dynamics of knowledge production in the social sciences. Hegemonic Western epistemological assumptions underpin the tacit belief that the researcher is an objective miner for data from the objectified respondent through an engagement that brackets out intersubjective relationality. This reinforces the Cartesian fallacy of hierarchical binaries and contributes to a culture of separation and domination which is anathema to justice. It is imperative for social justice that researchers think outside and beyond this binary to ensure that the knowledge production process guards against symbolic and epistemic violence.

This is an urgent task for all social justice-orientated researchers and particularly so for those working alongside communities organising in resistance to resource extractivism. The environmental injustice of extractivism devalues and exploits both people and places in the pursuit of profit for mining companies and transnational corporations. The communities impacted by extractivism are often at the periphery of society, economically disadvantaged and in many cases inhabited by minority groups. With little access to political power, these communities must mobilise to address procedural injustice in order to achieve recognition and environmental justice. Researchers seeking to understand and support these environmental justice movements must carefully consider our knowledge production practices if we are to avoid replicating the extractivist logic and aggravating the injustice experienced by communities.

In this chapter, I have reviewed decolonial and social movement scholarship which considers these ethical issues and engaged in a reflexive discussion of my own PhD research with the Irish anti-fracking movement. The design principles for anti-extractivist research which I set out offer a theorisation of how we might deepen our ethical practices as researchers in ways which prefigure more just and equitable knowledge production practices. This involves moving beyond managing risk towards fostering reciprocity and a deep relational accountability in the research process. The principles paint a picture of an expanded ethics, which centre human relationships, dialogue, critical reflection, mutuality and reciprocity in the shared task of freeing ourselves from injustice and 'staying with the trouble' (Haraway, 2016) of these troubling times. Beyond research design, this chapter makes a contribution to practice and policy. For communities, movements and social professionals, the principles for anti-extractivist research offer a framework to co-design research studies and to hold researchers to account for their ethical practices. For policymakers involved in designing ethics policies, it will be important to consider the issues raised in this chapter.

Finally, I acknowledge that these principles are ideals which I have not fully realised in my work, and I continue to strive reflexively to foster a laboratory research praxis. In this work, I seek ongoing relational accountability in community where I can listen deeply and be guided by the scholars and elders who have led the way in the struggle to decolonise methodologies and achieve epistemic justice.

Note

1   I drafted this chapter living on the unceded sovereign land of the Kaurna people and completed it in Mparntwe on Arrernte Country. I acknowledge, recognise and respect the ancestors, elders and families of the Kaurna and Arrernte people who are the traditional owners and custodians of the country on which I live and work. I developed my definition of research extractivism with thanks to Jacques Boulet (2018), whose writing helped me to think about this triple movement involved in research extractivism. This is discussed further later in the chapter.

References

Boulet, J. (2018) 'Research is relating in space and time', in M. Kumar and S. Pattanayak (eds) *Positioning Research, Shifting Paradigms: Interdisciplinarity and Indigeneity*, New Delhi: Sage.

Brinkmann, S. (2014) 'Doing without data', *Qualitative Inquiry*, 20(6): 720–5.

Brinkmann, S. and Kvale, S. (2018) *Doing Interviews*, London: Sage Publications.

Bryman, A. (2012) *Social Research Methods* (4th edn), Oxford: Oxford University Press.

Cieslik, K., Sinha, S., Leeuwis, C., Martínez-Cruz, T.E., Narain, N. and Vira, B. (2021) 'Some steps for decolonising international research-for-development partnerships', blISS blog [online], Available from: https://issblog.nl/2021/12/07/eadi-iss-conference-2021-some-steps-for-decolonising-international-research-for-development-partnerships/ [Accessed 29 August 2022].

Colectivo Mariposas (2022) 'Choosing to "stay with the trouble": A gesture towards decolonial research praxis', Undisciplined Environments blog [online], Available from: https://undisciplinedenvironments.org/2022/03/08/choosing-to-stay-with-the-trouble-a-gesture-towards-decolonial-research-praxis/ [Accessed 29 August 2022].

De Sousa Santos, B. (2018) *The End of the Cognitive Empire*, Durham, NC: Duke University Press.

Denzin, N.K. and Lincoln, Y.S. (2017) *The Sage Handbook of Qualitative Research*, London: Sage Publications.

Flacks, R. (2005) 'The questions of relevance in social movement studies', in D. Croteau, W. Hoynes and C. Ryan (eds) *Rhyming Hope and History: Activists, Academics, and Social Movement Scholarship*, Minneapolis: University of Minnesota Press, pp 3–19.

Foucault, M. (2002) *The Archaeology of Knowledge*, London: Routledge.

Foucault, M. (2020) *Discipline and Punish: The Birth of the Prison*, London: Penguin Classics.

Freire, P. (1996) *Pedagogy of the Oppressed*, London: Penguin.

Gaudry, A.P. (2011) 'Insurgent research', *Wicazo Sa Review*, 26(1): 113–36.

Gerlach, A. (2018) 'Thinking and researching relationally: Enacting decolonizing methodologies with an indigenous early childhood program in Canada', *International Journal of Qualitative Methods*, 17: 1–8.

Gorman, J. (2022) 'Rooting and reaching: Insights from Love Leitrim's successful resistance to fracking in Ireland', *Community Development Journal*, 57(1): 17–39.

Gorman, J. (2023) 'How to beat the fracking frenzy', The Commons Social Change Library, Available from: https://commonslibrary.org/how-to-beat-the-fracking-frenzy/ [Accessed 5 May 2023].

Graham, M. (1999) 'Some thoughts about the philosophical underpinnings of Aboriginal worldviews', *Worldviews: Environment Culture Religion*, 3(2): 105–18.

Haraway, D. (1988) 'Situated knowledge: The science question in feminism and the privilege of partial perspective', *Feminist Studies*, 14(3): 575–99.

Haraway, D. (1991) *Simians, Cyborgs and Women: The Reinvention of Nature*, London: Free Association Books.

Haraway, D. (2016) *Staying with the Trouble: Making Kin in the Chthulucene*, Durham, NC: Duke University Press.

Harvey, D. (2011) 'The future of the commons', *Radical History Review*, 109: 101–7.

Held, M.B.E. (2020) 'Research ethics in decolonizing research with Inuit communities in Nunavut: The challenge of translating knowledge into action', *International Journal of Qualitative Methods*, 19: 1–7.

Hui, A. (2023) 'Situating decolonial strategies within methodologies-in/as-practices: A critical appraisal', *The Sociological Review*, Available from: https://doi.org/10.1177/00380261231153752

Janasoff, S. (2007) *States of Knowledge: The Co-production of Science and Society*, London: Routledge.

Kouritzin, S. and Nakagawa, S. (2018) 'Toward a nonextractive research ethics for transcultural, translingual research: Perspectives from the coloniser and the colonised', *Journal of Multilingual and Multicultural Development*, 39(8): 675–87. DOI: 10.1080/01434632.2018.1427755.

Latour, B. (1993) *We Have Never Been Modern*, Cambridge, MA: Harvard University Press.

Latour, B. (2007) *Reassembling the Social*, Oxford: Oxford University Press.

Lerner, S. (2010) *Sacrifice Zones: The Front Lines of Toxic Chemical Exposure in the United States.* Cambridge, MA: MIT Press.

López, E., Vértiz, F. and Olavarria, M. (2015) 'Extractivism, transnational capital and subaltern struggles in Latin America', *Latin American Perspectives*, 42(5): 152–68.

Luchies, T. (2015) 'Towards an insurrectionary power/knowledge: Movement-relevance, anti-oppression, prefiguration', *Social Movement Studies*, 14(5): 523–38.

Martin, B.R., Nightingale, P. and Yegros-Yegros, A. (2012) 'Science and technology studies: Exploring the knowledge base', *Research Policy*, 41: 1182–204.

Martinez-Alier, J. (2001) *The Environmentalism of the Poor: A Study of Ecological Conflicts and Valuation*, Cheltenham: Edward Elgar.

Merton, R.K. (1973) *The Sociology of Science: Theoretical and Empirical Investigations*, Chicago: University of Chicago Press.

Milan, S. (2014) 'The ethics of social movement research', in D. della Porta (ed) *Methodological Practices in Social Movement Research*, Oxford: Oxford University Press, pp 446–64.

Ndhlovu, F. (2021) 'Decolonising sociolinguistics research: Methodological turn-around next?', *International Journal of the Sociology of Language*, 267–268: 193–201.

Nolan, C. and Gorman, J. (2023) 'Just transition champions: Reflections on climate-justice focused continuous professional development for community development workers', *IACD Practice Insights*, 20: 17–18.

O'Donovan, O. (2014) 'The commons, the Battle of the Book and the cracked enclosures of academic publishing', *Community Development Journal*, 49(suppl_1): i21–i30.

Owens, A. (2020) 'Going beyond extractive methodologies to research extractivism', WEGO-ITN blog, Available from: https://www.wegoitn.org/going-beyond-extractive-methodologies-to-research-extractivism/ [Accessed 29 August 2022].

Paasi, A. (2005) 'Globalisation, academic capitalism, and the uneven geographies of international journal publishing spaces', *Environment and Planning A: Economy and Space*, 37(5): 769–89.

Pascale, C. (2011) *Cartographies of Knowledge: Exploring Qualitative Epistemologies*, London: Sage Publications.

Pillow, W. (2003) 'Confession, catharsis, or cure? Rethinking the uses of reflexivity as methodological power in qualitative research', *International Journal of Qualitative Studies in Education*, 16(2): 175–96.

Popper, K. (2002 [1959]) *The Logic of Scientific Discovery*, London: Routledge.

Raftopoulos, M. (2017) 'Contemporary debates on social-environmental conflicts, extractivism and human rights in Latin America', *The International Journal of Human Rights*, 21(4): 387–404.

Rohracher, H. (2015) 'Science and technology studies, history of', in N. J. Smelser and P. B. Baltes (eds) *International Encyclopedia of the Social & Behavioral Sciences* (2nd edn), London: Elsevier, pp 200–5.

Sismondo, S. (2009) *An Introduction to Science and Technology Studies*, Chichester: John Wiley & Sons.

Smith, L.T. (2021) *Decolonizing Methodologies: Research and Indigenous Peoples*, London: Zed Books.

Solera, A. (2022) 'Transformative methodologies: Listening differently, hearing more clearly; A decolonial approach to fostering dialogue between plural knowledges', [online], Available from: https://issblog.nl/2022/02/08/transformative-methodologies-listening-differently-hearing-more-clearly-a-decolonial-approach-to-fostering-dialogue-between-plural-knowledges/ [Accessed 29 August 2022].

Strega, S. (2005) 'The view from the post-structural margins: Epistemology and methodology reconsidered', in L.L. Brown and S. Strega (eds) *Research as Resistance: Critical, Indigenous and Anti-oppressive Approaches*, Toronto: Canadian Scholars Press/Women's Press, pp 119–52.

Temper, L., McGary, D. and Weber, L. (2019) 'From academic to political rigour: Insights from the "Tarot" of transgressive research', *Ecological Economics*, 164, 1–14. Available from: https://doi.org/10.1016/j.ecolecon.2019.106379

Thambinathan, V. and Kinsella, E.A. (2021) 'Decolonizing methodologies in qualitative research: creating spaces for transformative praxis', *International Journal of Qualitative Methodologies*, 20: 1–9. Available from: https://doi.org/10.1177/16094069211014766

10

When objects speak louder than words: material ethnography in social justice research

Gloria Kirwan and Calvin Swords

Introduction

Objects embody meaning – they can embody the social, emotional and psychological experiences which people carry with them as part of their unique, individual journey in this world. Material ethnography provides researchers with a route into those meanings through the study of objects to which people attach meanings related to experiences in their lives. It is particularly useful in the context of research which involves populations whose experiences have been overlooked or undervalued in mainstream culture, as often those experiences lack a language that is readily accessible to either the researcher or the researched. This methodology facilitates the study of complex issues through the meanings which an individual attaches to objects which they associate with their lived experience of those issues.

The study reported here concerned an examination of the relevance of peer contact and peer support to mental health recovery (Kirwan and Swords, 2021). The authors adopted material ethnography as a portal through which they could reach an understanding of the experiences of members of a peer-led social club for mental health service users. Through the discussion of club-related objects chosen by the participants, the symbolic representations of those objects revealed much about the struggle to find safe spaces for social interaction for some people experiencing mental health problems. In particular, this study shed light on one peer-led group's struggle for self-determination and the right to associate, rights which surrounded the efforts of the participants to create a social space which they controlled. This chapter argues that material ethnography provides a powerful research tool for all researchers interested in social justice-based research.

This study confronts the taken-for-granted social segregation and silencing of people with severe and enduring mental health issues and finds hidden depths of meaning and emancipation in the conviviality of social contact at the peer-led club's weekly social gathering. The chapter will first provide some key background and context considerations. This will include a focus on exploring the connections between mental health, social justice, power and the idea of recovery in mental health service delivery. The authors will then explore the decision-making process surrounding the chosen methodology, which encouraged participants to not only tell their stories in a meaningful way but to construct feelings of solidarity and the need for collective action in response to the systemic oppression faced by the club's members. The findings from the material ethnography stage of the study will then be explored, with some important concluding remarks on the benefits of this research methodology for social justice research.

Research study context

In 2019, the authors of this chapter undertook a research project with a social club for mental health service users in Ireland (Kirwan and Swords, 2021). It is a peer-led club that operates with support from volunteers and family members. It supports people in the community living with a mental illness through providing a social outlet which is controlled and operated by the members themselves. The club is run on a Friday evening with a series of activities (snooker, table tennis, bingo, cards) and refreshments (tea/coffee, sandwiches) creating a space for people to 'be themselves'. In the summer months, outings and short holidays are organised by the club for its members. The club's ethos is informed by a strong belief in living a healthy and fulfilling life and one which is not defined or confined by a mental health diagnosis (Kirwan and Swords, 2021). The members share the responsibility of running the club, which aims to provide a support network and social space for people to find connection, hope and empowerment from the relationships that are fostered on a Friday night (Kirwan and Swords, 2021).

The authors of this chapter were approached by representatives of the club who were seeking assistance with research on the benefits of club membership and how the club supports the mental health recovery journey of its members. This chapter outlines the rationale underlying the choice of one element of the overall qualitative methodology used in this study and how this element – museum ethnography – provided an effective and safe means of information communication between the study participants and the researchers. Before outlining in detail one of the methods that we believe effectively facilitated participation in this study on the part of the club members, we will first outline the main human rights issues currently confronting mental health service users, not only in Ireland but across the world.

Mental illness and social injustice

In today's society, many groups grapple with multiple structures of inequality and injustice. Now more than ever, the concept of social justice is central to promoting change when seeking to improve the lives of disadvantaged groups (Sen et al, 2021). Kam (2014: 725) provides a description of what a social justice approach seeks to achieve: 'Social justice means challenging negative discrimination, recognizing diversity, distributing resources equitably, challenging unjust policies and practices and working in solidarity.' Societal attitudes and responses to mental illness have been arenas of contestation, inequality and social injustice. Despite disagreement on the causes of mental illness, the dominant response has been to construct mental distress as illness, to provide treatment for those afflicted and to protect society from the dangers mentally ill people are sometimes perceived to pose to themselves and others. Based on a public safety polemic, Ireland and many other jurisdictions have enacted legislation and deployed policy measures which include powers to limit the liberty and self-determination of people with mental illness in specific circumstances. At the same time, agreement remains elusive on the cause and nature of mental illness, and the merits of medical and non-medical treatments. Polarised views persist about how best to balance the individual rights of liberty and freedom versus the protection of the individual and/or the public in relation to the risks of harming others or self-harming behaviour which can sometimes arise in the context of mental ill-health.

Issues of social justice permeate many of these points of contention. For around 150 years, the involuntary detention of people with mental illness has been justified, legitimised and legalised through a paternalistic lens which argues that caring for mentally unwell people in segregated settings is morally superior to inhumane responses such as criminal incarceration or the destitution of the mentally unwell in society (Robins, 1986).

However, the erosion of individual liberty and self-determination lies at the heart of concerns regarding current societal responses to people who experience mental illness. The forced segregation from society of mentally ill individuals (sometimes referred to as involuntary detention or civic confinement) is not only experienced at the physical level of confinement. Less tangible segregation-related phenomena include the pervasive perception of mentally ill people as dangerous or different, leading to stigma, prejudice and denial of self-agency to make decisions about how they wish to live their lives on a day-to-day basis (for further discussion see Kirwan, 2017, 2018).

However, change is afoot, and increasingly there is acknowledgement that people with mental health issues are rights-bearers and that these rights have been hard won because of the historical depiction of people with mental illness as incapable of making rational decisions or acting independently.

This change is in its infancy, but the old guard perception of mentally ill people as lacking agency is steadily being replaced due to developments on a number of fronts.

First, within the global health agenda, there is a discernible evolution at a policy level regarding the recognition of health as a site of personal rights. The World Health Organization's (WHO) Alma Alta Declaration (WHO, 1978) laid a firm foundation for an inclusive agenda of 'health for all'. Over time, this inclusive agenda has developed beyond a vision of access to health care for all to one in which health care users exert influence on how health care is designed, delivered and evaluated. There has been a shift in the health discourse from viewing health care users as passive recipients of care to positioning them as agentic participants (Nabatchi and Leighninger, 2015). One consequence of this shift has been a model which incorporates the views and feedback of various stakeholder groups and which increasingly construes consumer empowerment and participation as essential elements of effective healthcare policy and delivery.

In this new configuration, the voices and opinions of mental health service users are regarded as important components of a citizen-responsive model of healthcare as envisaged in the WHO's (1997) Jakarta Declaration. Golightley and Kirwan (2019: 101) describe the essence of these developments in terms of the role of health care users, whereby the individual 'is recast as an empowered shaper of health outcomes, a role that reflects wider political efforts, beyond the realm of health care, to deliver on democratic and rights based ideas'. Indeed, the WHO (2013, 2021) has articulated an unambiguous recognition of mental health service users as rights holders in its recent mental health action plans and has overtly acknowledged the historical context of 'widespread human rights violations and discrimination experienced by people with mental disorders' (WHO, 2013: 7).

Golightley and Kirwan (2019) interpret these developments as a recasting of the role in society of mental health services users, whereby they have moved from passive, unheard patients to agentic, vocalised consumers of services. This new role brings with it the right to question established norms and practices, to confront elitist perspectives and, most importantly of all, to critically challenge how power is mediated within health service delivery (Brosnan, 2013). The insertion of a rights-based agenda into mental health care has drawn attention to the legacy of paternalistic approaches within mental health services. It is in this landscape that an increasing presence is emerging of mental health service user-commissioned research which seeks to highlight their situation and identify alternative responses which they believe can support their journey to recovery.

Simultaneously, alongside healthcare reform, systems of law have also displayed shifts regarding how the right to personal liberty versus protection of public safety are balanced against each other. Writing elsewhere, the first author has traced what she describes as the 'road to freedom' within Irish law, where a discernible amplification has occurred in mental health law jurisprudence regarding the vindication of the right to liberty (Kirwan, 2018), a right which Robinson and Scott-Moncrieff (2005) conceptualise as a 'touchstone right'. Gostin and Gable (2004) highlight the importance of respecting the rights of people experiencing mental health issues, but the legacy of past centuries reinforces for many mental health service users a feeling of disempowerment and the denial of self-determination regarding many areas of their lives. The United Nations has promoted the rights of people with mental illness at various times, particularly through the publication of the 'Principles for the protection of persons with mental illness and the improvement of mental health care' (UN, 1991) and more recently in the Convention on the Rights of Persons with Disabilities (UN, 2006), which Keys (2014) describes as a sea change in how the rights of people with disabilities are recognised. This includes how the right of individuals to be involved in decisions that affect them is envisaged.

Despite the gradual alignment of Irish law and policy with international best guidance regarding mental health care, there remains quite some distance to travel before mental health service users in Ireland – and in many countries across the world – are likely to feel or experience the full vindication of their rights to self-determination or to liberty. One key contributor to this was the shortcomings associated with the implementation of the Mental Health Act 2001 in November 2006 (Smyth et al, 2016). This legislation aimed to bring Ireland's response to 'involuntary admission on par with international standards of human rights' (Smyth et al, 2016: 555). However, a qualitative study completed in 2017 found that two thirds, or 34 of 50 service user participants, felt 'confined and coerced at various times over the course of their admission experience' (Murphy et al, 2017: 1129). In response to the somewhat slow pace of progress, service users have been self-mobilising for some time and have essentially become drivers of their own agenda in many respects. The recovery model in the field of mental health provides an increasingly significant example of the ways in which mental health service users have driven change in service delivery and service aims.

Understanding the mental health recovery journey

Recovery can be viewed as a personalised journey, focusing on an individual's growth towards developing and enhancing their quality of life beyond their mental illness (Pilgrim, 2008). It is a subjective experience, unique to everyone, which considers practical, existential and psychological components (Pilgrim, 2008). This interpretation of recovery provides hope to those receiving care from recovery-orientated services. It involves providing the opportunity for the individual to enhance their capacity for self-discovery and includes a holistic perspective towards self-care (Reeve, 1999), supporting the development of a hopeful mindset (Anthony, 1993) and locating meaning in an individual's life (Gersie, 1997). The focus is on 'all of us [needing] to come home to ourselves' (Gersie, 1997: 6). This involves people re-connecting with their own identity in a positive way, which is informed by a focus on restoration, rehabilitation and enrichment in life (Watts, 2012). This interpretation of recovery is defined as follows: 'It is a way of living a satisfying, hopeful and contributing life, even with the limitations caused by illness' (Anthony, 1993: 15).

Historically, recovery within the field of psychiatry was focused on the idea of 'clinical recovery' (Pilgrim and McCranie, 2013). The response on recovery was to eliminate symptoms, leading to an individual returning to full health (Swords and Houston, 2020, 2021). This was informed by the biomedical paradigm, which viewed mental illness as similar to any other illness – treatable through medical diagnosis and treatment (Norton and Swords, 2020).

The late 20th century saw the rise of the social movement known as the 'disaffected users of services' (Pilgrim, 2008). This movement of people with mental health problems emerged from the mental health consumerist and survivor movements, where experts by experience detailed their journeys towards wellness through alternative recovery pathways (Deegan, 1988, 1996, 2002). It provided a sense of hope to people who had negative experiences of services or who had suffered negative outcomes associated with the biomedical approach to mental illness (Brosnan and Sapouna, 2015).

Despite the reported successes of recovery-informed pathways, there has been a resistance to change within mainstream policy and service delivery, centring on two conflicting paradigms within services – recovery and biomedically informed approaches (Brosnan and Sapouna, 2015). Although the evidence base has found (Davidson et al, 2005) that biomedical interventions are not leading to high levels of clinical recovery, there remains a lack of acceptance of the emerging evidence base related to recovery models within mental health systems (Brosnan and Sapouna, 2015). This may in part be due to the central tenet of the recovery model, which shifts the power dynamic away from elitist professional knowledge (of the clinician, for example) and directs more emphasis towards the user of services becoming the expert on their own journey.

The significance of power within mental health services

Power also plays a significant role in the everyday social interactions within service culture (Kirwan, 2020; Swords, 2019, 2022; Topp et al, 2021). The relationships which take place in everyday life are often determined by relationships of power (Topp et al, 2021). This shapes 'health policies, services and outcomes' (Topp et al, 2021: 1). Power is grounded within the everyday interactions of health systems: 'Power dynamics – or the relational power that manifests in the interaction among individuals and organisations – also influence health systems, or the organizations, people and actions whose primary intent is to promote, restore or maintain health' (Topp et al, 2021: 1). Power not only exists in the influence it exerts on people and their behaviour but also on the access individuals have to desirable and necessary resources to live their life (Rose, 2018). It could also relate to how people living with mental health diagnoses are represented and perceived when voicing their views and opinions in respect of their challenges and aspirations. Often, this can be seen in mental health research in terms of how people are involved in the process, to what extent and how the findings correctly capture their experiences (Brosnan, 2013).

The members of the social club at the centre of this study believed that membership and participation in the club aided their recovery journeys in a variety of ways. However, they had found it hard to achieve recognition of the benefits of the club from the mainstream health services. It was the peer-led nature of the club which they felt differentiated it from other organised social settings, such as mental health day centres, where professional staff had control and oversight of the activities. They also believed members experienced a greater sense of freedom and independence as members of the club. Many members had never been asked their views on any aspect of their recovery journey, and it was important to ensure that the methods used to collect their viewpoints could accommodate and support the voluntary nature of the data collection while at the same time generating in-depth and valid data.

Material ethnography's role in promoting the voice of service users

There was an emphasis placed, in this research study, on how best the views of those involved in the social club could be reflected. The aim of this research was to investigate how members made sense of their experiences of being involved with the club and the extent to which their recovery journey was supported. The focus was also on supporting the club to create 'their own story' of the benefits of their membership. This included discussions on different research methodologies and methods that would possibly lead to participants feeling their contributions were meaningful and empowering (Lorenzetti, 2013). The aim also was that the research process would provide an opportunity for the development of solidarity among its members (Lorenzetti, 2013).

It was imperative to the researchers that the knowledge produced in the study was reflective of the members' experiences (Cresswell, 2013). Due to the study seeking to explore individuals' opinions, perceptions and experiences of the club, a qualitative enquiry was deemed the most appropriate approach (Bold, 2012). Qualitative approaches provide an opportunity for holistic exploration. This prevented participants from being confined to answering a specific set of questions (Bryman, 2012). Qualitative enquiry provides an opportunity for more in-depth levels of disclosure.

There was an emphasis on an approach to data collection which supported the process of service users being viewed as legitimate knowledge holders (Keogh et al, 2014). Studies that have adopted an approach which incorporates self-reports of those using services (that is, service users) have produced findings which are more likely to be an accurate reflection of each participant's experiences (Beresford, 2010; Kirwan, 2017). Consequently, the researchers believed strongly in facilitating a similar approach to the research methodology. Self-reporting is viewed as a core process of providing the space for an accurate representation of these views. Norton (1997: 410) states that it is necessary to establish an understanding of an individual's relationship with their world and how this relationship is 'constructed across space and time, and how people understand their possibilities for the future'.

Therefore, in line with Norton's (1997) perspective on meaning-making, the researchers were keen to understand the relationship that members had with the club, while also exploring how this intersected with their recovery journey. This led to the selection of semi-structured interviews and material ethnography as the methods for data collection (Bryman, 2012). The purpose of the interviews was to gather the viewpoints of members in relation to their experiences of membership. These interviews were semi-structured, meaning that questions were not rigid, allowing for exploration beyond the questions posed by the researchers (Bryman, 2012).

Research on mental health recovery has stated that there is a need to adopt methods which allow for 'opportunities to reveal insights that are beyond words' such as 'tacit knowledge' (Casey and Webb, 2019: 835). Casey and Webb (2019) claim that it is necessary to be creative when seeking to understand people's experiences. Therefore, the use of material ethnography provided an alternative, complementary method to capture the views of a wider range of participants in a format that was less intrusive but rich in its potential to reveal the participants' personal viewpoints and sentiments. It also encourages participants to symbolically explore their narratives of the club, enhancing solidarity and possibly empowering members to take collective action beyond this research study (Lorenzetti, 2013).

Material ethnography is a method of data collection which explores the insights of individuals through their identification and explanation of objects which they believe embody the meaning of an experience – in this case, the objects would symbolise the benefits of being part of a social club for those living with mental illness during their recovery journey (Doel, 2019).

Reflecting on the idea of material culture theory, Doel (2019) claims that this form of data collection provides an opportunity for exploration of complex topics and experiences using objects to illustrate meaning. Doel provides a lucid description of the value of using objects – 'things provide clues to a person's life' (Doel, 2019: 825). Other authors (Fiol and O'Connor, 2006; Pratt and Rafaeli, 2006) have found similar advantages in the use of object ethnography as a research method, arguing that the objects embody both physical and social meanings in relation to subjective experiences of people in our world (Broderick et al, 2019). Ultimately, material ethnography provides a tangible approach to research which seeks to support participants to self-report the meaning attached to their experiences (Fiol and O'Connor, 2006; Pratt and Rafaeli, 2006; Doel, 2019).

To make sure all members were given an opportunity to participate in the research, an open invitation was sent to all club members. Members who decided they would like to take part were invited to do so. Participants who wanted to take part were informed about the research, including what their involvement would look like and how data would be gathered and managed. The interviews took place in a designated room at the club. Both researchers have extensive experience of working and researching in mental health contexts, which they drew on during the data collection phase. Members of the membership-led Management Committee were always contactable when interviews were taking place in case anyone became distressed during their participation. To avoid risk of social desirability bias (Durand and Chantler, 2014), the researchers reiterated to participants that their anonymity and confidentiality were paramount throughout the research process. To avoid any bias in the data collected, the researchers had no prior involvement with the club or members before undertaking the research project. All raw data were managed and stored in line with Trinity College Dublin's policy on data storage.

The members of the social club were asked by the researchers to identify objects which illustrated the benefits of their membership. Members were asked not only to select objects which represented their association with the club but also to explain in their own words why the objects had been chosen (Turkle, 2007). They were invited to submit their explanation in written format if they wished – again, removing any pressure to express verbally to the researchers potentially quite strong emotions and feelings. This provided the club's members with autonomy and control not only over what objects were selected but also the meanings that were attached to them. According to Turkle (2007), objects support us in our thinking process regarding the meaning of our experiences. This includes our memberships of clubs, organisations and other social institutions.

There were research liaison members from the club who supported the members and the researchers. Members who were part of the membership-led committee were involved as research liaison members. These members had been involved in the club for many years, building trusting relationships with members over a sustained period. This was a straightforward process, with liaison members helping members of the club to take photographs of objects which captured the essence of their membership. These photographs were taken at the weekly gathering of club members. There were brief explanations written down about the positive meanings associated with the objects which had been photographed. These photographs and attached (anonymised) explanations were forwarded to the researchers, who were then able to gather a much more vivid understanding of the positive benefits of membership for club members. Reflecting on the historical and cultural influences on people's experiences of their mental health challenges, this approach supported their ownership of their views and how they were interpreted. Many of the research participants believed it was a very empowering experience.

Ethical approval was granted by Trinity College Dublin. The club is an independent organisation, supported 'by a membership-led Management Committee' (Kirwan and Swords, 2021: 23). The committee asked for this study to be completed and gave permission to the authors to be the selected researchers. Members of the club met the researchers several times prior to the start of the study, including information sessions about what the study was about. Informed consent from each participant was secured before any participation in the research. Throughout the research process, participants were reminded that they could withdraw their involvement and consent at any time.

Findings

The main research question asked of members was what they perceived as the benefits of the club for their own life. Members spoke about the range of activities available to them when they attend – there is something for everyone. In terms of the ethnographic data, members included pictures of the bingo cards, which are used in their weekly competitions in the club. For members, the bingo cards symbolise having fun and feeling comfortable when attending the club each week. One participant reflected on this experience when explaining the photograph of the bingo card:

> So what if you do not like table tennis or pool? Well we also run bingo when members request it. This is a great way to sit and chat to other members and is really good fun. The bingo is great and maybe after you get knocked out of one of the tournaments you still want to do something else or even to relax and do something less demanding – this is where the bingo comes in. We also have other board games like chess and checkers that individual members might like. (Participant 1)

This quote captures the essence of the benefits of the club for members. The opportunities for varied levels of participation provide members with a sense of involvement regardless of the level of engagement they want to have. Members expressed feeling a high level of support and companionship from their association with the club.

Members were also asked about the benefits of the club for their recovery journey. Due to the subjective, individualised nature of recovery as a journey, the analysis of this question centred around the 'CHIME' framework (Leamy et al, 2011). The CHIME framework was developed following the outcome of a systematic and narrative review of 1,100 papers on the idea of personal recovery, identifying that there were five necessary conditions for recovery:

- **C**onnectedness
- **H**ope and Optimism
- **I**dentity
- **M**eaning of Life
- **E**mpowerment. (Leamy et al, 2011)

In terms of connectedness, members took photographs of the refreshments available on club nights, including the following explanation:

> When the members arrive at the club the very first thing that they do when they come in the front door is sign in and order what they want from A and B [two club members] who staff the teas and coffees. They can choose between tea, coffee, cordial soft drinks or water. I think it is more than that though. *When anyone comes in they are welcomed* by the members and volunteers long before they take the short walk over to sign and order what they would like. *I feel this gives the members a real sense of belonging on a Friday night.* The members also choose some snacks that are laid out as you see in the photo. (Participant 2)

For the concept of connectedness, the researchers have placed emphasis on specific excerpts from the explanation. People are welcomed, with the refreshments contributing to a strong sense of belonging every week. Members also took photographs of the chairs and tables within the club, where they would sit together, which reminds them of the weekly social connectedness they experience. Another powerful explanation was provided about the tables and chairs:

> As you can see that around all the areas of competitions, there are tables and chairs. This is where members sit and chat and drink the tea and the coffee. This is just as important as anything else at the club. It is important because everyone sits down and talks. The conversation

is always flowing while the members wait to take a pool shot or for their name to be called to play table tennis. It is also a great way for members to catch up with everyone and see what they got up to that week. This helps with new friendships and if you know you have a friend, who goes to the club, it can be very encouraging for that friend to come along and participate with you. (Participant 3)

As outlined by Doel (2019), object provide clues into the meaning of people's lives. The meaning behind the tables and chairs is only brought to life through the material ethnography, with members of the club capturing the essence of their membership and its contribution to their recovery journey. The objects not only symbolised connectedness but also empowerment. Photographs were also included of the table tennis, which one member symbolised as contributing to increased levels of motivation and empowerment from the activities:

> The table tennis is run … every Friday night. This runs in conjunction with the pool tournament. Table tennis is more physical and requires a great deal of concentration. … if the members do not play pool, they play table tennis and some play both. Everyone has his or her own ability level from Beginner to Advanced players. Anyone can learn to play and everyone is always welcome to come and have a game. This is important to the members because it gives them something physical to do as in some games the pace is very high. The competition runs in much the same way as the pool does. In both competitions, it gives members something to look forward to each Friday. (Participant 4)

This member also explained that those attending the club feel a sense of autonomy and ownership over the club due to their involvement in the choice of activities each week: 'As a social club that is what we try to do – give the members a place to come on a Friday. Give them something to do that they want to do. Ask them 'what do you want to do next?' This applies to everything we do at the club' (Participant 1). Essentially, the club is led by its members, with each decision decided by all attendees of the club. Ultimately, the use of material ethnography provided a portal for the researchers to learn about self-determination and the right to associate free of professional surveillance, which encapsulates the experience of being a member of this club. Living with a mental illness often involves experiences of stigmatisation (Beresford, 2010), social exclusion (Boardman, 2011) and othering (Hughes, 2002). Furthermore, loneliness and isolation are often experiences felt by those living with enduring mental ill-health (Salokangas, 1997). In terms of stigma, this can be internalised by those living with mental illness, which is often associated with experiences of alienation from society and increased levels of distress: '[S]tigma and oppression experienced by mental health service users/survivors can become internalised, having an additionally damaging effect on their self-esteem and sense of self and possibly perpetuating their distress' (Beresford, 2010: 33). Such experiences can be negated by opportunities for participation in social activities (Sheridan et al, 2014). When talking about the benefits of club membership, those involved in this study made strong reference to social connectedness, a sense of belonging and togetherness. For members, being able to self-report their experiences of membership through material ethnography provided them with agency and freedom of expression. They held full ownership of their views on recovery and membership. They also had autonomy over how this was expressed, interpreted and reported.

Members' reflections on their participation in the research not only illuminated their experiences of the club but ignited even more motivation and empowerment to continue to develop and enhance the role of the social club in people's recovery journey. Ultimately, this was largely due to the use of material ethnography in conducting and completing the research. When the study was completed and published, members wanted to launch the report. The members believed that there should be one of these clubs in every part of Ireland and that the current reality of service provision and community support was inadequate for people on their mental health recovery journey. The research methodology supported members of the club to feel a sense of solidarity in terms of the benefits of their membership. It also extended beyond this, 'inciting collective action' among members for their positive experiences to be experienced by all those living with a mental illness in Ireland and beyond (Lorenzetti, 2013: 453).

What do the findings mean for social justice research, policy and practice?

These findings highlight the need to critically reflect on the role and involvement of individuals and groups affected by injustices and inequalities in social justice research. Material ethnography ignited the sharing of experiences that revealed participants' views on how membership of the social club bolstered their individual efforts to manage their recovery journey in positive ways and also revealed their collective desire for change in how mental health and recovery services are delivered beyond the social club itself. It is key to social justice research that, whenever possible, participants lead studies from start to finish. This is important because individuals and groups affected by unjust policies and practices can often have limited autonomy and agency (Sen et al, 2021). Working in solidarity (Kam, 2014) is only possible when individuals and groups feel heard, validated and motivated to seek a better world not only for themselves but others experiencing similar injustices. Material ethnography provided the necessary methodology for this to be achieved for the members of the social club and researchers. Finally, the findings have highlighted the need for social justice policy and practice to consider how we facilitate opportunities for autonomy and agency for the individuals and groups experiencing injustices in our society in their everyday lives. It is only then that we can truly begin to work in solidarity for real social change.

Conclusion

Reflecting on the concepts of human rights and social justice, our role as researchers is to promote the voices of groups in society who have been subordinated by mainstream culture. This chapter has demonstrated the value and possibilities associated with undertaking material ethnography when seeking to challenge the disparities faced by disadvantaged groups in society, in this case mental health service users. Material ethnography not only supports but empowers people to reflect, interpret and, at times, critically appraise the meaning-making experiences that have contributed to their reality of life in the social world. It also provides an opportunity for enhanced solidarity within groups who face systemic oppression to share their stories in more meaningful ways. Ultimately, this can lead to groups not only feeling ownership over their own narratives but also seeking collective change for those who share similar experiences within society.

References

Anthony, W.A. (1993) 'Recovery from mental illness: The guiding vision of the mental health service system in the 1990s', *Psychosocial Rehabilitation Journal*, 16(4): 11–23.

Beresford, P. (2010) 'Towards a social model of madness and distress? Exploring what service users say', Joseph Rowntree Foundation.

Boardman, J. (2011) 'Social exclusion and mental health: How people with mental health problems are disadvantaged: An overview', *Mental Health and Social Inclusion*, 15(3): 112–21.

Bold, C. (2012) *Using Narrative in Research*, Los Angeles: Sage Publications.

Broderick, G., McNicholas, J., Hegarty, R. and SAOL Project Participants (2019) 'Object poverty: Presented at the IASW National Social Work Conference 2019', *Irish Social Worker*, Winter: 19–34.

Brosnan, L. (2013) 'Service-user involvement in Irish mental health services: A sociological analysis of inherent tensions for service-users, service-providers and social movement actors', University of Limerick, Available from: https://researchrepository.ul.ie/articles/thesis/Serv ice-user_involvement_in_Irish_mental_health_services_a_sociological_ analysis_of_inherent_tensions_for_service-users_service-providers_and_ social_movement_actors/19832989

Brosnan, L. and Sapouna, L. (2015) 'Opportunities for social workers' critical engagement in mental health care', in A. Christie, B. Featherstone, S. Quin and T. Walsh (eds) *Social Work in Ireland: Changes and Continuities*, London: Palgrave Macmillan, pp 159–78.

Bryman, A. (2012) *Social Research Methods* (4th edn), Oxford: Oxford University Press.

Casey, B. and Webb, M. (2019) 'Imaging journeys of recovery and learning: A participatory arts-based inquiry', *Qualitative Health Research*, 29: 833–45.

Cresswell, J. (2013) *Research design: Qualitative, Quantitative, and Mixed Methods Approaches*, Thousand Oaks, CA: Sage.

Davidson, L., Borg, M., Marin, I., Topor, A., Mezzina, R. and Sells, D. (2005) 'Processes of recovery in serious mental illness: Findings from a multinational study', *American Journal of Psychiatric Rehabilitation*, 8(3): 177–201.

Deegan, P.E. (1988) 'Recovery: The lived experience of rehabilitation', *Psychosocial Rehabilitation Journal*, 11(4): 11–19.

Deegan, P.E. (1996) 'Recovery as a journey of the heart', *Psychiatric Rehabilitation Journal*, 19(3): 91–7.

Deegan, P.E. (2002) 'Recovery as a self-directed process of healing and transformation', *Occupational Therapy in Mental Health*, 17(3–4): 5–21.

Doel, M. (2019) 'Displaying social work through objects', *The British Journal of Social Work*, 49(3): 824–41.

Durand, M.A. and Chantler, T. (2014) *Principles of Social Research*, Maidenhead: Open University Press.

Fiol, C. and O'Connor, E. (2006) 'Stuff matters: Artifacts, social identity and legitimacy in the US medical profession', in A.E. Rafaeli and M.G. Pratt (eds) *Artifacts and Organisations: Beyond Mere Symbolism*, Mahwah, NJ: Lawrence Erlbaum Associates, pp 241–58.

Gersie, A. (1997) *Reflections on Therapeutic Storymaking: The Use of Stories in Groups*, London: Jessica Kingsley.

Golightley, M. and Kirwan, G. (2019) 'Social work and mental health', in R. Munford and K. O'Donoghue (eds) *New Theories for Social Work Practice: Ethical Practice for Working with Individuals, Families and Communities*, London: Jessica Kingsley, pp 100–16.

Gostin, L.O. and Gable, L. (2004) 'The human rights of persons with mental disabilities: A global perspective on the application of human rights principles in mental health', *Medical Law Review*, 63: 20–121.

Hughes, B. (2002) 'Bauman's strangers: Impairment and the invalidation of disabled people in modern and post-modern cultures', *Disability & Society*, 17(5): 571–84.

Kam, P.K. (2014) 'Back to the "social" of social work: Reviving the social work profession's contribution to the promotion of social justice', *International Social Work*, 57(6): 723–40.

Keogh, B., Higgins, A., Devries, J., Morrissey, J., Callaghan, P., Ryan, D. et al (2014) '"We have got the tools": Qualitative evaluation of a mental health Wellness Recovery Action Planning (WRAP) education programme in Ireland', *Journal of Psychiatric and Mental Health Nursing*, 21(3): 189–96.

Keys, M. (2014) 'Emerging issues in the law within a changing human rights framework', in S. McDaid and A. Higgins (eds) *Mental Health in Ireland, Policy, Practice & Law*, Dublin: Gill & MacMillan, pp 207–235.

Kirwan, G. (2017) 'Mental health service users' narratives of participation: Consensus, dissensus and paradox', Unpublished doctoral thesis, Trinity College Dublin.

Kirwan, G. (2018) 'The road to freedom: The journey from paternalism to liberty in Irish mental health law', Unpublished thesis, LLM, Trinity College Dublin.

Kirwan, G. (2020) 'Speaking truth to power: Mental health service users' experiences of participation in their diagnosis and treatment', *Social Work and Social Sciences Review*, 22(1): 137–56.

Kirwan, G. and Swords, C. (2021) 'Stronger together: The Troy Social Club model of peer-led participation and mental health support', Dublin: Troy Mental Health Association Social Club.

Leamy, M., Bird, V., LeBoutilier, C., Williams, J. and Slade, M. (2011) 'Conceptual framework for personal recovery in mental health: A systemic review and narrative synthesis', *British Journal of Psychiatry*, 199(6): 445–52.

Lorenzetti, L. (2013) 'Research as a social justice tool: An activist's perspective', *Affilia*, 28: 451–7.

Murphy, R., McGuinness, D., Bainbridge, E., Brosnan, L., Felzmann, H., Keys, M. et al (2017) 'Service users' experiences of involuntary hospital admission under the Mental Health Act 2001 in the Republic of Ireland', *Psychiatric Services*, 68: 1127–35.

Nabatchi, T. and Leighninger, M. (2015) *Public Participation for 21st Century Democracy*, Hoboken, NJ: John Wiley & sons.

Norton, B. (1997) 'Language, identity, and the ownership of English', *TESOL Quarterly*, 31(3): 409–29.

Norton, M.J. and Swords, C. (2020) 'Social recovery: A new interpretation to recovery-orientated services; A critical literature review', *The Journal of Mental Health Training, Education and Practice*, 16(1): 7–20.

Pilgrim, D. (2008) '"Recovery" and current mental health policy', *Chronic Illness*, 4: 295–304.

Pilgrim, D. and McCranie, A. (2013) *Recovery and Mental Health: A Critical Sociological Account* (1st edn), Houndmills: Palgrave Macmillan.

Pratt, M. and Rafaeli, A. (2006) 'Artifacts and organizations: Understanding our "objective" reality', in A.E. Rafaeli and M.G. Pratt (eds) *Artifacts and Organisations: Beyond Mere Symbolism*, Mahwah, NJ: Lawrence Erlbaum Associates, pp 279–88.

Reeves, A. (1999) *Recovery: A Holistic Approach*, Glouceter, UK: Handsell Publishing, City Works.

Robins, J. (1986) *Fools & Mad: A History of the Insane in Ireland*, Dublin: Institute of Public Administration.

Robinson, R. and Scott-Moncrieff, L. (2005) 'Making sense of Bournewood', *Journal of Mental Health Law*, 12 (May): 17–25.

Rose, N. (2019) *Our Psychiatric Future: The Politics of Mental Health*, Cambridge: Polity Press.

Salokangas, R.K. (1997) 'Living situation, social network and outcome in schizophrenia: A five-year prospective follow-up study', *Acta Psychiatrica Scandinavica*, 96(6): 459–68.

Sen, R., Kerr, C., MacIntyre, G., Featherstone, B., Gupta, A. and Quinn-Aziz, A. (2021) 'Social work under COVID-19: A thematic analysis of articles in "SW2020 under COVID-19 Magazine"', *British Journal of Social Work*, 52(3): 1765–82, Available from: https://doi.org/10.1093/bjsw/bcab094

Sheridan, A.J., Drennan, J., Coughlan, B., O'Keeffe, D., Frazer, K., Kemple, M. et al (2015) 'Improving social functioning and reducing social isolation and loneliness among people with enduring mental illness: Report of a randomised controlled trial of supported socialisation', *The International Journal of Social Psychiatry*, 61(3): 241–50.

Smyth, S., Casey, D., Cooney, A., Higgins, A., McGuinness, D., Bainbridge, E. et al (2017) 'Qualitative exploration of stakeholders' perspectives of involuntary admission under the Mental Health Act 2001 in Ireland', *International Journal of Mental Health Nursing*, 26: 554–69.

Swords, C. (2019) 'Recovery and co-production: Understanding the diverging paradigms and potential implications for social workers', *Irish Social Worker*, Winter 2019.

Swords, C. (2022) 'An exploration of how the concept of recovery in mental health is socially constructed and how it impacts on the delivery of mental health services: An Irish case study', [Unpublished], Trinity College Dublin, Available from: http://www.tara.tcd.ie/handle/2262/97765

Swords, C. and Houston, S. (2020) 'Exploring the concept of recovery in Irish mental health services: A case study of perspectives within an inter-professional team', *Irish Journal of Applied Social Studies*, 20(1): 31–46.

Swords, C. and Houston, S. (2021) 'Using social constructionism to research the recovery movement in mental health in Ireland: A critical reflection on meta-theory shaping the inquiry', *Irish Journal of Applied Social Studies*, 21(1): 52–73.

Topp, S.M., Schaaf, M., Sriram, V., Scott, K., Dalglish, S. L., Nelson, E.M. et al (2021) 'Power analysis in health policy and systems research: A guide to research conceptualisation', *BMJ Global Health*, 6(11): e007268, Available from: https://doi.org/10.1136/bmjgh-2021-007268

Turkle, S. (2007) *Evocative Objects: Things We Think With*, Cambridge, MA: MIT Press.

UN (United Nations) (1991) 'Principles for the protection of persons with mental illness and the improvement of mental health care'. Available from: https://www.ohchr.org/en/instruments-mechanisms/instruments/principles-protection-persons-mental-illness-and-improvement

UN (United Nations) (2006) 'Convention on the Rights of Persons with Disabilities'. Available from: https://www.ohchr.org/en/instruments-mechanisms/instruments/convention-rights-persons-disabilities

Watts, M. (2012) 'Recovery from "mental illness" as a re-enchantment with life: A narrative study', doctoral thesis, Trinity College Dublin.

WHO (World Health Organization) (1978) 'Report on the International Conference on Primary Care', Alma Alta, Geneva: World Health Organization.

WHO (World Health Organization) (1997) 'Jakarta Declaration on Leading Health Promotion into the 21st Century', Geneva: World Health Organization.

WHO (World Health Organization) (2013) 'Mental health action plan 2013–2020', Geneva: World Health Organization.

WHO (World Health Organization) (2021) 'Revised mental health action plan 2013–2030', Geneva: World Health Organization.

11

An expanded conceptualisation and definition of engaged research

Rory Hearne

Introduction

The dominant view within the academy, universities and among policymakers is that research is a process involving knowledge generation by academic experts. There is growing interest in, and increased university support for, 'engaged' research, which deepens research approaches to involve communities and civil society. However, such engaged research is too often limited to conceptualisations within the 'extractive' paradigm of research and places insufficient priority on Participatory Action Research (PAR). Such forms of participatory research are processes involving the co-construction of knowledge and social action with disadvantaged groups. There is a need, therefore, for a more expansive conceptualisation, definition and practice of engaged research, which is normatively critical and social justice- and social change-orientated, participatory in both process and outcome. This chapter provides such a framework for engaged, co-constructed, action research. It makes the case that this has an important value which enables the co-construction of new knowledge about inequality but within the research process also aims at the empowerment of marginalised groups through co-producing policy analysis, proposing solutions and bringing them into the policy and public spheres in forms of action research.

This chapter explores this participatory action approach to 'engaged' research through two case studies. The first is the application of an innovative research methodology, the Participatory Action Human Rights and Capability Approach (PAHRCA) in relation to homelessness in Ireland. The second is involvement in a campaign for a right to housing. As part of this, and drawing on experiences with other engaged research, the positionality and role of the academic and policy researcher in undertaking such engaged research for social justice is critically discussed. It considers how we can progress a praxis of social justice that promotes empowerment and social change, human rights and equality through our research. The key themes and concepts explored include: engaged research, PAR, empowerment, social change, and public policy transformation. The positive potential and the challenges for researchers undertaking engaged action research and critical public engagement on issues of social justice are also discussed. In the chapter, I provide an expansive conceptualisation and definition of the currently bounded 'engaged research' to one which emphasises co-production, empowerment for social change, public advocacy and action. This points to an important role for academic and policy researchers and social justice practitioners undertaking engaged research as partners with disadvantaged groups, researching for social change and social justice.

Engaged research: a critical discussion

International and national funders of research, along with universities, have increasingly encouraged academics to undertake 'engaged research', which seeks to involve the wider public as active participants in the construction of academic knowledge. Campus Engage, for example, is an initiative of Irish universities aimed at bringing researchers and communities together to address societal challenges in Ireland and promote engaged research. It defines 'engaged research' as 'a wide range of research approaches and methodologies that share a common interest in collaboration with societal partners' (Campus Engage, 2017: 4). Engaged research aims to 'improve, understand, or investigate an issue of public interest or concern, including societal challenges and sustainable development goals. It is advanced with societal partners rather than for them' (Campus Engage, 2017: 4).

There has been a criticism of some interpretations of what 'engaged research' actually means and how funding institutions' understanding of participation is too often limited to involvement with policymakers or a tokenistic engagement with the public and pays insufficient attention to the resources required to ensure genuine participation and empowerment of disadvantaged groups in particular. For example, writing about the UK experience, Heney and Poleykett (2022: 179) welcome the enthusiasm for engaged and participatory ways of working but argue that 'funding patterns, bureaucratic structures and an overreliance on people employed on casual contracts make it extremely difficult, often impossible, to do engaged research in British universities'. They found that their ability to undertake genuine participatory and engaged research was constrained by the way their institution 'imagined and materially supported engagement' (Heney and Poleykett, 2022: 179). It fell to individual researchers to try to overcome the structural barriers to engagement such as resource inequalities, which resulted in such engaged research not fulfilling 'its remit for inclusion and its radical potential' (Heney and Poleykett, 2022: 181).

There is a need therefore for a more critical assessment of the concept and practice of engaged research. What should it be aiming to achieve? What is its purpose? Furthermore, the role of academic research itself, and the academic, also needs to be interrogated.

Bourdieu (1991) finds that – given its capacity to represent and to name social experience – research carries significant symbolic power, particularly when authorised by the academy. This raises an issue central to this chapter and my work, which is the role academic research plays in society – in either affirming the status quo or challenging it. This section provides a discussion of approaches to the role of the academic researcher within the research process and how we define the research process itself.

In society today, academic social scientists are expected to play the role of 'experts' and 'technocrats' affirming the status quo, undertaking research that is defined and confined within the rules of the neoliberal political order (restricted to what is 'possible' within the confines of market-dominated ideologies and a managerial conception of politics that eschews publicly engaged interrogations of power and inequality). Policy recommendations are expected to be expressed in terms of 'best practices', 'guidelines' and 'standards', and not to emphasise power relations or the possibility of radically alternative views or models of society and the economy such as 'deliberation about contesting visions of the good' (Brown, 2015: 4). The role of the neoliberal social science academic is to stay within the university, securing research funding for their cash-strapped institution, undertaking research which is politically non-contentious and entering the public sphere only to act as an 'objective' commentator.

Universities consider that we should also only do research for which grant funding has been secured, to thus contribute to the financial viability of the university and enable the 'buy out' of our time. As a result, there can be a tension between time dedicated to engaged (often non-funded) research and the pressure to bring in funding. Engaged non-funded research should be valued equally as funded research within academia. We have come to approach the undertaking of research only when it receives funding. Therefore, who is to do research for and with communities who cannot provide funding? Or to do research where the agenda is set by the community, not the funding institution? Where is the time for research that is led and developed by civil society with academics, for its social value?

While there are many academics that play public roles for social justice and undertake critical and radical engaged research, the dominant discourse within neoliberal universities is that as academics we must eschew an overtly 'political' stance such as advocating and engaging in practices of radical research oriented towards societal transformation, or else face public opprobrium, lack of career progression, an inability to secure funding and pariah status in the neoliberal university. Within this dominant neoliberal paradigm, the following questions are not considered in a sufficiently profound way: What is the *actual purpose* of our research and knowledge production? Whose interests does it serve? How could research better contribute to the empowerment of disadvantaged groups and positive social change, for example in progressing the right to housing? What principles should underpin our research, what strategies can we use, and how should they frame our work?

As academics, we are too often told 'always be careful not to be political', even by our institutions and peers. We are told not to be overly critical of policy, of government, and while we may draw out proposals in our research, our job is not to advocate (never mind agitate) for such alternatives in the public sphere. What I mean by advocacy is taking a position in the public sphere that advocates and campaigns for policies that are critical of existing policies and goes a step further than simply knowledge dissemination but makes the case for alternative policies, for greater action. We are told simply to present our research – the knowledge we create –through various forms of dissemination. This can include to policymakers, but it is generally at a meeting behind closed doors.

The general rules of engaged research imposed by institutions and policymakers (of course, unwritten rules, just the 'culture' of how things should be done) is one whereby academics are to largely remain within academia and out of the public view, entering the public sphere only to present an 'objective' analysis once it is largely uncritical of the status quo.

However, there is a more unruly possibility, a more potentially transformative approach to research, which involves a shift in societal power dynamics. That is drawing on a PAR approach and co-creating new knowledge, with and by research participants affected by inequalities and bringing that into the public sphere in order to exercise the power of marginalised groups. The academic can and should be with them in that process.

An expanded concept of engaged research: Participatory Action Research

Strand et al (2003: 5) argue that engaged research is a means to 'democratize knowledge creation by validating multiple sources of knowledge and promoting the use of multiple methods of discovery and dissemination'. Campus Engage (2017) highlight how, from this perspective, the goal of engaged research is social action (broadly defined) for the purpose of achieving social change and social justice either directly or indirectly. But if engaged research is to achieve these outcomes, it needs to have a more solid theoretical and conceptual grounding in participatory theories and methodologies.

One such theoretical and methodological concept that would be useful in this regard and is central to engaged research is PAR, which is a longstanding theoretical and methodological approach to undertaking engaged research. PAR aims to generate knowledge in partnership with communities to empower the socially excluded in order to co-produce new knowledge about the reality of the impact of social and economic policies based on their lived experiences (Hearne and Murphy, 2019). It goes beyond just producing knowledge and includes, as part of its research process, the research participants taking constructive action on issues of inequality and injustice. Therefore, it is also a method of 'action' that brings new knowledge into the 'public sphere' of academic, NGO, policy and media debates in order to challenge social injustice (Gaventa and Cornwall, 2001).

The principles of PAR draw from Brazilian community educator Paulo Freire, who argued that people have a universal right to participate in the production of knowledge, and that action research involves a process whereby 'people rupture their existing attitudes of silence, accommodation and passivity, and gain confidence and abilities to alter unjust conditions and structures. Such action research is an authentic power for liberation that ultimately destroys a passive awaiting of fate' (Freire, 1974: xi). Freire highlighted the central role of the poor and oppressed in action research: the silenced are not just incidental to the curiosity of the researcher but are the masters of enquiry into the underlying causes of the events in their world. In this context, research becomes a means of moving them beyond silence into a quest to proclaim the world (Freire, 1974: 34).

Another useful theoretical approach to the conceptualisation of PAR is provided by economist and philosopher Amartya Sen. Sen argued it is 'essential to see the public not merely as "the patient" whose wellbeing commands attention, but also as "the agent" whose actions can transform society' (Sen and Dreze, 1989: 279).

These theories and understandings of engaged research challenge us to approach the purpose of research and policy analysis as not being only the interpretation of the world but as actively engaging in its transformation.

Academics as partners in social change

Such a PAR approach requires a different role than that of an 'objective' observer or expert, with the researcher instead becoming a 'partner in social change'. Drawing on Habermas, Fraser (1990: 77) explains that the 'public sphere' is a theatre in modern societies in which political participation is enacted. It is a space where 'citizens deliberate about their common affairs' and is 'conceptually distinct from the state: it is a site for the production and circulation of discourses' that can be critical of the state. However, Fraser highlights the need for a conceptualisation of the public sphere which enables 'critique of the limits of actually existing democracy in late capitalist societies' and should show the ways in which 'social inequality taints deliberation within publics', as some groups are more empowered in the public sphere than others. Fraser further proposes that there is a vital role and obligation for academics to be part of an 'unruly public' – to draw on our time, skills, knowledge and role to critically engage in this public sphere.

So how can we conceptualise and theorise a critical publicly engaged role for academic research as part of the 'unruly public'?

Academic research can have diverse roles and participate in forms of public engagement to ensure that co-produced knowledge contributes to society and social justice. Burawoy (2005) makes the case for a role for social scientists in promoting democratic solidarity to overcome neoliberalism – acting as 'public sociologists'. Social scientists can contribute to the public debate by providing information and knowledge, for example highlighting the extent, causes and consequences of extreme inequalities such as housing exclusion. However, as I have discussed earlier, it is not only the social scientist's own knowledge that is relevant; the production of knowledge should be democratised, as with PAR, involving those affected as well as the public.

The Italian political philosopher Antonio Gramsci provided a useful conception of the role of an 'organic intellectual' in society, whereby all men and women are 'philosophers'. In this context, citizens' daily lived experience and social movements are treated as 'knowledge producers', and the aim is to systematically generate counter-knowledge as a fundamental step in the process of social change (Cox, 2014: 965). The current hegemonic 'common sense' ideology is neoliberalism – the belief in the primacy, infallibility and allocative efficiency of the market, the individual as utility maximiser, the commodification and monetisation of everything and the removal of notions of a common society, solidarity and social support. However, this ideology has been deeply discredited by the 2008 financial crash, rising inequality and its failure to deliver economic freedom and prosperity for everyone. We are in a period that has echoes of that described by Gramsci when referring to the 1930s, where '[t]he crisis consists precisely in the fact that the old is dying and the new cannot be born; in this interregnum a great variety of morbid symptoms appear' (Gramsci, 1971: 275). Neoliberalism is in crisis, but there is a battle of ideas, and politics, for what replaces it. In this interregnum, one morbid symptom is the current authoritarian, nationalist, racist, sexist, extreme version of neoliberalism and financialised capitalism, which is in the ascendency in some of the most powerful countries in the world. The question we must ask and answer is what can challenge it and provide an alternative.

We can draw on Sen to provide a way forward here. Sen makes the important reflection, again drawing on Gramsci, that even if the goal is to change 'people's thinking and priorities' – as was the case for Gramsci – this still requires 'an engagement with the shared mode of thinking and acting' (Sen, 2009: 121).

Publicly engaged research for transformation can play a part in this task of providing a new common sense while also engaging with the old ways of thinking. This requires a kind of dual task, using language and imagery that communicate efficiently and well through the use of the existing 'common sense' while trying to make this language express proposals that would transform society (Sen, 2009). Drawing on the Gramscian concept of an 'organic intellectual', we can see a role for the academic researcher as a public sociologist or publicly engaged partner – not separate from the society and issues and struggles they are researching but part of them.

Working within and among social actors engaged in transformation, the publicly engaged academic can thus play a key role in contributing to the co-construction of common values and identity across the diverse groups required to enhance their collective capabilities to transform society (Burawoy, 2005). Academic research, therefore, should not be separate from civil society, policy debates, movements and communities but be part of them. Furthermore, we can apply Gramsci's conceptualisation of 'organic intellectuals' to understand the subjectivity and potential role of research participants, disadvantaged groups and those working with them in community development organisations or NGOs. Engaged research should aim to nurture and empower participants to see themselves as, and work with them to become, 'organic intellectuals' within the engaged action research process.

While community workers, grassroots activists, communities, civil society organisations and NGOs can and do play a major role in social change, empowerment and participation in relation to social justice and housing issues, it is not generally accepted that academic researchers play such a publicly proactive role in both advocating and campaigning for change and social justice.

Yet internationally, and historically, many academics have contributed to public debate and social change, indeed in actively shaping and building social movements for major societal change. In particular, academics have played an important role as critical voices who question and challenge inequalities and injustices and offer solutions and bring forward the perspectives and experiences of the excluded, disadvantaged and marginalised who would otherwise not be included or considered in policy and public debates.

A framework for participatory engaged action research

Academics and researchers can produce knowledge (like housing policy and analysis), but society and politics (social power) play a decisive role in whether or not that knowledge is used in a progressive, transformative way. Academics can also have major influence over the type and nature of research processes – whether they are done in extractive forms or through PAR, whether they empower or disempower. If we want to see change in policy and practice, therefore, academic research has to engage with politics and power.

Academics can play an important role in developing social power by undertaking research using an expansive conceptualisation of engaged research that includes participation for empowerment and social transformation, with participants becoming organic intellectuals and the academics as partners, through co-producing action research. This research process, by engaging in the public sphere in alternative and more socially active ways than just presenting to policymakers and in forms that educate, inform and empower the wider publics affected, can nurture solidarity and alternative value systems and policies. The current hegemony forecloses the possibilities of real social justice alternatives and asserts that inequality and neoliberal policies are natural, the most efficient and ultimately the only way to do things. However, these engaged processes can contribute to shifting the 'common sense' within civil society to create a counterhegemony of ideas and policies for a better, fairer and environmentally sustainable society. Thus engaging in a constructive form of Gramsci's 'War of Position'.

Based on my research and experience, I have identified several ways the academic researcher (and this can be applied to policy analysts and researchers, NGOs, human rights organisations, trade unions and community activists) can undertake engaged research that contributes to an egalitarian, socially and environmentally just and rights-based society. I have developed an analytical frame for such publicly engaged action/critical research (Hearne, 2020) which includes five strategies. These can also be applied to broader areas of social science, social work and the community and youth work fields:

1. Producing new 'knowledge', analysis and research of housing issues and policy, such as explaining the causes of housing crises and inequalities. Analysis from the normative framework of a human rights, social justice and environmental sustainability approach as an important counterbalance to the dominant market and neoliberal analysis. A rights and justice analysis should include policy alternatives that aim to empower, inform and inspire affected groups and the public, achieve cross-society solidarity and offer practical solutions to policymakers.
2. Work directly with vulnerable and excluded groups, communities and civil society to co-produce new knowledge and understandings of how social issues such as housing affect particular groups. A PAR approach is particularly effective. Existing policy and academic knowledge can be deepened and become more authentic through the direct experience of affected groups. Alternative policies can be co-constructed that better reflect the experiences and needs of those affected.
3. Engage with the policy process. Work with frontline workers and service providers, NGOs, state bodies, policymakers and elected representatives to gather their policy rationales and engage them in policy dialogue with those directly affected by social issues.

4. Be a public intellectual and advocate, bringing the voice of the excluded into the public political sphere along with new co-constructed knowledge and policy alternatives, through policy proposals, op-eds for the media, podcasts and speaking at public movement meetings.
5. Nurture solidarity across society. In partnership with civil society, facilitate and support the construction of structures and relationships of empowerment. Be part of social movements, campaigns and efforts to facilitate dialogue between diverse actors to develop common alternatives and action. Co-construct spaces for movements, civil society and wider public audiences through which social solidarity can grow, for example by creating spaces for dialogue, policy development and strategy formation.

The following section provides a case study of the application of this framework for engaged research to the area of homelessness.

Case study 1: Participatory Action Research with homeless families

Access to affordable, safe, secure and decent housing is essential for individuals' physical health, psychological well-being and living a life with dignity. A home provides the secure base from which to carry out all of life's functions (Hearne, 2020). Ireland has been experiencing a new housing crisis since 2013, characterised by housing shortages, rising rents and house prices and, most notably, the emergence of a new phenomenon of rapidly expanding family homelessness, particularly from 2015 onwards. Nationally, rental prices increased by 6.3 per cent on average each year between 2013 and 2019. Since the 1990s, low-income households unable to afford housing in the private market have increasingly been provided with housing 'benefits' – or supplementary rental supports – rather than traditional local authority (council) housing (Byrne and Norris, 2018). This policy shift away from the local authority building of social housing to a reliance on state subsidy to tenants which is then paid to private landlords resulted in the proportion of households in permanent social housing falling from 18 per cent of households in the 1960s to just 9 per cent in 2010 (Hearne, 2020). The majority (65 per cent) of new social housing provision under the national housing plan, Rebuilding Ireland (2016–21), came via private rental subsidy schemes such as the Housing Assistance Payment (Department of Housing, Planning and Local Government, 2016). This overreliance on the private rental market for social housing has exposed low-income households to increased evictions and homelessness and housing discrimination (Hearne and Walsh, 2021).

Homelessness increased from 344 families with 749 children in July 2014 to 1,616 families with 3,494 children in November 2022. This is a 370 per cent increase in the number of families recorded as homeless on a monthly basis, in Ireland in this period (Focus Ireland, 2021). These are families in emergency accommodation, such as bed and breakfasts, hotels and family hubs. These numbers do not capture the overall numbers of families and children experiencing homelessness in this period, as there is an ongoing exit of families from homelessness and then new families being made homeless. For example, in the first three months of 2022, 728 families were made homeless across Ireland. This means that around 1,400 children experienced the trauma of the loss of their home in the first three months of 2022 (Hearne, 2022).

Part of the public narrative expressed by policymakers during this crisis was to blame individuals and attribute the responsibility for homelessness to those experiencing homelessness. For example, a senior housing official in Dublin stated in a public forum and in the media that homelessness was 'created by bad behaviour' and there is a view among some policymakers that those in homelessness, particularly lone parents, are 'choosing' to stay in emergency accommodation in order to 'get a council house' (Hearne, 2020). Working with my colleague in Maynooth University, Mary Murphy, I undertook PAR with homeless families in 2017 and 2018 to try to understand the structural causes of homelessness, the role of the marketisation of housing policy and the impact of homelessness on families and children and advocate for co-constructed alternative policies in the public sphere. We did this as part of the H2020 European research project ReInVEST.

ReInVEST involved universities, research centres and NGOs across 13 European countries with 19 organisations and ran between 2015 and 2019. We worked with different 'vulnerable' and marginalised groups, such as people in mental health care (England), older jobseekers (Austria) and individuals and families who were homeless (Ireland).

As a researcher in the ReInVEST project, I was involved in co-producing the project's innovative and unique theoretical and methodological framework, the PAHRCA (Hearne and Murphy, 2017, 2018, 2019). The PAHRCA methodology drew on the capability approach and human rights theory in combination with PAR principles and methods. This new PAHRCA methodology aimed to co-construct new knowledge on the impact of austerity and marketisation of social policy and policies that could address these through PAR with academics, civil society actors (trade unions and NGOs) and marginalised groups and citizens. It aimed to transform social policy through co-created action in the public sphere by marginalised groups supported by academic researchers and civil society organisation partners. In this methodology, academics do not act as 'experts' who hold the objective knowledge but as facilitators and educators, supporting marginalised groups and civil society organisations by identifying key issues affecting them and researching with (rather than on) them. Civil society organisations were conceived not only as gatekeepers for recruiting participants for research but as important holders of knowledge – and thus as research participants themselves – and as potential actors in societal transformation. Finally, marginalised people were not conceived as part of a social problem to be solved by the experts but as subjects of rights and agents of change who have unique and valuable knowledge to share about their situation, how to ameliorate it and the key actors to be involved in processes of advocacy and public action.

The theory and practice of PAHRCA is outlined in two guides we produced for academic researchers and NGO practitioners (see Hearne and Murphy, 2019; Hearne et al, 2019). PAHRCA involved five key steps, including: the lead researchers and/or civil society organisation developing partnerships with the NGOs/civil society group working with marginalised groups; identifying, meeting and trust building with marginalised group participants; the developmental and capacity building of the participants through creative participative education on human rights and capability approaches and policy; participative methods to co-create new knowledge; and the PAHRCA 'voice – action – outcome' approach – using the research findings and outcomes to influence social change (Hearne and Murphy, 2019).

We applied the PAHRCA methodology in partnership with an NGO, Focus Ireland, to engage individuals and families who were homeless in assessing the impact of the marketisation of social housing policy on homelessness (Hearne and Murphy, 2017). The research process involved the co-construction of new knowledge of their experience of homelessness and policy responses, through group discussion, drawings and other participative methods and an empowering educational process based on the right to housing undertaken with the families in their emergency accommodation.

The research process involved weekly meetings over a ten-week period with a group of 12 homeless families (the parents, not children) in a family hub and also involved peer researchers. We undertook trust-building exercises with the families and us as researchers and used participative research methods to enable them to express their views and experiences of homelessness (such as photo-voice,[1] role play and drawing). We also provided education and analysis of housing policy and the concept of a right to housing with them over a number of sessions. The co-constructed research process identified new critical perspectives on housing policy, such as the impact of discrimination by private landlords and the detrimental impact on children of emergency accommodation (Hearne and Murphy, 2018). The research also co-constructed rights-based policy proposals, such as the state (or the local authority) directly sourcing housing for those who are homeless and ensuring greater tenant security in private rental housing.

A key part of the PAHRCA research process was empowering the homeless families to bring their voice into the policy and public sphere through a dialogue between the homeless families and senior policy and political stakeholders including the Irish Human Rights and Equality Commission. During the dialogue, the homeless parents (mainly lone-parent mothers) clearly articulated their experiences in terms of the impact of policies on their well-being and rights, showing the research process provided them with a language and insight on housing policy and on the human right to housing. Following the dialogue, we produced a public policy document. This report was highly critical of existing policy but also proposed alternative policy pathways.

The publications were cited in national media, and the report was discussed in the national parliament. We presented the research results (along with peer researchers) at various seminars and conferences organised by NGOs, and we also advocated for the findings in the media.

The NGO, Focus Ireland, continued to support the peer researchers involved, who were formerly homeless themselves. They involved them in producing research on homelessness and an analysis and guide in peer and participative research and involvement of service users in service design (Hoey et al, 2018; Focus Ireland, 2021).

This research contributed to and influenced the public and policy debate and knowledge on homelessness and social housing policy in Ireland. The research contributed to a tentative policy shift in 2020 which committed to move away, over time, from the marketised provision of social housing subsidies and to a greater emphasis on the direct delivery of social housing by the Irish state. Moreover, it showed that the solution to the 'problem' of homelessness requires conceptualising housing as a human right to be provided on the basis of need through a non-market, decommodified approach.

In response to the research, the then Taoiseach in national parliament criticised me personally, including by referring to my political activism. This was a clear attempt to delegitimise the research and deflect attention away from its critique of government. This response by the Taoiseach was criticised for its potential chilling effect on academic freedom and critique (Clifford, 2017).

This critique of my legitimacy as an academic undertaking public engagement clearly articulates a view that we, as academics, are supposed to behave in a certain way, with certain decorum. We are to remain 'objective', not taking sides, such as advocating for tenants' rights or against the privatisation of public land. This points to an opposition to undertaking political research (in the understanding of political as contentious, conflictual and critical of existing policy, not 'party political'). It makes it more difficult for academics to engage in critical engagement in the public sphere. However, there must be a place and space for research engaging in a fundamental questioning of how we distribute resources, how we organise our society.

Case study 2: Home for Good – the experience of engaged (non-funded) research with the campaign for a right to housing

A second case study is my involvement with NGOs including the Simon Communities and Mercy Law Centre from 2017 up to the present day in a network to progress a campaign for putting a right to housing in the Irish Constitution. The aim was to build upon the longstanding claim of NGOs working in homelessness in Ireland for the need for a right to housing in order to get substantive change on housing policy and practice. For three years, we undertook research and networking, building up the case for the right to housing, engaging legal experts and communications and values analysis (Crowley and Mullen, 2019). As an academic researcher, I played the role of supportive advocate, providing strategic advice and research on a right to housing, including writing articles in the media, using my podcast, Reboot Republic, and organising academic/civil society conferences on the theme in Maynooth University. My research supported and engaged with the NGOs and those progressing the right to housing, so I was not acting in isolation but as part of, and supporting, the growth of a civil society power advocating the right to housing. The NGOs, activists, community groups and members of the public told me that my analysis and advocacy influenced them in terms of providing a vision, legitimacy and information on how a right to housing would progress the housing issue in Ireland. I also engaged with the UN Rapporteur on Adequate Housing and dedicated a number of episodes of Reboot Republic to discussing how a right to housing could be progressed in Ireland, including interviewing and questioning the future (and now current) Minister for Housing about his commitment to delivering a right to housing (Reboot Republic, 2019). In January 2020, we launched the network publicly as a campaign, 'Home for Good'. *The Irish Times* (2020) reported: 'A new advocacy group launched on Wednesday will put pressure on politicians to commit to a referendum on inserting the right to a home into the Constitution.' A commitment was included in the Programme for Government 2020 to progress a referendum on housing. This was clearly not a commitment on a referendum on a right to housing, and it was highlighted that the Fine Gael party, in particular, as well as representatives within Fianna Fáil, were very reluctant to progress a right to housing in the Constitution. A number of presentations were made to the Oireachtas Housing Committee by Home for Good members which were very effective in influencing the elected members of the merits of a right to housing referendum. I included the right to housing as a key framing and proposal in my 2020 book *Housing*

Shock (Hearne, 2020), and when the issue of the investor funds buying up an estate in Maynooth resulted in a public outcry, I responded in the public debate by linking this financialisation of housing directly with the failure to enshrine a right to housing in the Constitution.

Given the phenomenal response to this, I set up an online petition, with support from campaigning group Uplift, which had six demands, one of which was to put the 'right to housing in our Constitution'. This petition was signed by almost 40,000 people, and Uplift and I presented it to the government at the Dáil in October 2021. Further public protests around housing that I was involved in supporting, including the Raise the Roof campaign, also advocated for a right to housing.

In January 2022, the government set up a Housing Commission to examine various issues in housing, including progressing a referendum on housing. As part of their work, they held a conference in University College Dublin in May 2022, at which I presented my research on why a referendum to insert the right to housing was required (Hearne, 2022). The commission then held a public consultation which ended in September 2022. In order to maximise the public engagement and submissions, I worked with the Home for Good coalition in preparing a submission and held a public webinar for the public and NGOs and civil society groups, advocating for the referendum to be a clear insertion of the right to housing in the Constitution (Home for Good, 2022). We await the recommendations from the Housing Commission on this. It is clear that there is now significant momentum for a right to housing referendum. A major shift has taken place in public attitudes and values to housing. Opinion polls carried out by the Irish Human Rights and Equality Commission show that a majority support putting a right to housing in the Constitution (IHREC, 2021). This would be a transformation in how housing and housing inequalities are dealt with and approached through policy in Ireland. I have shown how, in my academic role, I have contributed through a form of (non-funded) engaged research, a form of public engagement, drawing on my research to intervene with the public debate, support and empower civil society and progress a right to housing.

Discussion: the importance of bringing co-constructed knowledge into the public sphere

I want to emphasise the importance of the aspect of bringing the knowledge into the public sphere in a form of critical advocacy as a key component of my expanded concept of engaged research in terms of progressing both empowerment and transformation. This explains why we should include these aspects within the engaged research process itself.

This public sphere engagement is vital because state actors, policymakers and government ministers are constantly engaging with and meeting powerful lobbyists (such as developers, banks and investor funds) who seek to orientate policy towards their interests. And rather than looking at policy holistically, and, in particular, from frameworks such as social justice, equality and human rights, policy remains focused on the needs of these powerful market interests. There is, therefore, an obligation on academics, through participatory empowerment and as a partner for social change, to provide a co-produced evidence-based critical analysis of policy being developed and force policymakers to consider this in an engaged active way. To provide a counter power to the power of the markets in policy.

This is vital engaged research that analyses policy development contemporaneously and its impacts in the real world, on ordinary people, and not just providing the statistics and data in isolation of policy analysis but actually engaging in research and critical analysis of the state and market responses to critical social issues. It is also vital that as researchers and intellectuals we offer our analysis and viewpoints on what we would consider to be beneficial solutions. This is an area that academics have shied away from, but I believe we have a responsibility to use our knowledge and expertise and intellect to offer considered opinions and solutions to the public sphere, even if they are radical and even if they are not immediately implementable. Academics are supposed to be big thinkers – imagining what could and should be. We have an ethical and moral responsibility to use our academic positions to intellectually develop solutions to societies' critical challenges and to put those solutions into the public sphere, to deeply engage through participatory action with the affected groups in society in a dialogue on the potential for these solutions and to engage in the public and media debate to make the case for them. For example, the dominant analysis of housing in the media has been provided by academic and policy economists who hold free market economics perspectives. Their analysis is presented as 'unbiased objective' analysis, but in the area of housing, such analytical frameworks are filled with inherent (and often purposefully hidden) biases that treat housing as a market commodity, which is actually totally unsuitable and inappropriate for understanding and developing policy responses that could provide housing in a way that would meet the human need for housing, and not just market demand.

Asset-based commodified home ownership and financialisation have been central to the rise and dominance of neoliberalism, which gained much of its support by undermining public housing provision (for example, UK Prime Minister Margaret Thatcher's pointed attack on council housing in the 1980s, followed similarly in Ireland from the late 1980s to the present day) and the promotion of home ownership as the ideal for society. But the public sphere of housing (in the Habermassian sense) is also a space where counter-ideas, movements and practices are undertaken by people based on cooperative, community, collective, equality and rights-based values that fundamentally challenge the neoliberal order. In Ireland, for example, there is a growing tapestry of cooperative housing networks and artists reclaiming spaces of dereliction and vacancy that are asserting a different value system for housing – as a human right to a home, rather than a property investment asset for vulture funds and private developers.

Housing systems themselves result from the particular political economy in a country, the balance of power and influence of different sectors and forces in society: who controls it, who exercises their power and how (Kemeny, 1995). In Ireland, the dominant forces shaping housing have been private developers, landowners, home owners, landlords and more recently vulture funds and domestic and international real estate firms and investors (Hearne, 2020). However, 'civil society' is also a (potential) power, although much less influential in shaping housing policy and practice at a national level. That is changing in Ireland.

Academics, policy analysts, NGOs, trade unions, community workers and the wider public are playing a growing role in forcing change in policy in housing in Ireland. Most recently, the shift to introduce a ban on evictions and a vacant property tax has resulted, in part, from the role of this civil society power exerting pressure on government. It shows that civil society (including community housing activists and publicly engaged academic researchers) can all play a role in supporting those who are excluded and currently 'powerless' to exercise and realise their power and win the battle of ideas within civil society for an alternative 'common sense' based on the right to housing for all.

What do my findings mean for social justice research?

The findings presented in this chapter highlight the limitations of some current forms of engaged research which do aim or work to achieve genuine participation and empowerment of groups and individuals affected by inequalities within the research. The lessons from empowering action research for social justice is that there is a need for significant additional resources including time and effort to achieve genuine participation of those affected by inequalities within the research process. There is also a need to address the inequality of resources between academics and those living in disadvantage, around barriers of capacity, resources, language, confidence and the trauma of oppression. This requires a critical reflection on the positionality of the academic researcher and to work to mitigate the privilege and power imbalance between academic and participants so that participants genuinely become a co-producer of the research and a co-actor, an actual equal, a partner. Engaged research, if it is genuinely based on the principles of empowerment as envisaged in PAR, requires power sharing and empowerment for transformation. It must necessarily disrupt existing power structures both within academia and wider politics and society. That necessarily requires a willingness on the part of the researcher to also become an equal partner, go to spaces and places which can be time-consuming and organisationally and emotionally difficult and complex, and an awareness of, and being attuned to, the culture and day-to-day realities of inequalities. It requires reflection and praxis, reflection on practice, and dialogue between researchers and participants.

What do my findings mean for social justice practice and policy, both in the Irish context and beyond?

These two case studies show the potential of applying an expanded conceptualisation and application of engaged research to a form of engaged action research in order to contribute to social justice through empowering disadvantaged groups and bringing new co-constructed knowledge into the public sphere as a form of advocacy.

The chapter highlights the importance of engaged research involving PAR in order to empower those affected by inequalities – co-constructing a new knowledge, including the unique experiential knowledge of those affected by inequality and bringing this into the public sphere.

For researchers, practitioners and advocates, the chapter points to a requirement to challenge ourselves and be willing to take action to become a partner for social change. Indeed, the public action component of engaged research for social justice is essential. Funders, universities and existing state institutions and elected government representatives need to understand this core aspect of engaged research for social justice. It necessarily requires rupture and conflict and a redistribution of power away from existing elite institutions to disadvantaged groups. That is the core challenge faced in undertaking engaged research, but it is also its potential for real empowerment and transformation for social justice.

Research and policy advocacy for social justice, then, need also to focus not just on lobbying/engaging with policymakers but also on trying to change the 'common sense', as Gramsci described it, that is, the public narratives and discourse, the popular consciousness and cultural attitudes to social inequalities, such as we have done in the area of housing as a human right, and thus adopt research strategies that strengthen and empower the social power – a counter power of alternative ideas and demand for social justice. Engaged research can be seen then as a legitimate form of public education and public empowerment through providing a critical co-constructed (with those affected by inequalities) analysis of policy, identifying and highlighting the lived reality of inequalities and bringing this into the public sphere as a process of public conscientisation and a critical challenge of, and presenting alternatives to, neoliberal policy.

Conclusion

The chapter provides a critical assessment of engaged research using a PAR framework and makes the argument for an expanded conceptualisation of engaged research to become 'participatory engaged action research' which aims to bring to the fore the voice, experiences, needs and policy analysis of those affected by inequalities. In this case, I have shown how homeless families, NGOs and those seeking affordable housing can be empowered to be brought into the public sphere. Two case studies were explored drawing on the framework of my expansive conceptualisation of engaged research to empower disadvantaged groups to extend the debate of what is considered 'possible' in the public sphere to inform and educate the public to better understand who is affected and how by housing issues and policy and to nurture cross-society solidarity.

In this chapter, I have critically engaged with and expanded our conceptualisation and definition of engaged research. I have shown ways that engaged research (including policy analysis) can be developed and undertaken to educate, inform and empower those affected by inequalities, those NGOs and civil society organisations working with those affected, and the wider public who are, as Sen described, potential (and necessary) allies in solidarity. This moves our understanding of engaged research to integrally involve empowerment and social change.

Furthermore, my conceptualisation of engaged research is that it cannot be just confined to specific one-off pieces of research but is an ongoing process of dialogical engagement – of interaction – that is about addressing a social issue, using our academic legitimacy, our role as 'experts', to be a critical public advocate and publicly engaged partner for social change, to challenge policy and politicians in the public sphere. This needs to be seen by academia and academic institutions as a valued and legitimate role and an aspect of engaged research. This is research as a critical public intellectual for social justice. As academics, we in social science are often reluctant to enter the public sphere because areas of engagement are outside our specific area of expertise. Yet, economists are considered experts on everything and give their view and analysis (predominantly the classical free market view of the world) on everything. Social scientists, sociologists and social policy researchers and academics also have general expertise on society and social issues and policy. We should claim that in the public sphere.

This chapter also proposes, therefore, a core role of 'partner for social change' for academics, policy researchers and social justice practitioners and emphasises the potential for playing this role within a radical conceptualisation of engaged research. Neoliberalism has created a metaphorical ideological cage for academics that allocates the role of bystander and observer to academics within financial capitalism. It is an economic system where the aim is to create what sociologist Pierre Bourdieu termed 'a utopia of limitless exploitation'. The academic's place is to stay within the walls of the university and play the role of knowledge producer and reproducer of the new workforce, and not to engage in normative or value-based research and engagement that articulates perspectives of social justice and human rights. In contrast to this 'neoliberal academic', Bourdieu argues for the necessity of working 'to invent and construct a new social order'. This is a central intellectual task of critically engaged academics. As academics, we are also citizens and members of the public, and this places an obligation on us to consider and develop ideas, policies and actions that could bring about a country, and wider world, without poverty, without homelessness and that ensures flourishing for all people while also protecting and nurturing our environment and climate. It is not enough for us as academics to simply produce new knowledge. We must produce it through processes that involve 'co-construction', forms of empowering action research that engage with communities and civil society to enhance their capacity and power. We should also try to play a role in bringing that co-produced knowledge into the public sphere – in order to empower those affected by inequalities, shape the public debate, educate and inform the public, challenge inequalities and the structural and policy causes of inequalities, and propose social justice alternatives. We must bring the knowledge in the university out into the community and into society so that we can improve society.

We can work to rupture silences about injustice and inequalities or we can allow the hegemony of the common sense to go unchallenged. It is not just about identifying inequalities but also challenging their persistence. It is not just about identifying solutions but arguing for them in the public sphere.

This is an expansive definition of engaged research. Importantly, it also includes non-funded research.

The challenge for us then is how we can undertake publicly engaged research which is research for empowerment and social change, using co-production/participation and public advocacy. A key method within this, I have shown, is to convert our research into publicly accessible ways that challenge the neoliberal 'common sense' – through deconstructing policy but also informing policy debates and co-constructing alternatives. It is about thinking about how we communicate these in the public sphere.

The Irish state and government policy need to recognise and accept that critical public academics, policymakers, NGOs and community and voluntary organisations have a vital role to play in raising awareness of issues affecting the most vulnerable, offering alternative knowledge and policy alternatives and thus enhancing democracy through empowering the most marginalised.

Note

[1] The photo-voice technique involved participants taking pictures of situations related to their daily personal lives, in a way that shows to other people 'as we see it'.

References

Bourdieu, P. (1991) *Language and Symbolic Power*, Cambridge, MA: Harvard University Press.

Brown, W. (2015) *Undoing the Demos: Neoliberalism's Stealth Revolution*, Cambridge, MA: MIT Press.

Burawoy, M. (2005) 'For public sociology', *American Sociological Review*, 70(1): 4–28.

Byrne, M. and Norris, M. (2018) 'Procyclical social housing and the crisis of Irish housing policy: Marketization, social housing, and the property boom and bust', *Housing Policy Debate*, 28(1): 50–63.

Campus Engage (2017) 'Engaged research: Society and higher education working together to address societal challenges', Dublin: Irish Universities Association.

Clifford, M (2017) 'If in doubt, spin it out, sums up approach to crisis', *Irish Examiner*, Tuesday, 22 August, Available from: https://www.irishexaminer.com/opinion/arid-20457488.html

Cox, L. (2014) 'Movements making knowledge: A new wave of inspiration for sociology?', *Sociology*, 48(5): 954–71.

Crowley, N. and Mullen, R. (2019) 'Framing the right to housing: A values-led approach', *European Journal of Homelessness*, 13(2): 31–44.

Department of Housing, Planning and Local Government (2016) 'Rebuilding Ireland', Dublin: Government of Ireland.

Focus Ireland (2021) *Peer Research in Housing and Homelessness: A Guidebook for Organisations, Researchers and Funders*, Dublin: Focus Ireland.

Fraser, N. (1990) 'Rethinking the public sphere: A contribution to the critique of actually existing democracy', *Social Text*, 25–6: 56–80.

Freire, P. (1974) *Pedagogy of the Oppressed*, New York: Continuum.

Gaventa, J. and Cornwall, A. (2001) 'Power and knowledge', in P. Reason and H. Bradbury (eds) *Handbook of Action Research: Participative Inquiry and Practice*, London: Sage Publications, pp 70–80.

Gramsci, A. (1971) *Selections from the Prison Notebooks*, London: Lawrence & Wishart

Hearne, R. (2020) *Housing Shock: The Irish Housing Crisis and How to Solve It*, Bristol: Policy Press.

Hearne, R. (2020) *Gaffs: Why No One Can Get a House and What We Can Do About It*, Dublin: HarperCollinsIreland.

Hearne, R. and Murphy, M. (2017) 'Investing in the right to a home: Social housing', HAPs and HUBS, Maynooth University.

Hearne, R. and Murphy, M. (2018) 'An absence of rights: Homeless families and social housing marketisation in Ireland', *Administration*, 66(2): 9–31.

Hearne, R. and Murphy, M. (2019) *Participatory Action Research: A Human Rights and Capability Approach; Part 1; The Theory*, Brussels: ReInVEST, Available from: https://www.ifz-salzburg.at/wp-content/uploads/2021/11/ifz-RE-InVEST_Part_1_The_Theory_2019.pdf

Hearne, R., Murphy, M. and Whelan, N. (2019) *Participatory Action Research: A Human Rights and Capability Approach; Part 2; The Practice*, Brussels: ReInVEST, Available from: https://mural.maynoothuniversity.ie/13435/1/MM_mussi_participation.pdf

Hearne, R. and Walsh, J. (2021) 'Housing assistance and discrimination: A scoping study on the "Housing Assistance Ground" under the Equal Status Acts 2000–2018', Dublin: IHREC.

Heney, V. and Poleykett, B. (2022) 'The impossibility of engaged research: Complicity and accountability between researchers, "publics" and institutions', *Sociology of Health & Illness*, 44(S1): 179–94.

Hoey, D. and Sheridan, S., with Haughan, P., Richardson, E. and Twomey, K. (2018) *Are You Still OK?*, Dublin: Focus Ireland.

Home for Good (2022) 'Home for Good submission to the public consultation on a referendum on housing', Available from: home_for_good_submission_to_the_public_consultation_on_a_referendum_on_housing.pdf

Irish Human Rights and Equality Commission (2021) IHREC Annual Poll 2021: An Amarach briefing on behalf of IHREC, Available from: https://www.ihrec.ie/app/uploads/2021/12/IHREC-Amarach-Research-Survey-2021-29122021.pdf

Kemeny, J. (1995) *From Public Housing to the Social Market: Rental Policy Strategies in Comparative Perspective*, London: Routledge.

Sen, A. and Dreze, J. (1989) *Hunger and Public Action, WIDER Studies in Development Economics*, Oxford: Oxford University Press.

Sen, A. (2009) *The Idea of Justice*, Cambridge, MA: Harvard University Press.

Strand, K.J., Cutworth, N., Stoecker, R. and Marullo, S. (2003) *Community-Based Research and Higher Education: Principles and Practices*, New York: John Wiley.

The Irish Times (2020) 'Lobby to Press Politicians over Referendum on Right to Home', Wednesday, 22 January 2020.

12

Social justice as tool and process in research: progressing insight into children's right to participation through Interpretative Phenomenological Analysis

Breda O'Driscoll and Gloria Kirwan

Introduction

Drawing on research conducted by O'Driscoll (2023), this chapter demonstrates how the adoption of a social justice lens can inform methodological research design decisions in the context of social research. This chapter reports on a research study in Ireland which investigated the views of social workers regarding the right of children to participate in decisions which will impact their life trajectories, in this instance, decisions that need to be achieved when children are the subject of child welfare concerns. The research reported here sought to uncover how social workers conceptualise their efforts to support the activation of the child's right to participate in such decisions regarding their safety and well-being, and the extent to which they perceive how their work supports the child's participation in these matters. This chapter demonstrates how Interpretive Phenomenological Analysis (IPA), as the main research methodology, served to illuminate the experiences of social workers involved in direct work with children including how their interventions can play a crucial role in determining the extent to which children are consulted, heard and listened to in the context of child welfare work.

Aims of the research on child participation in decision-making

There is limited in-depth knowledge of social workers' experiences of working with children's rights within child protection services and little knowledge which has been developed through the specific research lens of social justice. As the main goals of children's welfare services are to promote children's safety and well-being, and to protect their rights, social workers' lived experiences of working with children in these contexts must be explored and critiqued (Ferguson, 2016). It is vitally important to understand what motivates and influences social workers' actions in their direct work with children, but, at present, there is a dearth of knowledge concerning social workers' efforts to involve children in decisions that will affect their lives (Winter, 2010; Ferguson, 2014, 2016, 2018; Ruch, 2014; Ruch et al, 2016; Winter et al, 2016, 2019).

The participation of children in decision-making was explored in the study reported here through a specific focus on social workers' experiences regarding children's participation in child welfare assessments and child safety decisions in the Irish context. Thus, this research topic speaks to a social justice agenda regarding the rights of children to be viewed as social actors who must be heard and listened to in decisions that have the potential to influence their life trajectories, their outcomes in life and ultimately their destiny.

This chapter illustrates how the methodology employed in this research study helped to elucidate and interpret the meanings, practices and emotions which encircled their work with children as reported by the social worker-research participants. Thus, the methodology played an important role, it will be argued, in achieving a deep level of insight into the ways in which social workers recognise and facilitate the child's right to participate.

Background context to the study: children's right to participate in global and local contexts

Despite the widespread acceptance and continued focus at global, national and local levels on the needs and rights of children, there remains much work to be done to vindicate these rights for *all* children. UNICEF's 'The State of the World's Children' series of reports, published between 1980 and 2021 (UNICEF, 1980–2021), paint a discouraging picture of the global condition of children. These reports document the many challenges and inequities experienced by children across the world, including poverty, trauma, child labour, exploitation and unequal access to education and healthcare, alongside many other problematic issues. It is this wider context regarding the position and treatment of children by society (local and international) that provided the impetus for conducting research on social workers' views on children's participation in decisions regarding their welfare and safety. Thus, the study reported here was infused from its inception with a social justice perspective, and it was through this lens that critical interrogation of the research data became possible.

The evolution of awareness and recognition of children as rights-bearers has been a gradual process. Positioning children as rights-bearers opens up a rights-based landscape of childhood in which children and young people's viewpoints have currency and value. The ambition to construct an inclusive society where children's voices are heeded remains at present an unfinished project with a lot more work to be done to embed the rights of children into the fabric of society at local, national and global levels. The study reported here aimed to illuminate how professional actors, in this case social workers, interpret the right of children to participate in decisions that affect their lives.

The importance of improving the participation of children in society has gained currency over time. The United Nations Convention on the Rights of the Child (UNCRC) (UNCRC, 1989) is the most recent international iteration of the codification of children's rights, an exercise which stretches back to the Geneva Declaration on the Rights of the Child as adopted by the League of Nations in 1924 (League of Nations, 1924). Yet, despite this long-term effort to articulate and activate children's rights, the vindication of their rights remains somewhat elusive or completely absent for millions of children across the world. It is, therefore, necessary to continue to interrogate this topic.

This study fills a knowledge gap by investigating how service providers experience and consider not only the concept of children's right to participate but how they believe they support this type of participation. UNICEF (nd) highlights on its homepage that '[c]hildren need champions'. This chapter aims to shed light on the potential for social workers to act as champions of the child's right to participate in decisions regarding their welfare and illustrates how research with a social justice orientation can identify the processes through which the participatory rights of children can be upheld, promoted and ensured.

Conceptualising the right to participation in childhood

The UNCRC (UNCRC, 1989) articulates the 'Right to Participation' in Article 12:

1. States Parties shall assure to the child who is capable of forming his or her own views the right to express those views freely in all matters affecting the child, the views of the child being given due weight in accordance with the age and maturity of the child.
2. For this purpose, the child shall in particular be provided the opportunity to be heard in any judicial and administrative proceedings affecting the child, either directly, or through a representative or an appropriate body, in a manner consistent with the procedural rules of national law. (UNCRC, Art. 12)

Hart's (1992) definition of participation chimes with the UNCRC definition by proposing a view of participation which links it directly into the broader democratic agenda. Hart (1992: 5) construes the core of participation as "the process of sharing decisions which affect one's life and the life of the community in which one lives". In this light, participation at decision-making forums becomes the means by which "democracy is built and upheld; it is a standard against which democracies should be measured" (Hart, 1992: 5).

In line with Article 12 of the UNCRC, Bellamy (2003) emphasises the importance of promoting children's participation so that they can influence decisions that affect their lives, gain skills in participation and understand the benefits of participation. Similarly, Sanders et al (2017) argue in favour of a strengths approach through which children and young people are viewed as positive contributors in society. They argue that services, including services for youth at risk, need to adopt strategies of engagement and empowerment of young people. The United Nations Committee on the Rights of the Child advises that for children in the care of the state it is essential that the child's views are heeded in terms of care plans and alternative care arrangements as well as their contact with their family of origin (Kilkelly, 2011). Overtly, statutory services in Ireland state that they aim to work in a consultative way with children and young people. The study reported in this chapter aimed to understand and explore how this is enacted in Ireland within child welfare and protection services.

Why children's participation in decisions matters

The benefits of child participation have been highlighted in the literature, especially in relation to children who may already be disadvantaged, powerless or alienated (Bell, 2002; Cashmore, 2002; Sanders et al, 2017). Some authors suggest that children's participation supports the development of autonomy and resilience, as these are important life skills, thus enhancing children's ability to protect themselves in the future (Leeson, 2007; Vis et al, 2011). Research findings typically report that participation increases children's feelings of self-esteem, helps them gain a sense of connectedness, as well as increasing their competence in life skills (Munro, 2001; Bell, 2002; Leeson, 2007; Vis et al, 2011).

However, the research evidence also indicates that most children who are in contact with child protection and welfare services and those placed in care feel that they may have few or no opportunities to participate in decisions that affect their lives (Munro, 2001; Bell, 2002; Cashmore, 2002; Bessell, 2007; Leeson, 2007). Children in these contexts have been found to carry feelings of being ignored and overlooked, and this can compound their sense of helplessness and desperation (Leeson, 2007; van Bijleveld et al, 2015).

Child participation in decisions and the child welfare system in Ireland

Drawing on the rights articulated in the UNCRC (1989), the Irish Child and Family Agency (Tusla) has developed a comprehensive Participation Strategy, which outlines the steps necessary to ensure that 'a child or young person's views should be heard whenever decisions are being taken that affect their lives' (Tusla, 2015: 5). The participation of children in the decision-making process is articulated in Irish policy documents (the National Standards for the Protection and Welfare of Children [HIQA, 2012], the National Policy Framework for Children and Young People 2014–20 [DCYA, 2014], the National Strategy on Children and Young People's Participation in Decision-Making 2015–20 [Tusla, 2019] and in the Children's First Guidelines [DCYA, 2011]), thus entwining processes of protection, prevention and participation. According to Tusla (2015: 7): "Child protection must begin with proactive prevention, and a rights-based approach to child protection starts with prevention ... participation is also understood as one means towards effective prevention of, and protection from, child abuse and neglect."

Thus, social workers in the field of child protection in Ireland are tasked with involving children in the important decisions affecting their lives.

However, some commentators in other jurisdictions suggest that many children who have been the subject of child welfare and protection interventions may experience a lack of consultation regarding their views and needs, and that this lack of consultation or opportunity to express their wishes and preferences further compounds any other negative experiences that may be happening in their lives (Sanders et al, 2017; Winter et al, 2016).

The study reported here, titled 'Standing Tall with Children' (O'Driscoll, 2023), aimed to address the knowledge gap regarding what professionals working in the Irish context actually do to involve children in decisions by seeking to identify key aspects of their work that support a participation agenda.

To explore this phenomenon (children's involvement in decision-making), a qualitative methodology, IPA, was utilised in this study. An overview of this research methodology is provided in the next section, including how it was used in this study to better understand how social worker participants conceptualised and reflected on how they support the children they work with to be involved in key decisions in their lives.

Interpretive Phenomenological Analysis and its application in this study

This study was located across two, geographically distanced sites within Tusla, the Child and Family Agency's network of offices. Following an open call for participants which was disseminated with Tusla's permission through an internal gatekeeper, ten social workers were recruited to take part in the study, all of whom were professionally qualified and registered social workers with considerable child protection work experience. A small, homogenous participant sample is consistent with the IPA approach (Smith,

2012). Ethical approval was sought and received from the Research Ethics Committees in both Tusla and the School of Social Work and Social Policy, Trinity College Dublin.

In practice, the IPA method, as it was applied in this study, involved in-depth one-to-one interviews between the researcher and each research participant on an individual basis which allowed for the recalling and sharing of the participants' stories (examples), thoughts and feelings (O'Driscoll, 2023). Participants were invited to offer detailed accounts of their experiences. This methodology provided a route through which to capture the stories, thoughts and feelings of the social work participants, thus providing deep-level access for the researcher into the internal meaning-making processes underlying how social workers view and experience their work with children. As Ferguson (2016) suggests, the lived experience of social workers must be further explored if they are to understand and develop their role with regard to the promotion of children's rights; this study provided an opportunity and means to conduct research in answer to Ferguson's call.

The aim was to elucidate how social workers make sense of decision-making by children in the context of child protection and welfare services, and this methodological approach provided a means by which the study could "give voice to the concerns of participants; and [achieve] the interpretive requirement to contextualise and "make sense" of their claims and concerns" (Larkin et al, 2006: 102). By using an IPA methodology, it was envisaged that the research would yield rich insights into social workers' views (cares and concerns) on the phenomenon of decision-making in childhood (in the context of child protection and welfare services) "informed by the social workers' own relatedness to, and engagement with, the phenomenon" (Larkin et al, 2006: 117).

When conducting the interviews, open-ended and exploratory questions were asked, allowing the participants to share their views and experiences in their own words and with as much depth of feeling and experience as they chose to share.

Interview question-prompts addressed to the participants as a means of eliciting their views on children's decision-making included the following:

- What does involving children in decisions mean for you?
- Recall the most recent experience of involving a child in a decision which affected their life (describe, discuss, consider).
- Explore an experience in which you felt satisfied with the experience of involving a child in a decision which affected their life (recall and discuss issues arising).
- Explore an experience in which you did not feel satisfied with the experience of involving a child in a decision which affected their life (recall and discuss issues arising).

- Describe how you go about involving children, what does this entail and how is this experienced – what are the positives and challenges for you?

These interviews generated considerable amounts of data derived from detailed accounts by the social workers on how their work with children either supported or not the rights of children to be involved in decisions about their safety and well-being.

An IPA study will typically be made up of small, purposefully selected samples in specific contexts. IPA analysis aims to reveal meanings underlying the phenomenon under investigation, and this is achieved through repeated readings of the data transcripts.

Each case is examined in great detail before moving to the next case and then cautiously moving on to look for connections, patterns, similarities and differences across cases (Smith et al, 2009). In this way, IPA produces its account of shared meanings identifiable within the data. 'In a good IPA study it should be possible to parse the account both for shared themes, and for the distinctive voices and variations on those themes' (Smith et al, 2009: 38).

Adopting the IPA approach in this study facilitated what Larkin et al (2006: 114) describe as the identification of the participants' 'concerns and cares, their orientation toward the world, in the form of the experiences that they claim for themselves', and specifically in the context of this research it helped to shed light on how the social workers understand the phenomenon of decision-making in childhood.

The objective of this study was to examine through rigorous enquiry how social workers make sense of their experience of involving children in decisions in the context of child protection social work. By adopting the IPA methodology, it was possible to capture and critically analyse their views, feelings and experiences. As Smith and Nizza (2022) explain, IPA not only provides a method of gathering detailed information regarding people's lived experiences; it can also uncover how people interpret those lived realities and how they connect their inner thoughts (internal self) with their external, social worlds (external self). Positioning participants as experts in their lived reality, the IPA method supports researchers to identify the underlying emotional processes that are connected to experiences. 'Participants are considered experts in the topic under investigation, so their input is obtained to understand what has happened to them or to know what their thoughts and feelings in a certain topic are' (Smith and Nizza, 2022: 6).

Examining how people articulate and recount their personal experiences is an important aim for IPA investigators, as this enhances their ability to interpret sense-making processes that surround the topic under investigation. This aspect of the analysis in the IPA methodology is generally referred to as the ideographic aspect of the analysis (Smith et al, 2009), in other words, the study of the particular. IPA is concerned with the particular because of the depth it can add to the analysis in terms of revealing how particular phenomena are understood by particular people in particular contexts.

In their interviews in this study, the social workers had much to say on the topic of children's participation in decision-making and also on the social workers' efforts to support children to participate. The accounts provide rich descriptions and capture the emotional intensity of the work. They shed light on the encounters between social workers and children and on the obstacles and challenges to involvement of the children in decision-making.

This chapter selectively presents a sub-set of findings from this study in order to present how social workers engage with and reflect on their lived experiences of child participation in decision-making.

Findings

Analysis of the interview data revealed how the social workers described their work as complex in the context of child welfare and protection services; they configure the involvement of children in decision-making in child protection contexts as a multi-level and multi-layered process. Social workers shared what it is like to stand tall with children as they strive to ensure rights to protection, provision and participation. They shared how they aim to create a safe space for children, and the importance of building rapport with the child so that they will articulate their views and needs. The aim of their work, in the views of the social workers who participated in the study, must always be to ensure that the child's wishes and needs remain the central focus.

The analysis of the participant interviews found that social workers identify numerous obstacles to communication by social workers with children in the context of child welfare assessments and interventions. For example, children may have little prior experience of involvement in decision-making, and children may be fearful or under duress when meeting the social worker.

The social workers report often meeting children whose right to participation in general has been previously limited, unacknowledged, curtailed, ignored or rejected. At the time of commencing contact with the child, they reported that it is often the case that the child's voice has not been previously acknowledged or respected. Indeed, it is a rare experience for children to feel free to disclose abuse, discuss harm and to feel comfortable with seeking help. According to the social workers, a child who is being abused will be unlikely to have had the experience of having their wishes, worries and views acknowledged and will rarely if ever feel free to discuss their worries, particularly with a social worker or someone outside their family. Thus, helping a child who is actually experiencing neglect or abuse to speak about the reality of their lives is, in itself, a route to achieving other rights of the child, apart from participation rights, including the rights to safety and good health.

Some children may also come to the relationship with the social worker with little or no prior experience of a trusting and safe relationship with adults outside of their immediate social sphere. In some instances, the child's experience with one or more adults has been one in which they have been harmed (physically, sexually, emotionally). These children are often full of fear and typically do not feel free to talk openly about their worries or what is going on for them regarding the abuse they have experienced. They may be holding a secret inside for a long time. Social workers describe how challenging it can be for children to express their views and needs if they are full of fear, scared, inhibited or do not feel safe enough to open up or make decisions.

How social workers work with children to involve them in decisions in the context of child abuse and neglect

Despite these challenges, the social workers in this study reported feeling that they do often make connections and build trusting relationships with children. The social workers' accounts in the research interviews describe communications with children which aid children's participation as characterised by compassion and empathy: "I think they are the most vulnerable in society, that is a big statement, they have no rights, we see that being demonstrated all the time" (Maureen); "I don't know how they are even surviving, how are they managing to live" (Angela). The communication messages the social workers aim to convey to the child are that their story is important, their voice is valued and their worries should be heard.

The analysis revealed that the tasks that the social workers are engaged in to achieve the participation of children are varied and complex. The work which occurs is multi-level and multi-layered, shedding light on the multitude of tasks that the social workers do in order to achieve the outcome of children's participation or children's involvement in decisions.

Indeed, child protection social workers are tasked with involving children in decisions at each step of the child protection process. In line with Article 12 of the UNCRC (1989), the social workers aim to enable children to express their views, for the views to be listened to, taken on board and advocated for. Thus, ensuring that the views of the children influence the decisions made about the child. In order to achieve these desired processes, the social workers engage in a multitude of tasks, including two which are highlighted for the purpose of this chapter, namely 'tuning in' and 'building connections'.

Tuning in

Social workers in this study shared examples of participatory practice which illustrate the significance of empathy by social workers in their work with children. The social workers stress the importance of 'tuning in' to the child's situation and thinking about what the experience of life is like for the child before they meet with a child and at various significant points along the whole course of the intervention.

The social workers describe being ever conscious of the harm and negative impact of abuse and neglect that can be present in the child's life, and they will have a heightened awareness that the child may be frightened. They also have a strong feeling of hope and firm commitment to trying to work collaboratively with all involved in order to improve outcomes for children. The social workers see the child as being deeply embedded in their family. Each social worker shared examples of their practice that provide an illustration of the significance of empathy and tuning in to the child and tuning in to the child's situation:

'Social workers need to put themselves in the shoes of the child they meet. We don't know what their experience of life is like.' (Maureen)

'When they are talking to us, I always try to ask myself, "what is it like for the child?" What is going through their head? Maybe they are thinking, if I say this or that then things are going to be worse. So, we have to reassure the child. We can't guarantee them this, but we will certainly try not to make things worse for them.' (Lin)

Tuning in is a process of trying to work out what might be going on for this individual child and then pitching or regulating the social work response accordingly and in a way that serves to engage and involve the individual child. Tuning in is also a process of awareness and sensitivity to a variety of interdependent factors (child factors and factors in the child's environment) which may be impacting on the child. The social workers engage in a process of calibration to the specific individual circumstances in order to create as safe and as comfortable a space as possible for the child to speak with them.

Starting point

As one study participant succinctly stated, there is a need to engage with a child on their terms: "Start with the child and where they are at" (Geraldine). The social workers' accounts identify child-specific factors and environment factors which can have a significant impact on the child, the work of the social worker and on the practice of involving the child in decisions. The child–related factors that the social workers describe as having a significance are the individuality of the child, the child's agency and the history of contact they have had with services:

'Sometimes families and children haven't been identified to Tusla until it's very late and they have been struggling for years, they

come to us at a time of massive crises, they are all in reactive mode.'
(Deirdre)

'This scenario is very different to a child who is identified early
or presents early in crisis and whose family have had no negative
experience to date with services.' (Deirdre)

The social workers all suggest they aim to work on a case-by-case basis,
and as one of the participants, named in the study as 'Geraldine', explains,
she tries "to respond to the child where they are at". However, in order to
meet the child where they are at, they must first tune in to the child and
find out, gauge, assess, what is or might be going on for this child. This is
a complex process and answering the question of what is going on for a
particular child is no easy matter. Understanding where a child is at requires
a complex response and varied capacities and skills.

Each social worker stresses the critical importance of responding to every
child as a unique individual. The practice examples and social workers'
descriptions and analysis of their work shared by the study participants
highlight the variety of situations that they can meet within the course of
their everyday work. They shared examples of many different situations and
scenarios regarding individual children whose personality, age, specific and
unique issues all interplay in a multitude of ways.

In terms of understanding and tuning in to the child factors, the social
worker has the dual task of being prepared and tuned in to what might be
going on for the child, based on available information. The social workers
aim to be prepared to respond sensitively to whatever the child is worried
about and to their wishes and individual needs.

Environment

While working to make a connection with the individual child, the social
workers also reported how they aim to connect with the child's family and
environment. They are conscious of the impact of wider environmental
factors. All the social workers describe children who are often living under
severe stress and duress and whose families and communities may also be
struggling with serious issues such as domestic violence, drug and alcohol
misuse, mental health difficulties, gangland crime and warfare. These
difficulties are compounded when families are struggling with poverty, social
isolation, discrimination and other significant social issues:

'With some families it could be something like the family is struggling
because parents are unemployed and they are having a hard time, maybe
one parent has a disability and they are struggling to get kids to school

and to manage meals and other challenges. We can get help, we can offer supports, but it is the other more complex situations that pose a terrible challenge.' (Deirdre)

'Many children we see are living in families where there is domestic violence and where the level of violence is through the roof.' (Maureen)

'The stress and anxiety levels in households could be described as extreme.' (Adah)

'Sometimes drug traffickers target young children and teenagers in the estates, and then the kids owe them and then they have them. The kids have to go collect debts or they have to slash someone's faces or petrol bomb. If they don't pay the debt then the family are targeted, families' windows smashed out, family approached and if family don't pay, then more threats, more petrol bombs to the family home and so child and parents are highly stressed out and are all on high alert.' (Ana)

'The problems which cause most challenge are gangland terror, level of violence in homes, addiction and crime.' (Edel)

In these contexts, the child can present as experiencing a degree of pressure, coercion at times, and almost always a degree of fear, and a child may present as being under threat. The level, extent, impact and nature of the fear varies, but all social workers shared examples of children having a fear of consequences for themselves and others, fear for a parent, or feeling responsibility for siblings.

If a child is under duress, the social workers indicate they tune in to the extent to which the child feels they have permission to be actively involved in a dialogue with the social worker and the extent to which they can engage. The social workers aim to tune in to whether the child feels free to talk, to share, to think, to listen, to engage, to be involved.

One of the challenges of tuning in to a child and a child's situation is the sheer variety and complexity of situations that the social workers meet on a day-to-day basis. They attempt to respond to the individuality of the child and to each situation on a case-by-case basis.

Building connections with children

Social workers aim to make a connection with the child they are working with to try to help them understand what is going on for this child, how this child feels and how they can help this child.

The outcome of a successful encounter with a child is one where the social worker feels they have a good sense of what life is like for the child, how the child feels, what worries they have and how the social worker could help.

Accounts from the social workers indicate that they try to form a mutual understanding as the basis of a relationship with the children, but this is not always straightforward or easy to achieve.

Capacities used by social workers when making a connection

The social worker must have the capacity to develop purposeful relationships with children. The social worker must be very clear about their role, use child-friendly language and clear communication in general:

'I would say to them that I am their social worker, and my job is to make sure that children are happy and that they are safe and that if they had any worries and anything that made them feel sad that they can talk to me about it and we can try and get a plan and sort things out. I'd say that in a very child-friendly way. They should know who you are, what your role is.' (Bernie)

The social worker needs a strong capacity for building rapport, relationship and trust in order to build connections with individual children. They need capacity to do this delicate task, in an often intense and anxious atmosphere when stakes are high and while under pressure of time:

'We are asking kids to emotionally expose themselves to us, to be vulnerable when the only times when they may have been vulnerable before, they may have been abused, then we come in and say, please open up and tell me everything. They can't do that; they have been hurt. You have to tune in to that, you have to be sensitive, take the time to build a picture and build a relationship.' (Adah)

'[There are times] when a child doesn't want to talk to you, you can't push that, you can't force them, you're not interrogating them, and you need the right manner to do that.' (Geraldine)

'Other children have never met a social worker and have no prior experience of communicating or relating with an adult in this way. No prior experience of involvement on decisions. Their experience of adults has been with someone who has harmed them. They can be nervous of adults.' (Maureen)

Dialogue

As discussed, child protection social workers are tasked with involving children in decisions at each step of the child protection process. In line with UNCRC Article 12 (UNCRC, 1989), there is an expectation that a social worker will take on board the views of the child. The encounters described by the social workers in this study are much more than this, however, as they describe a dialogue which can be highly reflective and which generates insights between child and social worker:

> 'We have to try and help children to tell us what is going on, for good as well as because we are worried about abuse. Tell us the positive things, it is not all about the risks. It's about balancing the risk, who in the family helps with certain things … whose around that can support them so that we can draw on that and draw up safety plans from it.' (Ana)

> 'I am amazed at … how honest they are, they have just told us something really important about something very personal … the social workers can develop relationships with them, where children will trust them, and will trust that the social worker will listen to what they are saying and will be honest with them … So much skill is needed to bring to a child that has had years of abuse and help them feel safe enough to talk to you about what life is like for them.' (Maureen)

The dialogue results specifically in the co-creation of a view in the form of words to be shared with parents and others that will influence the decision-making that is taking place concerning the child:

> '[I]t's subtle. You don't just walk into children and say right what do you want, and we are all going to carry that out. You have to be able to read things at different levels. You need, you recognise on an emotional level, what are children trying to tell you, what is it that is the best decision for the child, what is it that the child wants and needs, and you know something, they are the experts in their own situation. We also have to try and interpret what they are telling us or trying to tell us based on the other pieces of information that we have and to try to make the right decision.' (Adah)

There is also a second phase to the dialogue approach in situations where risk to the child is identified. In such situations, dialogue is about sharing information between the parties in order to produce a child safety plan:

'Look children's safety, everything about it, it is all about the child, what I would strive for, and I hope everyone would strive for is that the child's voice is listened to, the child's needs are met.' (Laura)

'The safety plan is the child's plan. It is all about the child. Everything about the child.' (Geraldine)

Maureen (pseudonym of one of the research participants) offers examples of very young children who she says "had incredible insight into the situation for their families", and many of the study participants gave examples of children who have "grasped the process" and where dialogue has worked well.

The social workers' accounts illuminate the conditions required for dialogue between child and social worker:

'Once the child has a safe space and once they get used to the process and they trust the social worker and once they feel they are free or have permission from parents to participate fully, then there can be a dialogue which can form understanding between social worker and child.' (Melissa)

Discussion

As noted earlier, expert commentators have previously highlighted the dearth of knowledge that exists regarding the involvement of children in decisions concerning their welfare and safety, and the role that social workers can play in facilitating this type of participation by children (Ferguson, 2016, 2018; Middel et al, 2021).

This study adds knowledge by illuminating how social workers think and feel about children's participation rights, and the role they can play to involve children. The analysis of the data identified social work skills which are named here as 'tuning in' and 'making a connection' with the child as relevant in this regard.

The study confirmed the view that the participation of children is a highly charged and emotive phenomenon in the context of child welfare and protection work (Ruch, 2014), in which the accomplishment of role-related expectations (that the social worker will include children as participants in decision-making processes) is overladen and interjected with emotions on the part of the social workers, such as feelings of protection, responsibility and compassion. This study found that these reactions inform how professional service providers strive to ensure the involvement of children in decisions that affect them.

Any child who has been neglected and/or abused has been in a position where their right to protection from abuse and neglect (UNCRC, Article 5) has already been infringed, and their safety undermined. Social workers describe working with the child (and others) to ensure that these violations cease and aim to conduct this work in a way which amplifies the child's wishes, worries, concerns and feelings (in line with the child's right to participate in decisions as set out in the UNCRC, Article 12).

Capacities required of the social worker for dialogue

The research findings suggest that social workers need a specific skillset to support their work with children aimed at enhancing a child's participation in child welfare decisions.

The communication style and language used must be responsive to the individuality of each child. Social workers must provide clear and transparent information alongside guidance and support in enabling a child to form a view (Kilkelly, 2011). As with other stages of intervention, the social worker must maintain a safe and comfortable emotional and physical space to help a child form and express a view and to engage in dialogue.

The children may also be experiencing much stress and be under duress caused by environmental factors. In engaging in dialogue with a child, the social worker must ensure the child feels free to talk, to share, to engage. The study findings indicate that the social workers are required to be sensitive, encouraging, reassuring, interested in children's lives, responsive to a child's pace, and being patient. This requires a high skill level and most likely requires opportunities for critical reflection on one's performance and reactions to different scenarios.

In line with IPA methods (Smith et al, 2009), the data generated in this study were interrogated rigorously, and a series of themes were identified which were important for all of the social workers. The theme of social justice was a thread running through all the accounts. Principles of social justice came across strongly and consistently in the practice examples, and there emerged a point of connection across the data which displayed the desire on the part of the participants to work positively so that children's right to participate in decision-making in child welfare contexts could be facilitated.

The researcher found that really listening to the experience of the social workers and then reflecting and striving to understand and make sense of their accounts using a rigorous interpretive methodology of data analysis served to critically appraise how they performed and enacted a commitment to promoting the right of children to be involved in decisions that are central to their well-being and safety.

The act of listening helped to connect the researcher with the underlying emotions, worries and perspectives of the social worker, that inform direct work with children in the context of child welfare and protection social work. It revealed how the attitudes of the social workers are informed by a social justice value base which prioritises the rights of the child, and in particular, the importance of including all stakeholders in decisions, especially those who are not regularly listened to or heeded.

What do the findings mean for social justice research, policy and practice?

The 'Standing Tall with Children' study (O'Driscoll, 2023) showcases original research on children's participation which has broad implications for social justice research, policy and practice. The study focuses attention on empowering practice with children who suffer abuse and neglect in their homes, a population who are hard to reach in many respects and particularly hard to reach for research purposes. Limitations and infringements on these children's rights make them one of the most vulnerable and disadvantaged groups in society. The findings shine a light on suffering, disadvantage, rights recognition and empowering practice, providing a window into children's lives, lives most often hidden from view, where children are not often seen or heard.

The study is a good example of research which explores issues for those in society who are denied the most basic of human rights, and it illuminates the process of social work intervention which is empowering and which aims to ensure full recognition and realisation of rights for all children, encompassing, but not limited to, the right to be free from fear and abuse, the right to protection, the right to provision and the right to be heard and have influence.

This study's findings position the social worker-research participants as children's rights champions. Exploring and shedding light on their struggle to achieve social justice for their service recipients, the social workers are identified in this study as key actors who intervene in the lives of children whose rights to protection, provision and to be heard have been violated or infringed, due to physical, sexual, emotional abuse and neglect. The study's findings demonstrate a strong commitment on the part of the social workers to deliver social justice and ensure children are free from fear and abuse, are provided for, are recognised and valued as rights holders and have their needs met. The study identifies and highlights the struggles and challenges for the social workers which this work entails.

An important aspect of this research is bridging the gap between social justice research and social justice practice (and vice versa) and ensuring a partnership between researcher and practitioner. The study presents a model for partnership between researcher and practitioner that culminates in the co-creation of knowledge regarding how to involve children in decisions, and it illuminates how the use of an IPA methodology is particularly suited to a partnership-based research approach. The rigorous process of sense-making, culminating in the co-creation of knowledge, involves the researcher making sense of the practitioner who themselves are making sense of the phenomenon of involving children in decision-making, a process referred to in this methodology as the double hermeneutic.

Another key tenet of this social justice research is that it results in a concrete translation of findings into policy and practice.

Obligations on the social worker are set out in concrete terms in legislation, in policy and under the UNCRC (1989). There is clarity among the social workers of what their obligations are and what they must do to protect children and ensure their safety and well-being. Policy sets out clear expectations regarding hearing the voice of the child and taking their views into account. However, there is little by way of how they must do this. There is an absence of analysis and guidance regarding implementation. This study considers the 'what' as well as the 'how' by considering the implications for *how* policy gets implemented, at grassroots level and on the front line of services to children who need protection.

The study findings make it explicit that the social workers operate from a social justice-oriented values base and that they apply social justice principles to all their interventions. Key to this is placing the child at the very centre of all intervention and ensuring recognition for the child as a rights holder and also simultaneously aiming to ensure the child's needs are met. Social workers demonstrate respect and regard for the child's wishes, worries and needs and put these front and centre stage.

The study lays the groundwork for a comprehensive rights-based model of participatory practice. It has implications for practice in child protection but also for intervention with children in all social work practice arenas.

Conclusion

The IPA method used in the collection and analysis of data for the study, titled 'Standing Tall with Children', enabled a deep illumination not only of how social workers describe their work in the context of these multiple factors but how they think about what they do, what they value and what they would like to change in that regard. The social workers interviewed in the study reported here identified key aspects of their work that support the participation of children in decisions, namely tasks such as tuning in, making a connection and building dialogue with children. The end goal of this form of research for social justice is to achieve structural recalibration (van de Sande and Byvelds, 2015), in this instance in relation to recognising the value of listening to, heeding and including the views of children – not only in relation to the issue examined in this specific research study but hopefully and intentionally with an eye to the wider participation of children across many systems in society. This chapter positions the concept of participation as a foundational cornerstone of social justice and explores how social workers in child welfare and protection services deal with the issue of participation in the decisions of the children with whom they work. The study reveals this realm of interactions between social workers and children as a complex, multi-dimensional space where many factors play a role in determining the degree to which children can exercise their right to be heard and heeded regarding their safety, welfare and future life outcomes.

While this research focus may at first appear narrow and targeted, it forced appraisal of big issues related to how the state interacts with children at risk and how the child's voice is heard by the state in those circumstances, and furthermore it is argued here that this is likely to reflect the extent to which society in general regards children as competent social actors who, by right, need to be included in decision-making processes in relation to issues that have long-term implications for their welfare and well-being. It emerged in the findings that social workers, when guided by social justice values, strive to tune in and connect with the children they work with and aim to ensure that children are involved in decisions about them. However, it is clear this is complex and difficult to navigate terrain, requiring high levels of commitment, skill and self-reflection on the part of the social workers. The methodology used to investigate this issue proved effective in unearthing this complexity and how social workers think about, respond and reflect on their direct work with children.

References

Bell, M. (2002) 'Promoting children's rights through the use of relationship', *Child and Family Social Work*, 7(1): 1–11.

Bellamy, C. (2003) 'The state of the world's children 2003', New York: UNICEF.

Bessell, S. (2007) 'Adult attitudes towards children's participation in the Philippines, policy and governance', Discussion Papers, Crawford School of Economic and Governance, Australian National University, Available from: www.crawford.anu.edu.au

Cashmore, J. (2002) 'Promoting the participation of children and young people in care', *Child Abuse & Neglect*, 26(8): 837–47.

DCYA (2011) 'Children First: National Guidance on the Protection and Welfare of Children', Dublin: Government Publications.

DCYA (2014) 'Better Outcomes, Brighter Futures: The National Policy Framework for Children and Young People 2014–2020', Dublin: Department of Children and Youth Affairs.

Ferguson, H. (2014) 'Researching social work practice close up: Using ethnographic and mobile methods to understand encounters between social workers, children and families', *British Journal of Social Work*, 46: 153–68.

Ferguson, H. (2016) 'What social workers do in performing child protection work: Evidence from research into face-to-face practice', *Child and Family Social Work*, 21(3): 283–94.

Ferguson, H. (2018) 'Making home visits: Creativity and the embodied practices of home visiting in social work and child protection', *Qualitative Social Work*, 17(1): 65–80.

Hart, R.A. (1992) 'Children's participation: From tokenism to citizenship', Innocenti essays, no 4. Florence, Italy: UNICEF International Child Development Centre.

HIQA (2012) *National Standards for the Protection and Welfare of Children*, Dublin: Health Information and Quality Authority, Available from: https://www.hiqa.ie/reports-and-publications/standard/national-standards-protection-and-welfare-children

Kilkelly, U. (2011) 'A children's rights analysis of investigation statements', Dublin: Office of the Ombudsman for Children.

Larkin, M., Watts, S. and Clifton, E. (2006) 'Giving voice and making sense in interpretative phenomenological analysis', *Qualitative Research in Psychology*, 3(2): 102–12.

League of Nations (1924) 'Geneva Declaration on the Rights of the Child', Available from: www.un-documents.net/gdrc1924.htm

Leeson, C. (2007) 'My life in care: Experiences of non-participation in decision-making processes', *Child & Family Social Work*, 12(3): 268–77.

Munro, E. (2001) 'Empowering looked after children', *Child & Family Social Work*, 6(2): 129–37.

Middel, F., Post, W., Lopez Lopez, M. and Grietens, H. (2021) 'Participation of children involved in the child protection system: Validation of the Meaningful Participation Assessment Tool (MPAT)', *Child Indicators Research*, 14(2): 713–35.

O'Driscoll, B. (2023) 'Standing Tall with Children', Unpublished doctoral research Thesis, Trinity College Dublin, Ireland.

Ruch, G. (2014) '"Helping children is a human process": Understanding how social workers communicate with children through "practice near" research', *British Journal of Social Work*, 44(8): 2145–62.

Ruch, G., Morrison, F. and Holland, S. (2016) 'Exploring communication between social workers, children and young people', *British Journal of Social Work*, 47: 1427–44.

Sanders, J., Munford, R., Ballantyne, R., Heneghan, M., Allison, R. and Jackson, R. (2017) 'Conditional openness: Young people define practices for successful child protection interventions', *Journal of Social Welfare and Family*, 39(3): 261–78.

Smith, J.A., Flowers, J. and Larkin, M. (2009) *Interpretative Phenomenological Analysis: Theory, Method and Research*, London: Sage Publications.

Smith, J.A. and Nizza, I.E. (2022) *Essentials of Interpretative Phenomenological Analysis*, Washington, DC: American Psychological Association.

Tusla (2015) 'Towards the Development of a Participation Strategy for Children and Young People', Dublin: Child and Family Agency.

Tusla (2019) 'Child and Youth Participation Strategy, 2019-2023', Dublin: Child and Family Agency.

UNCRC (1989) 'United Nations Convention on the Rights of the Child', Geneva: United Nations.

UNICEF (nd) 'Home page: UNICEF for every child', https://www.uni cef.org/ [Accessed 5 January 2023].

UNICEF (1980-2021) 'The State of the World's Children', New York: UNICEF.

Van Bijleveld, G.G., Dedding, C.W.M. and Bunders-Aelen, J.F.G. (2015) 'Children's and young people's participation within child welfare and child protection services: A state-of-the-art review', *Child and Family Social Work*, 20(2): 129–38.

Van de Sande, A. and Byvelds, C. (2015) *Statistics for Social Justice: A Structural Perspective,* Manitoba, Canada: Fernwood Publishing.

Vis, S.A., Strandbu, A., Holtan, A. and Thomas, N. (2011) 'Participation and health: A research review of child participation in planning and decisionmaking', *Child & Family Social Work*, 16(3): 325–35.

Winter, K. (2010) 'The perspectives of young children in care about their circumstances and implications for social work practice', *Child & Family Social Work*, 15(2): 186–95.

Winter, K., Cree, V., Hallett, S., Hadfield, M., Ruch, G., Morrison, F. et al (2016) 'Exploring communication between social workers, children and young people', *British Journal of Social Work*, 47: 1427–44.

Winter, K., Morrison, F., Cree, V., Ruch, G., Hadfield, M. and Hallett, S. (2019) 'Emotional labour in social workers' encounters with children and their families', *British Journal of Social Work*, 49(1): 217–33.

13

The potential for Q-methodology in promoting human rights and social justice: a case of social workers in practice research

Johanna O'Shea

Introduction

This study was undertaken in Northern Ireland (NI) and aimed to explore probation officers' perspectives on the contribution of risk of harm assessments in sentencing decisions and their perspectives on risk management strategies in probation practice. The emergence of the risk society (Beck, 1992) and the 'rise of risk' (Kemshall, 2003) in criminal justice from the late 1980s/early 1990s onwards has seen the probation service being reconstructed by government, changing its direction from a primarily rehabilitative and welfare-oriented service to a law enforcement and public protection agency (see Garland, 2003; McNeill, 2004; Nash, 2005; Cavadino et al, 2019). Legislation, policy and practice on 'dangerousness' often stem from serious case reviews and are linked to the worthy organisational aim of public protection. They also, however, arguably force probation practitioners, who in NI are qualified social workers, to neglect a social justice focus and adopt risk control measures against probationers more traditionally associated with police and prison staff practices.

Promoting social justice is a core commitment of the social work profession and one that distinguishes it from other professions (Solas, 2008; Grant and Austin, 2014; Deepak et al, 2015; Harrison et al, 2016). Indeed, the definition of social work as adopted by the International Federation of Social Workers (2014) explicitly includes social justice and human rights as principles central to social work:

> Social work is a practice-based profession and an academic discipline that promotes social change and development, social cohesion, and the empowerment and liberation of people. Principles of social justice, human rights, collective responsibility and respect for diversities are central to social work. Underpinned by theories of social work, social

sciences, humanities and indigenous knowledges, social work engages people and structures to address life challenges and enhance wellbeing. The above definition may be amplified at national and/or regional levels. (International Federation of Social Workers, 2014)

Probation Officers in NI are qualified social workers and have signed up to Standards of Practice which explicitly include social justice as an underpinning value: '[D]emonstrating social work values and principles, including the promotion of rights, social justice, equality and inclusion' (NISCC, 2019). Nicotera (2019) notes that there is no clear definition of what social justice means for social work. Various definitions emphasise equal opportunity and access, or focus more on equity, fair play, advocacy, social action and empowerment, whereas others underscore the centrality of promoting human rights (Austin et al, 2014; Adams et al, 2016).

A key difference in NI, as part of the United Kingdom, is that probation policy often mirrors policies and practice guidance from England and Wales, where the link to social work was broken in the 1990s and where policies are not always compatible with sound social work practice or the underpinning value of social justice. This leads to tension in professional practice for some probation officers in NI, particularly in the work with individuals considered to pose a serious risk of harm to others, where a prevailing policy focus is on the social exclusion of offenders (Kemshall and Wood, 2007) to protect the public. This raises issues of what Fenton (2014) terms ethical stress, which is experienced by practitioners when they are required to practice in a managerial and gatekeeping manner that is not congruent with their values or conscience.

As a researcher, social worker and former practising probation officer, I was acutely aware of the challenge of engaging frontline probation officers in critical research. Having previously undertaken research with the agency on politically sensitive topics, I appreciated how potentially threatening objective and independent research could be perceived. Equally as a former practising probation officer, I could recall how guarded I was in a research interview that questioned practice and policy issues. Critical views were only shared cautiously and sparingly due to how disempowering the research process felt. I recall a lack of trust in the researcher to protect the information and not use it for their 'hidden' agendas that could be perceived as damaging to the organisation.

It was with this awareness that I sought to undertake research with frontline practitioners which would allow them to critically reflect on their practice and the organisational policies that impact on the lives of service users. Rountree and Pomeroy (2010) insist that researchers and practitioners must work together to ensure that our efforts are informed by the core value of social justice. As a 'hard-to-reach' population, people involved with the justice system are usually excluded from initiatives and research specifically designed to include the service user's voice (Beresford, 2013). Probation officers work daily on the front line of services and have relationships with service users involved with the criminal justice system and their communities. They therefore have invaluable professional experience and insight to offer on justice-related policy which significantly impacts on the lives of those they supervise and on their own practice.

Being cognisant of these requirements and the potential obstacles, Q-methodology was chosen for several features which seemed to fit well with such conditions. Q-methodology is a qualitative systematic method to investigate the perspectives of participants who represent different stances on an issue by having participants rank a series of statements and by applying statistical analysis to the study of human subjectivity (Ellingsen et al, 2010). The analysis identifies patterns of subjective opinions in the data, thereby revealing dominant socially constructed discourses on the subject of enquiry.

This chapter first provides a synopsis of the background to and purpose of the research. It then briefly considers the challenges in identifying a research method that would allow practitioners to engage in critically reflective processes on their practice and organisational policy. An overview of Q-methodology in a social constructionist epistemology is then presented before discussing the benefits of adopting this method in research on 'hard-to-reach' issues that directly impact on the lives of people involved with the criminal justice system. This chapter is therefore less concerned with the study's findings and focuses primarily on the method adopted and how it fits with research for social justice.

Background to research

Deering and Felizer (2019) trace the significant shift in redefining probation's ethos and purpose and penal policy more generally to the late 1970s and early 1980s. In keeping with theories of late modernity (Garland, 2001; Pratt, 2005), neo-conservative political ideas saw the rise of classical rational choice theories of crime, reinforcing beliefs that punishment should be used to ensure retribution and deterrence (Wilson and Kelling, 1982), and there was a need for incapacitation to manage the dangerous (Bagaric, 2001).

In this climate, probation practitioners were gradually becoming part of a penal system where state control was on the rise, and while they still promoted rehabilitation, their duties were increasingly concerned with assessing risk, providing pre-sentence reports, monitoring sentences and parole, and enforcing breach and later recall proceedings. Various legislative changes over the last 30 years have reinforced this shift and firmly changed the official identity of probation, arguably away from its social work roots and commitment to social work values including social justice and human rights.

The first decade of this century saw the gradual introduction of more and more risk control strategies in parallel with a decrease in both the direct provision of services and the funding of community-based service provision. The 'community protection model' (Connelly and Williamson, 2000), which emphasises treatment through programmes on the one hand and surveillance and incapacitation through restrictive requirements in the community on the other, transformed probation practice. It has arguably led to a deskilling of practitioners (Fitzgibbon, 2008) through the introduction of more and more standardised ways of working and by the removal of professional autonomy and discretion in decision-making.

These constructions of probation practice elicited discursive practices which were shaping and conditioning not only the everyday interactions of probation officers in direct work with justice-involved adults but also the partnership working with community-based organisations. As resources became stretched or redirected, what is considered effective practice with high-risk offenders shifted more towards risk control strategies (O'Mahoney and Chapman, 2007). This changed role for probation necessitated more and more cooperation and collaboration with security and punitive elements of the criminal justice system, such as the prison service and police, which in turn influenced how probation services operate (Nash, 2005, 2008), with direct work with community and voluntary organisations decreasing significantly. Probation moved towards more security-orientated, risk-averse practice which views service users as 'other' (Drake, 2011). Engagement with families and communities has taken a back seat in risk management strategies despite the rehabilitative, reintegrative, restorative potential they offer.

The Criminal Justice (NI) Order 2008 established 'public protection' custodial sentences, introducing the concept of dangerousness and increasing the powers of the court in certain cases involving violent or sexual offences to impose an indeterminate custodial sentence or extended custodial sentence. It also introduced the determinate custodial sentence which combines imprisonment with a period of supervision in the community, without the consent of the individual subject to supervision. The new arrangements marked a turning point in the history of probation practice in NI. Importantly, the notion of working with individuals on the basis of consent, a principle that the Probation Board for NI had always upheld with pride (PBNI, 2002), would become irrelevant in this new world. As one probation officer reflected at this time: "[P]robation officers used to write reports to keep people out of prison; now we write them to put people in prison" (O' Shea, 2023: 19).

The concept of risk has therefore gained huge significance in probation practice. Using standardised tools, an assessment of 'risk of serious harm' is triggered in cases where the individual has been convicted of violent or sexual offences or where they have a history of such offending. The study on which this chapter draws was primarily concerned with this assessment, which can result in an individual being categorised as at 'significant risk of serious harm' a categorisation which can have very significant consequences for them. Risk assessment in this context has been socially constructed to focus primarily on *risk factors*, some of which are in fact redefined *needs*. Furthermore, protective factors are largely neglected in the consideration. The ramifications of a person being sentenced to a public protection sentence is far reaching for them, their family and their community, so there is clearly a dilemma in relying on fallible tools (Drake et al, 2014) to guide sentencing for offences not yet committed.

McSherry (2014: 780) suggests that 'taking away a person's liberty ... because of who they are and what they might do, rather than what they have done, not only breaches human rights, but focuses resources at the wrong end of the spectrum'. The criticality of probation officers' assessments has therefore increased in terms of pre-sentence report recommendations to inform sentencing decisions by the court. The information used in these assessments and the weight given to different pieces or sources of information is hugely significant given the implications for the individual's human rights.

Furthermore, the stringent enforcement and risk control policies adopted by probation under the mantle of public protection have led to transcarceration effects (Lowman and Menzies, 1986), whereby the boundaries between control levels in custody and the community become more and more blurred. It becomes increasingly evident that the assessment and management of risk has become a defining feature of probation practice at the expense of social justice-focused and rights-based practice. In fact, human rights considerations are increasingly portrayed by politicians and the media as an obstacle to the efficient and effective operation of the criminal justice system and the aim of public protection (Canton, 2009; Drake and Henley, 2014). Drake and Henley (2014: 145) suggest that as the shift towards more and more populist forms of democracy developed, deep divisions were drawn, and discourses emerged distinguishing between 'victims of crime (deserving of sympathy and compassion) and offenders (in need of tough responses)'.

Purpose and challenges of this study

This study aimed to explore these constructions in terms of how probation practitioners evaluate the impact of risk on probation practice and their capacity to promote social justice and human rights-based practice. People involved with the justice system represent the most excluded, stigmatised and traumatised among their peers (Dijker and Koomen, 2003; LeBel, 2012). The ethical promotion of social justice- and human rights-focused practice are therefore fundamental to sound social work practice in this field. Rountree and Pomeroy (2010) argue that social workers are tasked with partnering with undeserved and oppressed populations to create social change – populations largely excluded from major spheres of public and economic life (Strier, 2007).

However, researching such topics where practitioners' views can be captured is challenging where a culture of organisational professionalism (Evetts, 2003) and compliance exists. Organisational professionalism is described by Evetts (2003) as a discourse of control, incorporating rational-legal forms of decision-making, hierarchical structures of authority, the standardisation of work practices and accountability. Occupational professionalism on the other hand is the more traditional historical form and involves a discourse constructed within professional groups themselves that involved discretionary decision-making in complex cases, collegial authority, the occupational control of the work and is based on the trust in the practitioner by clients and employers (Evetts, 2003). The dominance of organisational professionalism over occupational professionalism brings with it certain tensions in professional practice for probation officers in NI given that they strongly identify and align themselves with the social work profession which seeks to promote social justice and human rights-based practice.

Jiwani and Krawchenko (2014) discuss the obstacles to undertaking research interviews with public servants in a climate of information control and constrained, even vetted, communications by government agencies. The search for an optimal research method was very much influenced by these tensions and considerations that objective research may be viewed with suspicion and as threatening to an organisation, allowing little or no space for critical research. Asking directly and probing about probation practice concerns, for example in semi-structured interviews, might have been too challenging for probation officers and put them in a position of feeling they were being overly critical of organisational policy and disloyal to their employer.

It was therefore essential to adopt a method which allowed participants to engage meaningfully, taking account of these concerns, but which also stimulated thought and discussion around macropolitical and structural issues, for example populist and punitive criminal justice policy versus human rights- and social justice-informed practice. Research for social justice needs to enable participation in research in a way that is just, non-threatening and takes account of the participant's concerns and needs. The challenge was to identify a research method which would give the participants control over the process and facilitate conditions whereby they could engage meaningfully and proactively to reflect on oppressive practice and policy issues. Q-methodology was decided upon as an optimal method in this regard. The remainder of the chapter outlines the methodology before discussing how certain features of it provided the basis for transformative social research to take place.

An overview of Q-methodology

A social constructionist epistemology assumes that knowledge is context-specific and subjective with the aim of exploring multiple and constantly changing knowledges and understandings (Burr, 2015). Social constructionism was considered the most appropriate perspective/lens through which to analyse the data as it provided rich insight into probation officers' constructions of key concepts such as risk, dangerousness, rights, fairness and justice and an understanding of how these concepts shape probation practice.

Social constructionism shares common philosophical roots with interpretivism in that meaning is created and negotiated by human actors. However, macrosocial constructionism for example differs from interpretivism due to its emphasis on power, language and interaction as mediators of meaning. Furthermore, it accepts the ambivalent sense that concepts, however socially constructed, correspond to something real in the world, which is reflected in our knowledge (Hjelm, 2014).

Socially constructed discourses on an issue can be revealed through Q-methodology studies. Q-methodology was developed by Stephenson (1935, cited in Lee, 2017) in his letter to *Nature* suggesting the correlation of people instead of variables in factor analysis. He describes Q-method as a qualitative systematic method to investigate the perspectives of participants who represent different stances on an issue, by having participants rank a series of statements and by applying statistical analysis to the study of human subjectivity (Ellingsen et al, 2010).

Subjectivity and Q-methodology are indelibly connected. Stephenson (1953), believed he could study subjectivity under the behaviourism tradition. While he did not negate the existence of consciousness in the human mind, he thought it did not offer much for behavioural science. Instead of consciousness, he decided to explore subjectivity, which for Stephenson is not to be understood as a mental concept or an aspect of mind or consciousness. It is not some isolated mind stuff that exists inside us or is inward-looking and is somehow separate from the real world of objects (Stephenson, 1953). On the contrary, subjectivity is a behaviour or activity, and it is an activity that is best understood relative to its impact upon the immediate environment. For Stephenson (1953, cited in Lee, 2017: 60): 'Dreaming is as much behaviour as is jumping a stile or dashing a hundred yards. All is a matter of interacting with this or that situation. Inner experience and behaviour are thus alike. Both are matters for objective, operational, definition and study.' Subjectivity, in operant terms, then, is simply the sum of behavioural activity that constitutes a person's *current* point of view. Stephenson believed that subjectivity could be operationalised so that individuals' perceptions of topics could be explored systematically (Watts and Stenner, 2012). He therefore developed inverted factor analysis, which involves comparing the variance and revealing patterns of association among a series of variables (which in Q are the participants, not traits) and where items (statements on a topic) of a Q-sort have been considered relative to one another and placed along a continuum (for example, most agree – most disagree) to identify and holistically describe a whole viewpoint or the construct of a social discourse (Watts and Stenner, 2012, 2017).

Q-methodology is variously described in the literature as a qualitative method (Shinbourne, 2009; Stenner et al, 2017) or a mixed-methods design (Coogan and Herrington, 2011; Hothersall, 2017). The ontological position of Q-methodology is linked to human conceptions and interpretations. The epistemological stance is on the subjective nature of knowledge, which clearly fits more closely with interpretivism and social constructionism and therefore qualitative methods. Q-methodology relies on some quantitative techniques in the design phase (such as allocating several statements confined to a specified number of places on a normally distributed grid) and on statistical analysis in the data analysis stage (by systematically identifying patterns between persons across the entire dataset). However, it arguably remains primarily a qualitative research method because the underpinning theory of Q-methodology is the study of subjectivity, in other words the study of subjective perspectives, attitudes and beliefs or socially constructed discourses on a topic.

Q-method involves sorting statements related to a particular topic on a normally distributed grid. It is a data reduction technique insofar as analysis reduces the data to a few Q-sorts or gestalts that capture whole viewpoints (or social constructions), each of which represents a cluster of participants or a typical viewpoint. Q-studies reveal a relatively small number of factors (viewpoints) or 'a limited independent variety of socially sedimented orientations, positions or points-of-view on a theme' (Stenner et al, 2008: 222) despite the 'enormous number of sorting configurations available' (Watts and Stenner, 2012: 43). These gestalts or 'stories' represent a dominant discourse shared by a cluster of participants on these issues. Although individuals complete the sorting exercise independently of each other, the emergence of statistically significant patterns or distinctive viewpoints accounting for a high percentage of variance therefore supports the theory of social constructionism, that is, the dominance of certain social discourses on an issue. Q-methodology serving a social constructionist position, therefore, will view factors as representing discourses with smaller numbers or individual participants representing, in microcosm, less dominant discourses. Stainton Rogers and Stainton Rogers (1990) argue that this also highlights Q-methodology's usefulness to explorations of power and discourse. If discourse and power are intrinsically connected (Foucault, 1980), and social constructionism critiques this, then Q-methodology draws out the majority and therefore dominant discourses as well as the minority discourses available on an issue. However, such assertions can be challenged, as Ho (2017: 681) highlights that in a Q-study '[o]ne cannot guarantee that all possible viewpoints [and therefore discourses on a topic] are uncovered or representative of the views supported by all individuals in the population'.

Advantages of using Q-methodology for research on and for social justice

McKeown and Thomas (2013) discuss the enormous range of applications in Q-methodology, spanning hundreds of different problems across the spectrum of the social and behavioural sciences. This study demonstrated that its versatility lends itself very well to undertaking transformative research to advance a social justice agenda. Details of the study are presented briefly here before the positionality of the researcher and the specific benefits of using Q-methodology in each phase of the study are discussed.

Participants in this study were practising probation officers in NI or retired probation officers, having retired in the previous five years (to ensure they had practice experience of risk of harm assessments in the period since the introduction of the 2008 legislation). The response rate was 33 participants: 30 serving probation officers (out of a potential 150) and three (out of a potential five) retired probation officers. Several features of Q-methodology at different stages of the research process proved optimal to facilitate and encourage meaningful engagement with probation officers 'on the ground' to stimulate thought and discussion around macropolitical and structural issues, for example populist and punitive criminal justice policy versus human rights- and social justice-informed practice.

Positionality of the researcher

I outlined in the introduction my previous roles as a social worker and practising frontline probation officer, as well as my experience as a research participant when I was still in practice. My own views on probation practice and the dominance of the 'risk agenda' on my practice undoubtedly influenced my decision to undertake this study. I was acutely aware then that my engagement in the research process and the interpretation of the data could be influenced by my own thinking and agendas (as discussed by Marsh et al, 2017). Reflexivity helped me to reflect upon my interconnectedness as a researcher and the context being researched. Wickens et al (2017) assert that the reader is more likely to identify bias than the researcher. However, this view is contested, and it is suggested that through reflexivity and through 'proper research and scientific design' (Pillow 2003 cited in Wickens et al, 2017: 865) all matters become knowable, implying that the researcher can mitigate against the effects of bias. I mitigated against the effect of conscious bias in this study through the consistent use of reflection and dialogue with supervisors, colleagues and probation practitioners. Furthermore, I adopted rigorous qualitative methods in the study to systematically research the phenomena under enquiry, to ensure as far as possible that the findings are reliable and valid. My professional background also brought with it considerable benefits in terms of building rapport with and gaining the trust of research participants, who clearly had confidence in my working knowledge of the subject matter.

Unique features of Q-methodology are considered in the following sections. Each phase of the study is discussed in sequence here for practical reasons, although in reality the process was iterative throughout with constant reflection and re-engagement with the data at all stages of the research process.

Study design and preparation

The developments of the Q-statements or 'concourse' as referred to in the literature is one of the most important tasks in the study design phase to ensure that all key ideas are included on the topic. This is essential to achieve what Watts and Stenner (2012) refer to as the 'carpet tile' effect and also to ensure that each statement covers one idea only with no conceptual gaps or overlaps (as discussed by Watts, 2009).

Several different models exist for developing the Q-statements – solely based on the literature, for example, or from a variety of sources such as conversations with probation officers and other experts (for example, retired probation officers). Including statements on the complexities of the issues was important to ensure that they were relevant for practitioners and reflective of current practice. As a key objective of the study was to capture the views of frontline probation officers, including statements on key experiences and dilemmas from practice was crucial to the credibility of the research.

One scoping focus group took place with five probation officers where discussion on issues was initiated in relation to risk of harm assessments before then allowing the discussion to flow and develop. Prompts included questions of how certain factors were taken into consideration or weighted in practice. A lengthy meeting took place with a retired probation officer to further develop ideas on risk assessment and management practices and policy.

Key concepts raised by practitioners were issues related to promoting an individual's human rights and a practice commitment to fairness; relationship-based social work that promoted re-integration with family and communities;

access to services; and finally due process rights in criminal justice and probation practice. Written notes were taken during the focus group and meetings. These notes were combined with issues arising from the literature to develop the initial Q-statements with the provisional categorisation in three distinct categories:

a. Risk control based on external measures (for example, curfews, electronic tagging, hostel accommodation requirement). Example of a statement: *Imposing and monitoring highly restrictive requirements on clients is compatible with good social work practice.*
b. Risk management based on internal controls (for example, relationship-based work; goal-oriented and desistance-focused work). Example of a statement: *With all these constraints, controls, and standardised systems, the power of the working relationship and my social work background/profession is no longer essential to undertake this role.*
c. Risk management and rights (for example, promoting due process rights, human rights-informed practice). Example of a statement: *A client's and victim's rights should be balanced and given equal consideration.*

Pilot study

Fifty-four statements were initially written before being reworked several times to avoid overlap, eventually settling on 46 statements. These Q-statements were piloted on four occasions with ex-probation officers for clarity of the statements and the comprehensiveness of the coverage of the subject matter. The pilot study was particularly valuable in ensuring the language used in the statements was as clear as possible and was language familiar to practitioners. Statements were phrased in both positive and negative language so participants could rank on whichever side of the curve fitted best with their view. Any ambiguous statements or words were changed to reflect current practice and jargon in the organisation. For example, the statement 'I'm not sure if I can manage risk and promote human rights' was considered too vague and was reworded to 'I can still promote a client's human rights when I enforce risk management plans.'

Pilot interviews 1 and 2 also tested an unstructured distribution (where respondents can choose how many statements to place in any given column) and structured distribution (where respondents can only place statements in the number of available boxes in a column). It was felt the unstructured distribution led respondents to only use the middle area of the grid, and they struggled to make decisions on which statements should be placed at the outer ends of the grid (+4 and −4 or strongly agree/strongly disagree) choosing more moderate positions such as −2 and +2 and the values in between those numbers for most statements. Pilot interviews 3 and 4 tested a structured distribution of the statements, before this mode was adopted. It was observed that using the structured distribution, participants generated a more thoughtful sort (McKeown and Thomas, 2013) because they took longer over the process, and although they were more challenged to reach a decision, they also discussed their reasoning more, providing some key insights and rich data. It was at such times that participants began to explore more macro issues in terms of populist and punitive policies versus relationship-based or rights-based practice.

The final range selected was a normal distribution grid with a total of nine columns labelled from 'tend to agree' to 'tend to disagree' (as discussed by Webler et al, 2009) on either side of the grid. While this instruction meant participants were forced to choose which statements they felt most strongly about (by placing statements on the outer extremes of the grid), it still allowed participants to choose moderate rather than absolute viewpoints and ensured they could always qualify their choices and not be seen to be openly critical of their organisation's policy and procedures and possibly be perceived as disloyal to their employer. Such considerations were critical to a research design process where participants could feel they were engaging in a just process which offered them choice and control with no hidden agendas.

Changes were made after each pilot interview until 39 final statements were decided upon. Sixteen of these statements were directly related to human rights and social justice issues in practice. A large poster size normally distributed grid with 39 squares across nine columns ranging from 'tend to agree' to 'tend to disagree' with two squares at each of the extremes was used in the fieldwork (see Figure 13.1).

Figure 13.1: Example of a Q-grid (O' Shea, 2023: 163)

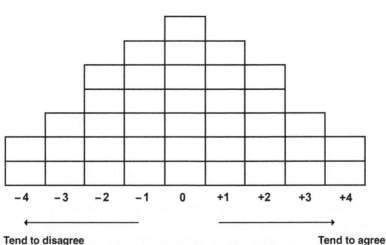

The fieldwork

The Q-sorting exercise can be undertaken as part of an interview with the researcher or as a standalone exercise manually using a computer programme. In keeping with the ethos of engaging probation officers meaningfully on sensitive and possibly controversial issues, this study adopted the approach of participants ranking the statements while discussing their decisions either during and/or after the exercise (as described by Watts and Stenner (2012). This approach was preferred as it was felt that it would facilitate conditions where practitioners could engage in the research process and critically reflect on their practice at their own pace with the practitioner being able to control when and how they engaged in discussion with the researcher. Again, this was considered crucial to empowering the participants to set the research agenda and direct the process.

Venues for the fieldwork were chosen by participants at a time and place convenient to them and for the practising probation officers were invariably the participants' place of work. There was some concern that the venue may compromise the participants' readiness to address sensitive issues or consider a critical stance towards their organisation's policies, but this was mitigated against as far as possible by ensuring that a closed office was always pre-booked for the interview in line with advice from McGrath et al (2019). In the case of the retired probation officers, they chose their home or in one instance a quiet local café as the venue. Interviews took between 45 minutes and one hour. A clear and consistent three-step instruction was given to each participant as follows:

Step 1: Read all the statements and sort them into three preliminary piles, under the categories 'tend to agree', 'tend to disagree' or 'neutral/ not sure'.

Step 2: Re-read the statements and begin to place them on the grid using as far as possible the number of available squares in each column allowing for some flexibility.

Step 3: Check the distribution and rearrange the cards if desired, but now ensure that all cards are placed using the allocated squares of the grid only.

This ranking process proved to be an indirect and useful research method to elicit clear views on the sensitive and controversial issues, including issues around social justice and human rights. Importantly, it allows participants to build a rapport, naturally and slowly, with the researcher before engaging in more meaningful discussion. Jiwani and Krawchenko (2014) attest to rapport being fundamental to quality research with public servants. The extra control participants had over when to share thoughts and decisions on the ranking of particular statements during the interview process proved invaluable in putting participants at ease and ensuring that they only discussed those statements they wished to comment on. In fact, participants often spent a lot of time at the end of the sorting process reflecting on practice developments and elaborating on the impact of policy and practice issues for service users.

Silent periods during the data collection process were therefore the 'norm' and useful for periods of reflection rather than being perceived as 'awkward pauses' as is potentially the case with other methodologies. Furthermore, the process involves the participant actively 'doing something' (sorting and re-sorting statements), which naturally allows time for reflection while also allowing space for discussion during the sorting exercise. This differs from other methods such as the use of questionnaires for surveys or in semi-structured interviews, where participants are usually required to answer as the interview progresses with limited opportunities to quietly reflect.

The Q-method process allows participants to re-sort statements until they are satisfied with their distribution, allowing them to consider their own priorities and make changes to 'their answer' before finalising it. This process furthermore facilitated participants making connections between statements and issues and encouraged discussion around macro-topics and trends. Again, this differs from other methodologies where participants cannot usually undo or change individual answers given. For example, Step 3 – the process of elimination to determine the choosing of statements for the outer extremes of the curve – generated a lot of discussion and often came later in an interview when a participant had relaxed more into the process. Participants were very particular about which four statements they wanted to place the greatest emphasis on, suggesting that meaningful results were obtained via this method. Overall, participants reported enjoying the research process and feeling more in control of it, in comparison to their experience of other research methods.

Given the need for discussion around 'hard-to-reach' issues which included taking a critical stance on organisational policy, ensuring confidentiality and anonymity in the write up of the results was crucial. Q-method offers increased protection around these issues for participants as their data are analysed along with the data from 32 others to identify patterns and reveal clusters and composite individuals. The write up of the results centres on the interpretation of these composite individuals rather than individual opinions, thereby offering an extra layer of protection for participants. Making participants aware of this type of analysis from the outset seemed to contribute to their willingness to engage in conversations on critical social justice and human rights issues in practice.

Q-data analysis method

A number of unique features of Q-data analysis contribute to the wider theorisation of probation practice, thereby highlighting key social justice and human rights issues. The statistical analysis of the data and a manual exploration of the factor arrays revealed a three-factor solution which was statistically significant and shared by a group of practitioners in the Q-sample. Further analysis of these factors using the qualitative interview data revealed three distinctive viewpoints which orientated their practice towards risk led practice; relationship based/strengths led practice; and rights led practice.

Conceptual space diagrams were used to complement the narrative and bring clarity to the position adopted by the probation officers on differentiated components of practice against the impact of risk-focused practice. Conceptual space diagrams are based on an analytical technique suggested by Watts and Stenner (2012) to depict differences between viewpoints extracted from a Q-methodology study. The distinctive positions of the viewpoints are plotted using two-dimensional space in order to demonstrate how particular ideas are central or secondary to each of the three distinct viewpoints.

These diagrams invite the reader to conceptualise the viewpoints visually (see Figure 13.2). The axes of each conceptual space diagram are defined using dominant concepts and ideas from the findings, for example around human rights and social justice issues.

Figure 13.2: Example of a conceptual space diagram (O' Shea, 2023: 291)

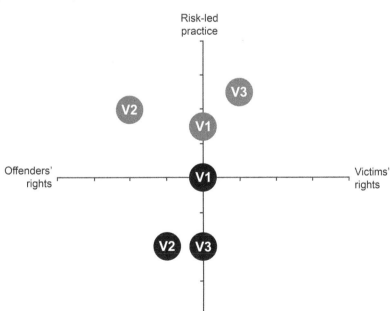

A viewpoint is charted by its number preceded by V, standing for viewpoint, within the diagram. The original diagrams proposed by Watts and Stenner (2012) were adapted further to add a second position for each viewpoint – the grey circle charts where the viewpoint currently constructs practice, and the black circles indicate where the viewpoint thinks practice should be. This disparity is important to convey the level of congruence a viewpoint has with how probation currently operates in the area of risk of harm and dangerousness. The depiction therefore incorporates the conceptualisation of improved practice, thereby offering a new lens to further advance the theorisation of probation practice.

While the distinct orientations of practitioners are important, the contribution to the debate goes further than these different orientations and takes a broader perspective on practice. The findings show that within each cluster, different perspectives co-exist on specific areas of practice. They also show consensus on some issues across the viewpoints. The theoretical contribution then is less concerned with specific practice strategies or methods and is more philosophical in that it is concerned with how a significant number of frontline practitioners think about what the main focus of probation practice should be, namely a social work agency with a key emphasis on relationship-based and social justice-/human rights-focused practice.

Conclusion

This chapter has considered how research on 'hard-to-reach' issues can be undertaken with frontline probation officers where practitioners may have concerns when taking a critical stance on organisational policy and practice. The focus of the study was the impact of the risk agenda on probation practice and how this predominates over relationship-based and social justice-/human rights-based social work practice. While the research drawn upon in this chapter was undertaken in NI, where the context of probation practice is, due to historical reasons, somewhat unique, the main focus of the chapter has been on Q-methodology. The research method adopted needed to take account of the potential sensitivity around some of the issues being explored, and to this end Q-methodology was identified as an optimal research method. Q-methodology offers an innovative approach to qualitative analysis through a 'quantification of patterned subjectivities' (Shemmings, 2006: 147), enabling statistically significant viewpoints to be identified in datasets.

Meticulous preparatory groundwork of the Q-study such as literature reviewing, engagement with practitioners and piloting proved invaluable in developing a relevant Q-set of statements to work from. Key concepts raised by former practitioners were issues related to relationship-based and social justice-informed social work, including due process and human rights informed approaches in probation practice.

This study has demonstrated how Q-methodology provides a rigorous, robust and innovative method which can be used to highlight social justice and human rights issues in probation practice through facilitating in-depth discussions and engagement with frontline social work practitioners. The data analysis method, in particular the use of conceptual space diagrams, allows for viewpoints on significant issues such as human rights to be plotted against the impact of risk-focused practice. The diagrams furthermore can be adapted to incorporate the conceptualisation of improved practice to convey the level of congruence a viewpoint has with how practice currently operates in a particular area, thereby offering a new lens to further advance the theorisation of social justice and rights-based probation practice. The outcomes of the research showed that probation officers overwhelmingly professionally identified with the social work and understood relationship building as key to engaging with people involved with the justice system. The 'ethical stress' as identified by Fenton (2014) and the tension between organisational and occupational discourse (Evetts, 2003) was evident for a significant number of participants, who regarded social work, social justice-oriented and rights-based practice as opposed to risk control strategies as fundamental to their work. This study therefore provides important evidence of frontline probation practitioners' commitment to social justice- and human rights-informed social work practice.

Furthermore, the process of Q-methodology as adopted in this study facilitates research for social justice as it offers unique features for engagement of participants and gives participants increased control over the research process. The creativity of the Q-sorting process appealed to participants. Several features of the method have been highlighted as particularly suited to undertaking research around sensitive and potentially controversial topics with frontline public service practitioners. These included the indirectness of the method in eliciting clusters of viewpoints, the flexibility in pacing the interview, the appropriate use of silence to allow reflection and the added control the participant has over the process in finalising their answer. The process provides the basis for deeper reflection on practice and organisational policy and is thereby a socially just method to engage participants who may otherwise be reluctant to participate in research on such issues.

This research on social work practice revealed that Q-methodology offers significant potential in ensuring fairness and more genuine engagement of research participants at various stages of the research process, and yet it is underused in social work research (Ellingsen et al, 2010).

This chapter demonstrates the advantages and versatility of Q-methodology to enable participation in research in a way that is just, non-threatening and takes account of the participant's concerns and needs. The method is clearly applicable in social research generally across a range of settings and lends itself very well to undertaking transformative research to advance a social justice agenda.

References

Adams, M., Bell, L.A., Goodman, D.J. and Joshi, K.Y. (2016) *Teaching for Diversity and Social Justice*, New York: Routledge

Austin, M.J., Branom, C. and King, B. (2014) 'Searching for the meaning of social justice', in M.J. Austin (ed) *Social Justice and Social Work: Rediscovering a Core Value of the Profession*, Thousand Oaks, CA: Sage Publications, pp 1–17.

Bagaric, M. (2001) *Punishment and Sentencing: A Rational Approach*, London: Cavendish.

Beck, U. (1992) *Risk Society: Towards a New Modernity*, London: Sage.

Beresford, P. (2013) 'Theory and practice of user involvement in research: Making the connection with public policy and practice', in *Involving Service Users in Health and Social Care Research*. London: Routledge, pp 15–26.

Burr, V. (2015) *Social Constructionism* (3rd edn), London: Routledge.

Canton, R. (2009) 'Nonsense upon stilts? Human rights, the ethics of punishment and the values of probation', *British Journal of Community Justice*, 7(1): 5–22.

Cavadino, M., Dignan, J., Mair, G. and Bennett, J. (2019) *The Penal System: An Introduction* (6th edn), London: Sage.

Connelly, C. and Williamson, S. (2000) 'Review of the research literature on serious violent and sexual offenders', Crime and Criminal Justice Research Findings no. 46, Edinburgh: Scottish Executive Central Research Unit.

Coogan, J. and Herrington, N. (2011) 'Q methodology: An overview', *Research in Teacher Education*, 1(2): 24–8.

Deering, J. and Felizer, M. (2019) 'Hollowing out probation? The roots of transforming rehabilitation', *Probation Journal*, 66(1): 8–24.

Deepak, A.C., Rountree, M.A. and Scott, J. (2015) 'Delivering diversity and social justice in social work education: The power of context', *Journal of Progressive Human Services*, 26: 107–25.

Dijker, A.J. and Koomen, W. (2003) 'Extending Weiner's attribution-emotion model of stigmatization of ill persons', *Basic and Applied Social Psychology*, 25: 51–68.

Drake, D. (2011) 'The "dangerous other" in maximum-security prisons', *Criminology and Criminal Justice*, 11(4): 367–82.

Drake, D. and Henley, A. (2014) '"Victims" versus "offenders" in the British political discourse: The construction of a false dichotomy', *The Howard Journal*, 52(2): 141–57.

Drake, D., Havard, C. and Muncie, J. (2014) 'The dubious "science" of risk prediction in criminal justice', International Centre for Comparative Criminological Research, Available from: https://www.crimeandjustice.org.uk/resources/dubious-science-risk-prediction-criminal-justice [Accessed 5 December 2022].

Ellingsen, I.T., Storksen, I. and Stephens, P. (2010) 'Q methodology in social work research', *International Journal of Social Research Methodology*, 12(5): 395–409.

Evetts, J. (2003) 'The sociological analysis of professionalism: Occupational change in the modern world', *International Sociology*, 18(2): 395–415.

Fenton, J. (2014) 'An analysis of "ethical stress" in criminal justice social work in Scotland: The place of values', *British Journal of Social Work*, 45(5): 1415–32.

Fitzgibbon, D.W. (2008) 'Deconstructing probation risk and developments in practice', *Journal of Social Work Practice*, 22(1): 85–101.

Foucault, M. (1980) *Power/Knowledge*, New York: Pantheon.

Garland, D. (2001) *The Culture of Control: Crime and Social Order in Contemporary Society*, Oxford: Oxford University Press.

Garland, D. (2003) 'The rise of risk', in R.V. Ericson and A. Doyle (eds) *Risk and Morality*, Toronto: University of Toronto Press, pp 48–86.

Grant, J. and Austin, M.J. (2014) 'Incorporating social justice principles into social work practice', in M.J. Austin (ed) *Social Justice and Social Work: Rediscovering a Core Value of the Profession*, Thousand Oaks, CA: Sage, pp 357–69.

Harrison, J., Van Deusen, K. and Way, I. (2016) 'Embedding social justice within micro social work curricula', *Smith College Studies in Social Work*, 86: 258–73.

Hjelm, T. (2014) *Social Constructionisms: Approaches to the Study of the Human World* (1st edn), New York: Red Globe Press.

Ho, G.W.K. (2017) 'Examining perceptions and attitudes: A review of Likert-type scales versus Q-methodology', *Western Journal of Nursing Research*, 39(5): 674–89.

Hothersall, S.J. (2017) '"Everyday knowledge": A mixed-methods study using factor analysis and narrative approaches to explore social worker's knowledge', *Social Work & Social Sciences Review*, 18(1): 15–30.

International Federation of Social Workers (2014) 'Global definition of social work, approved by the IFSW general meeting and the IASSW general assembly', Available from: https://www.ifsw.org/what-is-social-work/glo bal-definition-of-social-work/ [Accessed 9 January 2023].

Jiwani, F.N. and Krawchenko, T. (2014) 'Public policy, access to government, and qualitative research practices: Conducting research within a culture of information control', *Canadian Public Policy*, 40(1): 57–66.

Kemshall, H. (2003) *Understanding Risk in Criminal Justice*, Maidenhead, UK: Open University Press.

Kemshall, H. and Wood, J. (2007) 'Beyond public protection: An examination of community protection and public health approaches to high-risk offenders', *Criminology & Criminal Justice: An International Journal*, 7(3): 203–22.

LeBel, T.P. (2012) 'Invisible stripes? Formerly incarcerated persons' perceptions of stigma', *Deviant Behavior*, 33: 89–107.

Lee, B. (2017) 'The fundamentals of Q methodology', *Journal of Research Methodology*, 2(2): 57–95.

Lowman, J. and Menzies, R.J. (1986) 'Out of the fiscal shadow: Carceral trends in Canada and the United States', *Crime and Social Justice*, 26: 95–115.

Marsh, D. and Furlong, P. (2017) 'A skin not a sweater: Ontology and epistemology in political science', in V. Lowndes, D. Marsch and G. Stroker. (eds) *Theory and Methods in Political Science*, London: Palgrave Macmillan Education, pp 177–98.

McGrath, C., Palmgren, J. and Liljedahl, M. (2019) 'Twelve tips for conducting qualitative research', *Medical Teacher*, 41(9): 1002–6.

McKeown, B. and Thomas, D.B. (2013) *Q Methodology*, London: Sage.

McNeill, F. (2004) 'Correctionalism, desistance and the future of probation in Ireland', *Irish Probation Journal*, 1(1): 28–43.

McSherry, B. (2014) 'Throwing away the key: The ethics of risk assessment for preventative detention schemes', *Psychiatry, Psychology and Law*, 21(5): 779–90.

Nash, M. (2005) 'The probation service, public protection and dangerous offenders', in J. Winstone and F. Pakes (eds) *Community Justice: Issues for Probation and Criminal Justice*, Cullompton: Willan Publishing, pp 16–32.

Nash, M. (2008) 'Exit the polibation officer? Decoupling police and probation', *International Journal of Police Science and Management*, 10(3): 302–12.

Nicotera, A. (2019) 'Social justice and social work, a fierce urgency: Recommendations for social work social justice pedagogy', *Journal of Social Work Education*, 55(3): 460–75.

Northern Ireland Social Care Council (NISCC) (2019) 'Standards of practice and conduct for social workers', Available from:https://niscc.info/app/uplo ads/2020/09/standards-of-conduct-and-practice-for-social-workers-2019. pdf [Accessed 6 September 2023].

O'Mahony, D. and Chapman, T. (2007) 'Probation, the state and community: Delivering probation services in Northern Ireland', in L. Gelsthorpe and R. Morgan (eds) *Handbook of Probation*, Cullompton: Willan, pp 155–78.

O'Shea, J. (2023) Public protection, probation practice and related sentencing issues: A Northern Ireland Case Study. PhD Thesis available at Ulster University Repository. Unpublished Document.

Pillow, W. (2003) 'Confession, catharsis, or cure? Rethinking the uses of reflexivity as methodological power in qualitative research', *International Journal of Qualitative Studies in Education*, 16: 175–96.

Pratt, J. (2005) 'Elias, punishment and decivilisation', in J. Pratt, D. Brown, M. Brown, S. Hallsworth and W. Morrison (eds) *The New Punitiveness: Theories, Trends, Perspectives*, London: Routledge, pp 256–71.

Probation Board for Northern Ireland (PBNI) (2002) 'Corporate plan 2002–2005', Belfast.

Rountree, M.A. and Pomeroy, E.C. (2010) 'Bridging the gap between social justice research and practice', *Social Work*, 55(4): 293–5.

Shemmings, D. (2006) '"Quantifying" qualitative data: An illustrative example of the use of Q methodology in psychosocial research', *Qualitative Research in Psychology*, 3(2): 147–65.

Solas, J. (2008) 'Social work and social justice: What are we fighting for?', *Australian Social Work*, 61(2): 124–36.

Stainton Rogers, R. and Stainton Rogers, W. (1990) 'What the Brits got out of the Q: And why their work may not line up with the American way of getting into it!', *The Electronic Journal of Communication*, 1(1), Available from: http://www.cios.org/EJCPUBLIC/001/1/00113.html [Accessed 5 December 2022].

Stenner, P., Watts, S. and Worrell, M. (2008) 'Q methodology', in C. Willig and W. Stainton Rogers (eds) *The SAGE Handbook of Qualitative Research in Psychology*, London: Sage, pp 215–39.

Stenner, P., Watts, S. and Worrell, M. (2017) 'Q methodology', in C. Willig and W. Stainton Rogers (eds) *The SAGE Handbook of Qualitative Research in Psychology* (2nd edn), London: Sage, pp 212–37.

Stephenson, W. (1953) *The Study of Behaviour: Q-technique and Its Methodology*. University of Chicago Press.

Strier, R. (2007) 'Anti-oppressive research in social work: A preliminary definition', *British Journal of Social Work*, 37: 857–71.

Watts, S. (2009) 'Social constructionism redefined: Human selectionism and the objective reality of Q methodology', *Operant Subjectivity: The International Journal of Q Methodology*, 32(1): 29–45.

Watts, S. and Stenner, P. (2012) *Doing Q Methodological Research: Theory, Method and Interpretation* , London: Sage.

Watts, S. and Stenner, P. (2017) 'Q-methodology 1: Design and theory', Training Webinar. Unpublished.

Webler, T., Danielson, S. and Tuler, S. (2009) 'Using Q method to reveal social perspectives in environmental research', Greenfield, MA: Social and Environmental Research Institute.

Wickens, C.M., Cohen, J.A. and Walther, C.S. (2017) 'Reflexivity in the interstices: A tale of reflexivity at work in, during, and behind the scenes', *International Journal of Qualitative Studies in Education*, 30(9): 863–76.

Wilson, J.Q. and Kelling, G.L. (1982) 'Broken windows', *Atlantic Monthly*, 249: 29–38.

14

Reflecting as a pracademic in policy land: using research and practice to advance social justice in the hate crime policy domain

Seamus Taylor

Introduction

Having spent 25 years working in social justice policy and practice, and close on 15 years in academia, I identify as a practice-informed academic and an academic seeking to inform policy and practice. Such an orientation has been described as that of a pracademic. In this chapter, I outline and reflect upon how I have sought to use this pracademic melding of research, policy and practice experience to advance social justice in the hate crime domains in England, Wales and Ireland.

There is a relatively small body of literature on academics engaging with the policymaking process (Le Grand, 2006; Avey and Desch, 2014; Talbot and Talbot, 2014). There is an even smaller body of literature on academics contributing to the hate crime policy domain (Chakraborti and Garland, 2014; Giannasi, 2014; Hall, 2014). There is a gap in the literature on academics – on pracademics who start out in the policy domain and who transition to academia and seek to engage in both. This chapter begins to explore aspects of that gap.

Perspectives, key concepts and positionality

In this chapter, I use some concepts and terms and refer to some perspectives throughout. At the outset, I set out my understandings and position in relation to these perspectives, concepts and terms.

I start with social justice. Social justice is a widely used concept today. Although widely used, it has varied understandings, and to some extent it is a contested concept. I would identify a few broad perspectives on social justice, all concerned with a focus on social identities and economic inequalities. These perspectives I identify as social justice liberalism, critical social justice and anti-social justice.

In Western liberal democracies, social justice liberalism is broadly reflected in academia and in some governmental policy domains. Social justice liberalism is a broad approach concerned with ensuring equality of opportunity, reasonable accommodations, group-conscious policies, minority-specific and targeted policies both in terms of identity-based inequalities and economic inequalities. An excellent contemporary application of a progressive social justice liberalism approach to the analysis of criminalising hate is to be found in the work of Walters (2022).

Critical social justice is espoused in parts of academia and in social movements and to a much lesser extent in governmental policy domains. Critical social justice places emphases on structural, systemic, cultural and institutional inequalities and occasionally on individual experiences of inequality. Critical social justice places an emphasis on whole of society and whole of government transformative strategies to substantially reduce inequalities. Critical social justice includes a range of perspectives: some place emphases on substantial reduction in societal inequalities, while others emphasise equal outcomes. Some within critical social justice place emphases on the connections between discourse, language and power and emphasise that a focus on social justice requires disruption and replacement of inequalities embedded in discourse and language. Some are influenced by the work of neo-Marxists and some by the work of those writing in the Foucauldian tradition.

Anti-social justice contributors tend to dismiss a concern with social justice as a hollow rallying slogan rather than a serious approach to understanding and addressing injustices in society. Anti-social justice approaches are again quite varied: they range from viewing justice as resulting from a freely operating market society with a minimal state – it delivers natural justice through to contributors who critique identity inequalities as fundamentally destabilising of society. They also include more polemical critiques of what has been termed 'woke culture', 'political correctness' and more recently the #MeToo movement, the Black Lives Matter movement and the trans equality movement. Some talk in terms of critical social justice academics and advocates as 'the new puritans', viewing social justice as a postmodern religion that has captured the Western world (Doyle, 2022), social justice approaches as a modern 'madness' (Murray, 2019), including antiracism as a 'mania exposed' (Lewis, 1998).

Given the constraints of a book chapter, the preceding discussion is a broad overview of social justice perspectives today. I tend to identify with substantial aspects of the critical social justice approach, while also identifying with aspects of the liberal social justice approach as offering stepping stones to more critical justice outcomes. I welcome the critique of the anti-social justice perspectives while often disagreeing with them. Overall, I tend towards the view that no one perspective on social justice fully mirrors the realities of the social injustices that we are called upon to analyse and address. That said, elements of critical social justice and liberal social justice can assist our understandings and actions.

I now turn to the term hate crime. Like social justice, it is a widely used term in academia, policy and popular debate in Western liberal democracies. Until relatively recently, the policy and practice domain were in advance of theorising on hate crime (Iganski, 2008, 2010). That is no longer so, as there is now a flourishing multi-disciplinary field of hate studies (Perry, 2001, 2009; Iganski, 2008; 2010: Hall 2013; Schweppe and Walters, 2016; Walters 2022). There are numerous academic texts and articles dedicated to defining hate crime, its parameters, victims, manifestations and impacts, and how best to respond to hate. Again, given the constraints of a book chapter, I can only provide an overview of perspectives on hate crime.

A helpful explanation of hate crime for policy and practice purposes is that proffered by the Organization for Security and Co-operation in Europe, which regards hate crime as a criminal offence with a bias element (OSCE, 2009). This captures the essentials of hate crime in that there is a base criminal offence such as assault. It also captures that the base criminal offence is aggravated by a bias element – it is that bias element which makes it a hate crime. That might be a biased motivation, a demonstration of bias at the time of offending or biased targeting of the victim. Having defined the issues, the challenge moves to which biases or prejudices are to be protected under hate crime legislation. Most countries start out with a focus on race or religion, which extends over time to cover sexuality, disability and gender identity. Few cover gender, although the Irish Hate Crime Bill (2021) does. Walters (2022) provides a groundbreaking and very well-evidenced and argued rationale for the inclusion of group identities in hate crime protections which experience subordination and lack of power linked with group identity. He argues that it is by appreciating that hate crime is an attack on group identity that we can fully understand its distinct harms, indeed its boundaries, as a concept (Walters, 2022). While Walters has provided the leading theoretical argument for criminalising hate, Barbara Perry provides a particularly insightful understanding of what hate crime represents sociologically. Perry conveys this through the concept of hate crime as 'doing difference'. Perry conceives of hate crime as a means through which the unequal social order is reproduced in society. Hate crimes are message crimes, through which an individual victim or victims are put back in their place in society, and through which the wider group which shares that victim group identity are reminded of their place in the unequal social order, thereby reproducing that hierarchical social order. Through theorising the doing of difference, Perry has provided the leading sociological understanding of hate crime at the individual, community and societal levels (Perry, 2001).

Taking these perspectives on social justice and hate crime together raises questions for me as a pracademic interested in contributing to policy. I bring a blended critical–liberal social justice perspective to the hate crime domain. I identify with Perry's perspective on hate crime as 'doing difference' in society. Yet the application of hate crime law is in the main an individual-level response to societal challenges. If I solely pursued a critical social justice approach, I might well prioritise a transformative national equality strategy across all of society over the pursuit of hate crime law. I might well dismiss hate crime law as simply the state's slip from structural-level inequalities to individual-level responses, which neglects the most significant systemic inequalities. Here is where I draw upon the blended critical–liberal social justice approach. I view hate crime as but one instrument, albeit an essential policy and practice instrument, in advancing a more socially just society. Here I would favour having both hate crime law and a national equality strategy, the blended healthy magpie approach of critical–liberal social justice. I recognise the parameters of the policymaking process – in my contributions, I seek to act responsibly as an academic committed to social justice but recognising, accepting and working within existing feasibility, technical and political parameters of the policymaking process.

Given the focus of the main research study considered in this chapter on Disability Hate Crime, I wish to consider the terms disability and disabled people. I define disability in terms of the legislation as a functional impairment that may be physical, sensory or learning. I favour the use of the term disabled people rather than people with disabilities. This reflects my socialisation within the social model of disability, which views disabled people as people who are primarily disabled by society's physical, structural and attitudinal barriers linked to the functional impairments which they have. Some people in Ireland use and favour the alternative term people with disabilities.

Another concept I use in this chapter is that of outsider–insider perspectives. The concept of the outsider has a long history in the social sciences both in the study of deviance and in applied social studies more widely. I am influenced by a range of uses of the outsider–insider concept (Becker, 1963; Walters, 2001). For this chapter, I conceive of insiders as those who are on the inside of the policymaking process, specifically policy officials and politicians. I conceive of outsiders as those who are on the outside of the policymaking process but who may nevertheless be seeking to influence the policymaking process. Outsiders to the policymaking process include academics, NGOs, individuals, trade unions, think tanks and other stakeholders. I explore these concepts later as a pracademic – an academic who is now on the outside but who has worked on the inside of the policymaking process. I reflect whether it is possible to bridge the outsider–insider binary.

The research study underpinning this chapter

While this book chapter draws upon the range of my research and policy and practice experience, it is also based on a research study which was undertaken between 2012 and 2018 in England and Wales and which was built upon with the subsequent analysis conducted on developments between 2018 and 2020. The main research study sought to explore the contributions of activism, politics and policymaking to the development of Disability Hate Crime policy in England and Wales. It explored the challenges of a focus on vulnerability in the Disability Hate Crime area and the explanatory value of ableism as a prejudicial ideology fuelling Disability Hate Crime. The research study was based on a qualitative methodology which comprised in-depth interviews with key informants in activism, politics and policymaking. It also involved an analysis of Disability Hate Crime cases, through access to the Crown Prosecution System (CPS) case management system. Finally, the research study involved a critical analysis of key policy documents on the topic of Disability Hate Crime.

The organising concepts used in this research study

The central organising concepts used in this research study are informed by the work of Kingdon (2011) on the policy streams approach and by the work of Bacchi (2009) on problematisation and problem representation in policymaking.

Kingdom's model of public policy conceives of the policy environment as comprising three streams: a problem stream, a policy stream and a politics stream. It highlights the concept of a window of opportunity through which a new policy can emerge. Kingdon also emphasises issues of 'fit' in terms of acceptability of a policy proposals feasibility, technical fit, political fit and values fit. Bacchi has developed a more critical framework for analysis of public policy underpinned by critical social constructionism known as 'What's the problem represented to be?', where the central emphasis is on problematisation and problem representation. I devised an adapted organisation and analytical framework for this research study that fits with the Disability Hate Crime topic and my social justice orientation. I replaced Kingdon's problem stream with an activism and problematisation stream influenced by Bacchi, considered alongside the policy stream and the politics stream. This adapted policy stream approach was used throughout the research study, and it provides an organising analytical lens rather than a complete conceptual framework.

Key informant interviews

Interviews were conducted with 55 key informants drawn from among activists, criminal justice practitioners, policy officials and politicians.

Interviews lasted 70 minutes on average. Interview topics included: What is hate crime, and how is it conceived? What is Disability Hate Crime, and how does it relate to wider hate crime? What were the contributory factors to the development of the Disability Hate Crime agenda? What were the challenges to the emergence and development of the Disability Hate Crime agenda? What is the influence of a focus on vulnerability in relation to Disability Hate Crime? What were the roles played by activism, politics and policy activity in the development of the Disability Hate Crime agenda?

Documentary analysis

A range of policy-related documents have been produced on Disability Hate Crime from 1997 up to 2020. In this research study, I analysed around 20 policy-related documents. I analysed documents in the activist stream, the policy stream and the politics stream. Documents were appraised in terms of the following questions: What are the key themes in the document? Are there implicit themes? Does the document relate to a genre of documents? How does the document conceive of and problematise disabled people? Does the document address and problematise the issue of vulnerability? How does the document conceive of and problematise hate crime and Disability Hate Crime? What, if any, are the silences in the policy document? Are there other ways of conceiving the issues addressed in the document? What are they?

Analysis of individual cases of Disability Hate Crime

As part of this research study, I negotiated access to the CPS computerised case management system of prosecution cases for the years 2013–14. To secure access to these completed cases, I had to have security clearance. I undertook an initial screening of 548 cases. I then analysed 15 cases in detail, 12 from the CPS system in which disabled people had been victims of targeted incidents or targeted crime. All cases were anonymised. While 12 cases were secured through the CPS case management system, the final three were accessed via NGOs and the independent statutory sector, which was a purposeful extension to the case study sample to secure non-crimed cases, that is, cases that had not formally entered the criminal justice system.

If a strength of the key informant interviews lay in building understanding through the perspective of living experts and that of documentary analysis lay in building understanding of codified representations of the issue in policy, then the key strength of individual cases lay in advancing understanding through an analysis of the empirical material contained in a diversity of individual cases perceived as Disability Hate Crime. In a study focused on policy and practice development, it enabled a critical consideration of the issues in practice. Taking the three research methods together provided for a triangulated study which enabled analysis in terms of the overall research questions of why and how Disability Hate Crime emerged as and when it did into the hate crime domain in England and Wales.

In terms of analysis of the research findings, I undertook NVivo analysis of the key informant interviews and that started with an initial identification of 170 open thematic codes, leading to 33 categories and eventually six overall themes. These six themes formed the basis of the study's thematic chapters on agenda setting, agenda development, agenda institutionalisation, the challenge of vulnerability and the under-recognition of ableism in Disability Hate Crime. I also analysed the 20 documents and the 15 case studies using thematic analysis. The analysis allowed for integration across the research methods.

Threading a social justice focus through the research study

The social justice focus of this research study goes back to my interest in undertaking this study. My interest was ignited when I was involved in the development of hate crime policy as Director of Equality and Diversity in the CPS for England and Wales from 2004 to 2009. During this time, I contributed to the development of a CPS Disability Hate Crimes policy among other hate crime policies. There was a growing activism around Disability Hate Crime, and there was a sentencing uplift provision in place which recognised Disability Hate Crime. I sensed that the emerging agenda on Disability Hate Crime might challenge the criminal justice system and how it had constructed hate crime. I sensed a pervasive policy construction of disabled people as vulnerable. This seemed likely to present challenges when focusing on Disability Hate Crime. As I became immersed in the policy responses to Disability Hate Crime, I began to wonder if it may prove particularly challenging to find a home in the hate crime domain for disability hostility. These reflections and the finding of a home in hate crime for disability hostility was I felt important to advance social justice for disabled people.

Before I embarked on the research study in detail, I undertook a series of pre-research visits to England and Wales. I spent 1.5 weeks meeting a range of activists, policy officials and equality-related organisations to help inform the scoping and planning of the research study. I met with a range of activists in this pre-research phase given my commitment to parity of consideration of the contributions of the range of actors concerned with Disability Hate Crime. This engagement with activists from the outset reflected my commitment to social justice and to giving voice to those most impacted by Disability Hate Crime.

As I embarked on the research study, my social justice orientation was reflected at each stage in the research planning and execution. From the outset, I consciously planned to give parity of consideration to the insights of activists alongside policy officials and politicians. I could have undertaken a study which focused the key informant interviews on policy officials and politicians, and I could likewise have analysed policy documents solely from government and statutory bodies. I consciously focused the key informant interviews equally on activists alongside policy officials and politicians, and I equally analysed documents from the NGO sector that contributed to agenda development on Disability Hate Crime. This was informed by my social justice orientation.

In terms of analysis of the research findings, I foregrounded relevant findings articulated by activists, namely the issue of the overfocus on vulnerability and the under-recognition of ableism as the prejudice underpinning Disability Hate Crime. I highlighted these themes as activist interviewees stated without exception that they objected to their categorisation as inherently vulnerable by criminal justice agencies. In doing so, I enabled the voice of disability activists to be heard in a policy area where it had been neglected. I also gave a focus to ableism as the fuelling ideology underpinning Disability Hate Crime. I did this based on my analysis of the evidence across the research methods, which demonstrated the lack of recognition of ableism as a prejudicial ideology that frames disabled people's experiences. I again was enabling the lived experience of disability activists to be heard in this policy area.

Key findings of the study

The main findings of the research study informing this chapter are:

- Activists triggered the Disability Hate Crime policy agenda in England and Wales.
- Activists built a time-limited strategic alliance with a leading politician to get Disability Hate Crime on the policy agenda.
- Policy officials brought forward proposals to include Disability Hate Crime within the hate crime domain in response to the strategic alliance of activists and this politician.
- Today, the Disability Hate Crime policy agenda has moved on, and policy officials lead the Disability Hate Crime agenda and respond to activist critique with infrequent strategic political intervention.
- Disability Hate Crime remains a somewhat unsettled policy agenda in the hate crime domain.
- The biggest challenge to settling Disability Hate Crime into the hate crime domain and responding to it appropriately is the undue focus on vulnerability in Disability Hate Crime cases.

There is a significant under-recognition of ableism as a prejudicial ideology that fuels Disability Hate Crimes.

There are possible ways through these challenges and this lack of recognition. A way through these challenges is to vary the test of legal proof in Disability Hate Crime cases. The test of legal proof in Disability Hate Crime cases could be varied to allow for proof based on proof of a hostile motivation or a demonstration of hostility or discriminatory selection because of disability identity.

More Disability Hate Crime cases are likely to secure justice if the law and legal policy guidance and practice can be amended to reflect the previous recommendation.

An issue to be considered in undertaking the main research study was that I am a non-disabled researcher researching a concern for many disabled people, that is, the issue of targeted hostility or hate crime. I was alert to this and to debates within the disability movement regarding this. In some instances, 'rejection of non-disabled researchers occurred at the beginning of the British disability movement' (Shakespeare, 2000: 195). This rejection has been revisited more recently. It is increasingly acknowledged that because someone is disabled, they do not have 'automatic insight into the lives of other disabled people' (Shakespeare, 2006: 195). There is also a recognition that this rejectionist stance risks adopting an essentialist position where only disabled people can contribute to disability issues. The more recent social progressive perspective on disability acknowledges the role that non-disabled researchers can play and identifies a way forward through alliances between disabled and non-disabled people. There is a recognition that non-disabled researchers can make a positive contribution to the social situation of disabled people (Shakespeare, 2000: 196). This is the social justice-committed and critically reflective position from which I, as a researcher, approach the topic of research on hate crime and Disability Hate Crime in particular.

Using research and practice experience to seek to influence policy in England and Wales

The research study referred to earlier took place between 2012 and 2018. Co-terminus with this research study, the Law Commission for England and Wales launched a first Hate Crime Project in 2012 led by Professor David Ormerod QC (Law Commission, 2012). The project went through standard Law Commission project stages of initiation, pre-consultation, consultation, policy development and report submission to government. The Law Commission's first Hate Crime Project followed a request from the Ministry of Justice to review the existing hate crime-aggravated offences and explore the case for extending them to the areas of disability and gender identity. The Law Commission issued a consultation paper in 2013 and received 157 written responses. They considered these responses and issued their final report and recommendations to government in 2014. I made a submission to the Law Commission Review. The Law Commission issued their review report in 2014. They concluded that they had been constrained by the terms of reference of their review, which only allowed them to consider extending an exact replica of existing hate crime law on aggravated offences in racist and religious crimes to disability and gender identity offences. This was a model for hate crime law protections devised in 2003 to address the specifics and patterned features of racist crime. The Law Commission thus recommended that, rather than inappropriately extend the racist and religious-aggravated offences to disability and gender identity, a wider review of hate crime law be commissioned, which would not be constrained by a list of aggravated offences identified for racist crime and not suited to the specifics of Disability Hate Crime devised over ten years earlier. The Law Commission further recommended that if the government were not minded to immediately review the laws, then the existing aggravated offences, as applied to racist and religious crimes, should be extended to disability and gender identity-based hate crimes. I made a submission to the Law Commission consultation response. I arranged for the Law Commission lead officials to present on the Hate Crime Law Review and engage in consultation with the London CPS Hate Crime Scrutiny and Involvement Panel. In my consultation response, I made the point as concluded by the Law Commission – that the review was constrained by the Terms of Reference, which only allowed for an extension of the racist and religious offences exactly as they are to disability and gender identity. I pointed out that this did not allow for the specifics of the different discriminations to be addressed. I also made the point that there should be parity of protection across all hate crime strands, and the law should move away from the current unevenness in protections which amounts to a hierarchy of protections.

The government did not respond to the Law Commission Review for some considerable time. Then in 2018 the Law Commission was asked by government to conduct a wider review and to consider how hate crime laws should operate and how to ensure that the criminal law provides consistent and effective protection (Law Commission, 2019).

This was a much broader review, not constrained by only considering reforms to existing laws. The Law Commission launched the second review in 2019 and undertook a range of pre-consultation exercises. The Law Commission launched a consultation paper in September 2020, and 2,473 written responses were received. I made a written submission to this consultation on the review of hate crime law and arising from this written submission was requested to have a meeting with the lead Law Commissioner and lead officials supporting the Hate Crime Law Review. The Law Commission published their final review report in 2021, and as

I write this book chapter, the government are yet to respond to this latest Law Commission Review.

In responding to both Law Commission Hate Crime Reviews consultations in 2013 and in 2020, I conveyed my social justice background in policy, practice and academia. I drew upon the evidence bases both in practice and from my research. In the more recent Law Commission Review, I drew upon the evidence base in the research study I undertook from 2012 to 2018. I also drew upon prosecution service annual hate crime case data. These submissions were referenced in the subsequent reports of the 2014 and 2020 Law Commission Reviews. The final report of the Law Commission's Hate Crime Law Review in 2021 reflected a number of my and others submission recommendations including recommending parity of protection across hate crime strands and adding prejudice to the definition of hate alongside hostility. The Law Commission final report, however, did not reflect my recommendation to include in the law the provision for a discriminatory selection test to apply in targeted crimes against disabled people. The evidence base from my academic research and my policy work convinced me of the need for a test of proof in Disability Hate Crime cases based on biased selection of a disabled person as victim. The Law Commission went part way to meet this concern that I and others were raising by adding 'prejudice' to the definition alongside hostility, thereby perhaps making it 'easier' to secure disability-related prosecutions. The Law Commission's overarching commitment to parity of protections across the protected grounds seemed to take precedence over doing full justice to the specific needs of one protected ground, namely disability. Reflecting my social justice commitment, I have argued that the available evidence warrants provision of a varied legal geometry of protections that reflect the different manifestations of the different discriminations. Racism is not the same as sexism, or heterosexism or transphobia, and none of these are the same as ableism. They share a commonality as prejudicial ideologies based on group identity. However, these prejudices have different histories, manifest differently and warrant elements of both differentiated and common policy responses. This aspect of the social justice argument, based on a differentiated legal response, in disability, while backed by leading scholars such as Walters (2017), has to date proved a step too far for the Law Commission and for government.

Using research and practice experience to seek to influence policy in Ireland

In 2020, the Irish government published a report entitled 'Legislating for hate speech and hate crime in Ireland'. The government then undertook public consultation on its hate speech proposals but not on its hate crime proposals.

Since then, it has published the Heads of the Criminal Justice (Hate Crime) Bill 2021. It facilitated the undertaking of a pre-legislative scrutiny of the Heads of the Criminal Justice (Hate Crime) Bill 2021 in November 2021 by the Oireachtas Justice Committee. The Justice Committee published a report of the pre-legislative scrutiny of the Hate Crime Bill in April 2022, and the Minister for Justice (July 2022) announced that the full Hate Crime Bill would be published in the autumn, which has now occurred. Between 2020 and July 2022, the government's Hate Crime Bill proposals evolved considerably, indicating inputs from stakeholders to the policymaking process on hate crime law may well be influencing the evolving focus on hate crime law. I have made submissions, engaged with politicians, civil servants and NGOs at each stage in this policy development process. I made a response to the Hate Speech Consultation. I made a written submission to the Justice Committee pre-legislative scrutiny committee. I emphasised my practice experience in the hate crime field alongside my academic research. I was invited to give oral evidence to the Justice Committee. I submitted an Opening Statement to the Justice Committee. I linked and liaised with relevant NGOs in the hate crime field in advance of the Justice Committee. This linking and working with NGOs was critical to the progress achieved. In my opening submission, I emphasised my background in practice – in developing and implementing hate crime policy in a neighbouring criminal justice system. I built on this through drawing upon the research study underpinning this chapter. I gave evidence and answered politicians' questions over a two-hour period. I stressed the importance of evidence-based policymaking – that what matters is what works and what the available evidence demonstrates. I illuminated my argument with evidence from cases. I made three substantive arguments:

- that Ireland should adopt a test of legal proof in hate crime cases based on a two-limbed legal test of proof of motivation, and or proof of demonstration of hostility at the time of offending;
- that Ireland, in keeping with the spirit and provisions of the Good Friday Agreement, should provide parity of protection in hate crime law equivalent with the hate crime legal provisions in Northern Ireland;
- and finally, that Ireland's hate crime law should include specific provisions to address the specifics of Disability Hate Crime through inclusion of a discriminatory selection test as a third limb of legal proof that could be applied in Disability Hate Crime cases.

The Justice Committee produced its scrutiny report in April 2022 and adopted the first two of my recommendations, recommending a two-limbed legal test of proof of hostility based on motivation and/or demonstration of hostility and recommending that the government pursue equivalence in the

Hate Crime Bill with the existing legislation in Northern Ireland. Following publication of the Justice Committee report, I linked with justice officials at senior levels together with senior levels of other criminal justice agencies. I provided further evidence on the feasibility of a demonstration test of proof based on evidence from two neighbouring jurisdictions. I made both written submissions and met with senior officials in criminal justice agencies. Then in July 2022 the Minister for Justice announced that the full Hate Crime Bill would be issued in the autumn of 2022 and have a two-limbed test of legal proof based on motivation and/or demonstration of hostility and thereby achieve equivalence with the law in Northern Ireland. Neither a two-limbed legal test of proof nor jurisdictional equivalence with Northern Ireland was present when the government first issued its Hate Crime Bill proposals and Heads of the Hate Crime Bill in 2020 and 2021. It indicates a governmental process listening to evidence-based argument that I and in particular activists from the NGO sector have been articulating. The government issued the full Hate Crime Bill in October 2022, and it has now had a reading in the Oireachtas, where it was introduced by the Minister for Justice, Helen McEntee, in early November 2022. The Bill, known as the Criminal Justice (Incitement to Violence or Hatred and Hate Offences) Bill 2022, contains my key recommendation in relation to providing for proof in hate crime cases based on a demonstration of hostility. However, the Bill does not define hatred or hate, and it does not include provision for a discriminatory selection test of proof in Disability Hate Crime cases. At the time of writing this chapter, we are awaiting the return of the Bill to the Oireachtas. I continue to seek to influence the Bill through liaison with policy officials, politicians and NGOs. I decided to focus my influencing efforts on the definitions of hatred and hate and the retention of the demonstration test of proof. Taking a pragmatic approach, I ceased seeking to secure a discriminatory selection test of proof, as it has not been engaged with at all by policy officials or politicians. This was a difficult decision to make based on my research study findings and on my social justice orientation – both point strongly to the need for a discrimination test of proof in Disability Hate Crime cases. However, considering the policymaking process as it is unfolding, I made a judgement that it is a policy step too far for the policy domain in Ireland to engage with at this stage. It is, however, an issue that I will not cease to promote in the future based on the research evidence and seek to have it considered when the legislation comes up for review.

Reflections on seeking to influence hate crime policy

It is challenging to reflect on these case studies in policymaking. Challenges arise due to the recency of the policy proposals under consideration, one of which, the Hate Crime Bill in Ireland, is still going through the legislative process; the direct involvement of the author in both policy case studies and the potential issues raised for reflection, distance and potential bias; and the different nature of the two case studies. The former case study in England and Wales is focused on seeking to influence the Law Commission who make proposals for legal policy reform but do not make policy per se, and the latter focused on Ireland, which is a classic example of legislative policymaking. Notwithstanding these potential challenges, there is value in a preliminary reflection on these case studies in the context of the wider literature and the concepts introduced at the outset of this chapter.

In terms of the guiding concepts of social justice and hate crime, I am clear that while significantly informed by a blended critical–liberal social justice perspective, I recognise that hate crime as a state policy domain is at best a social liberal response to just one manifestation of what can be deep-seated systemic inequalities. I recognise that hate crime policy is tertiary-level social policy – it is intervening to mop up a mess at an individual level after what has occurred which may well be an acting out of the doing of difference at societal level. Coming from a blended critical–liberal social justice perspective, I would argue in the first instance for a whole of government and a whole of society national equality strategy. Within this, I would advise that a central emphasis be placed on education for respect for diversity of individuals and groups in society. I would advise that opportunities be maximised for respectful engagement through education, sports, the arts and culture, the media, the youth and community development sectors, social media, wider civil society and politics. I would advise that substantial inequalities that minoritised groups face be addressed, thereby helping to foster social cohesion and unity through diversity. Within this broader transformative national strategy, I would advise that there be a distinct focus on hate crime to address those hopefully less frequent circumstances where group identity is violated, leading to hate crime which harms the victim, the community and social fabric. I nevertheless recognise that we work in a context where a transformative national equality strategy does not exist and a focus on hate crime remains an issue and an important one to respond to. In the circumstances, I am guided by a pragmatic approach while retaining my social justice orientation.

In terms of the other guiding concepts, the evidence from these case studies appears to indicate some value in a pracademic base of expertise in seeking to contribute to policymaking. Through complementing, supplementing and amplifying academic research-based arguments, it can on occasions perhaps provide a grounded added dimension that policy officials may be open to. It can perhaps enhance the legitimacy of the pracademic's contribution through the perceived experience and authority that a grounding in practice can bring to evidence-based argument. It may help open policy officials' doors and give for a certain ease of shared understanding and a shared discourse on the 'policy problem' to be addressed and a shared appreciation of the feasibility of alternative policy proposals. It can place pracademic and policy officials on the same policy page at least some of the time and help the exchange in terms of appreciation of each other's challenges and constraints.

The value of the outsider and insider concepts are again illustrated through reflection on these case studies. The same points arise as in reflection on the pracademic role. The pracademic is the role through which the outsider and insider positionings get expressed. To start as an academic, one is clearly an outsider to the policy process. As an academic with former policymaking experience, one remains an outsider to the formal policy process. However, as a pracademic, one may have a level of 'bridging experience' which can ease exchange with policy officials involved in policymaking. There may on occasions be a more ready acceptance by policy officials that this academic knows what is involved when you have a policy problem to fix. This can be valuable in policy networking and the building of relationships with policy officials which are so important in seeking to engage with the policymaking process. There can also perhaps be a more ready appreciation by the pracademic of the political and feasibility parameters within which policy officials operate.

Reflecting on these case studies in both England, Wales and Ireland, the concept of 'fit' in terms of feasibility fit or technical feasibility, policy and political fit and values fit are all well illustrated. Evidence from the policy studies literature indicates that a policy proposal is more likely to be accepted by policy officials and implemented if it fits with an established way of doing things, if it fits with a broad incremental approach (Kingdon, 2011) – disability protection was accepted into the hate crime policy domain in England and Wales when what seemed to be required was a simple adding to the list of race, religion, sexuality and gender identity as protections. This was accepted because it was seen to be a feasibility fit – by compromising on the need for a different policy approach to disability hostility, disability got a home in the hate crime domain.

In Ireland, the acceptance of a dual-limbed legal test of proof of hostility appears to have been accepted based on a combination of political fit, feasibility fit and values fit. The original Heads of Criminal Justice Hate Crime Bill 2021 in Ireland did not contain a demonstration test of hostility. It was based solely on a motivation test of hostility. Policy officials began to engage substantially with inclusion of a demonstration test of hostility following politicians' pre-legislative scrutiny and their publication of a Scrutiny Report (April 2022) backing a demonstration test. They received a clear political indication that there was a fit between the views of the all-party Justice Committee and the inclusion of a demonstration test of hostility. It was also recognised that there was a political fit at another significant level – the level of all-island relations and legal protections. The Good Friday Agreement of 1998, the basis of the current peace process in Ireland, contains a commitment to parity of human rights and equality protections, which is a parity commitment, not replica legal provisions. Following submissions which pointed out the significant disparity in the proposed hate crime law between what exists in Northern Ireland and what was proposed for Ireland, the Justice Committee in their final report recommended that the provisions in Ireland should provide parity of protection with the hate crime law in Northern Ireland. In taking this into account, they were taking account of the wider context of political relations on the Island of Ireland and between Britain and Ireland.

Furthermore, there was a broad values fit between being progressive on hate crime law and the range of human rights and equality measures taken in Ireland in recent decades which seek to place Ireland at the forefront of progressive liberal democracies committed to human rights and equality and an open society and economy. From 1998 onwards, these have been reflected in employment equality legislation, equal status legislation, human rights legislation, legislation for same sex marriages, legislating for provision of abortion, ratifying UN conventions on aspects of equality and indeed seeking and securing a place on the UN Security Council.

All these aspects of 'fit' – feasibility, political and values fit – were issues which I raised throughout this process seeking to inform the development of social justice-orientated hate crime law in Ireland. It of course remains to be seen whether the current reasonably progressive proposals of the Irish government on hate crime will survive the journey through the legislative process. There is a considerable legislative journey yet to be followed, and a progressive hate crime law cannot be assumed at this stage.

Drawing out the lessons from this chapter for social justice research

Reflecting on the lessons that can be learned from this research and case studies for future social justice research, I identify the following:

- If we wish to undertake social justice research, we should make that explicit in the research aims and objectives from outset.
- We should be clear about our value-committed approach to social justice at the outset of our research. We should not undertake value-committed research under a veil of value neutrality.
- We should then explicitly build a social justice focus into every key stage of research planning, methodology, fieldwork. We should mainstream the social justice focus into every stage of a research project. This should involve us thinking about social justice dimensions at each stage, acting for the inclusion of social justice dimensions, and delivering on the social justice dimensions of a research project.

- We should design our research to give voice to those who are the intended beneficiaries at every key stage from research planning through fieldwork through to analysis.
- We should not only explicitly commit to the principle of do no harm through our research but also explicitly commit to the principle of furthering social justice through our research.
- We should give a parity of consideration to the experiences of the intended beneficiaries of our research alongside others involved in the research.
- We should invest the time, the considerations and resources required to undertake social justice research in genuinely inclusive, respectful ways.

Lessons for academics on seeking to influence social justice policy and practice in the Irish context and beyond

Reflecting on the lessons that can be learned from these case studies in engaging with social justice policymaking and practice, I identify the following (please note that some of these apply beyond social justice policy and practice, and some apply in particular to social justice):

- We need to familiarise ourselves as academics with the steps in the formal government policymaking process. Ascertain at which stages it is appropriate to intervene and how to intervene.
- There is a need to recognise the importance of policy networking in the relevant policy domains. The policy village on any one policy agenda tends to be quite small and sometimes niche. If possible, make yourself known to the lead government officials and politicians. Establish your expert credentials based on either a particular research study or based on your cumulative experience overtime.
- Researchers should recognise and accept that most public and social policy initiatives in Western liberal democracies may align somewhat with a liberal or at most a social liberal approach to justice. Very few policy proposals will reflect a critical social justice approach. As an academic, you need to acknowledge these policymaking parameters. As a result, you can at most expect to contribute sometimes to policy reform rather than routinely to transformative policy change. That said, it is important to retain a focus on changing the wider policy narratives so that better futures can not only be imagined but realised. That is central to the academic role.
- If as an academic you subscribe to a critical social justice orientation, you can retain your commitment to this orientation, but accept that if you wish to influence policy, you must often be prepared to contribute to and see incremental and partial change en route to possible realisation of longer-term commitments.

- Recognise that as an academic you are an outsider to the policymaking process, and that you contribute on that basis.
- Recognise that if you are a pracademic, you may on some occasions be able to bridge aspects of the worlds of academia and policymaking to good effect for all involved.
- Recognise the importance of communication to the policymaking audience. Clarity of communication for an intelligent, non-expert audience is key. Digestible, accessible two-page summaries of research evidence are valued by policy officials and politicians.
- Use summary comparative analyses of international policy and practice including in terms of how other jurisdictions are addressing the same policy agenda.
- Demonstrate that you appreciate the importance of fit for the acceptance of policy proposals, in terms of feasibility fit, technical fit and political fit.
- Be responsive when you engage in policymaking. Policy officials are often working to tight turnaround times. If you wish to influence, then you often need to engage and respond in short timeframes.
- Always act responsibly and do not compromise on academic integrity, values commitments and evidence on longer-term solutions while seeking to contribute constructively to and within the constraints of policymaking.

Concluding points

In a context where there is limited literature on the interactions between academics and the policymaking process and less on the interactions between pracademics and the policy process, this chapter provides an initial reflective contribution on one pracademic's recent experiences in the hate crime policy domains in England and Wales and Ireland. It highlights issues of social justice orientation and the opportunities and constraints on advancing this in the hate crime policy domain. It highlights issues of what it means to be a pracademic and linked issues of outsider and insider status in the policy process. It explores areas of potential constructive exchange between pracademics and policy officials. It explores the issues of 'fit' between a pracademic's proposals and policy officials and politicians' sense of what fits in terms of feasibility, political acceptability and values fit. It explores these issues in terms of case studies on hate crime policymaking in England and Wales and in Ireland. Through this initial exploration, I also identify some lessons learnt for academics seeking to influence policymaking. I conclude that this is a terrain worthy of further exploration – a terrain rich for pracademics and their critics. The challenge for pracademics is to strike the balance between seeking to influence the policymaking process and reflecting through research how such influence occurs. Hopefully this chapter has identified some avenues to explore to better understand such influences.

References

Avey, P. and Desch, M. (2014) 'What do policy makers want from us? Results of a survey of current and former senior national security decision makers', *International Studies Quarterly*, 58: 227–46.

Bacchi, C. (2009) *Analysing Policy: What's the Problem Represented to Be?*, Frenchs Forest, NSW: Pearson Australia.

Chakraborti, N. and Garland, J. (2014) *Responding to Hate Crime: The Case for Connecting Policy and Research*, Bristol: Policy Press.

Doyle, A. (2022) *The New Puritans: How the Religion of Social Justice Captured the Western World*, London: Constable.

Giannasi, P. (2014) 'Academia from a practitioner's perspective: A reflection on the changes in the relationship between academia, policing, and government in a hate crime context', in N. Chakraborti and J. Garland (eds) *Responding to Hate Crime: The Case for Connecting Policy and Research*, Bristol: Policy Press.

Le Grand, J. (2006) 'Academia, policy and politics', *Journal of Health Economics, Policy and Law*, 1: 319–22.

Hall, N. (2014) 'The adventures of an accidental academic in policy land: A personal reflection on bridging academia, policing, and government in a hate crime context', in N. Chakraborti and J. Garland (eds) *Responding to Hate Crime: The Case for Connecting Policy and Research*, Bristol: Policy Press.

Iganski, P. (2008) *Hate Crime and the City*, Bristol: Policy Press.

Iganski, P. (2010) 'Hate crime', in F. Brookman, M. Maguire, H. Pierpont and T. Bennett (eds) *Handbook on Crime*, London: Willan Publishing, pp 351–65.

Kingdon, J. (1995) *Agendas, Alternatives, and Public Policies* (updated 2nd edn), Springfield, IL: Pearson.

Lewis, R. (1988) *Anti Racism: A Mania Exposed*, London: Quartet Books.

Murray, D. (2019) *The Madness of Crowds: Gender, Race and Identity*, London: Bloomsbury.

Perry, B. (2001) *In the Name of Hate: Understanding Hate Crimes*, New York: Routledge.

Sanders, P. (2011) *The Rise of the Equalities Industry*, London: Civitas.

Schweppe, J. and Walters, M. (2016) *The Globalization of Hate: Internationalizing Hate Crime*, Oxford: Oxford University Press.

Talbot, C. and Talbot, C. (2014) 'Sir Humphrey and the professors', Commissioned Report, Manchester University.

Walter, B. (2001) *Outsiders Inside*, London: Routledge.

Walters, M. (2022) *Criminalising Hate: Law as Social Justice Liberalism*, Cham, Switzerland: Palgrave Macmillan.

Williams, J. (2020) *The Corrosive Impact of Transgender Ideology*, London: Civitas.

Williams, J. (2021) 'Rethinking race: A critique of contemporary antiracism programmes', London: Civitas.

15

Concluding thoughts

Kathryn McGarry, Ciara Bradley and Gloria Kirwan

Drawing this edited collection to a close, we reflect on the key lessons arising from the various contributions as well as what these contributions mean for the story of research for social justice when taken together. In doing this, we hope to have cemented some key understandings of what social justice means in research and for researchers, as well looking forward to the potential for harnessing and strengthening social justice approaches across the social sciences.

As outlined in our introduction to this volume and developed in many of the chapters, a social justice agenda reflects the philosophical commitment of researchers (Creswell, 2009). While the notion of rights is assumed in all research which adheres to basic ethical standards, promoting an explicit social justice-based approach to research moves beyond rights as a duty and responsibility of the researcher to rights as a lens for thinking about and operationalising research. Indeed, the impetus for this edited collection came from the need to gather together key ideas on translating the 'what' of social justice into the 'how' of social justice research. Our aim in bringing this collection together has been to explore what social justice means for research, how our research endeavour is shaped by and shapes issues of social justice and how we can advance and promote agendas for social justice through our knowledge production.

The various contributions in this edited collection tell us stories of how the social world has shaped particular experiences of power and knowledge, and how our research activity can compound oppressive practices or work to challenge and displace the lack of parity which has long imbued our social world. Inspired by critical feminist thinkers such as Haraway (1988), we remind ourselves as we bring this collection together of the commitment, the motivation and the promise that awaits when we locate ourselves and our research 'doings' within a social justice frame:

> I am arguing for politics and epistemologies of location, positionality, and situating, where partiality and not universality is the condition of being heard to make rational knowledge claims. These are claims on

people's lives. I am arguing for the view from a body, always a complex, contradictory, structuring, and structured body, versus the view from above, from nowhere, from simplicity. (Haraway, 1988: 588)

Heidegger explains that '[e]very inquiry is a seeking ... Every seeking gets guided beforehand by what is sought' (Heidegger, 1962: 24). Research is not and cannot be neutral: it is shaped by our theory of knowledge, guided by what we believe can be known and how. Paradigms and hence methodologies matter politically because they create different realities (Bacchi and Rönnblom, 2014). Baker et al (2004: 169) encourage us to acknowledge this inevitability. Bacchi and Eveline (2010) challenge us as researchers to confront our own 'politics of doing', and as practitioners committed to social change, we acknowledge that our research can never be an objective, value-free enterprise. Rather, in bringing this collection together we are calling for the recognition of the potential for knowledge building and the use of knowledge to advance or erode rights. The various contributions to this volume shed light on the importance of this recognition and, through the different research case studies presented, allow us to explore roadmaps for how we can advance a social justice agenda through research.

Drawing on such important works provides a useful basis to explore some of the biases which have fostered undemocratic research practices and compound the kinds of injustices social researchers are tasked with revealing. Indeed, our edited collection provides an important picture of how and where social injustice occurs in research as well as how and where critical research can disrupt and displace such injustice and promote an ethic of care, a standard for equality and a parity of participation which better reflects the original promise of the transformative potential of social research.

Key learning from this collection

What are we actually doing when we commit ourselves to social justice in our research? How are our understandings of social justice in research shaped, and how does this in turn shape the kinds of research practices we endeavour to uphold?

Foregrounding the collection, we explored the theoretical frameworks which underpin a social justice approach in research.

We draw much learning from the work of political theorist Nancy Fraser. Fraser's theorisations on the politics of justice describe three principal nodes through which justice claims are framed and organised, namely the *what* of justice (what constitutes the injustice and conversely the justice); the *who* of justice (who is the subject of justice and who is entitled to consideration/make justice claims); and the *how* of justice (how should we determine the grammar for reflecting on justice, how should we determine criteria and/or procedures for resolving disputes about the what and the who [Fraser, 2009: 54]). For researchers committed to social justice, our core concerns then can be organised around uncovering the 'what', facilitating justice claims for the 'who' and documenting and disseminating the 'how' of our research for social justice work. Our collection then has challenged us to reflect on the 'ontological politics' (Mol, 1999) which shape the lived realities we wish to observe in our research and which shape the kinds of knowledge we produce. Bacchi and Rönnblom (2014) argue, as set out by McGarry in Chapter 2, that research practice cannot be separated from what we observe, as paradigms, and therefore research methodologies, have political resonance – they shape different realities. McMahon in Chapter 5 further explores this through her poststructural analysis of youth work policy.

While the various contributions in this volume draw on different approaches and theoretical influences for engaging with social justice, as Taylor describes in his journeying into 'pracademia' in Chapter 14, we see a commonality across all of the chapters in confronting how our research practice shapes realities and how our questioning of the 'what', the 'who' and the 'how' of our research endeavour is a fundamental first step in genuine, reflexive engagement with research for social justice.

Returning to Bacchi and Eveline's (2010: 326) critical ideas on the 'politics of doing', the kind of research approach we choose to undertake and the 'practices which give it life' have real life consequences: creating new knowledge, sustaining and strengthening existing knowledge, challenging taken-for-granted assumptions or embedding established ideas. The knowledge and knower are indeed shaped through the research practice and (i) decisions around what knowledge is produced, as Gorman (Chapter 9) describes in his anti-extractivist approach in this volume, and in a different context as described by O'Shea in her Q-methodology approach, as well as O'Driscoll and Kirwan in their chapter on phenomenological design; (ii) access to knowledge production, explored in the work of Melaugh and O'Hara in their chapter on Participatory Action Research with people who use drugs (PWUD); (iii) recognition and validation as a knower, as described in Bradley and Kavanagh's chapter on challenging stigma and centring the voices of women, and also explored in McGarry's chapter on epistemic privilege; (iv) the means of knowledge creation as explored by Donovan in his chapter on advancing arts-based research for social change; and (v) the political ramifications of the knowledge that is produced explored in the chapters here by Taylor on policymaking, McMahon on poststructuralism, Hearne on 'engaged research' and McMahon, Bradley and Tierney on social justice praxis in practitioner research. Taken together, these become the core concerns of a research for social justice agenda. Simply put, our research matters.

Key learning for social justice research, policy and practice

The chapters which comprise this collection shed a light on social justice research as a 'politics of doing' through various examples. Our contributors all provided useful reflections on the lessons arising from their work for social justice practice, and we take a look now at some of the key learning which motivated this collection:

A social justice lens

Bradley and Kavanagh (Chapter 3) argue that 'there is an imperative for researchers to identify and make explicit in their research the ontology and epistemology that guides their work and how it impacts their research practice'. McGarry (Chapter 2) similarly argues the need for research for social justice to become a lens for 'how our practices for acquiring knowledge and the effects those practices have are critical spaces for scrutiny in terms of the manner in which they either perpetuate marginalisation or dismantle taken-for-granted ideas about the natural order of things'. Indeed, this idea is exemplified by Meehan (Chapter 6) in her research with deaf and hard-of-hearing women as she encourages '[e]mbedding strong principles of equity and accessibility into the research process and working from a starting point of valuing diverse and deaf ways of seeing and knowing the world [to] support building a rich, insightful analysis that challenges audism'.

A social justice ethic

Gorman (Chapter 9), reflecting on his learning from his environmental justice research, describes the need to move beyond mere ethically informed research to embed a social justice ethic in our research design:

> The design principles for anti-extractivist research which I set out offer a theorisation of how we might deepen our ethical practices as researchers in ways which prefigure more just and equitable knowledge production practices. This involves moving beyond managing risk towards fostering reciprocity and a deep relational accountability in the research process.

This point is further illuminated in the work of Kirwan and Swords (Chapter 10), who argue: 'Working in solidarity (Kam, 2012) is only possible when individuals and groups feel heard, validated and motivated to seek a better world not only for themselves but others experiencing similar injustices.'

Positionality and reflexivity

The idea of reflexivity is often an ornamental idea in research, as Bradley and Kavanagh (Chapter 3) argue: 'Reflexivity is as central to analysis and interpretation in research for social justice, as it is for engagement with participants, yet reflexivity in this process is often neglected.' McGarry similarly describes reflexive practice as part of the 'politics of doing' of social justice research: 'Advancing an agenda for change involves engaging in research practices which are transformative not simply in terms of the knowledge that is produced but in terms of critical praxis as a "politics of doing" (Bacchi and Everline, 2010) for social justice.' This point is further elaborated in the learning from the chapter by McMahon, Bradley and Tierney (Chapter 4) where they state: 'Knowledge production has implications for how communities, young people and social issues are problematised and for the solutions policymakers and practitioners seek to apply (Bacchi, 2009).' For Meehan (Chapter 6), our critical lens allows for spaces to emerge where established ways of thinking can be disrupted to allow for a reimagining of lived lives, illuminated through her work with deaf and hard-of-hearing women: 'It [a social justice approach] offers another way of thinking about and understanding disability, deafness and sexuality through dismantling the vulnerability framework and suggesting the flourishing framework as a way to ask new questions, garner new perspectives and by which to understand deaf sexuality.'

Creative methodologies for social change

McMahon (Chapter 5) describes the move away from researching people's views of policy in Poststructuralist Policy Analysis (PPA) looking instead at the discursive effects of policymaking and the learning this methodology has for social justice research:

> Undertaking a PPA has implications for the conduct of social justice research because it requires a shift from focusing on researching people and their views on policy as well as their experiences of policy and policy enactment to a focus on researching discourse and the 'vita activa' of texts and documents. (Prior, 2016)

O'Shea (Chapter 13) provides an interesting example of a methodology with implications for social justice research, arguing '[t]his research on social work practice revealed that Q-methodology offers significant potential in ensuring fairness and more genuine engagement of research participants at various stages of the research process'. In Donovan's chapter (Chapter 7) on art-based research for social justice, he reflects on the key learning as he describes how the arts have the potential to trespass the enclosure of rights and thereby disrupt the power of taken-for-granted ways of seeing the world. It shows how people 'tell stories in many ways' (Brannelly and Barnes, 2022: 145) and how 'patient listening' (Brannelly and Barnes, 2022: 146) hospitality on the part of the researcher is essential for those stories to be heard and for the seeking of 'just outcomes' for those telling their stories (Brannelly and Barnes, 2022: 19).

Meaningful participation and co-creation

A number of our contributors draw attention to the importance of meaningful participation, partnership and co-creation. O'Driscoll and Kirwan (Chapter 12) describe one of the most important aspects of their research as 'bridging the gap between social justice research and social justice practice (and vice versa) and ensuring a partnership between researcher and practitioner. The study presents a model for partnership between researcher and practitioner that culminates in the co-creation of knowledge regarding how to involve children in decisions.' Melaugh and O'Hara's research with PWUD found that social justice approaches provide the most appropriate framework for creating conditions of parity in research relationships: '[S]ocial justice research, because of its adherence to the principles of participation, access, equity and human rights, is named as an approach that supports meaningful engagement with PWUD.'

For Hearne (Chapter 11), meaningful participation for social justice researchers requires partnership and action: 'For researchers, practitioners, and advocates, [there is] a requirement to challenge ourselves and be willing to take action to become a partner for social change. Indeed, the public action component of engaged research for social justice is essential.'

Social justice research for transformative policy and practice

How our research impacts policy and practice takes on a particular meaning when we employ a social justice lens and approach in our research endeavour. Our contributors reflected on what this methodological approach means for the policy environment and practice in the social professions. Taylor (Chapter 14) reflects on the realities of the policymaking process relative to an ambitious social justice research agenda:

Very few policy proposals will reflect a critical social justice approach. As an academic, you need to acknowledge these policymaking parameters. As a result, you can at most expect to contribute sometimes to policy reform rather than routinely to transformative policy change. That said, it is important to retain a focus on changing the wider policy narratives so that better futures can not only be imagined but realised. That is central to the academic role.

In his contribution on 'pracademia' or the bridging of academia and policymaking, Taylor makes useful suggestions for engagement on policy issues: 'Recognise the importance of communication to the policymaking audience. Clarity of communication for an intelligent, non-expert audience is key. Digestible, accessible two-page summaries of research evidence are valued by policy officials and politicians.'

Where to from here

Our original ambition in bringing this collection together was to explore and harness learning from our research to advance the theory and practice of social justice and conversely to draw on different approaches to social justice praxis to inform and develop methodologies for social change. While the various contributions in this edited volume provide timely and welcomed avenues of exploration in the conceptualisation, design and operationalisation of social justice frames in our research, they also raise key questions to inform our research practice into the future: How can we work with and alongside communities in ways that challenge and transform? How can we address an ethics of care in our research and commit ourselves to anti-oppressive research practice? What does inclusion and voice really mean in our research? Who and what really matter in our research, and how can we reflect this in our research doings? Building from this foundation, we have at our disposal some critical practices which we can further shape, which we can hold up in a new light to consider and reflect upon, and which can help to bring to life our 'politics of doing', our research for social justice.

References

Bacchi, C. (2009) *Analysing Policy: What's the Problem Represented to Be?*, Frenchs Forest, NSW: Pearson Australia.

Bacchi, C. and Eveline, J. (eds) (2010) *Mainstreaming Politics: Gendering Practices and Feminist Theory*, Adelaide: University of Adelaide Press.

Bacchi, C. and Rönnblom, M. (2014) 'Feminist discursive institutionalism: A poststructural alternative', *NORA – Nordic Journal of Feminist and Gender Research*, 22(3): 170–86.

Baker, J., Lynch, K., Cantillon, S. and Walsh, J. (2004) *Equality: From Theory to Action*, New York: Palgrave Macmillan.

Brannelly, T. and Barnes, M. (2022) *Researching with Care*, Bristol: Policy Press.

Creswell, J.W. (2009) *Research Design: Qualitative, Quantitative and Mixed Methods Approaches* (3rd edn), Thousand Oaks, CA: Sage.

Fraser, N. (2009) *Scales of Justice: Reimagining Political Space in a Globalizing World*, Cambridge: Polity Press.

Haraway, D. (1988) 'Situated knowledges: The science question in feminism and the privilege of partial perspective', *Feminist Studies*, 14(3): 575–99.

Heidegger, M. (1962) *Being and Time*, Oxford: Blackwell.

Kam, P.K. (2014) 'Back to the "social" of social work: Revising the social work profession's contribution to the promotion of social justice', *International Social Work*, 57(6): 723–40.

Mol, A. (1999) 'Ontological politics: A word and some questions', *Sociological Review*, 47(S1): 74–89.

Prior, L. (2016) 'Using documents in social research', in D. Silverman (ed) *Qualitative Research*, London: Sage, pp 171–86.

Final 39 Q-statements used in fieldwork

1. External management controls as they currently operate are absolutely necessary for public protection.
2. Risk assessment can be reactionary and based on insecurity after a fresh arrest/charge.
3. Those subject to the most stringent controls and monitoring are often those who cannot cope with such tight constraints, and they subsequently fail – it becomes breach.
4. I have discretion in the formulation of risk management plans to promote protective factors.
5. The assessments are based on the best available evidence, and this is necessary for the purposes of public protection.
6. Imposing and monitoring highly restrictive requirements on clients is compatible with good social work practice.
7. Hostel accommodation may be useful for monitoring purposes, but it is not always a protective factor.
8. Risk management plans give me much more scope to enforce recall.
9. External controls are not always balanced with protective factors.
10. Risks can be bolstered at the PSR stage to make an argument and I can lose sight of the protective factors.
11. Information which is used to recall somebody can subsequently be dismissed by a court.
12. I can build risk management strategies on strengths-based approaches.
13. I have the scope in my practice to involve the client in contributing to risk management plans.
14. I can often access resources for the client which help bolster internal controls/strengths.
15. I have scope in my work to hold on to our social work values that bring people with you.
16. Through the practice of risk assessment/management, I underestimate a lot of clients.
17. Risk assessment/management doesn't allow me to engage with people on a human level.
18. An over focus on risk assessment and management means we lose sight of the fact that we are dealing with traumatised and very damaged people.
19. Long-term recall damages the working relationship, and there is no scope for damage limitation.

20. I feel supported by my organisation to apply risk assessment and management strategies in a way which is compatible with social work values.
21. I think my assessment and views carry a lot of weight at risk management meetings.
22. Management of risk often automatically means completing programmes.
23. I have scope in my practice to do individual work with clients considered to pose a risk of harm to others.
24. Media attention plays a huge role in ROSH cases.
25. My analytical skills are fostered in risk assessments.
26. We have devalued our own position by allowing our assessments to become mechanistic.
27. Key to getting these people on board is building that relationship.
28. With all these constraints, controls and standardised systems, the power of the working relationship and my social work background/profession is no longer essential to undertake this role.
29. Our focus is often on risk management by external controls but still includes assessment of 'need' and rehabilitation.
30. A social work background is still key to balancing risk management with strengths-based work.
31. The information upon which I am basing the assessment can be vague, and it is not always reliable, for example community or police allegations.
32. I have no concerns when recalling somebody to prison based on allegations of behaviour as this is the best evidence available at that time.
33. I can balance the rights of victims and service users in my risk assessment and management plans.
34. I can be pressurised by police to recall somebody and therefore allow them circumvent processes where much more stringent levels of evidence are required.
35. I can still promote a client's human rights when I enforce risk management plans.
36. Victim's rights take precedence over the client's rights in risk assessment and management.
37. Some interventions identified in assessments as potentially reducing risk are not available in prison to allow prisoners to demonstrate this reduced risk.
38. I tend to err on the side of caution when identifying risks, and this can undermine a person's rights.
39. A client's and victim's rights should be balanced and given equal consideration.

Q-study grid

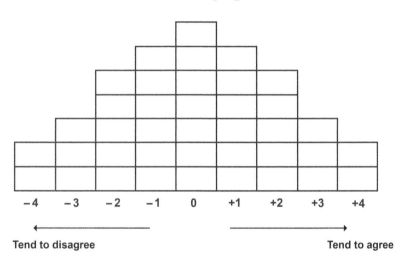

−4 −3 −2 −1 0 +1 +2 +3 +4

Tend to disagree   Tend to agree

Index

References to figures appear in *italic* type; those in **bold** type refer to tables. References to endnotes show both the page number and the note number (231n3).